The Global Architecture of Multilateral Development Banks

This book explores the evolution of the 30 functioning multilateral development banks (MDBs). MDBs have their roots in the growing system of international finance and multilateral cooperation, with the first recognisable MDB being proposed by Latin America in financial cooperation with the US in the late 1930s. That Inter-American Bank did not eventuate but was a precursor to the World Bank being negotiated at Bretton Woods in 1944. Since then, a complex network of regional, sub-regional, and specialised development banks has progressively emerged across the globe, including two significant recent entrants established by China and the BRICS.

MDBs arrange loans, credits, and guarantees for investment in member states, generally with the stated aim of fostering economic growth. They operate in both the Global North and South, though there are more MDBs focussing on emerging and developing states. While the World Bank and some of the larger regional banks have been scrutinised, little attention has been paid to the smaller banks or the overall system. This book provides the first study of all 30 MDBs and it evaluates their interrelationships. It analyses the emergence of the MDBs in relation to geopolitics, development paradigms, and debt. It includes sections on each of the banks as well as on how MDBs have approached the key sectors of infrastructure, human development, and climate.

This book will be of particular interest to researchers of development finance, global governance, and international political economy.

Adrian Robert Bazbauers is a Lecturer in International Public Sector Management, School of Business, UNSW Canberra, Australia.

Susan Engel is an Associate Professor in Politics and International Studies, University of Wollongong, Australia.

Routledge Explorations in Development Studies

This Development Studies series features innovative and original research at the regional and global scale. It promotes interdisciplinary scholarly works drawing on a wide spectrum of subject areas, in particular politics, health, economics, rural and urban studies, sociology, environment, anthropology, and conflict studies.

Topics of particular interest are globalization; emerging powers; children and youth; cities; education; media and communication; technology development; and climate change.

In terms of theory and method, rather than basing itself on any orthodoxy, the series draws broadly on the tool kit of the social sciences in general, emphasizing comparison, the analysis of the structure and processes, and the application of qualitative and quantitative methods.

Media Power and Hegemony in South Africa
The Myth of Independence
Blessed Ngwenya

Economic Neoliberalism and International Development
Edited by Michael Tribe

Critical Reflections on Public Private Partnerships
Edited by Jasmine Gideon and Elaine Unterhalter

Political Participation and Democratic Capability in Authoritarian States
Lien Pham and Ance Kaleja

The Global Architecture of Multilateral Development Banks
A System of Debt or Development?
Adrian Robert Bazbauers and Susan Engel

For more information about this series, please visit: https://www.routledge.com

The Global Architecture of Multilateral Development Banks

A System of Debt or Development?

Adrian Robert Bazbauers and
Susan Engel

Routledge
Taylor & Francis Group
LONDON AND NEW YORK

First published 2021
by Routledge
2 Park Square, Milton Park, Abingdon, Oxon OX14 4RN

and by Routledge
52 Vanderbilt Avenue, New York, NY 10017

Routledge is an imprint of the Taylor & Francis Group, an informa business

British Library Cataloguing-in-Publication Data
A catalogue record for this book is available from the British Library

Library of Congress Cataloging-in-Publication Data
Names: Bazbauers, Adrian Robert, author. | Engel, Susan N., author.
Title: The global architecture of multilateral development banks : a system of debt or development? / Adrian Robert Bazbauers and Susan Engel.
Description: Abingdon, Oxon ; New York, NY : Routledge, 2021. | Series: Routledge explorations in development studies | Includes bibliographical references and index.
Identifiers: LCCN 2020042575 (print) | LCCN 2020042576 (ebook) | ISBN 9780367440244 (hardback) | ISBN 9781003007128 (ebook)
Subjects: LCSH: Development banks. | International finance.
Classification: LCC HG1975 .B39 2021 (print) | LCC HG1975 (ebook) | DDC 332.1/53—dc23
LC record available at https://lccn.loc.gov/2020042575
LC ebook record available at https://lccn.loc.gov/2020042576

ISBN: 978-0-367-44024-4 (hbk)
ISBN: 978-1-003-00712-8 (ebk)

Typeset in Goudy
by codeMantra

For Freya and Ragnar

Contents

Tables

Acknowledgements

Adrian would like to thank the inexhaustible love and support of his Mum and Dad. Mum, thank you for more than I can include here. Dad, as always, I am 'maintaining the rage.'

Susan would like to thank her family too. To my partner Ian thanks for the love, care, and engaging conversations; to my sons, Mika and Till, thanks for keeping me grounded, and to my Dad, Wally, for always being there. Thanks to our Australian International Political Economy colleagues for their collegiality, support, and inspiration, I will single out Adam David Morton and Susan Park who have been informal mentors and role models (whether or not they know it). Thanks to my 'NGO friends' who keep me focussed on what is real, in particular Sally Stevenson from Indigo Foundation and Rayyan Hassan from the NGO Forum on the ADB, who even kindly read a chapter or two.

The authors would both like to thank the hard work of Nadeen Madkour, the best research assistant we could hope for.

Acronyms and abbreviations

AfDB	African Development Bank
AfDF	African Development Fund
AfDI	African Development Institute
AIF	ASEAN Infrastructure Fund
AIIB	Asian Infrastructure Investment Bank
AFESD	Arab Fund for Economic and Social Development
AMF	Arab Monetary Fund
AoA	Articles of Agreement
AsDB	Asian Development Bank
AsDBI	Asian Development Bank Institute
AsDF	Asian Development Fund
ASEAN	Association of Southeast Asian Nations
BADEA	Arab Bank for Economic Development in Africa
BBVA	*Banco Bilbao Vizcaya Argentaria*
BCEAO	Central Bank of West African States
BDEAC	Development Bank of Central Africa States
BDEGL	Development Bank of the States of Great Lakes
BEAC	Bank of Central African States
BIS	Bank for International Settlements
BMCs	Borrowing Member Countries
BNDES	Brazilian National Bank for Economic and Social Development
BOAD	West African Development Bank
BRI	Belt and Road Initiative
BRIC	Brazil, Russia, India, and China
BRICS	Brazil, Russia, India, China, and South Africa
BSEC	Black Sea Economic Cooperation
BSTDB	Black Sea Trade and Development Bank
CABEI	Central American Bank for Economic Integration
CACM	Central American Common Market
CAF	Development Bank of Latin America
CARICOM	Caribbean Community
CCT	Conditional Cash Transfer

CDB	Caribbean Development Bank
CEB	Council of Europe Development Bank
CEI	Central European Initiative
CEMAC	Central African Economic and Monetary Community
CFAF	*Communauté Financière d'Afrique Franc*
CHEXIM	China Export-Import Bank
CIFs	Climate Investment Funds
CMEA	Council for Mutual Assistance
COBAC	Central African Banking Commission
COMESA	Common Market for Eastern and Southern Africa
CRA	Contingent Reserve Arrangement
CRAs	Credit Rating Agencies
DAC	Development Assistance Committee-Development Cooperation Directorate of the OCED
DFI	Development Finance Institution
DPLs	Development Policy Loans
EAC	East African Community
EADB	East African Development Bank
EAEU	Eurasian Economic Union
EBID	ECOWAS Bank for Investment and Development
EBRD	European Bank for Reconstruction and Development
EC	European Community
ECAs	Export Credit Agencies
ECF	European Co-Financing Facility
ECLA	Economic Commission for Latin America
ECOWAS	Economic Community of West African States
ECO	Economic Cooperation Organisation
ECOWAS	Economic Community of West African States
ECOWAS Fund	Fund for Cooperation, Compensation, and Development of the ECOWAS
EDB	Eurasian Development Bank
EDI	Economic Development Institute
EEC	European Economic Community
EFSD	Eurasian Fund for Stabilisation and Development
EFSI	European Fund for Strategic Investments
EIB	European Investment Bank
EIF	European Investment Fund
EMDEs	Emerging Markets and Developing Economies
ERDF	ECOWAS Regional Development Fund
ERIB	ECOWAS Regional Investment Bank
ESG	Environment, Social, and Governance
ESF	Exchange Stabilisation Fund
ETDB	ECO Trade and Development Bank
EU	European Union
EURASEC	Eurasian Economic Community

FAO	Food and Agriculture Organisation
FSO	Fund for Special Operations
G77	Group of 77
GAD	Gender and Development
GCF	Green Climate Fund
GCI	General Capital Increase
GDP	Gross Domestic Product
GEF	Global Environment Facility
GET	Green Economy Transition
GFC	Global Financial Crisis
GHG	Greenhouse Gas
GMS	Greater Mekong Sub-Region
GNI	Gross National Income
HIPC	Heavily Indebted Poor Countries
IAB	Inter-American Bank
IADB	Inter-American Development Bank
IBEC	International Bank for Economic Cooperation
IBRD	International Bank for Reconstruction and Development
ICB	International Competitive Bidding
ICD	Islamic Corporation for the Development of the Private Sector
ICIEC	Islamic Corporation for the Insurance of Investment and Export Credit
ICSID	International Convention on the Settlement of Investment
IDA	International Development Association
IDFC	International Development Finance Club
IFAD	International Fund for Agricultural Development
IFC	International Finance Corporation
IFI	International Financial Institution
IFSD	Solidarity Fund for Development
IIB	International Investment Bank
IIC	Inter-American Investment Corporation
ILO	International Labour Organisation
IMF	International Monetary Fund
IOs	International Organisations
IPCC	Intergovernmental Panel on Climate Change
IPE	International Political Economy
IR	International Relations
IRTI	Islamic Research and Training Institute
IsDB	Islamic Development Bank
ISI	Import Substitution Industrialisation
ITFC	International Islamic Trade Finance Corporation
KSTA	Knowledge and Support Technical Assistance
LIBOR	London Inter-Bank Offered Rate
MDB	Multilateral Development Bank

MDF	Multilateral Development Finance
MDGs	Millennium Development Goals
MFD	Maximising Finance for Development
MIF	Multilateral Investment Fund
MIGA	Multilateral Investment Guarantee Agency
NAM	Non-Aligned Movement
NCF	Nordic Climate Facility
NDB	New Development Bank
NDCs	Nationally Determined Contributions
NDF	Nordic Development Fund
NEFCO	Nordic Environment Finance Corporation
NGO	Non-Governmental Organisation
NIB	Nordic Investment Bank
NIE	New Institutional Economics
NIEO	New International Economic Order
Nopef	Nordic Project Fund
NTF	Nigeria Trust Fund
OAS	Organisation of American States
OBOR	One Belt, One Road
OCR	Ordinary Capital Resources
ODA	Official Development Assistance
OECD	Organisation for Economic Cooperation and Development
OFID	OPEC Fund for International Development
OIC	Organisation of Islamic Cooperation
OPEC	Organisation of the Petroleum Exporting Countries
PEFF	Pandemic Emergency Financing Facility
PFF	Public Sector Finance Facility
PIDB	Pacific Islands Development Bank
PPPs	Public-Private Partnerships
PRSPs	Poverty Reduction Strategy Papers
PTA	Preferential Trade Area
RDB	Regional Development Bank
SALs	Structural Adjustment Loans
SARS	Severe Acute Respiratory Syndrome
SCI	Selective Capital Increase
SDF	Special Development Fund
SDFU	United Special Development Fund
SDGs	Sustainable Development Goals
SDRs	Special Drawing Rights
SECALs	Sectoral Adjustment Loans
SEI	Sustainable Energy Initiative
SICA	Central American Integration System
SIDA	Swedish International Development Cooperation Agency
SMEs	Small and Medium Enterprises
SPV	Special Purpose Vehicle

SRDB	Sub-Regional Development Bank
SUNFED	Special United Nations Fund for Economic Development
TAF	Technical Assistance Fund
TASF	Technical Assistance Special Fund
TCD	Technical Cooperation Division
TDB	Eastern and Southern African Trade and Development Bank
TRTA	Transaction Technical Assistance
UAE	United Arab Emirates
UK	United Kingdom
UN	United Nations
UNDP	United Nations Development Programme
UN-ECA	United Nations Economic Commission for Africa
UN-ECAFE	United Nations Economic Commission for Asia and the Far East
UN-ECLA	United Nations Economic Commission for Latin America
UNESCO	United Nations Educational, Scientific and Cultural Organisation
UNFCCC	United Nations Framework Convention on Climate Change
UNICEF	United Nations Children's Fund
US	United States
USSR	Union of Soviet Socialist Republics
WAD	Women and Development
WAEMU	West African Economic and Monetary Union
WAMU	West African Monetary Union
WAMZ	West African Monetary Zone
WBI	World Bank Institute
WDR	World Development Report
WHO	World Health Organization
WID	Women in Development

1 Introduction

When we started this book, our major motivator was to understand the role of the system of multilateral development banks (MDBs) in promoting both debt and development. Despite the 2007–8 Global Financial Crisis (GFC), it was clear that debt was again rapidly building in many countries and that the development paradigm was shifting, partly thanks to Chinese influence. While scholars had written about the impact of some of the MDBs, it seemed odd to us that there was no comprehensive picture or analysis of the MDB system; and in this work, we identify 30 of them. Since commencing the book, COVID-19 emerged, which added a whole new level of urgency to our task because multilateral development finance (MDF) is a major source of finance for many Global South countries in their response to the health, social, and economic consequences of the pandemic. Debt build-up was a global concern prior to COVID-19, with the World Bank calling the build-up in emerging markets and developing economies (EMDEs) between 2010 and 2018, the 'largest, fastest and most broad-based increase' in the past half century (Kose et al. 2020, 111). Yet, states around the world, especially the poorest, need additional resources to limit the scale of the pandemic's human tragedy.

As the saying goes, we have seen this film before, and we know how it ends – with another debt crisis. In just the past four decades, the major crises have been the 1982 Developing World Debt Crisis, 1997 Asian Financial Crisis, and 2007–8 GFC. Of course, history does not repeat itself and each crisis had specific drivers, features, and triggers but all involved a significant debt build-up, unregulated financial 'innovations,' and a trigger – often a banking or financial crisis, though this time it may be a virus.

The MDBs were key building blocks of the post-Second World War financial order and they have multiple ways they operate in that system (Culpeper 1997). They:

1 Provide states with increased access to finance;
2 Signal a state's creditworthiness to private financiers and thus promote the expansion of private sector lending across the globe;
3 'De-risk' projects to bring in private finance;
4 Advocate financial liberalisation by persuasively 'educating' policymakers and, when that fails by attaching coercive policy conditionalities to loans;

5 Develop 'innovative' (i.e., risky) financial instruments to underpin their loans and encourage EMDEs to utilise them; and
6 Expand debt relations within countries via policy diffusion, loans to governments and financial intermediaries, and projects supporting the financialisation of households.

The MDBs have been players in the handling of each new debt crisis. Yet, the building blocks analogy is problematic because the international financial system does not have a solid foundation. The regulatory regime relies, on the one hand, on inter-state cooperation, which is increasingly hard to achieve, and, on the other hand, on rules for private finance that they have themselves established to suit their own interests. There is no orderly default mechanism for states.

The development banks have shaped thinking about what development means and how to go about it. The World Bank is a leader in this field. Over 25 years ago, George and Sabelli (1994, 5) compared the Bank's role in development discourse to the medieval Christian church, arguing that it 'has a doctrine, a rigidly structured hierarchy preaching and imposing this doctrine and a quasi-religious model of self-justification.' There is still truth in that comparison; core elements of the neoliberal banking doctrine remain, though the Bank has evolved its thinking in a range of areas and understanding the detail is vital. What is less understood is how the 29 other MDBs operate: what are their similarities and differences? It is our hope to shed some light on these questions by exploring the system of MDBs.

MDF is a mechanism through which regional and international organisations arrange loans, credits, and guarantees for investments in countries, generally with the aim of fostering economic growth. The MDBs are a key source of MDF. All MDBs follow the mould of the World Bank, which commenced operations in 1946. Since then, their number and type have flourished. Regional, subregional, and specialised MDBs have emerged across the globe. While the flow of MDB creation turned to a trickle in the late 1970s, it did not stop, even in the neoliberal age of the 1980s on, which was seemingly hostile to the public facilitation of capital. Some banks have faced near-catastrophic challenges, but we have found only one MDB not currently operating, though it still exists on paper. So, here are further important questions: why do new MDBs keep getting created and why have they persisted? The two most recent MDBs established in the mid-2010s – the BRICS-led New Development Bank (NDB) and China-led Asian Infrastructure Investment Bank (AIIB) – reignited debate on the MDBs and their role in the global order. And yet there is still no book-length study of the MDB system.

To understand what the MDBs do, one need look no further than their name (Babb 2009, 6): their ownership is *multilateral*, in contrast to national development finance institutions (DFIs); they focus on *development*, taking a predominantly economic approach; and, they are *banks*, mainly providing loans and not grants like some other aid agencies. Most of the MDBs have charters – or Articles of Agreement, as they tend to be called – modelled upon the World Bank.

They are organised as shareholding corporations, with the size of their capital bases determining their lending capacity. They originally prioritised lending for infrastructure but have come to work in a range of sectors. Our approach covers all MDBs. We do not make artificial distinctions between those working in the Global North and South as some research has done.

The staff of the World Bank and five regional development banks (RDBs) number over 24,000. If we add in the 24 sub-regional and specialised development banks, that number would be closer to 30,000, which compares to the United Nation's 44,000 employees but with a narrower field of operations. The MDBs also contract thousands of consultants and indirectly influence tens of thousands of recruits on the projects they fund. In 2018, the 30 MDBs in our study had a total capitalisation of over $1.3 trillion and some $222.7 billion in new lending commitments.[1] Many commentators like to point out that the scale of MDB loans relative to private markets is low (see Ahluwalia et al. 2016). There is some truth in that. According to the International Monetary Fund (IMF), total global public and private debt reached $188 trillion in 2018. Still, the MDBs and other public DFIs 'are the pin on which the upside down pyramid of investment is crowded in from the rest of the private sector and bilaterals, who are reassured that their risk is controllable because of the presence of IFI capital in a country, sector, project, company or bank. It is the underwriting function' of MDBs that is vital to bilateral and private finance (Bracking 2009, 54).

Investments can often be beneficial to a state's development, but debt-based operations are more complicated. Debt is a 'matter of morality' (Graeber 2014, 8). Debt predated money but as bullion money became the basis for daily human relations, debt became something else, something unlike any other obligation thanks to the fact that it 'can be precisely quantified. This allows debts to become simple, cold, and impersonal – which, in turn, allows them to be transferable' (Graeber 2014, 13). Yet, despite often horrific and violent consequences, debt relations have expanded at an incredible pace since the Second World War and particularly since the financial liberalisation of the 1970s that went along with the rise of neoliberalism. The rapidity with which debt was again pushed on states and people and hailed as the solution to poverty, low growth rates, and even climate adaptation after the GFC was astonishing. Financial innovation and financialisation are again on the rise, with the latter being 'where the financial sector grows faster, or appropriates a larger share of profits than, manufacturing or trading in goods and services' (Gabor 2018, 1).

The rest of this chapter is occupied, first, with outlining our somewhat eclectic theoretical framework, which is influenced by both Critical Theory and Constructivism. Our book is deeply informed by our theoretical engagement, but as a text on the entire MDB system we have a lot of material to cover, thus we keep our theoretical musings short. The second part of this chapter defines what we mean by MDF and the MDBs and explains how we have categorised the MDB system. In this process, we outline the structure of the book and the key questions driving it.

1.1 Theorising the MDBs: Critical Theory and Constructivism

The MDBs embody a set of theoretical ideas and their work is framed by sets of beliefs and ideas too. As John Maynard Keynes (1973, 383), the lead theoretical architect of the MDB system, famously put it, even '[p]ractical men [and women] who believe themselves to be quite exempt from any intellectual influence, are usually the slaves of some defunct economist.' This book is a collaboration of two scholars of International Relations (IR), or more precisely from the field of International Political Economy (IPE), meaning we have a strong focus on the international level and the intersection of politics and economics. The MDBs are important case studies in this regard. Indeed, there are only a handful of other formal international organisations (IOs) that are as important to this intersection as the MDBs.

While the authors of this book share an overarching IPE framework, we diverge in theoretical approach. Susan Engel adopts a neo-Gramscian/Critical Theory lens and Adrian Robert Bazbauers draws on Constructivism and Organisational Sociology. Both of us have seriously engaged with each other's approach and we consider there is overlap between the two approaches but equally that theoretical eclecticism is a strength.

The three core tenets broadly uniting Constructivist IR (see Copeland 2006, Park 2018, Wendt 1995) can be explored to reveal commonalities and differences with neo-Gramscian scholarship. First, Constructivism seeks to understand global social relations. While mainstream IR/IPE theories Neo-realism and Neo-liberalism attempt to predict causal outcomes, Constructivism seeks to understand social interactions. The Italian neo-Marxist Antonio Gramsci (1971) does have moments in his writing where he tends to determinism (Anderson 1976), but, as with contemporary neo-Gramscian scholarship, Susan focusses on Gramsci's historicist mode (Engel 2010). Thus both approaches share a focus on social relations, but a neo-Gramscian account interrogates how elites construct hegemonic power and how working classes might progress positive social change and human well-being (Engel 2010, Rupert 1998).

The second core tenet uniting Constructivism is the view that the world is socially constructed through the social relations of actors sharing intersubjective meanings; ideas, rules, and norms are constitutive and shape actor behaviour appropriate for their fields, a point explored by Adrian in analyses of the World Bank (Bazbauers 2016, 2018, 2019a, 2019b). Gramsci had similar concerns in his analysis of hegemony, focussing on leadership, alliances, and networks as well as ideas and ideology, which not only organise human action and thought but frequently produce a reductionist 'common sense' (Gramsci 1971, Simon 1991). Norms, which Constructivists label standards 'of appropriate behavior for actors with a given identity' (Finnemore and Sikkink 1998, 891), certainly have much overlap with Gramscian scholarship, although neo-Gramscians contend that this literature lacks sufficient engagement with power and does not give enough attention to the social relations of production (Wills 2017).

Constructivism's third common tenet is that non-material factors are positioned above material ones in understanding global social relations. Constructivist IR does not dismiss material factors entirely, however. Wendt (1999, 96) argued that 'brute material facts' exist, constraining but not determining ideational factors; it is 'not ideas all the way down.' The contrast with the material-focussed Neo-realism and Neo-liberalism is clear. For Constructivists, material features exist, but their meaning is shaped through social action producing intersubjective understandings. Gramsci's approach to the material and non-material is best understood through his concept of the 'historic bloc,' which is Gramsci's term to explain how dominant groups predominate for long periods (Simon 1991). Historic blocs emerge from the production and the distribution of goods and services but are also based in culture, religion, theory, and ideology (Lears 1985), in other words there is a dialectical relationship between the material and non-material. Gramsci took a dynamic approach to studying historic blocs and encouraged attention to both short-term non-structural changes and long-term structural changes. Overall, while both approaches share an interest in the material and non-material, material interests are more prominent in neo-Gramscian analysis.

Applied to the MDBs, our approaches view the IOs as embedded in broader social orders, in our case a focus on their role in debt dynamics as a way they reproduce contemporary social relations. The reader will see that Susan's neo-Gramscian view of debt relations as capitalist and often exploitative frames much of the analysis on this issue. The shared concern with ideas means that the book engages extensively with the development paradigms at play in the MDBs at the macro, meso, and micro levels, trying to both deconstruct them and understand their relationship to practices that might best progress human well-being. Adrian's Constructivist analysis emphasises the role of internal organisational traits – like bureaucratic and normative structures – and external institutional characteristics – such as social networks and intersubjective meanings shared within MDF – and is visible in the study of the individual MDBs and how they constitute a system.

1.1.1 The MDBs from a Critical Theory perspective

Key ontological and epistemological priorities of a neo-Gramscian approach are outlined above. One concept, however, needs further explanation: hegemony. Hegemony occurs when a dominant class builds an effective historic bloc that controls the social system predominantly through consent rather than coercion and force (Cox 1983, Gill and Law 1993). A hegemonic system sees subservient classes acceding to the dominant one because of their consent to practices and ideologies established by the dominant class, which restrict alternatives, frame thought, and instil legitimacy, thus establishing a 'common sense' for all members of a community (Cox 1992). Hegemonic common sense can be resisted, however, and an historic bloc can breakdown through (i) an 'organic crisis' that destroys the social, economic, and political relations of a hegemonic system, (ii) a 'passive revolution' by the dominant group from above to resist potentially transformative change, and (iii) the actions of a counter-hegemonic movement, whereby subaltern classes undermine the historic bloc (Morton 2007, Murphy 2005, Rupert 1998).

Robert Cox (1986, 1996, 1992, 1983) was one of the first scholars to apply Gramsci's concepts to the global arena, constructing a schema to analyse hegemonic and non-hegemonic forces globally by considering the levels of social forces, states, and world orders. At the level of world orders, the historic bloc concept is deployed as a transnational entity. These are organic, involve more than one class, and include 'government institutions and civil societies of a number of countries including weak states' (Gill 1986, 211). IOs play a significant role in world orders, legitimising hegemonic norms, co-opting the elites of developing countries, and absorbing counter-hegemonic narratives (Cox 1986). Given that 'world hegemony is thus in its beginnings an outward expansion of the internal (national) hegemony established by a dominant social class' (Cox 1996, 137), neo-Gramscian analyses of IOs have tended to emphasise the role played by the US and *pax Americana* in establishing global governance actors like the World Bank and IMF and the role such IOs play in securing a transnational historic bloc designed to reinforce US intellectual and cultural hegemony, notably on economic policy. Susan's earlier work on the World Bank took this approach (Engel 2010); however, she has shifted views somewhat, influenced by work challenging the state-centric conception of hegemony, which argues it is increasingly incompatible with a globalised world. It is vital to move towards a transnational framing that recognises horizontal connections between social forces across and between national and transnational institutions (Robinson 2005, 2015).

This approach helps to explain the emergence of the two new MDBs: the AIIB and NDB. While the BRICS do reflect shifting structural power at the level of world orders (see Bond 2016 for a summary of analyses), a transnational capitalist approach highlights that the MDBs do not challenge the ideational base of the world order. Indeed, they support it. At best, as Stephen (2014, 914) argues, the BRICS 'pose a within-system challenge to global governance: they challenge its most liberal content, while becoming dependent on, and engaging with, its existing institutional structures.' Such a within-system challenge may produce a more multipolar, diverse international system, but it is unlikely to displace the inegalitarian order itself (Robinson 2014); variability in the system does not mean the historic bloc is being substantively challenged. This is not to say that states are irrelevant. Significantly, the US retains quite a degree of power over the World Bank and several other MDBs and has not been willing to relinquish that control and 'BRICS capitalism exhibits a greater role for state regulation and public sectors… What this simply tells us is that "varieties of capitalism" produce "varieties of integration" into global capitalism' (Robinson 2015, 17–18).

This brings us to one final point: the global system has been managing structural crisis resulting from capitalism's tendency to overaccumulation and the resultant inequality for some time, but the crisis is becoming more acute. One of the World Bank's key roles was to ensure that capital was provided where it was most needed, initially in the context of capital shortages. However, as the Keynesian, modernisation, welfare model was overturned, inequalities increased (Piketty 2014) and the propensity for capital to accumulate more rapidly than could be productively reinvested in the production or exchange of goods and services grew (Harvey 2005, 2010, Soederberg 2006). The MDB system is supportive of the ways capitalism has tended to deal with crisis. Harvey (2010) identified three key avenues. One is a spatial fix, meaning geographical expansion and spatial reorganisation. Here the growth and expansion of the MDBs has allowed the greater penetration of economies that would not normally be regarded as 'bankable.' A second fix is temporal – excess capital is invested into long-term activities, which take many years before returning capital to circulation. Infrastructural investments by the MDBs are classic examples of this and the current focus of the MDBs on de-risking projects for the private sector rather than investing themselves facilitates greater reach. The third fix is where the preceding two intertwine: 'spatio-temporal' fixes. Again, MDB projects do this, including signalling investment feasibility to private capital; the capacity to influence capital markets and shape government policy is of greater consequence than the money the MDBs lend.

1.1.2 The MDBs from a Constructivist perspective

Constructivism is not a substantive theory of international politics but rather an attempt to understand social relations and the fluid intersections between the global, regional, and national. Drawing from sociology, Constructivism sees social reality as built on collective understandings produced and reproduced by people; 'people always construct, or constitute, social reality, even as their being, which can only be social, is constructed for them' (Onuf 1989, 1) – hence the term 'Constructivism.'

In understanding the behaviour of IOs, Constructivist IR/IPE is often positioned in contrast to the rationalist principal-agent model. The model proposes that principals, such as states, delegate authority to agents, such as IOs, to perform tasks for the principal thereby maximising benefits and reducing costs for the principal (Snidal and Tamm 2018). Beyond ontological and epistemological distinctions, a central difference between the two relates to the autonomy of IOs from their principals. Whereas the principal-agent model argues that 'member governments *sometimes* empower their IO agents with real decision-making authority' (Nielson and Tierney 2003, 242 emphasis added), Constructivists tend to regard IOs as far more autonomous.

Barnett and Finnemore (1999) argued that IOs have their own bureaucracies and authority and are thus empowered to act autonomously of their principals. IO autonomy is significant in recognising that the MDBs are not simply artefacts controlled by shareholders but are capable of exercising their own authority (Snidal and Tamm 2018). While the US is influential in the World Bank, even there its power varies over time and by issue. In the MDB system, the distribution of internal shareholder power varies greatly too, as does the relative power of shareholders to influence their MDBs. This creates an opportunity to explore in detail the autonomy of the MDBs relative to their principals (Humphrey and Michaelowa 2013), especially when analysing the institutionalisation of behavioural norms in the MDF architecture (Hanlon 2017, 546).

The focus of Constructivism on institutional fields derives from Organisational Sociology and seeks to understand IOs not just in terms of inter-state relations but in reference to organisational dynamics and their broader social relations in producing and reproducing intersubjective meanings (Koch and Stetter 2013). This has led to a central focus on institutions, which Scott (2008, 48) defines as 'comprised of regulative, normative, and cultural-cognitive elements that... provide stability and meaning to social life.' An institutional field is the architecture of procedures, routines, norms, and conventions that surround organisations within their field. For the MDBs, this means the institutional field of MDF, which they, in turn, shape. A key insight coming out of the literature that is very relevant to the MDB system is the process of institutional isomorphism – this work highlights how IO operations become normalised and their organisational behaviour and culture similar over time due to social influence, coercive and persuasive forces, and socialisation (Acharya 2009, Finnemore and Sikkink 1998, 2001, Park 2006, 2014).

Constructivist IPE aligns with new institutionalism, which is comprised of numerous theoretical strands (see Lowndes and Roberts 2010), of which the sociological variant is the most relevant here. New institutionalism posits that organisational behaviour is not reducible to rational or functional pursuits (Bell 2011, DiMaggio 1998). Organisations of course need to ensure their own effectiveness, but the drive to demonstrate legitimacy is, in fact, more important (Frandsen and Johansen 2013). Organisational convergence derives from the pursuit of legitimacy, an end-state facilitated by the production and reproduction of social facts through institutional isomorphism. Three forces drive institutionalisation (DiMaggio and Powell 1983, 150–2): (i) coercive isomorphism derives from formal pressures, such as legal regulations, exerted on actors to conform to prescribed behaviour; (ii) mimetic isomorphism arises in places of industry ambiguity leading new organisations to model themselves on more established organisations; and, (iii) normative isomorphism relates to professional and occupational standards that produce conformity in an industry. These forces are all visible in MDF and help the MDBs demonstrate their legitimacy and thus survival.

Institutional processes are not passive. Power relations pervade institutional structures and not only are such structures powerful in conditioning behaviour, but organisations exercise power in shaping their institutional fields (Lawrence and Buchanan 2017); Constructivists regard this as the production and reproduction of social facts. The World Bank, for example, has exercised considerable influence in shaping MDF. Further, isomorphic processes are not neat and tidy. Organisations adapt and change in often difficult and confusing ways, contingent upon internal organisational exigencies and rational bureaucratic factors.

IOs are thus defined by their formal bureaucratic structures and juridical personalities as well as their social embeddedness in global institutional fields (Abdenur and Folly 2015). Further, the staff employed by them are socialised and normalised into the formal and informal practices of their organisations while also being sought by IOs for their expertise, experience, and socialised skills necessary to align with organisational and institutional priorities (Malkin and

Momani 2016). IO staff members emerge from and are socialised within communities of practice (Haas 1992), or are sought out as they already possess beliefs derived from their training and experience in related organisations. Demonstrating linkages to neo-Gramscian thought, we can say that those employed by MDBs are part of a transnational technocratic elite institutionalised within particular normative frameworks (Robinson 2015).

1.2 Structure of the book

MDF involves regional and international organisations arranging loans, credits, and guarantees for investment in economic development. The focus on *multilateral* finance means we exclude bilateral finance provided by states to other states and to the private sector for development purposes. This, unfortunately, means excluding some quite important areas of development finance, including:

1. Government-sponsored or quasi-governmental export credit agencies (ECAs, sometimes called export-import banks): these provide credit, insurance, and guarantees to facilitate a country's exports. ECAs preceded the MDBs – as outlined in Chapter 2 – and they operate in around 85 countries today. They are significant creditors to EMDEs, they work with the MDBs, and they are a key part of the broader DFI network that few scholars have explored, one exception being Bracking (2009).
2. Bilateral aid agencies that include loan programmes in their development assistance. The US initially developed loan schemes in a de facto form through the 1954 Agricultural Trade and Development Assistance Act, which allowed local currency repayment for US agricultural products. In 1957, the US established the Development Loan Fund, which has been through several titles and seemed in danger of being defunded, but competition from China saw the US establish the International Development Finance Corporation in 2019. A range of other bilateral aid agencies also provide loans, including established donors – such as Japan and Germany – and some new ones, like Thailand.
3. Domestic development banks: these generally commenced with a domestic mandate but have expanded to provide development finance to other states as well. The BRICS have become important players in this area. The China Development Bank, for example, is twice the size of the World Bank and has increasingly engaged in cross-border projects, as has the large Brazilian Development Bank (BNDES). The MDBs sometimes lend to domestic development banks as financial intermediaries.

The function of the MDBs as lenders and guarantors evolved out of the long history of debt, money, inter-state lending, and inter-state cooperation. This is the focus of Chapter 2, which offers a brief *longue durée* record of these topics. The direct ancestors of the MDBs are the ECAs, set up in the Global North just after the turn of the 20th century, to assist exporters but their focus on geostrategic allies and former colonies led them to have a developmental element. Further, US financial cooperation with Latin America included discussions on forming an inter-American bank from the late 1880s and in 1939 a Mexican delegation proposed that this bank should channel investment to promote economic development in the Americas (Villaseñor 1941). Thus, Chapter 2 demonstrates that, rather than being an American idea, the MDBs may well be a Mexican one. Still, the first MDB did not come into being until the US was behind the idea at the 1944 Bretton Woods Conference, where the establishing agreement of the International Bank for Reconstruction and Development (IBRD) – alongside its 'sibling,' the IMF – was signed.

Chapters 3 and 4 tell the story of the evolution of the 31 MDBs, 30 of which are functional (see Table 1.1). Chapter 3 starts in 1946, when the IBRD – today known as the World Bank, alongside its concessional arm, the International Development Association (IDA) – became operational and outlines the key issues and debates that shaped its creation. It explores the expansion of the MDB system from 1956 to 1979, when a further 21 MDBs were founded. The early growth of the MDB system is linked to the post-war Keynesian, welfare, modernisation model (Fine 2001) and the mandates of most MDBs from this period reflect this. The chapter concludes with the first major post-war debt crisis, the 1982 Debt Crisis, demonstrating on the MDBs relationship with, and response to, debt.

Chapter 4 analyses the period from 1980 to 2020, an era when a further eight still-functional MDBs were established. The focus is again on the interrelationships between the MDBs, geopolitics, debt, and development discourse. The chapter thus explores the evolution of neoliberalism, which came to dominate thinking in the World Bank and many other MDBs, particularly in the policy prescriptions they suggested to developing countries between 1980 and 1997, a period known as the Washington Consensus era. With the 1997 Asian Financial Crisis, hardline Washington Consensus prescriptions were discredited and, in the attempt to revitalise neoliberal development discourse, the post-Washington Consensus era began. It combined some core neoliberal ideas with the Millennium Development Goals (MDGs) and a global interest in poverty alleviation to produce a small window of time where the global development agenda was somewhat more progressive and human centred. However, this period closed with the 2008 GFC and was replaced with the retroliberal development agenda (Murray and Overton 2016) and the re-emergence of a more state-centric, nationalist discourse promoting debt-not-grants and an excessive focus on infrastructural investment.

Chapter 5 examines the formal structure of the MDBs, using the World Bank as a model. It delves into how their structures have shaped them as organisations, exploring voting rights and capital subscriptions. We highlight how the MDBs need to issue bonds on international capital markets to raise funds, which has given capital markets and credit rating agencies considerable influence over them. The banking and development agendas of the MDBs frequently conflict, with banking norms often taking precedence. The chapter also explores governance structures and loan types, terms, and conditions. Despite the rapid growth

Table 1.1 Development banks by type

Decade	*Specialised*	*Regional*	*Sub-regional*
2010s	Asian Infrastructure Investment Bank (2015) New Development Bank (2014)		
2000s			Eurasian Development Bank (2006) ECO Trade and Development Bank (2005)
1990s		European Bank for Reconstruction and Development (1991)	Black Sea Trade and Development Bank (1997)
1980s			Pacific Islands Development Bank (1989) Eastern and Southern African Trade and Development Bank (1985) Development Bank of the States of Great Lakes (1980)[a]
1970s	International Fund for Agricultural Development (1977) OPEC Fund for International Development (1976) Nordic Investment Bank (1976) Islamic Development Bank (1974) Arab Bank for Economic Development in Africa (1974) Arab Fund for Economic and Social Development (1971)		ECOWAS Bank for Investment and Development (1975) Development Bank of Central African States (1975) FONPLATA Development Bank (1974) West African Development Bank (1973) International Investment Bank (1970) Development Bank of Latin America (1970) Caribbean Development Bank (1970)
1960s		Asian Development Bank (1966) African Development Bank (1963)	East African Development Bank (1967) International Bank for Economic Cooperation (1963) Central American Bank for Economic Integration (1960)
1950s	Council of Europe Development Bank (1956)	Inter-American Development Bank (1959) European Investment Bank (1958)	
1945	World Bank (global)		

a No longer functional.

in private finance since the 1980s, many private financiers will not lend to low-income countries and there are many projects that they will not fund in middle- and high-income countries because of perceived financial risk, thus the MDBs persist and new ones have been created.

Chapters 6 through 8 analyse the key features, priorities, and frameworks of the 29 MDBs established after the World Bank. Loosely adapting Wihtol's (2014) typology, we divide the MDBs into regional, sub-regional, and specialised development banks. The RDBs are 'regional' in that their mandates support African, Asian, Latin American, and European development, collaboration, and integration. The sub-regional development banks (SRDBs) resemble the RDBs, except that they are typically much smaller and serve sub-regions, such as East Africa or the Caribbean. The specialised banks are more disparate but are unified as niche development financiers; for example, they finance agricultural interventions or provide Islamic development finance.

Chapter 6 focusses on the RDBs, the first of which was the European Investment Bank (EIB) in 1958, a product of the fast-evolving post-war European integration project. EIB was quickly followed by the Inter-American Development Bank (IADB) in 1959 from Latin America. The African Development Bank (AfDB) was established in 1964, emerging remarkably quickly after post-war African decolonisation; between the 1940s and 1960s, the number of independent African states increased from a handful to over 30. The Asian Development Bank (AsDB), founded in 1966, was more a case of a regional power – Japan – pushing the creation of an MDB. Chapter 6 also examines the outlier in RDB creation – the European Bank for Reconstruction and Development (EBRD), established in 1991 at the height of the Washington Consensus era with the aim of assisting the post-Cold War transition of Soviet states from communism to capitalism.

Chapter 7 turns to the 15 SRDBs, which Culpeper (1997, 54) described as a 'stratum' of MDBs 'that lies below the regional banks; they generally serve a group of borrowers that share borders or geographical or other characteristics and that stand apart from their neighbours in other ways.' We would add that they were frequently the product of a concern that capital needs were not being met by the World Bank and RDBs and, notably in sub-Saharan Africa, were often the financial arms of formal sub-regional groups. There are some success stories among them, such as the Development Bank of Latin America (CAF) today rivalling the IADB in Latin America, but also stories of failure – the Development Bank of the States of Great Lakes (BDEGL) collapsed in 1993 due to conflict between its members.

Chapter 8 covers the nine specialised banks. These MDBs either have memberships that do not fall along regional lines or have a specialised focus on an area of development, like agriculture or infrastructure. The largest group of these banks is one that we broadly call the 'Arab-led MDBs': the Arab Fund for Economic and Social Development (AFESD), Arab Bank for Economic Development in Africa (BADEA), Islamic Development Bank (IsDB), and OPEC Fund for International Development (IsDB). With Arab countries as their largest shareholders, they emerged from pressure imposed on oil exporters after the 1973 oil price shock to expand their international contributions and they did this partly through MDBs. The specialised banks also include the two most recent entrants to the MDB system: first, the NDB, which was established in 2014 and whose membership is currently limited to the five BRICS countries, and, second, the China-led AIIB established in 2015 that prioritises infrastructural investments.

Chapters 9 through 11 explore three of the main areas of MDB operations: infrastructure, climate finance, and human development. As Chapter 9 outlines, infrastructure has always been central to the MDBs. It was a key concern after the destruction of the Second World War and underpinned the Keynesian, welfare, modernisation model. While declining in importance as human needs entered development discourse, it regained its top spot during the current retroliberal era. Infrastructure is vitally important for development but at the same time it is a complicated field. Large projects mean complexity and the likelihood of technical errors, mismanagement, and corruption goes up, as do environmental and social consequences. Problematic infrastructure projects were the key drivers of the MDBs establishing safeguard policies and inspection panels. The retroliberal push for increased infrastructure funding could be very useful for some countries, but is equally likely to provide many failures, leaving a debt legacy that will last many years.

Chapter 10 analyses the development of MDB environmental policies and lending programmes. Despite their culpability in a range of what can only be described as environmental disasters up to the 1980s, the MDBs are now prominent financial agencies in a range of environmental initiatives, including the Global Environment Facility (GEF). Certainly, on paper at least, their environmental policies and safeguards are among the best in the world, but as mainstream development financiers they have taken a long time to reduce their portfolios of carbon projects. Further, the MDBs have promoted the use of innovative financial instruments to expand the climate finance regime. While these instruments may be built on strong financial structures, questions emerge whether they are well suited to assist countries adapt, mitigate, and build resilience to climate change.

Chapter 11 discusses human development, focussing on education, health, and gender. Prior to the 1970s, most MDBs had not funded social projects as they preferred investments with easily quantifiable economic returns. With the introduction of basic needs, absolute and relative poverty, and human development to development discourse, the MDBs slowly began to broaden their understanding of development. Yet, the small percentage that the MDBs allocated to fund such projects prioritised investing in people to improve their productive capacity not improving their quality of life. Further, the MDBs only belatedly – and somewhat reluctantly – came to acknowledge the role of women in development starting in the 1980s, which evolved into gender policies, programmes, and safeguards. While considerable strides have been made over the past few decades, the MDBs continue to approach gendered inequalities as problems that can be 'fixed' through the application of the right resources, focussing on creating economic opportunities for women and not addressing structural gendered imbalances.

Note

1 In this study, \$ = US dollars, € = Euros, £ = British pounds, and any other currencies are as specified.

Bibliography

Abdenur, Adriana Erthal, and Maiara Folly. 2015. "The New Development Bank and the Institutionalization of the BRICS." *R/evolutions* 3:66–92.

Acharya, Amitav. 2009. *Whose Ideas Matter? Agency and Power in Asian Regionalism*. New York: Cornell University Press.

Ahluwalia, Montek Singh, Lawrence Summers, Andrés Velasco, Nancy Birdsall, and Scott Morris. 2016. *Multilateral Development Banking for This Century's Development Challenges: Five Recommendations to Shareholders of the Old and New Multilateral Development Banks*. Washington, DC: Centre for Global Development.

Anderson, Perry. 1976. "The Antinomies of Antonio Gramsci." *New Left Review* 100:5–78.

Babb, Sarah. 2009. *Behind the Development Banks: Washington Politics, World Poverty, and the Wealth of Nations*. Chicago, IL and London: The University of Chicago Press.

Barnett, Michael, and Martha Finnemore. 1999. "The Politics, Power, and Pathologies of International Organizations." *International Organization* 53 (4):699–732.

Bazbauers, Adrian Robert. 2016. "The World Bank as a Development Teacher." *Global Governance* 22 (3):409–26.

Bazbauers, Adrian Robert. 2018. *The World Bank and Transferring Development: Policy Movement through Technical Assistance, International Political Economy Series*. Cham: Palgrave Macmillan.

Bazbauers, Adrian Robert. 2019a. "The Relational Dynamics of World Bank Survey Missions." *International Journal of Public Administration* 42 (1):28–40. doi: 10.1080/01900692.2017.1390763.

Bazbauers, Adrian Robert. 2019b. "World Bank Technical Assistance: Participation, Policy Movement, and Sympathetic Interlocutors." *Policy Studies*:1–19. doi: 10.1080/01442872.2019.1581156.

Bell, Stephen. 2011. "Do We Really Need a New 'Constructivist Institutionalism' to Explain Institutional Change?" *British Journal of Political Science* 41 (4):883–906. doi: 10.1017/S0007123411000147.

Bond, Patrick. 2016. "BRICS Banking and the Debate over Sub-imperialism." *Third World Quarterly* 37 (4):611–29.

Bracking, Sarah. 2009. *Money and Power: Great Predators in the Political Economy of Development*. London: Pluto Press.

Copeland, Dale C. 2006. "The Constructivist Challenge to Structural Realism." In *Constructivism and International Relations: Alexander Wendt and His Critics*, edited by Stefano Guzzini, Anna Leander and Barry Buzan, 1–2. Abingdon, Oxon: Routledge.

Cox, Robert W. 1983. "Gramsci, Hegemony and International Relations: An Essay in Method." *Millennium: Journal of International Studies* 12 (2):162–75.

Cox, Robert W. 1986. "Social Forces, States and World Orders: Beyond International Relations Theory." In *Neorealism and Its Critics*, edited by Robert Keohane, 204–54. New York: Columbia University Press.

Cox, Robert W. 1992. "Multilateralism and World Order." *Review of International Studies* 18 (2):161–80.

Cox, Robert W. 1996. "Gramsci, Hegemony, and International Relations: An Essay in Method." In *Approaches to World Order*, edited by Robert W. Cox and J. Sinclair, 124–143. Cambridge: Cambridge University Press.

Culpeper, Roy. 1997. *Titans or Behemoths?* London: Lynne Rienner.
DiMaggio, Paul. 1998. "The New Institutionalisms: Avenues of Collaboration." *Journal of Institutional and Theoretical Economics (JITE) / Zeitschrift für die gesamte Staatswissenschaft* 154 (4):696–705.
DiMaggio, Paul, and Walter Powell. 1983. "The Iron Cage Revisited: Institutional Isomorphism and Collective Rationality in Organizational Fields." *American Sociological Review* 48 (2):147–60. doi: 10.2307/2095101.
Engel, Susan. 2010. *The World Bank and the Post-Washington Consensus in Vietnam and Indonesia: Inheritance of Loss.* London: Routledge.
Fine, Ben. 2001. *Social Capital versus Social Theory: Political Economy and Social Science at the Turn of the Millennium.* London: Routledge.
Finnemore, Martha, and Kathryn Sikkink. 1998. "International Norm Dynamics and Political Change." *International Organization* 52 (4):887–917.
Finnemore, Martha, and Kathryn Sikkink. 2001. "TAKING STOCK: The Constructivist Research Program in International Relations and Comparative Politics." *Annual Review of Political Science* 4 (1):391–416. doi: 10.1146/annurev.polisci.4.1.391.
Frandsen, Finn, and Winni Johansen. 2013. "Public Relations and the New Institutionalism: In Search of a Theoretical Framework." *Public Relations Inquiry* 2 (2):205–21. doi: 10.1177/2046147x13485353.
Gabor, Daniela. 2018. *Understanding the Financialisation of International Development through 11 FAQs.* Washington, DC: Heinrich Böll Stiftung North America.
George, Susan, and Fabrizio Sabelli. 1994. *Faith and Credit: The World Bank's Secular Empire.* London: Penguin Books.
Gill, Stephen. 1986. "Hegemony, Consensus and Trilateralism." *Review of International Studies* 12 (3):205–22.
Gill, Stephen, and David Law. 1993. "Global Hegemony and the Structural Power of Capital." In *Gramsci, Historical Materialism and International Relations*, edited by Stephen Gill, 93–124. Cambridge: Cambridge University Press.
Graeber, David. 2014. *Debt: The First 5,000 Years.* Brooklyn, NY: Melville House.
Gramsci, Antonio. 1971. *Selections from the Prison Notebooks of Antonio Gramsci.* Translated by Quintin Hoare and Geoffrey Nowell Smith. London: Lawrence and Wishart.
Haas, Peter. 1992. "Epistemic Communities and International Policy Coordination." *International Organization* 46 (1):1–35.
Hanlon, Robert J. 2017. "Thinking about the Asian Infrastructure Investment Bank: Can a China-Led Development Bank Improve Sustainability in Asia?" *Asia & the Pacific Policy Studies* 4 (3):541–54. doi: 10.1002/app5.186.
Harvey, David. 2005. *The New Imperialism.* Oxford: Oxford Unviersity Press.
Harvey, David. 2010. *The Enigma of Capital: And the Crises of Capitalism.* Oxford: Oxford University Press.
Humphrey, Chris, and Katharina Michaelowa. 2013. "Shopping for Development: Multilateral Lending, Shareholder Composition and Borrower Preferences." *World Development* 44:142–55. doi: 10.1016/j.worlddev.2012.12.007.
Keynes, John Maynard. 1973. *The General Theory of Employment, Interest and Money.* London: Macmillan for the Royal Economic Society.
Koch, Martin, and Stephan Stetter. 2013. "Sociological Perspectives on International Organisations and the Construction of Global Political Order: An Introduction." *Journal of International Organizations Studies* 4 (Special Issue):5–13.
Kose, M. Ayhan, Peter Nagle, Franziska Ohnsorge, and Naotaka Sugawara. 2020. *Global Waves of Debt: Causes and Consequences.* Washington DC: World Bank.
Lawrence, Thomas B., and Sean Buchanan. 2017. "Power, Institutions, and Organisations." In *The SAGE Handbook of Organizational Institutionalism*, edited by Royston

Greenwood, Christine Oliver, Thomas B. Lawrence and Renate E. Meyer, 477–506. London: SAGE Publications.

Lears, T.J. Jackson. 1985. "The Concept of Cultural Hegemony: Problems and Possibilities." *The American Historical Review* 90 (3):567–93.

Lowndes, Vivien, and Mark Roberts. 2010. *Why Institutions Matter: The New Institutionalism in Political Science*. Basingstoke: Palgrave Macmillan.

Malkin, Anton, and Bessma Momani. 2016. "An Effective Asian Infrastructure Investment Bank: A Bottom Up Approach." *Global Policy* 7 (4):521–30. doi: 10.1111/1758-5899.12357.

Morton, Adam David. 2007. *Unravelling Gramsci: Hegemony and Passive Revolution in the Global Political Economy*. London: Pluto Press.

Murphy, Craig N. 2005. *Global Institutions, Marginalisation, and Development*. London: Routledge.

Murray, Warwick E., and John Overton. 2016. "Retroliberalism and the New Aid Regime of the 2010s." *Progress in Development Studies* 16 (3):244–60. doi: 10.1177/1464993416641576.

Nielson, Daniel L., and Michael J. Tierney. 2003. "Delegation to International Organizations: Agency Theory and World Bank Environmental Reform." *International Organization* 57 (2):241–76.

Onuf, Nicholas. 1989. *World of Our Making: Rules and Rule in Social Theory and International Relations*. Columbia: South Carolina University Press.

Park, Susan. 2006. "Theorizing Norm Diffusion within International Organizations." *International Politics* 43 (3):342–61. doi: 10.1057/palgrave.ip.8800149.

Park, Susan. 2014. "Institutional Isomorphism and the Asian Development Bank's Accountability Mechanism: Something Old, Something New; Something Borrowed, Something Blue?" *The Pacific Review* 27 (2):217–39. doi: 10.1080/09512748.2014.882394.

Park, Susan. 2018. "Constructivism." In *International Organization and Global Governance*, edited by Thomas G. Weiss and Rorden Wilkinson, 146–56. Milton: Routledge.

Piketty, Thomas. 2014. *Capital in the Twenty-First Century*. Cambridge, MA: Belknap Press.

Robinson, William. 2005. "Gramsci and Globalisation: From Nation-State to Transnational Hegemony." *Critical Review of International Social and Political Philosophy* 8 (4):559–74.

Robinson, William. 2014. *Global Capitalism and the Crisis of Humanity*. Cambridge: Cambridge University Press.

Robinson, William. 2015. "The Transnational State and the BRICS: A Global Capitalism Perspective." *Third World Quarterly* 36 (1):1–21.

Rupert, Mark. 1998. "(Re-)Engaging Gramsci: A response to Germain and Kenny." *Review of International Studies* 24:427–34.

Scott, W. Richard. 2008. *Institutions and Organizations: Ideas and Interests*. Los Angeles, CA: Sage.

Simon, Roger. 1991. *Gramsci's Political Thought: An Introduction*. London: Lawrence & Wishart Ltd. Original edition, 1982.

Snidal, Duncan, and Henning Tamm. 2018. "Rational Choice: From Principal-Agent to Orchestration Theory." In *International Organization and Global Governance*, edited by Thomas G. Weiss and Rorden Wilkinson, 135–45. Milton: Routledge.

Soederberg, Susan. 2006. *Global Governance in Question: Empire, Class and the New Common Sense in Managing North-South Relations*. London: Pluto Press.

Stephen, Matthew. 2014. "Rising Powers, Global Capitalism, and Liberal Global Governance: A Historical Materialist Account of the BRICs Challenge." *European Journal of International Relations* 20 (4):912–38.

Villaseñor, Eduardo. 1941. "The Inter-American Bank: Prospects and Dangers." *Foreign Affairs* 20 (1):165–74.

Wendt, Alexander. 1995. "Constructing International Politics." *International Security* 20 (1):71–81. doi: 10.2307/2539217.

Wendt, Alexander. 1999. *Social Theory of International Politics*. Cambridge: Cambridge University Press.

Wihtol, Robert. 2014. *Whither Multilateral Development Finance?* Tokyo: Asian Development Bank Institute.

Wills, Joe J. 2017. *Contesting World Order?: Socioeconomic Rights and Global Justice Movements*. Cambridge: Cambridge University Press.

2 Debt, development, and the emergence of multilateral development finance

> Some of the most intricate and momentous problems of foreign investment are connected with loans to alien Governments. *It has been said that the possession of a national debt is one of the first signs of civilisation.* Borrowers are always eager to lend where there is a chance of big profits, and the Governments of weak and backward countries [sic] often fall an easy prey to the wiles of financiers, when they are faced with difficulties, internal or external.
>
> (Hobson 1914, xx–xxi emphasis added).

This chapter start with a brief *longue durée* examination of the emergence of money and debt. It examines state debt as the precursor to the creation of various kinds of state and multilateral development finance (MDF). It analyses the factors that led to the establishment of the first multilateral development bank (MDB) – the International Bank for Reconstruction and Development (IBRD), commonly known as the World Bank – in 1944, following earlier proposals for an Inter-American development bank. Positioning MDF within a longer tradition of finance and debt demonstrates its place in the web of globalised finance that slowly emerged since the creation of money. Early state debt mostly financed warfare and empire building, while modern MDF has evolved to focus primarily on development, though war and the arms trade have not been absent. Financial innovation took off from the 1800s and the creation of MDF was part of this. As we shall see in later chapters, the MDBs now play a significant role in spreading financial innovation.

Debt is not, and never has been, an innocent instrument. Regardless of whether it was utilised for warfare, business, or development, money-debt's logic turns moral questions about debt and credit 'into a matter of impersonal arithmetic' (Graeber 2014, 14). Debts must be repaid regardless of the legitimacy of those that took them out or the purposes for which they were taken. Positioning MDBs within a broader expansion of credit relations is vital to the purposes of this book. The MDBs have enhanced the legitimacy of debts – because as banks, they need to ensure they themselves are repaid – and expanded its reach across the world in the context of a post-war financial system that has no orderly mechanism for nation-states to default on debt. The poor, as taxpayers, have borne disproportionate responsibility for debt repayment.

The chapter also examines the more immediate inspirations for the creation of the IBRD. This is important because, in much of the literature, the origins of MDF are either a bit of a mystery or the outcome of Anglo-American negotiations at the 1944 Bretton Woods Conference, which produced the Articles of Agreement of the IMF and IBRD. However, recent historical research has helped correct this and, piecing together the different histories, we posit five key precedents for MDBs, taking analysis well beyond Anglo-American negotiations into US-Latin American cooperation, broader international cooperation, and also to the role of new ideas and hegemonic change.[1]

The first precedent is the growth in international cooperation from the mid-1800s and the related belief in human capacity to organise. These helped set the enabling environment for change. The second factor, a contextual one, is the change in international hegemony produced by the First World War, the inter-war chaos, and the Second World War. Even with a transnational theoretical focus, it is clear that the Bretton Woods twins – the IMF and IBRD – were the product of US global hegemony, which was firmly in place by the end of the Second World War. Keynesianism and New Deal politics are the third precedent to MDBs explored in the chapter. Keynes' academic analysis provided a theoretical backbone for increased economic cooperation between states, explaining why markets left on their own would not necessarily produce good economic or social outcomes.

The fourth precedent to the IBRD is less well known but very important, namely, US economic cooperation with Latin America. This produced a 1940 proposal for an Inter-American development bank, well before the proposal for the IBRD (Diaz-Bonilla and del Campo 2010, Helleiner 2014, 2017, Scott-Smith and Rofe 2017). This was a grander proposal than the IBRD and the later iteration of the IADB that emerged in the 1960s. What is equally interesting is that this proposal emerged out of loans that were already being provided to the region through the US Export-Import (Exim) Bank. This link to Exim banks is less well-known and scholars working on development rarely consider the MDBs as part of a larger MDF system (Bracking 2009). The final factor considered in this chapter is US economic planning during the Second World War, which drove thinking about the post-war system.

Taken together, this chapter paints a new picture of MDF's emergence, one that highlights the tension between MDF's progressive origins in internationalist ideals of producing a fairer, more inclusive global system and its state-centric origins in promoting a Western world order based on markets and debt. This is significant because this new analysis demonstrates how many of the strengths and limitations of the IBRD were inherent in its development and subsequent MDBs have reproduced this dynamic.

2.1 The growth of inter-state private and public debt

State debt is vital background to the emergence of the MDF system. It is a largely capitalist phenomenon, although the state system predates capitalism and hence understanding MDF's origins demands a dialectical understanding of capitalism and the state system (Bieler and Morton 2018). As Graeber (2014) argued, money (or bullion) debt owed by empires and states was historically closely linked to war and violence making, whereas credit money systems have generally gone hand-in-hand with more peaceful human epochs. MDF emerged late in the most recent bullion debt era, which started around 1450. It was designed to address war debt and reconstruction problems but became increasingly part of a credit money system promoting development not warfare. At face value, this suggests that MDBs could be part of a more human-friendly future. However, at least two challenges stand in this path. First, so long as debt remains capitalism's tribute mechanism and there is no mechanism to manage default by states, a shift to credit debt will not reduce the violence traditionally associated with debt collection. Second, development itself is a complex and contested term and MDBs have generally promoted a rather emaciated vision of development as growth plus a minimalist vision of poverty reduction as getting people above the international poverty line of $1.90 a day (Cammack 2004).

Debt and credit have, in fact, been around for a lot longer than money. People in different parts of the world long had informal systems of credit. Money in its bullion form began to appear around 800–500 BCE in Europe, India, and China. Graeber (2014, 213) argued that the single key reason for the rise of money was the increase in warfare because '[b]ullion predominates, above all, in periods of generalized violence'; money can be stolen and used to pay soldiers and empires need taxation to fund warfare. Graeber's first period of bullion money, 800 BCE to 600 CE, saw extensive warfare and the concomitant creation of great empires. As Graeber argued, cash and barter are usually limited to contexts of low trust involving strangers or people who are not credit-worthy, but money provided a problematic mathematical precision to debt that was enforceable, though only with the help of sovereign or state violence. You might lose your home or need to sell your wife or children to pay your debts but that's 'incidental to the creditor' (Graeber 2014, 14). The debt peonage that came from this system resulted in large-scale social unrest and sometimes revolt, so that rulers regularly instituted general debt amnesties to resolve tensions. In contrast, the Middle Ages saw the return to credit money (not a reversion to barter), the fall of empires, bans on slavery across most parts of Eurasia, and an increase in living standards for many ordinary people. The age of capitalist empires, which Graeber (2014, 214) dates from around 1450, saw a return to bullion, slavery (in particular the North Atlantic slave trade), and generalised violence through both inter-state violence and the colonial project. While the core of Graeber's argument is important, 1450 was a marker in the emergence of the state system, and capitalism appeared much later, from the late 18th century.

Bullion money and conflict were central to the emergent states system. Historically, monarchs and rulers of various kinds borrowed predominately to fund their wars and conflicts (Kindleberger 1984). Indeed, it seems likely that inter-state lending started with loans to allies or nations at war, though private lending was mostly driven by trade (Hobson 1914). Moving into more modern times, borrowing by states was mostly wars-driven too. States and their predecessors borrowed through a range of mechanisms: early on it was common for monarchs to take mostly short-term loans directly from wealthy individuals and later from banks and, as borrowing from banks developed, loan terms lengthened. States also started issuing annuities and later bonds that guaranteed the purchasers a long-term income stream. These were initially to finance wars, but later they backed state infrastructure and development projects. In either case, creditors have been willing to inflict violence directly or economically on those who cannot pay back such debts.

Public or sovereign debt in Europe is generally said to have begun around 1200 CE in both city-states and the growing large centralised monarchical states, though it began earlier in China. The large European states generally borrowed domestically, but they began to borrow internationally too. English King Edward I borrowed extensively from the Ricciardi of Lucca from 1272 to 1310 and defaulted on the debts. In the mid-16th century, the Fuggers from southern Germany are credited with developing 'financial intermediation, borrowing from wealth-owners and lending to a king' (Kindleberger 1984, 45). Money lending was, of course, risky and Geisst (2013, 47) expresses the common view that 'lending to sovereigns in general was riskier than lending to established merchants.' However, according to Stasavage (2016, 3), the primary lenders to European states were merchants who had gained wealth from long-distance trading and wanted to diversify their risk. This highlights the important point that lending always involves two sets of interests – the lenders and the borrowers – and both sets pursue interests and systems that suit their needs. There have always been winners and losers in the relationship, which has changed over time, often reflecting the relative political weight of the parties (Stasavage 2016). The MDBs were established to reduce risk thus enabling expanded lending to (less credit-worth) countries, but they have always promoted the political interests of lenders.

The city-states began long-term borrowing or fund-raising through annuities and securities from the early 13th century, with the large monarchical states only following a few centuries later. This aligns with Arrighi's (1994) argument that Italian city-states were the economic hegemons of the 13th and 14th centuries, with the Dutch taking over in the 16th and 17th centuries, the British in the mid-18th century, and the US from the Second World War. Great Britain was slow to issue long-term sovereign debt; it sold its first Treasury order, or what we would now call government bond, in the late 1660s and its first annuity to the public in 1692, the latter to finance a war with France (Geisst 2013, 101–3). MDBs' primary source of funds today is from issuing bonds. Britain expanded the system with the creation of the Bank of England in 1694 amid the Nine Years' War, as a corporation of London merchants that could sell government tradeable securities. The Dutch had also already established a national bank in 1609 and these banks became lenders to the crown often to finance wars (Geisst 2013, 106–9). Expansion in the scale of European conflict generated scale and innovation in finance.

After the Reformation in the 16th century, religiously based strictures against usury started to fade and the modern state system began to emerge. International Relations scholars tend to regard the 1648 Peace of Westphalia, which ended the

Thirty Years' War in Europe, as a key marker, though the transition started earlier. This was a time of exploration and commerce, and national and commercial debt was central to expansion (Geisst 2013, 97). Colonialism was largely an extractive venture, whether through plunder, extraction of natural resources, or cash crop production for European markets. Still, extraction and plantations often required investment. The British and Dutch East India Companies – established in 1600 and 1602 – played a key role in international investments. They were initially private companies, yet their existence was bound up with their respective states and the Dutch East India Company was a pioneer of foreign direct investment (FDI). Both public and private investments were central to the formation of colonies (Mikesell 1966), and plantations became a key driver of private investment (Hobson 1914). The colonial states' investments in their colonies sometimes lasted past their colonial role. For example, the British crown had investments in the US after independence (Geisst 2013, 131). These investments were a way of returning capital to the colonial powers.

Colonial era sovereign borrowing was mostly from private banks rather than other states, though during wars allies lent to each other. Britain utilised debt across the 18th century to build canals, towns, factories, and to fund industrial agriculture facilitated by the enclosure of the commons (Hobson 1914). The British made government loans to its ally Austria during the Napoleonic Wars and the French raised funds through borrowing and annuities to support the US in the American War of Independence (Kindleberger 1984), while both the British and US sought loans in Holland (Hobson 1914). The French state sold assets to fund Napoleon's wars and such wartime borrowing often produced very complex transactions. Common causes of state-to-state debt were indemnities and war reparations (see Kindleberger 1984, ch 13) and the repayments frequently produced problems similar to those in the first era of bullion debt, namely, direct financial hardship leading to poverty and instability. The state system and emergent capitalism had granted autonomy to money and built up a political and military system to ensure repayment regardless of the cost to people (Graeber 2014).

By the 19th century, complex financialisation of loans was compounding problems created by bullion war debt. The century saw two large waves of sovereign defaults that influenced later thinking. Both hit Latin America and also several other states and were preceded by speculative waves and economic crises. Indeed, as Toussaint (2019) argued, before each of the debt crises from the 19th to the 21st centuries, there was a boom in central states resulting in surplus capital being recycled into peripheral states. And the subsequent crises in peripheral states have, for the most part, been caused by external factors like a financial crash or a recession in the core states. This contrasts to the mainstream narrative that blames over-indebtedness in the periphery for the crisis. In the case of the 1820s crisis starting in Latin America, Toussaint (2019) pointed to the London Stock Exchange crash as the precipitator but the terms of the speculative loans made to states as the underlying driver. Perhaps the most problematic case was a bond issue by Mexico in 1824. Bonds to the value of £3.2 million were issued by Mexico's broker B.A. Goldschmidt & Co at 5% interest. But investors rarely pay the full or par price for bonds and, in this case, they paid just £58 for a £100 bond. This changes the effective interest rate from 5% to 8.6%. In addition, B.A. Goldschmidt & Co took a further £750,000 in commission and fees, so Mexico ended up with £1.1 million from £3.2 million in debt issued (Toussaint 2019, Wynne 1951). The resulting defaults in 1825 included all independent Latin American countries, four US states, Greece, and later Portugal. The loan mania leading to defaults in the early 1870s again in Latin America was even more extreme and its effects longer lasting. One of its more notorious impacts was the 1902–3 naval blockade of Venezuela by the UK, Germany, and Italy. This resulted in the Second Hague Conference of 1907 creating a convention to limit the use of force in debt recovery where debt is owed by one government to another (Hobson 1914).

Financialisation continued after the First World War, feeding into the Great Depression from 1929 and another debt crisis, discussed later. The idea for the IBRD came from concerns about the ugly loans made during this mania as well as the problem of war debts creating instability. Yet, by the late 2010s, MDBs were focussed on leveraging billions of dollars of lending into trillions, despite the evidence that such debts will become a weight around the neck of borrowing countries as soon as the next crisis hits. Writing in 2020, an economic crisis seems to have been triggered by a virus rather than a banking crisis, but the underlying causes are financial innovation and debt build-up and the consequences will almost certainly be long-lasting and severe. It will involve repayments to MDBs being made from recycled bilateral grant aid or from each other's loans as has occurred in the past (Bracking 2009).

Banks started to develop various mechanisms for settling accounts between them and lending to each other during crises, which provided the logic for the creation of an international settlement bank that was one of the building blocks in the emergence of MDF. Similarly, states and national banks, after their creation, lent to each other during financial crises. This led governments to discuss creating a lender of last resort, like the IMF, for a couple of decades before its actual establishment, discussed below.

After this brief detour into the long-term growth of states, money, and debt, the chapter takes a more in-depth look at the factors that led up to the establishment of the first MDB. We pick up the story in the 1800s, when Britain was still at the centre of global finance, before the US took over this mantle between the two world wars. The picture of boom and bust financial markets was well established. By the 1880s, international capital flows were on a large scale and there were significant flows to foreign governments at the national, state, and municipal level mostly through securities. But, from this time until the eve of the First World War, the level of finance flowing to governments declined significantly, though flows to private ventures continued (Mikesell 1966, 4). Lending was tending to occur in bursts of about 20 years, followed by busts and defaults (Eichengreen 1991). Some of these loans, especially those to Latin and Central America, produced not just defaults but also concerns about exploitative lending practices and conditions. The forerunners of MDF were wider than just the boom and bust debt cycle though and include thinking about the possibilities for international cooperation.

2.2 Five key factors behind the emergence of MDBs

2.2.1 The growth of international cooperation

Nascent international cooperation was a key factor in the emergence of the MDBs. One of the first attempts at a mechanism for promoting international peace and stability was the Concert of Europe, established in 1815. It failed but set the precedent for cooperation and international organisations dedicated to pragmatic economic and technical cooperation did ultimately prove successful. Interestingly,

> in earlier international organizations, voting power was determined purely by financial contributions, ensuring that the most economically powerful members would prevail. This was the case in the International Telegraphic Union established in 1865 and, subsequently, in the Universal Postal Union, the International Wine Office, and the International Institute of Agriculture, all of which were created by 1914.
>
> (Woods 1999, 42)

The voting proposed for, and adopted by, the IMF and World Bank and most subsequent MDBs seems to derive from this precedent. The distribution of power in the IBRD initially reflected the economic hierarchy at the end of the Second World War and this legacy has been hard to overcome with the US determined to maintain its control. As Pieterse (2011, 26) said, 'even if hegemonic capacity isn't what it used to be, the habits of hegemony and of following hegemony linger.'

Still, the key point, as Mazower (2012) argued, is that between the late 1700s and the 1830s Europeans started to conceive not just of inter-state politics but also of an international political system acknowledging diverse peoples and forms of government. Systems of international organisation took a leap forward after the First World War, though most proposals and organisations were not able to overcome state rivalries and the forces of isolationism – especially in the US, the emerging hegemon.

2.2.2 The First World War, inter-war chaos, and changing international hegemony

The First World War was a nodal point in the decline of British hegemony and the rise of the US. War debts were one significant factor in this shift. The inter-war period (1918–39) saw a range of proposals for international cooperation, including in the financial terrain, though few successes. Still these provided the inspiration for later efforts. The ideas, and failures, of earlier cooperation attempts and the Great Depression were key motivators driving renewed cooperation efforts during and after the Second World War.

During the First World War, there were large government-to-government war and relief loans in particular from the US, Britain, and France to their allies and, subsequently, to support reconstruction (Mikesell 1966). However, there was no formal cooperation to assist countries recover from the war individually or collectively. Interestingly, Imperial China's leader Sun Yat-sen unsuccessfully proposed 'to the Paris Peace Conference of 1919 the creation of an "International Development Organization" that could mobilize international long-term lending to support China's development' (Helleiner 2017, 29). After the war, many countries faced political and economic chaos and for some this was exacerbated by the terms of the Treaty of Versailles, which concluded the war. The Great Powers established the League of Nations, though it was largely a failure. They attempted to organise financial cooperation through the League, starting with a conference in Brussels in 1920. Discussions on the monetary system and exchange rates at the conference were not successful but those for lending did continue. The proposals at these conferences provide a lineage for the Bretton Woods twins.

One proposal for the Brussels conference sent to delegates by Léon Delacroix, Prime Minister and Finance Minister of Belgium, was to set up an International Bank of Issue, which has a range of similarities to the IBRD (Oliver 1975). Its purpose was to issue interest-bearing gold bonds in exchange for securities like rights over customs duties, minerals, harvests, and so on. The bonds were to be issued to importers to pay for countries' imports of productive goods. Shares in the Bank were to be purchased in gold and voting power determined by the number of shares held, as in the IBRD. But the proposal lacked a guarantee that the bonds would be redeemed and sufficient incentive for nations that would not borrow to join (Oliver 1975).

M.C.E ter Meulen, the Dutch delegate, working off Delacroix's ideas, developed a plan for a Central Commission, which would allow individual states to issue interest-bearing bonds. It proposed using government revenues as securities and to give those securities to importers to use as collateral with exporters. The Central Commission was to be appointed by the League of Nations, which suggested that creditors' interests would be protected, and the bonds were to be 5–10 years, longer than Delacroix's, aiming to give borrowers more chance of recovering. The ter Meulen Plan was accepted and a Commission was established but, in 1922, the scheme was abandoned without making any loans. One of the reasons for this was the development of alternative sources of finance, in particular the 1919 US Edge Act provided long-term credits to support exports and, in the same year, the UK established an Exports-Credit Scheme (Oliver 1975). Export-import banks are, in fact, a key predecessor to the MDBs and they remain as siblings in the contemporary MDF system.

There were several other plans for economic cooperation in the 1920s and 1930s of lesser and greater ambition, the most important being John Maynard Keynes' 1930 plan for a Supranational Bank. This was the predecessor to his International Clearing Union Plan that was the alternative to US Treasury official's, Harry Dexter White's, plan for the post-war economic and financial order. Keynes' proposal was focussed on short-term adjustment finance, but other plans had long-term development aspects. What is notable is that there was significant debate on the topic in the inter-war years.

By the mid-1920s, the post-war chaos seemed to settle, and private international finance began to flow again. In contrast to the 19th century when flows to emerging regions mostly financed wars, these flows financed many productive investments (Mikesell 1966). Equally, however, many loans were reckless and excessive and there were mass defaults in the 1930s, resulting in private long-term lending slowing to almost a stand-still; it was even slower to recover after the Second World War. The defaults were caused, or aggravated, by the Great Depression, which started in 1929 with a financial crisis in the US. It spread internationally initially because Germany relied on US loans to pay its war reparations to Great Britain and France, and they, in turn, relied on these funds to pay their war debts to the US and other countries. Global lending collapsed and countries resorted to trade protectionism and currency devaluations which only exacerbated the crisis by contributing to a collapse in global trade. Mikesell (1966, 3–4) argued that the collapse of private lending in the inter-war years was in large part responsible for the establishment of the 'complex of national and international public lending agencies' that grew in the post-war era as there was clear evidence that free markets were not providing the necessary credit. The defaults of the 1930s produced the idea that loans for reconstruction and productive investments should be based on the recipients' ability to repay. In other words, creditors should set conditions that were conducive to repayment and growth (Mikesell 1966, 19–20). Here is a key logic for MDF – coordination of creditors and debtors needs. The focus on fair terms between creditors and debtors is no longer as prominent in many MDBs but the broader idea of the need for economic cooperation between nations has remained.

In 1931, US President Herbert Hoover put in place a one-year moratorium on war debt repayments from all nations and this became permanent (Mikesell 1966, Rohrer 2006). The chaos of the inter-war years and unregulated debt informed the US approach in the Second World War – from March 1941, under the Lend-Lease programme, the US supplied whatever goods were declared by President Roosevelt as 'in the interest of national defense' to more than 38 nations and repayment was as 'the President deems satisfactory' (Kimball 2003). Between $42 and $50 billion of aid was given and repayment frequently came in the form of post-war agreements rather than cash or bullion. Before and during Lend-Lease, many nations had taken on debt, and Britain only paid back the last of this debt in 2006 (Rohrer 2006).

Despite the failure of the League of Nations' attempts at economic cooperation, international monetary cooperation expanded during the inter-war period (Mikesell 1966). Cooperation between the emerging system of Federal Reserve Banks began in the 1920s (Ahamed 2009) and the Bank for International Settlements (BIS) was established in 1930 to manage the flow of German reparations and to formalise cooperation between central banks. German reparations were suspended shortly after the BIS was established but it continued to operate as a clearing house. It was set up as a corporation with shares owned by central banks, except for the US where private banks purchased the shares (Mikesell 1966, 14–15). This is like the IMF and IBRD, which are structured as state-owned shareholder-based institutions. The US Exchange Stabilization Fund was established in 1934 to promote exchange rate cooperation, which means it is a direct predecessor of the IMF. However, before the Second World War, the US was not willing to underpin an international system and the UK no longer had the capacity to do so (Arrighi 1994, 271, Ikenberry 1992, 306), thus cooperation was still largely piecemeal.

2.2.3 Keynesianism and the New Deal

Along with the shift in hegemonic power from the UK to the US, a vital part of the emergence of MDF was the arrival of a new theoretical and ideological framework, a new 'common sense' around economics (Engel 2010). The Great Depression, the rise of communism, and the increasing organisation of labour saw academics and politicians alike agreeing that high rates of unemployment were not just sub-optimal, but also dangerous in that they could lead to chaos or revolution. The Great Depression was tangible evidence that free markets do not always produce ideal economic and social outcomes. The new faith in human capacity to organise and the practical example of socialist states, which had grown industrially during the Great Depression, opened the door to the idea of state planning, which became a buzz-word in politics (Hobsbawm 1999).

These experiences and ideas were given a theoretical baptism by Keynes who homed in on the importance of the demand-side of the economic equation and the negative impact of deflationary policies. He started this focus in *A Tract on Monetary Reform* (1923) and bought together his ideas in his magnum opus, *The General Theory of Employment, Interest and Money* (1936). He argued that there was not necessarily a direct relationship between savings and investment and that confidence affects investment. The level of both aggregate demand and investment might not be enough to create full employment and that investors were too interested in short-term profits not long-term societal gains. This provided a case for government investment to increase demand and direct investment to its most productive uses. The 'Keynesian revolution' was in fact a two-headed animal – 'first, the theoretical revolution in economic analysis; and, second, the practical revolution in governmental policies' (Meade 1975, 82). The revolution in government policies did not always strictly follow Keynes' ideas, for example, in the growth of the welfare state, but the governmental revolution was more important than the economic one (Meade 1975), and it greatly improved the life experience of most people in Western countries. Overall, 'there was a profound change in the approach of liberal capitalist states to the role of government intervention in the economy – there was a new openness to the idea of economic planning and of state participation in the economy' (Engel 2010, 19). These changes further opened the door to expanded economic cooperation at the international level too.

The Second World War deepened US economic dominance as its economic productivity expanded and control over the financial system shifted to New York (Arrighi 1994, Kennedy 1989). US political isolationism was put to rest for many decades and the US became the global hegemon able to lead international organisation building. Indeed, the US government began planning for the post-war economic and political order from the autumn of 1939 (Gardner 1980), prior to becoming directly involved in the war! Its first focus was the post-war monetary and economic system, not the organisation of peace and security (Ikenberry 1992). US economic planning is discussed a little more below but first we turn to its economic cooperation with Latin America.

2.2.4 US economic cooperation with Latin America: from export-import banks to development banks

Discussion of regional economic and financial cooperation started in earnest with the First Pan-American Conference of 1889–90, in other words prior to the European discussions of the inter-war years. This conference proposed the idea of a private International American Bank to facilitate trade and investment in the region (Diaz-Bonilla and del Campo 2010). The then US President supported the idea, but it did not pass the Congress. Still it was reaffirmed at the Second Pan-American Conference in 1898, before disappearing. The 1913 Federal Reserve Act, in addition to setting up a decentralised reserve system, dealt with many of the issues that had concerned the first conference by allowing US banks to finance overseas trade, to operate accounts in other countries, and to establish agencies and branches abroad (Diaz-Bonilla and del Campo 2010). The issue of improving trade and investment relations, specifically exchange rates and adequate credit flows to Latin America, was again discussed during the First World War but little came of it. In the 1920s another credit binge took hold.

By the 1930s, the US was concerned about countering the appeal of Nazism and statist and nationalist economic policies in Latin America, which had grown during the Great Depression. The Depression had hit Latin America hard with the prices of its main primary commodities exports dropping from 1928. In fact, the 'Pan-American Agricultural Conference of 1930 contemplated the creation of an Inter-American Agricultural Bank' extending rural credits and finance for trade, but dropped the idea fearing subjugation to Wall Street (Diaz-Bonilla and del Campo 2010, 26).

Franklin D. Roosevelt's election in 1932 changed relations with Latin America with the 'Good Neighbor' policy renouncing US military intervention in the region. The policy was expanded over time to include a financial partnership promoting development (Helleiner 2014). The Seventh Inter-American Conference in 1933 proposed greater economic and financial cooperation through an agency comprising a Board, Consultative Committee, and an Inter-American Bank, which was to be like a central bank for the continent. Yet again, the US did not pursue implementation due to Congressional opposition. The US did though formally established an Export-Import (Exim) Bank in 1934 and, towards the end of the 1930s, it started providing the equivalent of development loans to some Latin American countries (Mikesell 1966, 13).

The language in Executive Order 6581 that established the Exim Bank has clear parallels to the IBRD's Articles of Agreement (AoA). It states that, in creating the Exim Bank, Congress aimed:

> to remove obstacles to the free flow of interstate and foreign commerce which tend to diminish the amount thereof, to provide for the general welfare, by promoting the fullest possible utilization of the present productive capacities of industries, to reduce and relieve unemployment, to improve standards of labor, and otherwise to rehabilitate industry...
>
> (Roosevelt 1934)

The IBRD's AoA (World Bank 2012) promote 'private foreign investment,' the 'development of productive facilities,' and the 'development of the productive resources of members, thereby assisting in raising productivity, the standard of living and conditions of labor in their territories.' New Deal, Keynesian principles permeate both documents. Like the IBRD, the Exim Bank was set up with capital stock divided into shares, though all were held by the Secretary of State and Commerce. Further, the IBRD followed the US Exim Bank's procedure of providing funds on receipt of invoices rather than establishing a deposit in the name of the borrower and of investigating the usefulness of projects, although as an MDB it abandoned the Exim's tied aid (Oliver 1975, 90).

A memorandum to the President in October 1938 by White under guidance from Treasury Secretary Henry Morgenthau urged large-scale economic aid to Latin America and China to secure peace and make the Good Neighbor policy effective (Diaz-Bonilla and del Campo 2010). White was the US Treasury Department official who drafted the first plans for what became the IMF and World Bank, and he had New Deal views and supported statist development models in line with US Treasury views.

A 1939 consultation meeting with Latin America's foreign ministers 'asked again for the creation of a new financial institution' with a multilateral focus and not a bilateral one like the US Exim Bank (Diaz-Bonilla and del Campo 2010, 32). The Mexican delegation presented a draft for the institution which included a range of clearing house and exchange stabilisation functions, many of which had been discussed earlier. However, 'on this occasion the Mexican Delegation expressly added the following: (f) To act as a channel for the investment of capital which will promote sound economic development in the American Republics' (Villaseñor 1941, 166). Indeed Kirsty Thornton (2017) attributed this addition to Eduardo Villaseñor, then Mexico's Undersecretary of the Ministry of Finance and Public Credit, and noted that Mexican officials had been discussing long-term development finance for at least 15 years prior to Bretton Woods. The US tried to deflect this request through expansion of the Exim Bank in 1940 and an agreement that it could lend to governments not just the private sector. Still, US views about a regional state-backed investment mechanism started to change; they became more open to the idea. In this context, the Inter-American Financial and Economic Advisory Committee began work on a draft charter for an Inter-American Bank (IAB), which is the chief direct progenitor of the MDBs.

The plan combined a clearing house, a stabilisation fund (like the IMF), and a development bank promoting the growth of industry and infrastructure. It was also to promote research, provide technical advice, and promote and publish data (Diaz-Bonilla and del Campo 2010). Like the IBRD, its first purpose was promoting the productive use of capital (Federal Reserve Bulletin 1940). Its structure was a bank with a capital base of $100 million, made up of 1,000 shares of $100,000. This follows the inter-war plans for an institution by Delacroix and became the model for the Bretton Woods twins. Voting was linked to shareholding and important decisions required a four-fifths majority, though the US was not going to have veto power as it did with the IMF and IBRD. Administration was to be vested in a Board of Directors meeting at least four times a year, rather than a permanent presence as the IMF and IBRD have. The proposal flagged the idea of an executive committee to make decisions between Board meetings, like the IBRD's Executive Directors who are responsible for day-to-day decision-making. The draft charter also outlined that any medium- or long-term loans needed a report from experts before approval.

From the US side, drafting was led by the State Department and White worked on it along with Emilio G. Collado who also worked on the IBRD. Oliver (1971, 4) argued the White's stabilisation fund and bank plan were 'an outgrowth of the Inter-American Bank proposal, though it embodied his own thoughts and the thoughts which had been expressed during earlier discussions within the Treasury Department.' Reading the proposed charter for the IAB that seems clear, although, in terms of the IMF, the US Exchange Stabilization Fund and other developments influenced White's thinking too (see Diaz-Bonilla and del Campo 2010, Helleiner 2017). In a footnote, Oliver (1971, 24) argues that Collado, Assistant State Department Chief, Division of American Republics was a major author of the Convention for the Establishment of an Inter-American Bank and 'may really have been the individual most responsible for the conception' of the IBRD. He was later the IBRD's first US Executive Director. In an oral history, Collado (1974) stated:

> In that committee we had a proposal for an inter-American bank. We actually wrote a treaty for an inter-American bank which was signed by half the American Republics, including the United States, but it was never ratified. It's a long story as to why it was never ratified. Harry White was one of the principal authors of this with Adolf Berle, who was the Assistant Secretary of State at the time. I got to do a great deal of the work and this was usually the rule. Actually a great deal of thought was put into an inter-American bank proposal at that time and it had some rather innovative aspects which never survived into the World Bank. It had access to the credit of the Federal Reserve System in a way that was never further put into some of the later proposals and maybe that's why it never got adopted.

The focus on White, Collado, and Berle, it seems to us, obscures the leading role of the Latin American delegations, in particular Mexico; indeed, *The Washington Times* critically labelled the IAB 'a Mexican-inspired institution' (Diaz-Bonilla and del Campo 2010, 39). The proposed operational powers of the IAB exceeded those of the IMF and World Bank and the 'sheer ambition of the bank project proved intimidating' (Diaz-Bonilla and del Campo 2010, 39). The US never ratified the charter after stiff opposition from sections of Congress and private banks. The latter is not surprising given the IAB had a broad mandate including making loans to private individuals and business. Indeed, Villaseñor (1941) argued that this should be its primary function.

2.2.5 US economic planning and the Bretton Woods Conference

Economic planning by the US and its allies has been outlined and debated in depth (see inter alia Block 1977, Gardner 1980, Helleiner 2014, Van Dormael 1978) and Chapter 3 explores the outcomes of that planning. This section simply outlines some of the key topics of debate and what was not agreed upon and not debated. The US State Department began economic and political planning in 1939, prior to becoming directly involved in the Second World War (Gardner 1980). The State Department had a *laissez-faire* approach and adopted, at times, aggressive tactics to push its trade agenda. The Treasury had been more influenced by the chaos of the inter-war years and was committed to planning. They became the key US negotiators and found common ground with the British and others on the need for a post-war monetary system (Ikenberry 1992). Still, the Bretton Woods institutions were shaped by the trade-offs needed to get approval from Congress, which was dominated by *laissez-faire* views (Gardner 1980, Scammell 1983). The planning negotiations aimed to create a stable trading order with reduced tariffs and limited non-tariff barriers to trade, cooperation in exchange rates and settlements to avoid the competitive devaluations of the inter-war years, building on the nascent central bank cooperation of that period, and to promote economic expansion after the war.

Negotiations between the US and its allies were based on the *Suggested Plan for a United and Associated National Stabilization Fund and a Bank for Reconstruction and Development of the United and Associated Nations*, drafted by White first in 1941. The plan was circulated for comment in mid-1943 and did not include a plan for the Bank. When the Bank plan was published it was no longer a central international bank as the IAB proposal was for the Americas, it had become an international lending agency (Block 1977). The British, led by Keynes, produced their own proposal for the Stabilization Fund – the International Clearing Union. Negotiations before and at Bretton Woods, though, were based on the White plan. There were 44 nations present, including strong representation from Latin America and the USSR. Still, it is often presented as an Anglo-American affair. There is some truth in this, but recent historical research has reclaimed the role played by other states, in particular in the developmental focus of the World Bank (Scott-Smith and Rofe 2017).

The IMF that emerged out of Bretton Woods was designed to manage a fixed exchange rate system with gold and US dollars the core units of account, act as a multilateral clearing house of funds between nations, supplement international liquidity for states, and impose conditions on states in regular deficit if they wished to access further liquidity from the Fund. Keynes had wanted both countries in surplus and deficit to be pressured to adjust but this did not suit US interests at the time; US interests did not consider that they would ever face regular deficit, as is the case now. Conditionality was also built into the IBRD's AoA, and, as sibling organisations, the World Bank has often acted as an enforcer of IMF conditionality, especially from the 1980s with the emergence of the Washington Consensus (more on this in Chapters 4 and 5).

Trade negotiations did not get far at Bretton Woods, dominated as it was by representatives from ministries of finance, though for the US orderly exchange mechanisms and convertibility were core to trade. The IMF dealt with short-term balance of payments deficits, while the World Bank was to provide long-term loans for reconstruction and development. This sounds comprehensive but there were key topics for the financial order not addressed. First, the movement of private capital – the system encouraged immediate liberalisation of countries' capital account. In fact, most of the world did not achieve this for some decades and attempts at premature liberalisation were the cause of a number of crises for developed countries (Scammell 1983). Capital movement's capacity to cause instability for developing and emerging economies dramatically expanded after the liberalisation of finance markets from 1973 with the end of fixed exchange rates. In the 1980s, many developing countries were pushed to open their capital accounts through IMF and World Bank conditionality often resulting in financial crises. The scale of international financial movements and lending is a significant cause of instability for developing countries and something that MDBs promote (Bracking 2009). Second, there are many weaknesses in the regime for supervising and regulating banking and finance, domestically and internationally, as was all too clear in the 2007–8 GFC. These weaknesses are a problem for the Global South, where debt can easily build up for a host of reasons. Virtually no matter how a state came to power, they can put a country into debt and this debt must be repaid by citizens. Third, there was no mechanism to deal with long-term default by states established at Bretton Woods. White's first draft of the IMF and IBRD did include a role in debt restructuring but this disappeared in later drafts (Helleiner 2017), presumably because it was too politically contentious for the world's largest creditor, the US, where powerful Wall Street interests wanted to ensure debtor paid up. The IMF and World Bank have taken up some of this role, though they have no legal power in managing relations with private creditors. Further, because of the tendency to bail-out failed governments and banks, the finance system has created an enormous moral hazard that favours the interests of elites (Bracking 2009). The MDBs face virtually no risk of non-repayment.

2.3 Conclusion

This chapter demonstrated that MDF was a logical step in the evolution of state borrowing initially for war and later for development. Debt from complex but largely unregulated private finance produced instability that Western democratic states could not tolerate and, at the same time, an overall dearth of financial flows to newly independent states. The dire impacts of the boom and bust cycles of international finance produced domestic and international forces promoting control and regulation but it was incomplete. Indeed, the very mechanisms created to facilitate flows to developing countries have created instabilities as there are few or no mechanisms to ensure public and particularly private debt is created for useful purposes by representative, effective regimes.

Some of the tensions embodied in MDF derive from its origins. State lending to other states has always been fraught and war credits often fed into post-war instability. The debates about economic cooperation by the League of Nations after the First World War led to the first proposals for institution building in this area and the creation of the BIS. However, the first formal development finance institutions were export-import banks, dating back to 1919 and they were designed with the developmental interests of the already industrialised world in play. The US Treasury was aware in the 1930s that Exim banks created political tensions (Oliver 1971). Nevertheless, the US Exim Bank came to provide something like concessional development finance to Latin America during the 1930s, assisted by concerns in the US Congress about the rising popularity and influence of Nazi Germany in the region. The US Treasury was also acutely aware of the failures of private institutions to provide adequate credit to developing regions, let alone ones at reasonable interest rates and for well-researched projects, which were likely to promote development and progress.

It seems clear that the first proposal for a regional body to provide MDF came from Mexico and not the US. Mexico, at the time, was pursuing a fairly radical economic nationalist developmental policy and actively sought to represent and promote the interest of poorer states (Thornton 2017). Given the relative progressiveness of the Roosevelt Administration and the concerns about the rise of Nazism, they supported the idea and helped develop a proposal for the IAB. The IAB 'combined the functions of (a) an investment bank; (b) an international stabilization fund with some Central Bank powers; (c) an ordinary commercial bank, and (d) a centre of technical and economic research to promote economic development' (Diaz-Bonilla and del Campo 2010, 39). In other words, it had broader functions than the subsequent proposals for the IMF and IBRD at Bretton Woods. These origins support Helleiner's (2014, 2017) recent accounts of Bretton Woods as having a greater developmental focus than has been presented in the histories of the World Bank to date. What Helleiner perhaps misses are that in structuring these organisations as banks – bound up with, and indeed reliant on, the international banking sector and money markets – the institutional structures created would prioritise banking needs not developmental ones. White thought that the institution's disinterested analysis of projects would be enough to differentiate it from older forms of finance capital. He said:

> In the past movement of capital have been regarded as, frankly, imperialist. They usually led later to difficulties of one sort or another. The other country did not like to pay; the interests built up were frequently supposed to be tyrannous. We are still liquidating many of the nineteenth-century messes which were occasioned by the *somewhat violent and not too enlightened motives of capital.*
>
> (White cited in Oliver 1975, 97, emphasis added)

Yet MDBs have not overcome the violence of capital, rather, as Graeber (2014) argued, debt as violence continued and has only been partially hidden by the impersonal structures of the modern state system and capitalism. Structural features were more influential in shaping the IBRD and MDF than the, at times, progressive aspirations of its founders to a 'New Deal in international economics' whose goals included supplying 'the huge volume of capital that will be needed abroad for… the attainment of world prosperity and higher standards of living' (Memo to Roosevelt quoted in Helleiner 2017, 28). State-backed MDF still remains subject to cycles of credit expansion followed by crisis. The repayment imperative sees basic services cut to the poor to pay back debt. Across the world, austerity policies result in increased disease and death, but such cuts disproportionately impact the poor in the Global South.

The MDF system was designed to ensure that debts were used productively but it did not include any mechanism for dealing 'expediently and humanely with a bankrupt government' (Soederberg 2006, 96–7). The IMF was focussed on currency stability and convertibility and short-term loans to countries facing balance of payments crises. This latter topic, along with increased surveillance of states, became its main focus after the end of the Bretton Wood mark I system, as the period from their establishment to the demise of the gold standard in 1971 and fixed exchange rates in 1973 is sometimes called. Neoliberal conditionality grew too with lending. The Bretton Woods twins have guaranteed repayment and both organisations are arbiters of country creditworthiness. Both also act as *de facto* global debt collectors and not always, or indeed often, in humane ways (Soederberg 2006). For example, in the case of the Argentine default in 2001, even after the country reached a deal with its creditors, a small number of private investors defied the agreement buying up defaulted debt at cheap prices and suing the Argentine government through US courts to get a better deal on the debt. An agreement was only reached in late 2016 and the precedent set by the holdouts was a major setback for effective restructurings (Stiglitz 2013).

It is fascinating that today's emerging powers, in particular China, are largely following the patterns of credit creation established from the 1930s. China's development finance started through its export-import bank and national policy banks and, as the political costs of this system of tied aid started to become too high, they established their own MDB, the AIIB. It is not entirely surprising that a state-led economy like China would find comfort in the Keynesian ideas that dominated when the first MDBs were proposed and created, namely, that '[p]rivate investors cannot be counted on to finance world-wide economic development in the absence of government guarantees to reduce the risk of overseas lending' (Oliver 1975, 62). But the fact is that the record of MDBs in creating economic development has not been overwhelming yet the system of MDBs continues to expand.

Note

1 This analysis draws quite a bit on Mikesell (1966). He outlined four direct precedents for the emergence of the IBRD: first, the growth of private finance and lending; second, war loans, third, international monetary cooperation; and, finally, the establishment of export-import banks. However, he does not discuss the proposal for an Inter-American Bank, which is the key precedent for the IBRD.

Bibliography

Ahamed, Liaquat. 2009. *Lords of Finance: The Bankers Who Broke the World*. New York: Penguin Press.

Arrighi, Giovanni. 1994. *The Long Twentieth Century: Money, Power, and the Origins of Our Times*. London: Verso.

Bieler, Andreas, and Adam David Morton. 2018. *Global Capitalism, Global War, Global Crisis*. Cambridge: Cambridge University Press.

Block, Fred L. 1977. *The Origins of International Economic Disorder: A Study of United States International Monetary Policy from World War II to the Present*. Berkeley: University of California Press.

Bracking, Sarah. 2009. *Money and Power: Great Predators in the Political Economy of Development*. London: Pluto Press.

Cammack, Paul. 2004. "What the World Bank Means by Poverty Reduction and Why it Matters." *New Political Economy* 9 (2):189–211.

Collado, Emilio. 1974. *Oral History Interview with Emilio Collado*, edited by Richard D. McKinzie. Truman Library. Accessed 8 November 2018. https://trumanlibrary.org/oralhist/collado2.htm

Kimball, Warren. 2003. "Lend-Lease." In *The Oxford Companion to World War II*, edited by I.C.B. Dear and M.R.D. Foot. Oxford: Oxford University Press, online.

Diaz-Bonilla, Eugenio, and Maria Victoria del Campo. 2010. *A Long and Winding Road: The Creation of the Inter American Development Bank*. Australia: Lulu.

Eichengreen, Barry. 1991. "Historical Research on International Lending and Debt." *Journal of Economic Perspectives* 5 (2):149–69.

Engel, Susan. 2010. *The World Bank and the Post-Washington Consensus in Vietnam and Indonesia: Inheritance of Loss*. London: Routledge.

Federal Reserve Bulletin. 1940. Inter-American Bank, edited by Board of Governors of the Federal Reserve. Washington, DC.

Gardner, Richard N. 1980. *Sterling-dollar Diplomacy in Current Perspective: The Origins and the Prospects of our International Economic Order*, 3rd ed. New York: Columbia University Press.

Geisst, Charles R. 2013. *Beggar Thy Neighbor: A History of Usury and Debt*. Philadelphia: University of Pennsylvania Press.

Graeber, David. 2014. *Debt: The First 5,000 Years*. Brooklyn, NY: Melville House.

Helleiner, Eric. 2014. *Forgotten Foundations of Bretton Woods: International Development and the Making of the Postwar Order*. Ithaca, NY and London: Cornell University Press.

Helleiner, Eric. 2017. "What's Been Missing from Conventional Histories of Bretton Woods?" In *Global Perspectives on the Bretton Woods Conference and the Post-War World Order*, edited by Giles Scott-Smith and J. Simon Rofe, 17–34. Cham: Palgrave Macmillan.

Hobsbawm, Eric. 1999. *Age of Extremes: The Short Twentieth Century 1914–1991*. London: Abacus. Original edition, 1994.

Hobson, C. K. 1914. *The Export of Capital*. London: Constable and Company Ltd.

Ikenberry, G. John. 1992. "A World Economy Restored: Expert Consensus and the Anglo-American Postwar Settlement." *International Organization* 46 (1):289–321.

Kennedy, Paul. 1989. *The Rise and Fall of the Great Powers: Economic Change and Military Conflict from 1500 to 2000*. New York: Vintage Books.

Kindleberger, Charles P. 1984. *A Financial History of Western Europe*. London: George Allen & Unwin.

Mazower, Mark. 2012. *Governing the World: The History of an Idea, 1815 to the Present*. New York: Penguin Books.

Meade, James. 1975. "The Keynesian Revolution." In *Essays on John Maynard Keynes*, edited by Milo Keynes, 82–88. Cambridge: Cambridge University Press.

Mikesell, Raymond F. 1966. *Public International Lending for Development*. New York: Random House.

Oliver, Robert W. 1971. *Early Plans for a World Bank, Princeton Studies in International Finance No. 29*. Princeton, NJ: Department of Economics, Princeton University.

Oliver, Robert W. 1975. *International Economic Co-operation and the World Bank*. London and Basingstoke: Macmillan Press.

Pieterse, Jan Nederveen. 2011. "Global Rebalancing: Crisis and the East-South Turn." *Development and Change* 42 (1):61–79.

Rohrer, Finlo. 2006. "What's a Little Debt between Friends?" *BBC News Magazine*. Accessed 28 February 2018. http://news.bbc.co.uk/2/hi/uk_news/magazine/4757181.stm.

Roosevelt, Franklin D. 1934. Executive Order 6581 Creating the Export-Import Bank of Washington. The American Presidency Project.

Scammell, W. M. 1983. *The International Economy Since 1945*, 2nd ed. London: Macmillan Education Ltd.

Scott-Smith, Giles, and J. Simon Rofe, eds. 2017. *Global Perspectives on the Bretton Woods Conference and the Post-War World Order*. Cham: Palgrave Macmillan.

Soederberg, Susan. 2006. *Global Governance in Question: Empire, Class and the New Common Sense in Managing North-South Relations*. London: Pluto Press.

Stasavage, David. 2016. "What We Can Learn from the Early History of Sovereign Debt." *Explorations in Economic History* 59:1–16. doi: 10.1016/j.eeh.2015.09.005.

Stiglitz, Joesph. 2013. "The Vultures' Victory." *Project Syndicate*, September 4.

Thornton, Christy. 2017. "Voice and Vote for the Weaker Nations: Mexico's Bretton Woods." In *Global Perspectives on the Bretton Woods Conference and the Post-War World Order*, edited by Giles Scott-Smith and J. Simon Rofe, 149–65. Cham: Palgrave Macmillan.

Toussaint, Eric. 2019. *The Debt System: A History of Sovereign Debts and Their Repudiation*. Chicago, IL: Haymarket Books.

Van Dormael, Armand. 1978. *Bretton Woods: Birth of a Monetary System.* London: Macmillan Press Ltd.

Villaseñor, Eduardo. 1941. "The Inter-American Bank: Prospects and Dangers." *Foreign Affairs* 20 (1):165–74.

Woods, Ngaire. 1999. "Good Governance in International Organizations." *Global Governance* 5 (1):39–61.

World Bank. 2012. International Bank of Reconstruction and Development Articles of Agreement. Washington, DC: World Bank. Accessed 24 November 2020. https://www.worldbank.org/en/about/articles-of-agreement/ibrd-articles-of-agreement

Wynne, William Harris. 1951. *State Insolvency and Foreign Bondholders Vol II: Selected Case Histories of Governmental Foreign Bond Defaults and Debt Readjustments.* Washington, DC: Beard Books.

3 Development thinking, debt, and the multilateral development bank system: 1946–79

This chapter is the first of two chapters exploring the emergence of development ideas and how they link to (i) the advent of the MDB system and (ii) development in practice. Chapter 3 explores the period from the start of the Bretton Woods system at the end of the Second World War until the late 1970s, three decades through which the post-war Keynesian consensus melded with welfare state and modernisation model to dominate economic thinking (Fine 2001). It was also the largest period of MDB creation with 22 organisations established. The chapter pays special attention to the founding of the first MDB – the World Bank – as it provided the model for future development banks. Thus, this chapter begins with a brief outline of the Bank set within the context of the emergence of development thought. The second section of the chapter explores the impact of regionalism and the United Nations (UN) on the expansion of the MDB system, outlining how the marginalisation of the UN in favour of the MDBs profoundly shaped development practice and more. The third section explores the sub-regional expansion of the MDB system, while the final section returns to the issue of debt, which rapidly expanded in the 1970s laying the foundations for the so-called 1982 Third World Debt Crisis.

As Chapter 2 outlined, the theoretical tradition that most influenced the Bretton Woods institutions was Keynesianism. Keynes' (1973) work was aimed at saving capitalism from its tendency to crisis as well as ensuring high levels of employment and reasonable standards of living for all; he aimed to make capitalism work more effectively. Keynes argued that capitalism tended to boom and bust cycles and that contra neoclassical economics, there was no automatic system for adjustment rather government intervention was needed (Galbraith 1975, Roll 1973). Keynes also saw the need for international economic cooperation as these same forces were at work globally and coordination was vital, especially during crises. Indeed, he was a key participant at the July 1944 Bretton Woods Conference that created the World Bank. Keynesianism fed into the establishment of development economics in the 1940s and 1950s and helped consolidate the idea that the state was a key means to organise society and promote development (Berger 2004). Keynes' work also reflected changes that had already been taking place in many industrialised states, where the role and reach of the state was expanding. This has been called a revolution in practical governmental policy, and Meade (1975, 87) argues this was 'of much greater importance and significance for the welfare of mankind' than the revolution in macroeconomics produced by Keynesianism.

After the Second World War, influenced by Keynesianism, development thought was not particularly ideological, it was not 'left' or 'right,' rather there was general consensus that more government intervention was needed than previously (Rapley 2002). Other key influences on development thinking were Modernisation Theory, with its focus on emulating the political and social systems of the West, and Growth Theory, which focussed on expanding capital formation from savings and investments as crucial to accelerating economic growth. Fine (2001) usefully labelled the post-war consensus as the Keynesian, welfare, modernisation model. This was the general milieu as the World Bank was established – development studies and development economics were in their infancy and thinking focussed on a greater role for the state through planning. Statism, Modernisation Theory, and Growth Theory all saw debt as a useful way the state could obtain the capital necessary for investment and 'take-off,' though Structuralism and Dependency Theory would challenge many of these ideas.

3.1 The World Bank: a brief introduction

The World Bank commenced operations in 1946 as the IBRD but later grew into the World Bank Group, which today has five institutions: IBRD, International Finance Corporation (IFC) added in 1956, IDA in 1960, International Centre for the Settlement of Investment Disputes (ICSID) in 1966, and Multilateral Investment Guarantee Agency (MIGA) in 1988. Given that this book studies MDF, we focus on the Bank's MDF arms: the IBRD, IDA, and IFC. As per World Bank Group usage, the term 'World Bank' refers to the IBRD and the concessional lending arm, the IDA, which have different Articles of Agreement but share the same staff and headquarters. In contrast, the IFC invests purely in private enterprises via loans and guarantees and provides risk management and advisory services. The Bank is the largest development agency in the world with over 12,000 staff and 5,000 contractors in 2019. After a large capital increase agreed to in 2018, its total capital base is $312.9 billion, meaning that surpassed even the European Investment Bank (EIB) which has $275 billion in capital.

Most historical accounts of the World Bank largely present it as the product of Anglo-American negotiations. As outlined in Chapter 2, however, its origins are more complex than that, with proposals for international economic cooperation dating to the 1800s. The story of the Bretton Woods Conference, where the final details of the IMF and Bank were negotiated, has been told often and very well (see inter alia Block 1977, Gardner 1980, Oliver 1971) and hence is not retold here. Overall, Bretton Woods gave the IMF responsibility for promoting an orderly exchange rates system, providing short-term assistance to nations facing balance of payment crises and undertaking surveillance of global economic conditions. Of course, its role in the exchange rate system changed dramatically in the early 1970s with the end of the gold standard and the shift to floating exchange rates. The Bank was to provide long-term loans to promote reconstruction and development. As Chapter 2 outlines, both institutions reflected the growing belief in the importance of international organisation, and they had Keynesian social democratic aims. The Bank's primary architect, Harry Dexter White, intended the IBRD as an alternative to private banks, which had been too exploitative and crisis prone (Oliver 1975). But, like most things, the devil is in the detail and in setting up the IBRD as a bank, White created an institution that would institutionalise banking norms more than human development goals. Other MDBs largely followed the model framed by the Bank, with their structures outlined in Chapter 5. Still, the Keynesian ideals that imbued the Bank's creation remain an important influence on the institution and subsequent MDBs, often most visible in their purposes, one focus of this chapter.

Analyses of Bretton Woods have tended to argue that reconstruction was at the forefront of White's mind in establishing the IBRD (e.g., Oliver 1971). In fact, White also had a strong focus on development and the Latin American delegations – and Mexico's representatives in particular – ensured that development was higher on the Bank's agenda than would have otherwise been the case (Helleiner 2017, 2014, Urquidi 1996). US bureaucrats did use the funding of reconstruction as a way of selling the Bank to Congress (Gardner 1980) and most of the other large shareholders were engrossed by concerns with reconstruction and the Bank's early loans reflected this (Mason and Asher 1973).

The IBRD's main aim is facilitating investment 'for productive purposes,' promoting private foreign investment, and promoting 'long-range balanced growth,' productivity, and standards of living (World Bank 2012, 3). The MDB was designed to help capitalism function more effectively and in a socially acceptable manner. In line with the Keynesian project, growth was important not just for its own sake but for its impact on employment (Engel 2010). The Great Depression had demonstrated that the international economy would not, under its own momentum, provide investment at a level that would achieve near full employment. Once operational though, the Bank understood development as the expansion of capitalism. But as Amin (2014, 14) has argued, '[c]apitalism is not "a system of development",' rather it is about the expansion of capital and private property. The Bank demonstrates this point in the way that it has sidelined some of its purposes, including balanced trade and national accounts, standards of living, and employment. To illustrate, the Bank for years claimed that its prohibition on political activity prevented it from promoting the International Labour Organisation's Core Labour Standards (Murphy 2014) despite the fact that among its purposes is the promote of the 'conditions of labour'.

The focus on private investment, private markets for capital, and guaranteeing private loans was a key contribution of the European delegations at Bretton Woods. As the Bank's first official history noted, it 'was all but the universal expectation of the founders of the Bank that its primary function would be to guarantee private investments' (Mason and Asher 1973, 26). In practice, it focussed on direct lending to states. The clause on private investment also highlights how economic logic dominated Bretton Woods thinking which has 'colored the Bank's development efforts' ever since, as the Bank's second official history pointed out (Kapur, Lewis, and Webb 1997, 70). The purposes demonstrate belief in planning and management by experts, noting the need for prioritising 'useful and urgent projects' (World Bank 2012, 3). Finally, the clause highlighting 'the effect of international investment on business conditions' (World Bank 2012, 3) offered a limited promise of counter-cyclical investment on both a country and a world scale, a Keynesian view. This is an area where it rarely engaged up until the 2007–8 GFC.

In terms of what investments should be prioritised, the World Bank sets the agenda and continues to play a leading, indeed often hegemonic, role in shaping the development practices of other MDBs. Founding senior IBRD staff held that manufacturing and export industries should be funded by private investors, so they were excluded as was investment in state-run enterprises, other than utilities. The consensus that dominated IBRD lending for more than a decade was that public utilities – in particular electricity, dams, transport, and communications – provided the preconditions to economic growth and the expansion of private investment (Mason and Asher 1973). As Toussaint (2008) points out, in its first 17 years the Bank did not lend at all for education, health, drinking water, or waste-water treatment and certainly not for welfare. Bank staffers felt their contribution to economic growth was 'less measurable and direct than that of power plants' (Mason and Asher 1973, 151) though it is now clear that this is the most direct way to improve human well-being.

In its early years, the Bank made several loans to colonial powers to finance projects in colonies in direct contravention of the UN's commitment to self-determination (Kapur, Lewis, and Webb 1997). Once independent, former colonies were required to take over Bank debts contracted by former colonial entities regardless of how odious they were (Toussaint 2008). Further, a key loan condition from its earliest operations has been settlement of outstanding debts, making the Bank a debt collector enforcing a capitalist hegemonic principle. Table 3.1 outlines the main contributions of Bank Presidents until 1981.

Table 3.1 World Bank Presidents 1946–81

Name and Term	*Background*	*Legacy*
Eugene Meyer June–Dec 1946	Born in US, attended Yale University, wealthy banker, served in several government offices, owned Washington Post.	Recruited senior staff, mostly bankers. Laid some of the groundwork for the Bank, especially loan analysis backed by a research department. Adopted a conservative approach to gain Wall Street's confidence. Clashed with Executive Directors over authority.
John McCloy 1947–9	Born in US, attended Harvard University, trained as lawyer, served Assistant Secretary of War during World War II.	Accepted presidency on the basis that he would have strong executive authority relative to the Board of Executive Directors. Obtained funds from capital markets and to do so demonstrated 'sound' (read conservative) lending and staffing policies. Established the interest rate policy and negative pledge – that no other creditor would take precedence over the IBRD – and policy of not lending to countries that had not tried hard to settle on any defaults to other creditors. Started the shift from reconstruction to development financing.

(*Continued*)

Name and Term	*Background*	*Legacy*
Eugene Robert Black 1949–62	Born in US, attended University of Georgia, served in US Navy, worked as investment firm banker, saw himself as a development diplomat.	Built up the foundations of the Bank started by McCloy in terms of loan development, staffing, management, and access to US credit markets to raise capital. Emphasised conservative banking principles. Focused on projects that align with strong national development plans and launched the Bank's technical assistance program. Promoted a vision of development as modernisation and advocated the role of private sector finance, leading to the creation of the IFC in 1956. The concessional loan affiliate, the IDA, was established in the Bank in 1961, although he originally rejected the idea. Popular with Bank staff.
George David Woods 1963–8	Born in US, office worker at bond firm, investment banker.	Viewed the Bank as a development institution rather than just a bank. He expanded lending and introduced program loans and established the Bank's role in aid coordination and strengthened the IFC. Woods expanded research from country creditworthiness to a more comprehensive assessment and expanded economic staff. He shifted focus from large-scale investment to agriculture productivity, education, and population growth. To allay investor fears about private investments, he established ICSID in 1966. Decolonisation saw membership increase by one third.
Robert Strange McNamara 1968–81	Born in US, attended University of California and Harvard Business School, introduced quantitative management to US car industry, served as US Secretary of Defence, responsible for the Vietnam War strategy that analysed success by the number of enemy dead.	One of the most influential and transformative Bank Presidents and a spokesperson for developing countries. He applied his quantitative managerial program to achieving Bank expansion in lending volume, geographical reach and staffing, and diversifying sources of finance. Lending expansion came at the expense of quality. McNamara focused the Bank on inequality and poverty, basic needs, education, and rural development especially for smallholders. Strengthened aid coordination and research capacity. Successful in substantially increasing IDA replenishments through political lobbying. Responded to the OPEC oil crisis by expanding lending and introducing structural adjustment late in his term.

Source: Compiled by authors from a range of sources, basic details from World Bank website (2019).

3.2 The expansion of the MDB system: the role of the UN and regional politics

The World Bank's shift to lending to developing countries occurred in the context of early Cold War hysteria. Despite the Cold War, many newly independent countries were assertive about their developmental needs and they were motivated by the success of the Marshall Plan. They focussed on the need for external capital for the development and were concerned that continued reliance on primary products exports would lead to under-development. This latter concern was empirically demonstrated by the work of Raúl Prebisch (1950) and Hans Singer (1950), whose separately published work on First-Third World trade, titled the Prebisch-Singer thesis, showed that the price of primary commodities, the main exports of developing countries, was declining relative to the price of manufactured exports from the First World. The declining terms of trade meant Third World countries would either need to export more and more primary commodities, change the structure of production in their economies, or live with increasing under-development. Faced with this dilemma, developing countries made a revolutionary push for soft finance to be provided through the UN and not the IBRD (Shaw 2005). The call was originally made by the Indian economist Dr. V.K.R.V. Rao in 1949 and was championed in developing countries and by Singer over the next decade. In 1952, the proposal was labelled the Special United Nations Fund for Economic Development (SUNFED) and it provided the core ideas for what became the IDA. SUNFED was to provide highly concessional loans and grants and be replenished regularly (Shaw 2005). The World Bank originally opposed the idea, in particular low-interest, long-term loans, as it perceived such loans would reduce the creditworthiness of borrowers (Mason and Asher 1973, 389–90).

The US was also opposed to SUNFED and little happened in IOs in these years without their imprimatur. US initial aid efforts focussed on technical assistance and Congress was very hostile to proposals for grant aid, indeed isolationist elements opposed any expansion of aid (Engerman 2018). The growth of MDF was an attractive alternative to grant aid and US President Truman's famous Four Points Speech in 1949 opened the door for its further expansion (Peet 2003). Still, it took some time to convince Congress of this and an idea from a State Department official for an Asian Development Fund went by the wayside in 1955 (Engerman 2018). This was despite the famous Asian-African Conference taking place in Bandung in April 1955, where 29 Afro-Asian states met to promote economic and cultural cooperation and to oppose colonialism and neocolonialism; the Bandung Conference was a key step in the creation of the Non-Aligned Movement (NAM) in 1961.

The World Bank was focussed on expanding support for the private sector. President Eugene Black proposed the establishment of the IFC as a sibling to the IBRD, to fill a supposed void in private sector lending. The US originally opposed its establishment too, but reversed this as a way of being seen to respond to the SUNFED calls (Mason and Asher 1973, Shaw 2005). Thus, the IFC was established in 1956 'to further economic development by encouraging the growth of productive private enterprise in member countries, particularly in the less developed areas, supplementing' IBRD activities (IFC 2012). The US shift was influenced by Cold War concerns too, which is clear from the fact that it created its own Development Loan Fund in 1957 under the Mutual Security Act aimed at strengthening 'friendly foreign countries' through 'competitive free enterprise' (United States Committee on Government Operations 1960, 6).

Other MDBs started to appear at this time. The Council of Europe Development Bank (CEB) (1956) and EIB (1958) were established without US involvement and are both borrower-led banks in contrast to the IBRD. They were early attempts to create a regional European bloc, as well as rebuild and strengthen Western Europe following the Second World War and during the early Cold War years (Bussière and Willaert 2006, Griffith-Jones and Tyson 2013). The CEB is a specialised development bank and it initially focussed on the welfare element of the Keynesian, welfare, modernisation model. Its social mandate aimed to help solve Europe's problems focussing on the impact of refugees and displaced peoples. It established the idea of both a regional and specialised focus for the MDBs, demonstrating that MDBs could engage with social issues, something the IBRD had avoided. The EIB followed in 1958, established by the Treaty of Rome as part of the European integration project. It aimed to build a common market, facilitate European integration, and promote balanced growth, which set the region-building tone of the RDBs and returned to a modernisation, economic focus. Still, Keynesian social elements continued with its focus on 'balanced and steady development' (European Union 2002, 139). It claims not to be an MDB, but its structure and functions are so similar that we think that it doth protest too much (see Chapter 6). The EIB's focus on region-building – it prioritises funding to 'projects of common interest to several Member States' (European Union 2002, 140) – was explicitly replicated in later regional and sub-regional banks (see Chapters 6 and 7). It was also the first MDB to specify that it is not-for-profit, in contrast to the IBRD being formally a profit-making institution and other MDBs being a mix.

Next came the US-backed IADB, established in 1959. As noted in Chapter 2, the early ideas for an inter-American bank pre-date the IBRD, although formal negotiations fell through. It was resurrected in the post-war era by the 1957 Economic Conference of the Organisation of American States. By 1958, the US supported the proposal, first and foremost because the US was concerned that the Cold War was impacting its zone of influence (Tussie 1995). Further, as discussed in more depth in Chapter 6, the IADB was seen as a counterweight to the IBRD's rather monopolistic position (Phillips 2009) and as a response to the Bank's perceived inadequate attention to Latin America and regional interests in integration (Barria and Roper 2004, Krasner 1981, Tussie 1995).

The IADB started a new approach to the purposes of the MDBs, moving away from the IBRD's mandate of facilitating investment for productive purposes and promoting private investment to the broader goal of contributing 'to the acceleration of the process of economic and social development of the regional developing country members, individually and collectively' (IaDB 1996, 5). While this could be seen as broadly Keynesian, it also reflects the impact of structuralist and statist development ideas that came out of the UN's Economic Commission for Latin America (UN-ECLA), which were popular in the region (Tussie 1995). Indeed, it had more flexibility to direct loans to the private sector than the World Bank (Humphrey 2016). This follows the strategy of import substitution industrialisation (ISI), which was the main way structuralism was operationalised to change the structure of production and avoid under-development (Rapley 2002). ISI was a key strategy in Latin America from the 1930s and was adopted by many newly independent states after the Second World War as well.

Although conforming to the IBRD's banking model, the IADB was established with a concessional lending arm, the Fund for Special Operations (FSO). This indicated that it was possible to combine hard-nose banking functions with a social agenda. While Latin American states had a majority of votes in the main body, the US demanded a veto over FSO operations and insisted that the IADB be headquartered in Washington, DC (Humphrey 2016), demonstrating again the impact of geopolitics on MDBs. Technical assistance is included in the IADB's functions, which was not the case in the earlier MDBs. This likely derived from the experience of the IBRD, which found it could not develop a project pipeline without the provision of extensive advisory services (IBRD 1948). This is further demonstration that the network between the MDBs started early. The establishing agreements of the subsequent RDBs – the AfDB, AsDB, and EBRD – all include technical assistance in their functions.

The IADB supported the creation of other RDBs (Culpeper 1997). Still, the supporters of SUNFED at the UN continued their efforts and even started drafting statutes in 1957. US views had been shifting, which was clear by 1958, but they wanted a soft lending facility under their control rather than the UN, hence tied it to the World Bank. The US had other motivations for supporting the IDA too, they had been accumulating non-convertible foreign exchange through the US food aid programme sale of surplus agricultural commodities and saw the IDA as an outlet for these holdings (Shaw 2005). Further, it was clear that the outlook for developing countries was not great and that the IBRD could not provide the needed support. Indeed, a report on the US Development Loan Fund had noted the IBRD was more like 'the international equivalent of the Export-Import Bank rather than' a loan fund (United States Committee on Government Operations 1960, 33). In other words, the IBRD had a hard-nosed business focus. Once the US supported the IDA idea, the US Treasury Secretary took an outline for it to the IBRD, and they then filled out the details and the IDA was launched in 1960.

The consequences of this decision were profound. The UN 'became a residual organization in economic and social development programs' (Shaw 2005, 58). The World Bank, in contrast, with the IDA add-on increased its resources and client base and was able to move into whole new areas of work that were not self-liquidating like most IBRD lending, including poverty and the social sector. The IDA may have slightly reduced Bank reliance on Wall Street, but it increased the power of major donor states because of the need for regular resource replenishments (Kapur, Lewis, and Webb 1997). The desirability of IDA resources helped facilitate structural adjustment lending in the 1980s at the same time as donors, especially the US, intervened more in policymaking. Overall, the IDA add-on put the Bank in a tremendous position of power in relation to borrowers, meaning that it is not a servant of sovereign states – as the UN system was designed to be (Shaw 2005, 59). The Bank was meant to liaise with the UN system but in practice even liaison has been weak and there is a chasm between the two organisations. In another weakening of the UN system, a group of Northern states set up a coordination mechanism for donors in 1960 through the grouping of rich states, the Organisation for Economic Cooperation and Development (OECD), which came to be called the Development Assistance Committee (DAC). It gets to decide what counts as aid and has become an influential voice in development debates.

Despite the focus on poverty and social lending in the debate that produced the IDA, its purposes – like that of the IBRD – make no mention of poverty. The IDA aims to 'promote economic development, increase productivity and thus raise standards of living…,' which will trickle down to raise standards of living (World Bank 1960, 2). This is not surprising as the IBRD played a key role in drafting the Articles and President Black promised that the 'IDA will not be a "soft lender"' (cited in Kapur, Lewis, and Webb 1997, 155). To protect the IBRD's creditworthiness, the IDA was created under its own establishing agreement, which duplicates the IBRD's with three changes: first, the Articles identify developed and developing countries and link countries' access to the IDA to their status to ration its concessional resources, second, the IDA's voting structure is slightly more favourable to developing countries, and, third, the IDA can fund social projects. Even though they have separate Articles and finances, the IBRD and IDA function as one institution.

By the late 1960s, the World Bank was largely focussed on assisting poorer countries, having reduced lending to rich states, and diversified sectoral loan allocations (Kapur, Lewis, and Webb 1997, 140). This did not happen just through the Bank's own vision of course, but in the context of rapid decolonisation, demands from the Global South, and challenges to the Keynesian, welfare, modernisation development model. The IDA and retained IBRD earnings also facilitated expansion, though the big push took place under President McNamara (see Table 3.1), who turned his zeal for prosecuting the Vietnam War to combatting poverty or, to be precise, promoting redistribution with growth and later basic human needs. The Bank expanded into soft sectors including health, education, water supply, and agriculture. In a way, McNamara was re-inserting welfare into the Keynesian, welfare, modernisation model, but in a minimalist form with the focus on absolute poverty reduction rather than on equality and rights, which has continued to be the Bank's focus. The basic needs approach increased the level of intervention in developing countries at the same time as bolstering the legitimacy of the Bank as a development agency (Rist 1997). It was, in Gramscian terms, part of the hegemonic struggle to shore up capitalist development combining coercive and consensual elements (Engel 2010).

From 1969, the Nixon Administration supported McNamara's growth plans for the Bank, because they wanted to increase private US bank lending globally to centralise the role of the US dollar in international finance and hence shore up US hegemony (Gowan 1999, 22). The Bank was useful because of its role as a recycler of funds and signaller to private finance. In practice, basic needs lending expanded after 1974 when McNamara discovered the integrated rural development approach. By the later years of McNamara's Presidency, the Keynesian consensus was under attack and neoliberalism and structural adjustment came to dominate the Bank, which is discussed in Chapter 4.

3.3 Sub-regional and general expansion of multilateral development banking

From 1960 to 1977, a further 18 MDBs were added to the system, ten of these in the 1970s. Only two were from Europe, the rest from the rapidly growing number of newly independent states. MDBs continued to grow too following the collapse of the Bretton Woods monetary order and the first oil shock in the early 1970s. Eight new MDBs were established between 1974 and 1979, indicating that they may even have been a response to the chaos generated by this time. This section explores the logic of this expansion linking it to geopolitics and development ideas, though given the number of actors, the section paints a broad picture, with the details of each MDB explored in later chapters.

After the IDA, the next MDB was from the Latin American region, which had fought for and won independence earlier than most of Africa and Asia. It was a sub-regional development bank (SRDB) and, like all the subsequent early SRDBs, it aimed to promote the integration and development of a sub-region. And growth of both regions and sub-regions were seen by structuralism as an instrument for promoting economic transformation (Bruszt and Palestini 2016). The Central American Bank for Economic Integration (CABEI) was established in 1960 by five Central American states, which were all members of the IADB. This makes it the first MDB established without the backing of a First World state. As part of their treaty on economic integration they established a SRDB to support sub-regionalisation, possibly taking inspiration from the European integration project and the EIB, but examining its purposes reveals clear influences from UN-ECLA and structuralism. As Chapter 7 outlines, CABEI's objectives start with the aims visible in earlier MDBs of regional development and balanced economic and social development but go on to specify that it will support projects and programmes in infrastructure, industry, and agriculture that benefit and modernise the region. Thus, it incorporated ISI in its objectives more directly than the IADB. Further, CABEI's subscriptions were not weighted, so founding states had equal shareholdings (Cochrane 1965), though this changed with the introduction of non-regional and non-founding member states, which quite a number of the smaller MDBs did in the 1980s, as discussed in the next chapter.

Several Soviet states created the International Bank for Economic Cooperation (IBEC) in 1964. It started as something closer to the IMF, but post-Cold War reforms saw it become an MDB. Next from what was then Communist Eastern Europe and Russia was the International Investment Bank (IIB) in 1970, a Soviet competitor to the World Bank. Its original aims are worth quoting as they are at one level so different from all the other SRDBs yet, at another level, they share the view of development as industrialisation and growth. It aims to provide:

> long-term and medium-term credits primarily for the implementation of measures relating to the international socialist division of labour, specialization and co-operation in production, expenditure for the broadening of the raw materials and fuels base in the common interest and the building of projects in other branches of the economy…
>
> (IIB 1970, 344)

The IIB's aims have since been changed quite radically, which is discussed in more detail in Chapter 7.

The 1955 Bandung Conference helped stimulate the idea of pan-Africanism, and five African MDBs were created between 1964 and 1975, the first an RDB – the AfDB in 1964 – and then four SRDBs. The AfDB followed the IADB's purposes in promoting accelerated economic and social development, and it also specified that development must be sustainable. Like CABEI, and inspired by NAM and Group of 77 (G77) agenda of seeking independent development, it was formed without any superpower or First World engagement (Culpeper 1997, English and Mule 1996, Mingst 1990). The four African SRDBs originally had only regional developing country membership as well and all arose from sub-regional integration efforts, which the UN Economic Commission for Africa (UN-ECA) played a key role in (Humphrey 2019). Many of the regional integration and trade agreements are no longer operational yet the MDBs remain. The SRDBs are the:

- East African Development Bank (EADB), formed in 1967 to support the East African Community (EAC);
- West African Development Bank (known by its French acronym, BOAD), established in 1973 as part of the West African Monetary Union (WAMU);
- Development Bank of Central African States (known by its French acronym, BDEAC), set up in 1975 to support the Central African Economic and Monetary Community (CEMAC); and
- Fund for Cooperation, Compensation, and Development formed as part of a second West African initiative – the Economic Community of West African States (ECOWAS) – in 1975; in 1999, it was renamed the ECOWAS Bank for Investment and Development (EBID).

All four African MDBs have standard SRDB purposes, although the EADB includes a role for regional promotion and BOAD has a strong focus on mobilising domestic resources. These SRDBs demonstrate the conflicting forces at play in post-colonial Africa of fragmentation and cooperation – as in Latin America, economic cooperation was seen as vital to post-colonial development. Mostly the African SRDBs financed infrastructure and small and medium enterprises to support industrialisation (Delikanli, Dimitrov, and Agolli 2018).

Following the AfDB, the next RDB was the AsDB established in 1966. It did not have anti-colonial credentials being proposed by Japan, then an emerging regional and global power. The US originally opposed the MDB's formation but later changed mind, seeing it as a way to contain perceived Soviet and Chinese influence by fostering regional growth and cooperation (Dent 2008, Kappagoda 1995). With Japan and the US as its major shareholders, it adopted much more pragmatic and capitalist language in its Charter with the aim of fostering 'economic growth and co-operation' in the region (AsDB 1967, 2). Like the World Bank, the AsDB now articulates a poverty-free region as its mission. The AsDB mirrored earlier MDBs closely from its inception, with the first President Takeshi Watanabe attending IBRD and IADB meetings to see how they were run before the Asian MDB began operations (McCawley 2012). Notably, there are no SRDBs in South or Southeast Asia, though a couple emerged that cover Central Asia later.

The next two MDBs established were again in the Latin America and Caribbean region *circa* 1970 with a further one added in 1974, bringing the regional total to five MDBs. The Caribbean Development Bank (CDB) was established in 1969 to support regional and local financial institutions and the development of regional capital markets as well as the usual SRDB goals. The innovation of building local financial markets harks back to the failed attempts at creating an Inter-American Bank and is a reminder of the recent development of public and private financial markets in some parts of the Global South. The CDB originally had 16 regional members along with Canada and the UK as non-regional members. While additional stakeholders have been added including China in 1998, the US is still not a member. The famous development economist Sir W. Arthur Lewis was the CDB's first president. Lewis was a key founder of classical Growth Theory which posited that states need to focus on growth, not redistribution, and that poverty was an employment problem, making it a suitable topic for economists (Engel 2019, Todaro 1985). His work on the need to transfer labour from the supposedly inefficient rural subsistence sector to the industrial high productivity sector was quite influential at the World Bank. The logic of most MDBs today is still to fund the enabling environment for this growth model, but the model has gaps and investments in industrialisation often came at a high human and environmental cost.

The Development Bank of Latin America (known by the Spanish acronym CAF) was established in 1970 and like the CDB it was tasked with 'providing multiple financial services to clients in the public and private sectors' in order to achieve regional integration and sustainable development (CAF 2015, 9). It started operations without member states from the Global North. USAID, Canada, the IADB, and a few European states provided resources early on but stopped, leading it to struggle to gain enough financial resources to operate until later restructuring (Humphrey 2016). The Financial Fund for the Development of the River Plate Basin (known since 2018 as FONPLATA Development Bank), followed in 1974 to support the River Plate Basin. It still has just five regional members: Argentina, Bolivia, Brazil, Paraguay, and Uruguay. It has a strong focus on studies and technical assistance, though they are also empowered to act as a financial agent or broker for loans for members (FONPLATA 2018).

Next in the MDB chronology is the Arab Fund for Economic and Social Development (AFESD). Its founding documents were prepared in 1968 but entered into force in 1972 and it was the first of a group of four diverse MDBs whose common feature is their Arab country-led shareholding. The Arab Fund is an SRDB with the rather pragmatic aim of '[f]inancing economic projects of an investment character… to public or private organizations and institutions, giving preference to economic projects that are vital to the Arab entity and to joint Arab projects' (AFESD 2016). While it is best understood as an SRDB, we have included it in Chapter 8 as a specialised MDB alongside the other Arab-led MDBs as they are an interrelated group that emerged after oil prices started to increase in 1971 (Corm 2006). The Arab Bank for Economic Development in Africa (BADEA) was established in 1973. It was a response to the increasing anger in the Third World about rising oil prices but also reflected the Arab desire to replace Israeli influence in Africa and promote Arab access to raw materials (Shushan and Marcoux 2011). It was the first development bank whose aim was to promote linkages between two regions, by providing financing and technical assistance. It was quickly followed by the Islamic Development Bank (IsDB) in 1974, which is a specialised bank operated in accordance with Shari'ah financial principles that ban the practice of interest. Its capital was subscribed in a new accounting currency, the Islamic Dinar (Delikanli, Dimitrov, and Agolli 2018). Its purposes are economic development and social progress, with the level of focus on human well-being standing out among the MDBs. It has stuck to its original, albeit broad, sectoral focus on transportation, infrastructure, energy, agriculture, and social infrastructure and not shifted with trends like policy-based loans, conditionality, or safeguards (Kellerman 2019). Its membership is not limited to Arab states but to those with a majority Islamic citizenry, making it a unique MDB.

Next came the Organisation of Petroleum Exporting Countries (OPEC) Fund for International Development (OFID) in 1976, which has the very pragmatic aim of promoting cooperation between OPEC member states and developing countries by providing financial support to the latter, making it a bit like BADEA. Its membership is again not limited to Arab states; indeed, Venezuela is the third largest shareholder. Looking at shareholdings in these Arab-led MDBs, Saudi Arabia is the largest shareholder in all except the Arab Fund where Kuwait has a slightly larger stake (Shushan and Marcoux 2011). Libya has large stakes in the BADEA and IsDB and is the third largest shareholder in the AFESD and sixth in the OFID, which is a left over from Muammar Gaddafi's activist Islamic socialist agenda of the 1970s.

It is useful to follow the Arab-led MDBs with the International Fund for Agricultural Development (IFAD), established in 1977, because Arab states also played a key part in its formation. Intellectually informed by calls for a New International Economic Order (NIEO) in 1974, it is based on an amalgam of Keynesian and structuralist ideas. IFAD's direct heritage is that of a challenge between OECD DAC donors and OPEC states in 1974 to each put up around

$600 million for agricultural development in developing countries (Szasz 1999). This was following the early 1970s sub-Sahelian food crisis (Wihtol 2014) and a general increase in food insecurity aggravated by the 1973 oil shock. The negotiations took place in 1974 and 1975, just after the NIEO. IFAD's structure was coped from the World Bank, but its shareholder structure gave equal voting shares to three groups: DAC donors, OPEC, and G77 states. The G77 states argued very strongly that votes within each group should be equally distributed and not on the basis of contribution as DAC and OPEC states wanted (Szasz 1999). The compromise was that each group could decide how they distributed votes and elected board members. The DAC managed to constrain the organisation, however, by mandating that IFAD could not undertake project appraisals, instead having to rely on evaluations conducted by other financial institutions.

One final MDB was created before 1979, the Nordic Investment Bank (NIB), established in 1976. It had been discussed since the 1950s by the five Nordic states – Denmark, Finland, Iceland, Norway, and Sweden – but a more favourable political climate and the oil shocks provided the needed impetus (Dennis 2015). It was set up simply to supplement existing institutions and finance and notably did not have a mandate for sub-regional projects.

Overall, by 1979, there were 22 MDBs. MDB creation was very high in Latin America (five banks) and across much of Africa (five banks), excluding the southern states where apartheid South Africa still exerted hegemonic influence. There were three banks established in Europe including the very large EIB, four Arab-led banks, and just one Asian MDB. But by 1979, state debt in many developing countries had already started to build up to problematic levels, and this enabled the emerging neoliberal doctrine to be imposed on states through loan conditionality, which is discussed in the next chapter. But to conclude this one we explore the debt crisis.

3.4 MDBs, debt, and the developing world debt crisis

Using debt to finance investments was a key part of the post-war Keynesian, modernisation, welfare model, which the MDBs were a key part of. But they face a unique situation, having a limited clientele and, as detailed in Chapter 5, their non-concessional lending arms need credit-worthy borrowers to get good credit ratings, which allows them to borrow cheaply on financial markets and on-lend. Still, with a limited number of borrowers, MDBs often become debt-pushers. If they do not keep pushing new loans out the door, they run into the problem that borrowers are paying back more than is being lent in new loans. This is called the negative net transfer problem. For most countries, MDBs are not their largest creditors but as Chapter 1 outlined, they play a range of roles in the development finance system. Their role expanded over the decades, with the World Bank at the centre thanks to its repository of data and reports. After the first debt crisis, the World Bank also became a debt collector and lender of last resort.

Development banks walk a fine line between pushing debt and worrying that recipients have too much of it. Debt was a challenge in some countries as early as the 1950s; a number of Latin American states had existing debt portfolios and they had faced two large debt crises in the 19th century and one in the 1940s as we saw in Chapter 2. The World Bank rescheduled loans to Haiti in the 1950s on balance of payment grounds and in 1965 made two loans to Brazil to cover the maturities due on earlier loans (Kapur, Lewis, and Webb 1997). India's debt problems were notable from the mid-1960s, but it was cushioned by its high level of access to the highly concessional IDA, becoming its largest borrower; the IDA was colloquially referred to as the Indian Development Association. The IDA add-on enabled the IBRD to reduce its exposure to India and undoubtedly India only met some IBRD and other obligations thanks to IDA credits. Nevertheless, India asked the World Bank to lead a rescheduling in 1966 (Kapur, Lewis, and Webb 1997).

A large debt build-up occurred in the 1970s bolstered by low interest rates and financial innovations beginning with the Eurodollar market and syndicated loans, where a group of banks lends to a borrower. The oil price hikes of the 1970s had very negative impacts on oil importing developing countries by increasing their costs and reducing export prices, meaning they had to borrow to cover the immediate costs of the shock. The oil shock created large revenues for oil exporters called petrodollars and these, along with the end of the fixed exchange rates system, contributed to a large increase in liquidity in private banks. Like MDBs, private banks need to on-lend their funds to pay interest to depositors. Developing countries offered a seemingly lucrative market and there was profligate and very large scale lending (Bracking 2009, Scammell 1983). Debt accumulation was largest in Latin America with several sub-Saharan African countries following suit. On average, debt-to-GDP ratios for low-income countries increased from 13% in 1970 to 46% in 1982 (Kose et al. 2020, 62). Loans were also made to what can only be described as illegitimate, odious, or corrupt regimes (Toussaint 2019). And too many projects did not benefit local populations, or caused too much environmental, social, or human rights harm. Legal and illegal capital flight was a particular problem, as Caufield (1998, 132) noted, the 'amount of money that left the Third World during the lending boom is staggering. The World Bank estimates that between 1976 and 1984, capital flight from Latin America equalled the increase in the continent's external debt.'

The World Bank under McNamara had a liberal approach to debt and expanded Bank lending while encouraging developing countries to expand their access to private finance (Caufield 1998, George and Sabelli 1994, Toussaint 1999). The South was creating their own MDBs too, further expanding debt relations. While private sector lending accounted for most of the debt, MDBs signalled that countries were credit-worthy. It seemed for a time like the lending would be sustainable, though that was illusory. The immediate triggers for the debt crisis were the second oil shock in 1979 and the Volcker shock of 1981. The second oil shock led to a recession that hit the exports of developing countries very hard. Developed countries tightened their fiscal and monetary policy leading to increased interest rates globally and increased debt service payments. Paul Volcker, then Chair of the US Federal Reserve, almost doubled the US federal funds rate in 1981 to 20%, in what is often referred to as the Volcker shock. Given the power of the US dollar, it effectively sets global interest rates, still US banks also directly held 37% of the $600 billion developing country debt (Bracking 2009). In 1982, amid a global recession partly bought on by the Volcker Shock, Mexico defaulted on its loans. Quickly thereafter most private lending to developing states stopped and the debt crisis began. Some 40 states found themselves in arrears, 27 had to restructure debts and 16 of those were in Latin America and the Caribbean (Kose et al. 2020).

The IMF, World Bank, and larger MDBs thrive in financial crises. Borrowing increases and private finance looks to them as debt collectors and as a safe place to invest. In the 1982 crisis, the debt deals turned private debts into public ones; the private banks were largely paid and even received large fees for loan rescheduling. The Bank and other MDBs took on a larger share of developing country debt and became the global system's main debt collectors. They had done this in part using what George and Sabelli (1994, 55) aptly called McNamara's 'parting gift' to the World Bank: structural adjustment loans. These enabled the principles of the new Washington Consensus to be enforced upon developing countries with ferocity.

3.5 Conclusion

This chapter shows how MDBs were created during the modernisation or Bretton Woods era, which had a relatively non-financialised banking system in response to the excesses of the late 19th and early 20th centuries. The Cold War political context was a key factor in many of the MDB creation – many larger MDBs were created by the Western block and the US as the political hegemon of the time had to be supportive or at least not obstructive. The Soviet Union played a similar role for states then in its sphere of influence, but it was not as interested in MDBs and only the IBEC and IIB were established in its sphere. Some of the MDBs in Africa and Latin America reflected more structuralist development ideas.

The MDBs were designed to meet one of the shortcomings of capitalist finance; private banks can be risk averse, particularly in developing country contexts, and so national and multilateral development banks were meant to provide an alternative way to boost investment. However, the MDBs played a role in the growing financialisation of the 1970s by encouraging lending to the Third World and setting standards for it as well as by promoting new financial instruments, so they were a contributor to the developing country debt crisis. Financialisation took off during the 1980s, which is where Chapter 4 takes up the story: MDB creation in the neoliberal era.

Bibliography

AFESD. 2016. *Agreement Establishing the Arab Fund for Economic and Social Development*. Kuwait. Accessed 14 May 2020. http://www.arabfund.org/Default.aspx?pageId=429.

Amin, Samir. 2014. *Capitalism in the Age of Globalization: The Management of Contemporary Society*. London and New York: Zed Books.

AsDB. 1967. *Agreement Establishing the Asian Development Bank*. Manila: Asian Development Bank. Accessed 24 November 2020. https://www.adb.org/documents/agreement-establishing-asian-development-bank-adb-charter

Barria, Lilian A., and Steven D. Roper. 2004. "Economic Transition in Latin American and Post-Communist Countries: A Comparison of Multilateral Development Banks." *International Journal of Politics, Culture, and Society* 17 (4):619–38. doi: 10.1023/B:IJPS.0000031235.74193.a4.

Berger, Mark T. 2004. *The Battle for Asia: From Decolonization to Globalization*. London and New York: Routledge Curzon.

Block, Fred L. 1977. *The Origins of International Economic Disorder: A Study of United States International Monetary Policy from World War II to the Present*. Berkeley: University of California Press.

Bracking, Sarah. 2009. *Money and Power: Great Predators in the Political Economy of Development*. London: Pluto Press.

Bruszt, Lazlo, and Stefano Palestini. 2016. "Regional Development Governance." In *The Oxford Handbook of Comparative Regionalism*, edited by Tanja A. Börzel and Thomas Risse, 374–404. Oxford: Oxford University Press.

Bussière, Eric, and Emilie Willaert. 2006. *Council of Europe Development Bank: The Social Development Bank in Europe*. Paris: Council of Europe Development Bank.

CAF. 2015. *Agreement Establishing Corporación Andina de Fomento*. Caracas: Banco de Desarrollo de América Latina. Accessed 24 November 2020. https://www.caf.com/media/29934/caf-agreement-establishing-10032015.pdf

Caufield, Catherine. 1998. *Masters of Illusion : The World Bank and the Poverty of Nations*. London: Pan Books.

Cochrane, James D. 1965. "The Central American Bank for Economic Integration: A Descriptive Note." *Caribbean Studies* 5 (2):64–73.

Corm, Georges. 2006. "The Arab Experience." In *Regional Financial Cooperation*, edited by José Antonio Ocampa, 291–328. Washington, DC: UN ECLA and Brookings Insitution Press.

Culpeper, Roy. 1997. *Titans or Behemoths?* London: Lynne Rienner.

Delikanli, Ihsan Ugur, Todor Dimitrov, and Roena Agolli. 2018. *Multilateral Development Banks: Governance and Finance*. Cham: Palgrave Macmillan.

Dennis, Bengt. 2015. "Green Light at Third Attempt: How NIB Came to be Forty Years Ago." Nordiic Investment Bank. Accessed 20 May. https://www.nib.int/who_we_are/news_and_media/articles/1761/green_light_at_third_attempt_how_nib_came_to_be_forty_years_ago.

Dent, Christopher M. 2008. "The Asian Development Bank and Developmental Regionalism in East Asia." *Third World Quarterly* 29 (4):767–86. doi: 10.1080/01436590802052714.

Engel, Susan. 2010. *The World Bank and the Post-Washington Consensus in Vietnam and Indonesia: Inheritance of Loss*. London: Routledge.

Engel, Susan. 2019. "Development Economics: Classical, Neoclassical, Critical." In *Oxford Research Encyclopedia of International Studies*, edited by Renée Marlin-Bennett, 1–24. Oxford: Oxford University Press.

Engerman, David C. 2018. *The Price of Aid: The Economic Cold War in India*. Cambridge, MA: Harvard University Press.

English, E. Phillip, and Harris M. Mule. 1996. *The African Development Bank*. London: Lynne Rienner.

European Union. 2002. *Consolidated Versions of the Treaty on European Union and the Treaty Establishing the European Community*. Brussels: European Union. Accessed 24 November 2020. https://eur-lex.europa.eu/legal-content/EN/TXT/?uri=CELEX%3A12002E%2FTXT

Fine, Ben. 2001. *Social Capital versus Social Theory: Political Economy and Social Science at the Turn of the Millennium*. London: Routledge.

FONPLATA. 2018. *Financial Fund for the Development of the River Plate Basin Articles of Agreement*. Accessed 24 November 2020. https://www.fonplata.org/sites/default/files/paginas-fonplata/archivos/EN%20-%20Constitutive%20Agreement%20%28Update%202018%29.pdf

Galbraith, John Kenneth. 1975. "How Keynes Came to America." In *Essays on John Maynard Keynes*, edited by Milo Keynes, 132–41. Cambridge: Cambridge University Press.

Gardner, Richard N. 1980. *Sterling-dollar Diplomacy in Current Perspective: The Origins and the Prospects of Our International Economic Order*, 3rd ed. New York: Columbia University Press.

George, Susan, and Fabrizio Sabelli. 1994. *Faith and Credit: The World Bank's Secular Empire*. London: Penguin Books.

Gowan, Peter. 1999. *The Global Gamble: Washington's Faustian Bid for World Dominance*. London: Verso.

Griffith-Jones, Stephany, and Judith Tyson. 2013. The European Investment Bank: Lessons for Developing Countries. In *WIDER Working Paper*.

Helleiner, Eric. 2014. *Forgotten Foundations of Bretton Woods: International Development and the Making of the Postwar Order*. Ithaca, NY and London: Cornell University Press.

Helleiner, Eric. 2017. "What's Been Missing from Conventional Histories of Bretton Woods?" In *Global Perspectives on the Bretton Woods Conference and the Post-War World Order*, edited by Giles Scott-Smith and J. Simon Rofe, 17–34. Cham: Palgrave Macmillan.

Humphrey, Chris. 2016. "The Invisible Hand: Financial Pressures and Organisational Convergence in Multilateral Development Banks." *The Journal of Development Studies* 52 (1):92–112. doi: 10.1080/00220388.2015.1075978.

Humphrey, Chris. 2019. "'Minilateral' Development Banks: What the Rise of Africa's Trade and Development Bank Says about Multilateral Governance." *Development and Change* 50 (1):164–90. doi: 10.1111/dech.12467.

IaDB. 1996. *Agreement Establishing the Inter-American Development Bank*. Washington, DC: Inter-American Development Bank. Accessed 11 March 2020. https://www.iadb.org/en/legal-resource-center/historic-agreement-establishing-inter-american-development-bank

IBRD. 1948. Third Annual Report to the Board of Governors, 1947–1948. Washington, DC: International Bank for Reconstruction and Development.

IFC. 2012. *Articles of Agreement*. Washington, DC: International Finance Corporation. Accessed 24 November 2020. https://www.ifc.org/wps/wcm/connect/corp_ext_content/ifc_external_corporate_site/about+ifc_new/ifc+governance/articles/about+ifc+-+ifc+articles+of+agreement

IIB. 1970. Agreement Concerning the Establishment of an International Investment Bank. New York: United Nations – Treaty Series Volume 801, 1975. Accessed 11 March 2020. https://treaties.un.org/doc/Publication/UNTS/Volume%20801/v801.pdf

Kappagoda, Nihal. 1995. *The Asian Development Bank*. London: Lynne Rienner.

Kapur, Devesh, John P. Lewis, and Richard Webb. 1997. *The World Bank Its First Half Century, Volume 1: History*. 2 vols. Vol. 1: History. Washington, DC: Brookings Institution Press.

Kellerman, Miles. 2019. "The Proliferation of Multilateral Development Banks." *Review of International Organization* 14 (1):107–45. doi: 10.1007/s11558-018-9302-y.

Keynes, John Maynard. 1973. *The General Theory of Employment, Interest and Money*. London: Macmillan for the Royal Economic Society.

Kose, M. Ayhan, Peter Nagle, Franziska Ohnsorge, and Naotaka Sugawara. 2020. *Global Waves of Debt: Causes and Consequences*. Washington, DC: World Bank.

Krasner, Stephen D. 1981. "Power Structures and Regional Development Banks." *International Organization* 35 (2):303–28.
Mason, Edward S., and Robert E. Asher. 1973. *The World Bank Since Bretton Woods.* Washington, DC: The Brookings Institution.
McCawley, Peter. 2012. *Banking on the Future of Asia and the Pacific: 50 Years of the Asian Development Bank.* Manila: Asian Development Bank.
Meade, James. 1975. "The Keynesian Revolution." In *Essays on John Maynard Keynes,* edited by Milo Keynes. Cambridge: Cambridge University Press.
Mingst, Karen. 1990. *Politics & the African Development Bank.* Lexington: The University of Kentucky Press.
Murphy, Hannah. 2014. "The World Bank and Core Labour Standards: Between Flexibility and Regulation." *Review of International Political Economy* 21 (2):399–431. doi: 10.1080/09692290.2013.779591.
Oliver, Robert W. 1971. *Early Plans for a World Bank, Princeton Studies in International Finance No. 29.* Princeton, NJ: Department of Economics, Princeton University.
Oliver, Robert W. 1975. *International Economic Co-operation and the World Bank.* London and Basingstoke: Macmillan Press.
Peet, Richard. 2003. *Unholy Trinity: The IMF, World Bank and WTO.* London: Zed Books.
Phillips, David A. 2009. *Reforming the World Bank: Twenty Years of Trial – and Error.* Cambridge: Cambridge University Press.
Prebisch, Raúl. 1950. *The Economic Development of Latin America and Its Principle Problems.* New York: United Nations.
Rapley, John. 2002. *Understanding Development: Theory and Practice in the Third World.* Boulder, CO: Lynne Reinner Publishers Inc.
Rist, Gilbert. 1997. *The History of Development: From Western Origins to Global Faith.* Translated by Patrick Camiller. London and New York: Zed Books.
Roll, Eric. 1973. *A History of Economic Thought,* 4th ed. London: Faber and Faber Ltd.
Scammell, W.M. 1983. *The International Economy Since 1945,* 2nd ed. London: Macmillan Education Ltd.
Shaw, D. John. 2005. "Turning Point in the Evolution of Soft Financing: The United Nations and the World Bank." *Canadian Journal of Development Studies* XXVI (1):43–61.
Shushan, Debra, and Christopher Marcoux. 2011. "The Rise (and Decline?) or Arab Aid: Generosity and Allocation in the Oil Era." *World Development* 39 (11):1969–80.
Singer, Hans W. 1950. "The Distribution of Gains between Investing and Borrowing Countries." *American Economic Review* 40 (2):478.
Szasz, Paul C. 1999. "Establishment of the International Fund for Agricultural Development." *Studies in Transnational Legal Policy* 31–32:32–43.
Todaro, Michael P. 1985. *Economic Development in the Third World: An Introduction to Problems and Policies in a Global Perspective,* 3rd ed. New York: Longman.
Toussaint, Eric. 1999. *Your Money or Your Life! The Tyranny of Global Finance.* Translated by Raghu Krishnan and Vicki Briault Manus. London: Pluto Press.
Toussaint, Eric. 2008. *The World Bank: A Critical Primer.* Translated by Elizabeth Anne, Vicki Briault, Bertrand Declercq, Sushovan Dhar, Judith Harris, Raghu Krishnan, Marie Lagatta, Christine Pagnoulle, Véronique Renard, Gillian Sloane-Seale and Diren Valayden. London, Anne Arbor: Pluto Press in associatin with CADTM, Committee for the Abolition of Third World Debt.
Toussaint, Eric. 2019. *The Debt System: A History of Sovereign Debts and Their Repudiation.* Chicago, IL: Haymarket Books.

Tussie, Dianne. 1995. *The Inter-American Development Bank*. London: Lynne Rienner.
United States Committee on Government Operations. 1960. Operations of the Development Loan Fund. Washington, DC: US Government Printing Office.
Urquidi, Victor L. 1996. "Reconstruction vs. Development: The IMF and the World Bank." In *The Bretton Woods – GATT System: Retrospect and Prospect After Fifty Years*, edited by Orin Kirshner, 30–51. Armonk, NY: M.E. Sharp.
Wihtol, Robert. 2014. Whither Multilateral Development Finance? In *AsDBI Working Paper Series*. Tokyo: Asian Development Bank Institute.
World Bank. 1960. *International Development Association Articles of Agreement*. Washington, DC: World Bank. Accessed 10 March 2020. https://www.worldbank.org/en/about/articles-of-agreement
World Bank. 2012. *International Bank of Reconstruction and Development Articles of Agreement*. Washington, DC: World Bank. Accessed 24 November 2020. https://www.worldbank.org/en/about/articles-of-agreement/ibrd-articles-of-agreement.

4 Development thinking, debt, and the multilateral development bank system: 1980–2020

This second chapter on the evolution of the multilateral development bank (MDB) system starts in 1980 when neoliberalism captured the global political economy including the World Bank and other large MDBs. It journeys through a range of modifications to neoliberalism leading to the current era, which we call retroliberal following Murray and Overton (2016). There were nine MDBs established in this period, eight still functioning, thus by the end of 2020, there were 30 functioning MDBs, several with multiple financing arms. As with Chapter 3, the emergence of and shifts in the MDBs are linked to three factors: geopolitics, development discourse, and debt relations.

This chapter is divided into three periods, each linked to a major debt crisis that can be associated with calls capitalism's need for spatial fixes (Harvey 2010). The first period was high neoliberalism or the Washington Consensus era; it lasted from 1980 to 1997 and began and ended with debt crises. At the start, the Third World debt crisis saw large MDBs become debt collectors and impose the new orthodoxy of free markets, free trade, small government, and individual responsibility on recipient states. Only a few MDBs were created during this period, including the only MDB with a pro-democracy, pro-market mandate: the EBRD. The Washington Consensus era ended with the 1997 Asian Financial Crisis, by which time the social costs of fundamentalist neoliberalism had become too great, including increasing poverty and social inequalities. The post-Washington Consensus era of 1998–2009 was the response to the problems of orthodox neoliberalism. Poverty reduction seemed to replace economic growth at the top of the development agenda, supported by the 2000 MDGs and, later, the 2015 SDGs. However, the term *post*-Washington Consensus highlights the continuities with neoliberalism – the focus on growth and private markets had not disappeared and the poverty-reduction agenda was ultimately rather minimalist; still, there was a sense that the development agenda had become more progressive. This period saw the rise of China and leftist movements in Latin America, which resulted in an increased focus on the role of the state and new development paradigms aimed at challenging the Washington Consensus. The era closed when debt expansion in the US and Western and Central Europe achieved critical mass in the 2007–8 GFC.

The GFC changed development discourse, but not as significantly as would be hoped. The moniker *retroliberal* for the period 2010–20 highlights that policy responses to the GFC mostly shored up the position of capital over labour by socialising private losses while maintaining the privatisation of gains. Financialisation was only reined in for a brief moment, before again being unleashed in another example of how the practices of neoliberalism adapt to circumstances (Cahill 2014). Still, a more state-centric, nationalist era has emerged. Aid and development finance are again viewed in terms of the benefits they provide to donor states' firms rather than to poverty reduction. Further, in large part thanks to Chinese interests, infrastructure is again a key focus for development finance, which is a return to modernisation era thinking along with the revised fixation on economic growth. Hence the retro prefix makes sense; it hints at the retrospective and retrograde elements of development discourse in 2020, with the MDBs again at centre stage after having taken somewhat of a back seat during the early 2000s.

A major danger of this shift is its impact on debt. Already prior to the 2020 Coronavirus crisis, the IMF and World Bank were warning of growing debt, with the Bank calling the build-up of debt in EMDEs from 2010 to 2018 the 'largest, fastest and most broad-based increase' in the past 50 years (Kose et al. 2020, 111). COVID-19 is causing further debt build-up and may trigger a debt crisis, whereas the usual triggers of the past 50 years were financial or banking crises. It is an emerging context, yet it seems rather clear that the MDBs are again going to be key players in another debt crisis.

The three eras explored in the chapter each follows the same structure: first, changes in developing thinking are briefly analysed, second, changes in the World Bank are outlined, followed by a third section on changes in the other MDBs, and a fourth analysing the growth of new MDBs in each era.

4.1 The Washington Consensus era: 1980–97

The global shift from the Keynesian, welfare, modernisation model to neoliberal structural adjustment – or austerity politics – must be told in conjunction with that of the IMF and World Bank. This is because the policy prescriptions associated with this neoliberal approach were negotiated between the US and the Bretton Woods twins in Washington, DC, and hence are called the Washington Consensus (Williamson 1990). The policies reflected the resurgence of a strand of neoclassical economics propounded by scholars like Friedrich von Hayek and Milton Friedman, which rejected the post-war consensus and instead promoted the moral and economic priority of individuals and markets over society and the state. It was a broad project ushered in by a new politico-economic climate with the election of Margaret Thatcher in the UK, Ronald Reagan in the US, and Helmut Kohl in West Germany. There were neoliberal regimes elected or imposed through coups and other non-electoral mechanisms around the world, for example, the Augusto Pinochet regime in Chile. Multinational corporations promoted neoliberal approaches in ways that benefitted them. In Gramscian terms, neoliberalism's spread was through both consent and coercion. In examining the practices of governments, it is important to remember that they have been happy to implement a range of policies that are not always immediately in keeping with neoliberalism or may not appear to be neoliberal, but this pragmatic approach reinforces the legitimacy of that state and often serves particular capitalist interests. In the wake of financial and banking crises, the GFC being a case in point, governments have often resorted to Keynesian-type policies, but generally only as a temporary measure in order to deepen neoliberalism in the long run (Cahill 2014).

The Washington Consensus clustered around three broad commitments: macroeconomic stability, outward orientation, and domestic liberalisation (Fine 2001). In the early years, it tended to be implemented in two phases: first, short-term macroeconomic stabilisation carried out quickly via 'big bang' reforms, which was the focus of IMF programmes; and, second, long-term exhaustive microeconomic reforms including trade liberalisation, privatisation of state-owned enterprises, and then later utilities, changes to taxation, land titling to make land more easily alienable, labour market reform, and deregulation of banking and capital movement (Chossudovsky 1997). This latter programme tended to be implemented jointly by the IMF, World Bank, and RDBs. The Washington Consensus was based on a 'profoundly cynical view of the state in developing countries' (Toye 1993, 135).

The Third World debt crisis provided the IMF and World Bank the opportunity to implement neoliberal policies as loan conditions, which often supported US hegemony and made the Global South structurally more open to US goods and finance (Gowan 1999). As time passed, there was variation in the Bank's approach, mostly prompted by the failures of neoliberal austerity policies. The number of people living under the absurdly low $1 per day international poverty line increased in many regions. The 1980s were thus labelled the lost decade for developing countries, particularly those in Latin America and sub-Saharan Africa. For much of Africa, the debt crisis was not resolved until the late 1990s. In Latin America, where the 1980s debt relief schemes were targeted, growth remained low. The debt management processes also saw the Paris Club and multilaterals holding an increasing share of EMDE debt and the new loans they provided were often used to pay arrears on private sector debt.

There were two early additions to the Washington Consensus to try to improve performance. One was good governance, which initially meant multi-party elections but was expanded to include anti-corruption initiatives and the adoption of Western budgetary and auditing systems. The second was a focus on poverty and minimalist social safety; arguably without some focus on poverty, neoliberalism was in danger of collapsing. In 1990, the World Bank's influential World Development Report was grandly titled *Poverty* and on 31 December 1991, poverty appeared in the Bank's mission statement (Kapur, Lewis, and Webb 1997). Poverty reduction is the neoliberal alternative to redistribution and social democratic welfare systems because it is a minimalist idea that defines equity and equality as getting people above the international poverty line – now at $1.90 a day – and no more. It posits that getting out of poverty mostly involves individual pursuit of increased productivity (Cammack 2004) and re-awakens the distinction between the deserving and undeserving poor. In 1990, the UN Human Development

Reports first appeared too, demonstrating a re-emergence of the UN system in development space, as a timid challenger to World Bank.

The literature on the empirical and theoretical failures of the Washington Consensus increased over the 1990s. GDP in Latin America only returned to its pre-debt crisis level in 1993 (Kose et al. 2020). The IFIs 'big bang' reform approach in the former Soviet Union was a failure as was their response to the 1997 Asian Financial Crisis. This 1990s debt wave was mostly in East Asia and some other emerging economies and was predominately caused by an upsurge in private sector debt following liberalisation and deregulation, while the Brady bonds created as part of the resolution of the Latin American debt crisis stimulated the development of sovereign bond markets in developing countries. In the case of the Asian Financial Crisis, former World Bank Chief Economist Joseph Stiglitz (2000, 60) concluded that the IMF's response made the crisis 'deeper, longer and harder.' Sustained pressure on the Bank led it to claim by the late 1990s that it had moved beyond the Washington Consensus. What emerged, however, was merely a modified post-Washington Consensus.

While neoliberalism reigned at the World Bank, in academia in the 1980s and 1990s there was a flourishing of critical development approaches. These came from eclectic fields: concerns about the negative impact on women of the development project evolved into a sophisticated literature on gender and development; the environmentalist movement expanded, focussing attention on sustainability; scholars and activists highlighted the importance of grassroots concerns and indigenous knowledges; structuralism and Critical Theory continued to unpick the material interests at work behind development interventions; and, and the post-development school inspired by Foucault and post-structuralism explained the extent to which development was a neo-colonial and Eurocentric project that needed to be challenged from the grassroots (Willis 2005). The debate around gender, participation, and the environment were all taken up by the Bank, other MDBs, and the wider development community, though mostly in instrumentalist ways that ensured an expanded commitment to neoliberalism.

4.1.1 Key developments at the World Bank

At the World Bank, Reagan appointee Alden Winship Clausen ensured a neoliberal agenda was followed, though given that the organisation had been shaped by bankers, the shift was not always large (Engel and Bazbauers 2020). The initial debt crisis response plan – the 1985 Baker Plan – involved the IFIs and private banks providing additional resources to debtor states in return for structural adjustment. The 1989 Brady Plan also leveraged Bank resources and demanded further structural adjustment, so that the Bank became a key player in debt management (George and Sabelli 1994, Woods 2006). Developing country debt increased during the 1980s and more of it was owed to IFIs than to private sources (Bello 1994). Average annual Bank commitments grew from $5.36 billion in 1970–79 to $15.69 billion in 1980–89 and $22.03 in 1990–95 (Kapur, Lewis, and Webb 1997, 6), increasing Bank leverage over borrowing countries.

The World Bank's environmental failings started coming home to roost during Clausen's presidency. The infamous Polonoroeste project paving 1,500 kilometres of highway through Brazil's Amazon resulted in mass deforestation and immiseration of the local Amerindian tribes. The bad press for the Bank was a factor in the establishment of its first environment department in 1987 (Rich 1994). That did not stop them financing the Narmada Sardar Sarovar dam in India starting in 1988 that produced one of the world's largest social movements up to that time. Despite its very poor environmental track record, the Bank became one of the chief operational arms of the Global Environmental Facility (GEF) established in 1992. The issues of the MDBs and the environment are discussed further in Chapter 10. The Bank introduced an Inspection Panel in 1993 for project affected persons to have their concerns heard, with the US playing a key role in its establishment (Park 2017). Over the next decade, the AfDB, AsDB, IADB, and EBRD all adopted similar accountability mechanisms due to a combination of US pressure, institutional isomorphism, and pressure from civil society organisations (Park 2014, Uhlin 2016). This is evidence of an interconnected MDB system.

The period from 1980 to 1997 saw three one-term World Bank Presidents – Clausen, Barber Conable, and Lewis Preston – and their key contributions and major events are outlined in Table 4.1.

Table 4.1 World Bank Presidents 1981–95

Name and term	*Background*	*Legacy*
Alden Winship Clausen 1981–6	Born in US, attended Carthage College and University of Minnesota, lawyer, banker.	Led the Bank during the 1980s recession and developing world debt crisis. Strong focus on neoliberal free markets, structural adjustment, and coordination with the IMF. These policies damaged the Bank's global reputation. Priority investment areas were agriculture, energy, and sub-Saharan Africa. Introduced innovations in guarantees and co-financing with commercial banks. The Bank's poor environmental standards became a focus of NGOs and media.
Barber Conable 1986–91	Born in US, attended Cornell University, short legal career, long-term Republican politician first in New York state then House of Representatives.	The US' refusal to ratify Clausen's last budget forced Conable into a major, disruptive reorganisation, vacating all positions. The cuts reinforced dominance of neoliberal ideas in the Bank. He established the Bank's first environment department in 1987 and started negotiations on the GEF. Conable gained approval for a large IBRD capital increase in 1988 and IFC in 1991. Strengthened focus on poverty but in ways that promoted privatisation and proletarianisation. The Bank became increasingly involved in debt management.

Name and term	Background	Legacy
Lewis Thompson Preston 1991–5	Born in US, served as a Marine during WWII, attended Harvard University, long banking career with JP Morgan.	Reaffirmed the Bank's poverty focus and took a pragmatic, client-focused approach to management. Commissioned Wapenhans Report, which showed declining project quality inside the Bank. Established the Inspection Panel in 1993, and GEF had the Bank as a key administrator; Preston said development and environmental protection were complementary. Indigenous issues and resettlement gained attention after the disastrous Sardar Sarovar project in India; the Morse Commission report on it was prototype for the Inspection Panel. 24 new members joined IBRD and 20 IDA after collapse of USSR and many obtained loans.

Source: Compiled by authors from a range of sources, basic details from World Bank website (2019).

4.1.2 Key developments in other MDBs

Several MDBs were restructured in this era in response to either the debt crisis or the exigencies from the crises of the 1970s and the growth of globalised finance. Others, particularly the RDBs, became partners in pushing Washington Consensus policies on borrowing states (Babb 2009). Given the debt crisis centred on Latin America and the Caribbean, the IADB became a key player. In the Latin American RDB, there was a dramatic increase in their equivalent of adjustment programmes, indeed the US demanded that 25% of resources were devoted to such loans (Babb 2009, Kellerman 2019). There was also an increasing politicisation of lending policy, which regional member states protested with little success (Kellerman 2019). A large capital increase followed in 1988, so by 1994 it had become the region's main source of development financing. The IADB added new private sector financing and insurance arms in this period too.

The SRDBs in the region struggled, with CABEI losing its ability to remain a regional member-only MDB (Cevallos 1996); the first non-regional members were Taiwan and Mexico in 1992 and Argentina and Colombia in 1995 and 1997. In 1990, CAF also started expanding its membership to include 12 additional countries from Latin America and the Caribbean as well as Spain and Portugal and then 13 private regional banks because its 'finances were in a precarious state' (Humphrey 2016, 104). In order to renew its effectiveness and relevance, CAF restructured its corporate model to resemble the World Bank and IADB and hired consultants 'from Coopers and Lybrand and a former World Bank vice president to review the CAF's operations and make recommendations for overhauling internal process' (Humphrey 2016, 104).

Most of the African SRDBs were greatly affected by the economic downturn of the 1970s and this spilt over into the 1980s and even 1990s. Problems were compounded by failed member integration, lack of political commitment to regional actions, loan non-repayments worsening portfolio performance, reluctance to borrow from foreign donors, and deteriorating economic conditions in Southern Africa (Mistry and Kritzinger-van Niekerk 1998). The situation was so problematic for the EADB that it was almost dissolved during the late 1970s and early 1980s. The African SRDBs started admitting new members during the 1980s. Importantly, it was not just new non-regional member states but also MDBs, IFIs, national development banks, and even private banks, though the shareholdings tended to remain small.

The European-based MDBs were not particularly impacted by the debt crisis, and the Arab-led banks were setting up and expanding. The IsDB, in line with its distaste for conditionality, never offered structural adjustment programmes or policy-based lending (Kellerman 2019). Asia was also not hit particularly hard by the debt crisis and the AsDB slowly expanded, propelled by the addition of China as a borrower in 1986. The Asian RDB also started lending to the private sector in 1983, mirroring Washington Consensus trends. In regard to the specialised development banks, IFAD was restructured in 1995 making it more like the World Bank (Szasz 1999), and the NIB became a development group with the establishment of the Nordic Development Fund (NDF) in 1989, which is a regional financing mechanism linking Nordic countries to developing states.

4.1.3 New MDBs

MDB creation slowed but did not come to a standstill during the Washington Consensus era; five new banks were created between 1980 and 1997, though the Development Bank of the States of Great Lakes (BDEGL) established in 1980 was not operational long. It was another African SRDB founded to support a regional economic community, the Economic Community of the Great Lakes Countries. It was proposed in 1977 and became effective in 1980 and included two non-regional members: Belgium and the AfDB (The New Times 2009). Conflict between its regional member states of Rwanda, Burundi, and the Democratic Republic of the Congo led to its collapse in 1993. Discussions were held in 2009 about re-opening it but little seems to have happened.

The next MDB was the first of a sub-group of SRDBs focussed on trade and development, which combine the functions of an MDB with a multilateral version of national export-import banks. They are often focussed on regional infrastructure. The Eastern and Southern African Trade and Development Bank (TDB) was established in 1985. It came out of African regional integration efforts, and then called the Preferential Trade Agreement (PTA) of Eastern and Southern Africa – now called the Common Market for Eastern and Southern Africa – so it was initially called the PTA Bank. Southern Africa had remained outside earlier regional integration programmes but with Zimbabwe's transition to majority rule in 1980, the door opened for expansion south.

The Pacific Islands Development Bank (PIDB) came next in 1989. It was established by a group of US-associated states in the Pacific, which worried that the US was going to end aid (Mak and Naya 1994). Despite its name, it only covers

Micronesia and not any of the Polynesian or Melanesian Pacific Island states. Most of those states were already members of the AsDB, which has been the Pacific's 'principal multilateral development finance institution,' even though most Polynesian and Melanesian states are also members of the World Bank (Mak and Naya 1994, 36).

Established in 1991, the EBRD came in the wake of the collapse of communism and at the height of neoliberal fervour. It has the most political and neoliberal aim of any MDB, which is 'to foster the transition towards open market-oriented economies and to promote private and entrepreneurial initiative in the Central and Eastern European countries committed to and applying the principles of multiparty democracy, pluralism and market economics' (EBRD 2013, 4). Indeed, the EBRD is the only MDB with an explicitly political mandate. Its region was extended to include Mongolia and the Southern and Eastern Mediterranean after 2006, which has expanded its lending. It has adopted a persona more alike a commercial bank than a traditional MDB (Babb 2009), but it still operates as an MDB. It is the smallest of the RDBs but may benefit from an InvestEU programme that was being legislated in 2020.

The second trade and development bank of the period was the Black Sea Trade and Development Bank (BSTDB), which was established in 1997 and became operational in 1999. Like all SRDBs, it was linked to a regional cooperation forum and has as its first goal assisting the transition of member states towards economic prosperity as well as promoting regional projects and banking services. It originally thought that trade finance would be its bread and butter; however, its portfolio is dominated by project loans either directly or through financial intermediaries (BSTDB 2019).

The continued growth of MDBs during this period demonstrates that they were not incompatible with neoliberalism, indeed the EBRD was a neoliberal-inspired creation. Still, most MDBs were bound up with postcolonial developmentalism and, as this slowed, so too did the creation of new banks.

4.2 The Post-Washington Consensus era: 1998–2009

The post-Washington Consensus era began following the Asian Financial Crisis and it saw a large shift in the global aid agenda with a big push for debt forgiveness and poverty reduction resulting in increasing the concessional resources available to developing countries and developing country ownership of development pathways through the Aid Effectiveness Agenda. Politically, the shift built on the rise of large progressive social movements and centre left parties like those of Bill Clinton in the US (1993–2001) and Tony Blair in the UK (1997–2007), whose minimally progressive agendas were friendly to globalisation (Mawdsley et al. 2018). Large social movements included the anti-globalisation movement peaking in the Battle for Seattle in 1999, the landmark protests in Cochabamba, Bolivia against privatised water price hikes in 2000, and the Make Poverty History coalition. Economically, the growth of China and relative stability globally meant many developing regions started to emerge from the austerity-induced recessions of the 1980s and early 1990s. It is a mistake, however, to think that there were no crashes: Brazil in 1999, the dotcom bubble burst of 2000, and Argentina in 2001 were three of the largest and the pre-conditions for the next regional debt crisis began with the build-up of private sector debt in the US and Europe, leading to the GFC.

Ideationally, the MDBs drew mostly on the New Institutional Economics (NIE) strand of mainstream economics. NIE was an attempt to build on neoclassical economics by incorporating a theory of institutions (North 1998). By significantly expanding neoclassical analysis of market failures to include information failures and transaction costs, NIE produced a picture of markets as subject to extensive imperfections, in contrast to the neoliberal idea of perfectly functioning markets (Fine 2001, 2005). As Greenwald and Stiglitz (1986) outlined, this means that government intervention could be efficient in many more cases than neoliberal doctrine allowed. Stiglitz was World Bank Chief Economist from 1997 to 2002 but was fired for his somewhat unorthodox views, though his influence lived on. His review of neoliberal 'big bang' capital market liberalisation concluded that if attention was not given to the order and timing of reform, programmes can cause more harm than good (Broad 2004, Stiglitz 2002).

Beyond NIE, the Developmental State and Neostructuralist literature were important parts of the broader context of development thinking, drawing a critical eye on the failings of the Washington Consensus. The Developmental State literature, analysing the rapid post-war development of Japan, South Korea, Taiwan, Singapore, and Hong Kong, emerged in the early 1980s and had some impact on the post-Washington Consensus. This literature highlights that active states utilising macroeconomic and industrial policies, run by a developmental elite shielded to a degree from political competition, had been able to achieve high levels of industrial transformation and economic growth (Amsden 1989, Thurbon 2016, Wade 2018). One of the most successful development states, Japan, sought to have the World Bank acknowledge the role of the state and industrial policy in development, funding a Bank report titled The East Asian Miracle (1993) to recognise this. In the editing of the report, however, the role of the state was watered down to the point that the neoliberal development paradigm emerged unscathed (Wade 1996). Developmental States certainly influenced the AsDB. Neostructuralism in Latin America similarly aimed to challenge neoliberal dogma but still cast market forces as the primary driver of development, adding that without attention to policy and institutional interventions focussed on equity, markets would not flourish (Leiva 2008). Like the Development State literature, Neostructuralism created space for thinking about the role of the state in development, an important contributor to the unfolding post-Washington Consensus.

Despite these new approaches, the practice of the post-Washington Consensus generally extended the neoliberal approach to constraining the state in both monetary and fiscal policy and through devolution of power to statutory bodies like central banks (Carroll 2010, Engel 2010, Wade 2001,). Regulation and other mechanisms were utilised to create more space for private markets, not states. Curbing state – but not private sector – corruption became a major focus, which was linked to the existing good governance agenda, thus many MDB projects targeted 'reform' of government financial and auditing systems. In later years, the focus was on deepening marketisation through tendering out of activities once performed by the state in everything from infrastructure to healthcare, education, and welfare.

Still, the post-Washington Consensus had a stronger focus on absolute poverty reduction than its predecessor and some focus on the social costs of adjustment. It offered a more progressive approach to health and education investments by state and markets, though in practice did little to support these. The World Bank and other MDBs claimed to have abandoned one-size-fits-all approaches to development and created tailored country programmes, found in country programming documents. These frameworks were meant to be based on recipient government ideas as local ownership was a key element of the post-Washington Consensus.

The focus on poverty and local ownership was formalised in two international agreements that became a key part of the 2000s aid consensus. The first was the MDGs and the second the Aid Effectiveness Agenda. Both came out of the OECD DAC and, despite some progressive overtones, they represented the Global North shaping the global justice agenda. The OECD DAC started work in the area in 1995, but the work was initially done by a group of all male, rich country development politicians and bureaucrats whose focus was on practical issues of projects and policies, hence the use of results-based management with target-setting (Hulme 2009). Through years of politicking, a series of international development goals, as the DAC called them, evolved into the eight MDGs comprised of numerous targets and indicators approved by the UN Millennium Assembly held in 2000. The MDGs became a unifying framework for the MDBs and former World Bank President James Wolfensohn referred to them in 2002 as 'the hymnbook that we're singing from now' (cited in Bissio 2003, 157). Yet, as Saith (2006) argued, the MDGs were embedded in profoundly inegalitarian neoliberal relations and they sought not to change these, but only address the issue of absolute poverty. This is clear from the fact that the first MDG was to reduce the proportion of people living below the international poverty line of $1 a day, an accounting illusion that did not actually provide enough to allow people an average life expectancy (Hickel 2016).

The Aid Effectiveness Agenda emerged from the DAC, along with key statements made at High Level Forums in Rome (2003), Paris (2005), Accra (2008), and Busan (2011). The Agenda was a practical plan focussed on improving the quality and impact of aid policy and programmes and focussed on the practices of both donors and recipients. Ultimately a technocratic schedule devised by the Global North-led DAC (Booth 2008), the OECD (2011) itself acknowledged that donors did not progress the agenda as much as recipients. Nonetheless, all the larger MDBs and several smaller ones participated in Aid Effectiveness programmes, 13 out of the then 28 MDBs aligning behind institutional standards of behaviour. Notably, a few of the Arab-led MDBs were involved in these programmes but none of the smaller African SRDBs and only one of the Latin American SRDBs, the CDB.

4.2.1 Key developments at the World Bank

Clinton-appointed President James Wolfensohn oversaw the World Bank's transition to the post-Washington Consensus and expanded the poverty-reduction mission (see Table 4.2). Under Wolfensohn, the phrase 'Our dream is a world free of poverty' was grandiosely carved into the entrance of the Bank's refurbished headquarters in 1996 (Marshall 2008, 54). The Bank retained poverty reduction as its overarching mission since, even during the presidencies of conservative US Republican Party appointees Paul Wolfowitz and Robert Zoellick. Still, as Cammack (2004, 197) argued, Wolfensohn's Bank promoted the 'sustainable reproduction of capitalism' by ensuring micro-level incentive structures were in line with neoliberal macroeconomic ones. Wolfensohn further attempted to maintain the Bank's hegemony by shaping developmental thought through programmes like the Knowledge Bank initiative in 1996, designed to make the Bank the leading provider of development expertise, and the World Bank 'Doing Business' series starting in 2004, which reported on the ease of doing business in states across the globe and has been very influential (Banerjee et al. 2006). He also renamed structural adjustment loans as development policy loans in 2004 to distance the Bank from the most ideological aspects of the Washington Consensus (Bazbauers 2018). The Bank also helped launch the Heavily Indebted Poor Countries (HIPC) initiative for debt relief in 1996, although debts to the Bank were exempt until the 2005 Multilateral Debt Relief Initiative, to protect its preferred creditor status and credit rating. Despite progress, the conditions on debt relief advocated neoliberal prescriptions like limiting public expenditure and prioritising debt servicing over other needs.

World Bank lending spiked in 1998 and 1999 in response to the Asian Financial Crisis from an annual average of $22.03 billion in 1990–5 to $27.8 billion but rapidly declined to $15.3 billion in 2000. Yet, MDBs need to lend, so they steadily grew again to reach $24.7 billion in 2008, with the GFC then causing a further spike in loans. The relative stability of the 1999–2007 interregnum was not great for the IMF or Bank as their customers were reducing debt or able to borrow with few conditions and at competitive rates from other provides. Indeed, many countries were building foreign reserves explicitly to avoid having to turn to the IMF in the future. Still, the Bank remained vitally important to many smaller and poorer countries whose access to private finance was limited.

Co-financing expanded World Bank lending. This was mostly with official bilateral and multilateral partners. Between 1996 and 1999, co-financing ranged between 33.9% and 40.1% of the value of bank loans. As Bracking (2009) argued, these linkages highlight that there is not just an MDB system, but rather a system of interlinked development finance institutions. Still, an indication that MDF and the MDBs declined in influence over the 2000s was that by 2007 Bank co-financing was equal to just 25.5% of operations. Bank lending to the financial sector increased during this period through all three of its lending arms, particularly the IFC. Leading up to the GFC, the Bank was quite exposed to asset- and mortgage-backed securities, though the IADB was far more exposed (Kellerman 2019).

Table 4.2 World Bank Presidents 1995–2007

Name and term	*Background*	*Legacy*
James Wolfensohn 1995–2005	Born in Australia, acquired US citizenship specifically to gain the World Bank presidency, attended University of Sydney and Harvard Business School, investment banker with interest in arts and music, known as the 'Renaissance Banker.'	Launched the HIPC in 1996 along with the IMF Managing Director. He focused on corruption before the Asian Financial Crisis and more so after with institutional mechanisms established in 1999. This crisis highlighted the Bank's lack of inclusion, participation, and the shallow nature of its poverty reduction agenda, and they became key parts of the post-Washington Consensus along with influences from NIE. The 1997 Strategic Compact reform was designed to gain more resources for Bank in return for a streamlined institution. Launched the Comprehensive Development Framework and PRSPs in 1999 as frameworks for country lending and later as mechanisms for implementing the MDGs.
Paul Wolfowtiz 2005–7	Born in US, attended Cornell University, obtained PhD from University of Chicago, held a number of government appointments for Republican administrations.	Wolfowitz was a political appointee from the Bush administration, which did not support the Bank. Had a tumultuous relationship with the Bank Board. Focused on anti-corruption but forced to resign after giving his partner a position with a high salary.

Source: Compiled by authors from a range of sources, basic details from World Bank website (2019).

4.2.2 Key developments in other MDBs

The AsDB took an active response to the Asian Financial Crisis, but some of its IMF-style policies led to backlash. It adopted poverty reduction as its mission in 1999, predating the World Bank. It was partly the result of pressure from the US Treasury, which forced the Asian MDB to put a much greater share of its funds into social and environmental projects than it had in the past (Babb 2009). The AsDB and most of the RDBs adopted and expanded safeguard mechanisms to protect project affected people from harm, which has helped ensure loans benefit local communities, though many problem projects are still funded. The RDBs increased inter-agency harmonisation too and engaged with new financial instruments following the World Bank's lead.

The post-Washington Consensus era was a solid period for many of the sub-regional and specialised development banks. The smaller MDBs that would become influential during the 2010s began their expansion circa 2000, the CDB and CAF being two examples of this change in fortune, following organisational restructurings implemented during the 1990s. The focus on the private sector expanded in many smaller MDBs, for example, the AFESD's Board of Governors approved a revision of the MDB's Articles of Agreement in 1997 to better support the Arab private sector (AFESD 1997).

In Europe, the CEB broadened its mandate during the post-Washington Consensus era, through the 1997 Strasbourg Summit that advocated the CEB incorporate 'strengthening European social cohesion' into its mandate and the 2005 Warsaw Summit that called for building a free, democratic, and more inclusive European society; such changes reflected the greater focus on good governance in the post-Washington Consensus period. The EIB became the EIB Group during this period with the incorporation of sibling institutions addressing private sector financing and partnerships, reflecting the expansion of the World Bank into the World Bank Group with the IFC and MIGA.

In Africa, the misfortunes of the EADB continued into the 2000s, not as the result of the economic decline of its members but due to severe mismanagement of finances, leading to several high-ranking officials, including Director General Godfrey Tumusiime, being expelled; it posted losses of millions of dollars. In contrast, BOAD increased its private sector financing, along with a few other smaller MDBs. BOAD originally lent to regional member states but, from 2002, it provided loans to the private sector for development projects of regional significance plus lines of credit to small and medium private enterprises. This can be interpreted as the MDBs following the lead of the World Bank towards more private sector financing products in line with the post-Washington Consensus approach of market-led development.

4.2.3 New MDBs

Just two new MDBs were established between 1998 and 2009 and there was one unsuccessful proposal. The first new MDB, a trade and development bank, was established in 1996 by the Economic Cooperation Organisation (ECO) regional grouping comprised of mainly central Asian states. The ECO Trade and Development Bank (ETDB) was founded by three of the ECO states – Iran, Pakistan, and Turkey with Azerbaijan, Afghanistan, and the Kyrgyz Republic joining later. The ETDB aims simply to expand intra-regional trade and increase economic development. The second new MDB, the Eurasian Development Bank (EDB), was created in 2006 as another post-communist MDB mandated to develop and strengthen market economies, although its member states – the Russian Federation, Kazakhstan, Belarus, Armenia, Tajikistan, and Kyrgyzstan – remain far from model market economies.

The unsuccessful proposal was for a *Banco del Sur* (or Bank of the South), the idea for which was first raised in 2005 between Venezuela and Brazil. It was an expression of Neostructuralism and an indicator of new activism in the Global South. Its proposers were concerned that the South was still depositing large amounts of resources in Global North financial institutions and they wanted to create a new regional financial architecture (Pérez 2009–10, Rosales 2013).

Discussions occurred in 2006–7 between Venezuela and Argentina, and they were joined by Brazil and Ecuador. In 2009, an agreement to establish the MDB was signed with eight initial members. In responding to the demands of the different founding member countries, the functions proposed for the MDB were:

> to finance development projects in key sectors of the economy, aimed at improving competitiveness, scientific-technological development, infrastructure, creation and provision of services, intraregional productive complementarity, and the maximization of value added to raw materials produced in the countries of the region.
>
> (cited in Rosales 2013, 31)

Its proposed structure seems rather like a standard MDB: a proposed initial capitalisation of $20 billion, capital raised on bond markets, and weighted voting for large projects and structures matters but one country, one vote for simple operational matters. Its constituent agreement entered into force in 2011 but adequate capital was not paid-in to make it operational. Venezuelan President Nicolás Maduro attempted to revise it in April 2015, but it was not capitalised (Mares and Trinkunas 2016). The proposed *Banco del Sur* was a clear manifestation of Latin American Neostructuralism, and thus part of the broader post-Washington Consensus discourse. It also reopened discussion about the need for public development financing, which the NDB and AIIB continued in the 2010s.

4.3 Retroliberalism and the rise of debt: 2010–20

The progressive changes of the post-Washington Consensus era had come and largely gone by the early 2010s, with the focus turning to the retroliberal – or beyond aid – agenda. The quantity of resources delivered as opposed to the quality of aid effectiveness came to define MDB cooperation documents. The retroliberal agenda first emerged in the early 2000s and began as a slow political reconfiguration away from grant aid. As early as 2002, the International Conference on the Financing of Development in Monterrey made it clear that poor countries were responsible for their own development and that the private sector was expected to be the key course of finance going forward (Saith 2006). And, yet the retroliberal era did not fully emerge until around 2010, catalysed by the upheaval of the GFC.

Ideationally, it was hoped that the 2007–8 GFC would contribute to a broadening of development discourse. And, for a moment in the wake of the crisis, there was a brief flirtation with unorthodox policies, in particular Keynesian stimulus spending and financial controls in order to bail out capitalists but this was followed by a rapid return to austerity politics (Ortiz et al. 2020). The minor changes to regulations such as reforms to the Basel banking rules did not address the systemic risk that had been created by the liberalisation of financial flows, and financialisation revived after the crisis (Gabor 2020, Goldin et al. 2014). Mainstream donors and the MDBs maintained a broadly post-Washington Consensus mindset, but now with an increase emphasis on infrastructure, nationalism, and financialisation – promoting private investment and loans over grant aid. Thus, following Murray and Overton (2016), we label the period from 2010 to 2020 as the retroliberal era.

The term retroliberalism underscores that the policy response to the GFC benefited capital by socialising its losses and leaving labour income to pay for this through public debt. The practice of neoliberalism has always differed from the theory, with centre left and right governments adapting to serve business interests. In the current era, this means a return to a more state-centric and nationalist discourse focussing on the benefits that development aid and finance can provide to private and state firms rather than to poverty reduction. Retroliberalism has also marginalised the SDGs; they may get lip service, but they are no longer at the centre of development thinking. Significantly, the dramatic rise of China and its development strategy has put infrastructure again at the centre of development finance, a resurgence that broadly aligns with the modernisation mentality the World Bank pursued over its first two decades.

China's approach to rapid industrialisation differs radically from the minimalist state agenda of the Washington Consensus and China's influence on development has grown – by 2019, they were the third largest World Bank shareholder and were central to the formation of the NDB and AIIB. This has led scholars like Jakupec and Kelly (2019) and Lin and Wang (2017) to argue that China has created space for the Global South to adopt developmentalist approaches. However, like Yağcı (2016, 43), we argue that while China's experience may be informative for debates about developmentalism, China itself is not concerned with 'enlarging space for developing countries' trade relations and industrialisation efforts.' Rather, the contemporary inegalitarian capital order provides the foundations for China's development, which they support along with the associated global economic governance system (Bond 2015, Robinson 2015).

The expansion of China's mutual aid activities since 2008, notably the Belt and Road Initiative of 2013, was largely in response to domestic stagnation. Its aid promotes retroliberal policies – supporting open markets and broadly neoliberal fiscal and monetary policy, but with increased investment in infrastructure and less interference in state affairs including around human rights. Further, China's policies support their investors, whether they are seeking to source raw materials, outsource elements of low-wage manufacturing, or gain construction contracts outside China using Chinese inputs and labour. Indeed, it is not unwarranted to say that they are often 'kicking away the ladder for developing countries' (Chang 2002). A key issue here is China's extensive use of debt instruments, which previously had been very cautious about. During the 2010s, however, China's approach became a retroliberal one – largely neoliberal policies with a good dash of infrastructure spending, all wrapped up in debt.

China's expansion of debt relations has led the MDBs to expand their loan portfolios and the Global North to expand existing, and create new, bilateral development finance mechanisms, such as the US International Development Finance Corporation or Australia's Infrastructure Financing Facility for the Pacific. Private sector debt has rapidly grown too over the past decade, and in 2018 global debt reached a record high of 230% of GDP. Since 2010, debt in EMDEs 'has risen 54 percentage points of GDP to a historic peak of about 170% of GDP in 2018'

(Kose et al. 2020, xix). China itself has also rapidly expanded debt, but they have the advantage of most of their being owed to domestic sources.

Key contributors to the 2010s debt wave are the usual culprits of low interest rates and financialisation, as well as 'a rise of regional banks, growing appetite for local currency bonds, and increased demand for EMDE debt from the expanding non-bank financial sector' (Kose et al. 2020, xxi). The expansion in EMDE debt between 2010 and 2014 was predominantly private sector debt, but from 2014 to 2018 that reversed with publicly guaranteed debt making up the majority. In low-income countries, both public and private debt has grown and there has been a shift away from concessional finance and towards private creditors, although smaller sub-Saharan African states are still primarily reliant on official creditors (Bonizzi, Laskaridis, and Toporowski 2019). According to Kose et al. (2020, 10), this 'wave of debt buildup has been unprecedented in its size, speed, and reach' in EMDEs. It is also more global than previous debt build-up waves occurring since the 1970s, though debt in the Global North has been stable and there have been declines in debt in the Middle East, Eastern Europe, and Central Asia.

4.3.1 Key developments at the World Bank

World Bank President Jim Yong Kim, who led the MDB from 2012 to 2019, with his public health background, seemed to offer a progressive approach to development (see Table 4.3). By the time Kim left the Bank, however, the MDB had doubled down on financialisation. At the same time, networks between the MDBs and DFIs continued to grow. The International Development Finance Club was established by the IMF and Bank in 2011 to help DFIs set agendas on development finance and share know-how. It has six SRDBs and the IsDB as members of its private sector arm, along with Global North and South national development banks and one Exim bank.

World Bank commitments reached an all-time high in 2010 of $58.7 billion, and then dropped substantially to $29 billion in 2012. Yet, this lending interregnum was short. As the investment climate deteriorated mid-decade, states increased public spending, and President Kim announced his 'billions to trillions' agenda in 2013 that aimed to leverage Bank lending to shift from billions of dollars in investments to trillions. Between 2017 and 2019, average annual Bank commitments were $44.8 billion and IBRD gross disbursements were $18.5 billion and IDA gross disbursements totalled $14.9 billion (World Bank 2019).

The 'billions to trillions' agenda was followed by Maximising Finance for Development (MFD) in 2017, which sought to leverage official development finance to attract private investment but with a focus on 'innovative' financial instruments. The World Bank's 2018 large shareholding increase (detailed in Chapter 5) was core to this, though it was also likely partly driven by competition with the new MDBs and Chinese development finance. The increase substantially expanded Bank Group lending capacity and is linked to the IDA raising funds on money markets for the first time in its history. With the Trump regime in power in the US, it seems that the shareholder increase came at the price of Kim's resignation.

Table 4.3 World Bank Presidents 2007–20

Name and term	*Background*	*Legacy*
Robert B. Zoellick 2007–12	Born in US, attended Swarthmore College and Harvard, spent three decades between private sector firms (including Goldman Sachs) and government appointments in Republican administrations, including Deputy Secretary of State (2005–6).	World Bank President during the 2007–8 GFC, when lending increased to an all-time high. He oversaw the first general capital increase for IBRD in 20 years agreed to in 2010. Involved in an increase in shares for developing and transition countries and agreed to review their position every 5 years. Commissioned Zedillo Report released in 2009 on the World Bank Group's governance structures. Zoellick's presidency focused on good governance and anti-corruption and launched the World Bank's 'open data' initiative.
Jim Yong Kim 2012–19	Born in South Korea, migrated to the US with family at age 5, attended Brown University, obtained MD and PhD from Harvard University, co-founded public health NGO, served as a director in WHO, and worked as university lecturer and administrator.	Kim initiated another major and controversial reorganisation, some of it reversed in 2017. Originally focused on health and human development and approved Framework for Mainstreaming Citizen Engagement. Shifted to focus on financialisation through the Maximising Finance for Development initiative, which was linked to a large capital increase agreed to in 2018 and expanded the role of the IFC. This promoted privatised social services. Kim also set stronger targets for climate finance, ended financing for oil and gas exploration and extraction, and strengthened rules on lending to private banks with fossil fuel investments.
David R. Malpass 2019–	Born in US, attended Colorado College and University of Denver, Georgetown University economist, chief economist of Bear Stearns, held government appointments in Republican administrations.	Warned about the build-up of debt in EMDEs, including debt from IFIs. President during the COVID-19 pandemic, which to mid-2020 involved a $160 billion commitment, with strong emphasis on the IFC.

Source: Compiled by authors from a range of sources, basic details from World Bank website (2019).

The MFD initiatives shows that, despite the havoc wreaked by financialisation in the GFC, the World Bank has become a proponent of it being extended to aid and development finance; the 'overall strategy is to policy-engineer a shift towards securities-based financial systems and thus render DECs [developing and emerging countries] more amenable to the forces of financialised capitalism' (Gabor 2018, 16). While the overall strategy is clear, the precise methods for implementation are less so. One method is issuing new kinds of bonds, such as green bonds, IDA bonds, the world's first blockchain bond, and Indonesian women's empowerment bonds (World Bank 2019). A second method is the 'cascade approach' that identifies imperfections that may be stopping private capital from investing in projects. If addressing the imperfection is not enough, subsidies and guarantees may be needed to leverage private investment and only when such reforms are still not attracting private investment can public investment be considered (Gabor 2018). It thus combines an ideological preference for private investment over public regardless of profitability or efficiency, with a preference for financialised capitalism over traditional banking. For example, the Bank issued catastrophe bonds in 2016 through the Pandemic Emergency Financing Facility (PEFF), a mechanism pioneered by insurance companies to pay high interest rates on the basis that investors may lose some of or all their money. The Bank's PEFF bond had a complex set of triggers before they could be paid out, leading to an expectation that they would not be. But, the COVID-19 crisis met all the triggers and so investors lost their principal (Mackenzie 2020). The Bank created PEFF bonds to build a new market in securitised risk but given most investors are loss adverse, they will be less likely to purchase them again in the future (Mackenzie 2020). More to the point, such innovative financial instruments may have a strong structure, 'but from almost any angle, they look fundamentally ill-suited to protecting vulnerable people from diseases, disaster, or climate change' (Mackenzie 2020).

With Trump appointee David Malpass as the incumbent president (see Table 4.3), the Bank became more concerned with the growth of debt, which the IMF had been warning about for a few years. Yet, the COVID-19 pandemic has left no option but for a big increase in lending as bilateral donors are not increasing grant resources. The Bank has said they will provide $160 billion in frontloaded funds to help states respond to the crisis and other MDBs will private $80 billion. They are also frontloading grants through their COVID-19 Fast Track Facility, but more loans will follow.

In 2020, the Bank Group's ambitious mission was to end extreme poverty by decreasing the percentage of people living on less than $1.90 a day to no more than 3% by 2030 and to promote shared prosperity by fostering the income growth of the bottom 40% of people in every country. But, just like the MDGs, this formulation is an accounting illusion that narrowly focusses on inequality by promoting income growth. This brings us back to the centrality of the Bank's original purposes, which can be summarised as facilitating investment in productive purposes and promoting private investment and trade.

4.3.2 Key developments in other MDBs

The late 2000s and 2010s saw an across-the-board improvement in the organisational functioning and loan portfolios of the regional, sub-regional, and specialised development banks, particularly among a few smaller MDBs that had struggled during the 1980s and 1990s. Such improvements coincided with organisational restructurings, an expansion of capital availability, and new leadership. In the case of the RDBs, however, most of which had also lent counter-cyclically during the 2007–8 GFC, they had a larger decline in lending in the early 2010s than the World Bank, which has been attributed to downward pressure from credit rating agencies (Delikanli, Dimitrov, and Agolli 2018).

In the case of the SRDBs, successful reform occurred across several continents. In Africa, the EADB went from severe financial mismanagement during the 2000s to significant organisational restructuring and the recovery of outstanding loans under Director General Vivienne Yeda, who was appointed in 2009. As a result, Yeda received several financial and banking awards, including the African Banker of the Year Award in 2014. At the TDB, President Adamassu Tadesse, who received the same African Banker Award in 2019, spearheaded a dramatic reformation of the African SRDB, including growing equity capital and annual profits four-fold between 2012 and 2019, attracting 15 new shareholders, and receiving the TDB's first investment grade rating from Moody's in 2017 (Africa Fintech Summit 2019). The TDB's reform process began in 2000 and the overall result is that it is now substantially larger than the four African SRDBs that were created before it (Humphrey 2019). In Latin America, CAF came to rival the IADB and exceed World Bank Latin American and Caribbean commitments during the 2010s, which is indicative of the change in fortunes and expansion of operations of so many MDBs (Humphrey 2014, 2016).

In Europe, the NDF, after almost being dissolved in the 2000s, instituted a series of institutional reforms in 2009, shifting its mandate from soft loans for social and economic development to grants for climate change interventions in low-income countries (Amland 2018, Normann 2019). This was an attempt to not only satisfy the competing interests of its Nordic shareholders but also to better find its niche within MDF (Wihtol 2013). The CEB, its relevance revitalised in the 1990s with the collapse of the Soviet Union and reintegration of people from the former Soviet bloc into capitalist Europe, renewed its pertinence once again in response to the refugee crisis affecting Europe since the mid-2010s.

In Eastern Europe and Central Asia, the IIB underwent considerable restructuring in 2012. Following two decades of stagnation in the wake of the Soviet Union's collapse, new management entered the former Soviet-led MDB to make it a modern-day development bank. A revised agreement in 2014 saw it shift to a much more capitalist agenda of 'promoting economic growth, increasing the competitiveness of national economies, expanding trade and economic ties, and maximising investment interaction opportunities' (IIB 2018, 1). The IIB also entered debt capital markets in 2014, the first time in its history, and began issuing bonds in Russia, Slovakia, and Romania.

In a range of ways, the 2010s saw a closer alignment between the MDBs as to what a development bank 'should' look like. In addition to broad harmonisation efforts, another example is the increasingly close alignment on climate finance following the 2015 Paris Agreement (see Chapter 10) and further many MDBs followed the World Bank's lead in increasing their financial innovation engagement.

4.3.3 *New MDBs*

Two new MDBs emerged during the retroliberal era, the NDB and AIIB, and they were designed as traditional development banks. The NDB (2015, 1) adopts neutral language in its purposes, aiming to 'mobilize resources for infrastructure and sustainable development projects in BRICS and other emerging economies and developing countries,' and the AIIB (2015, 2), largely duplicating the AsDB's Charter, has a strong profit focus prioritising 'infrastructure and other productive sectors,' despite being founded by an ostensibly socialist state. The absence of references to poverty reduction in the NDB and AIIB's founding documents speaks to them being business-link banks, at odds with the SDGs; the new MDBs conform to the 'GDP-centred, Northern-development-model approach' (Dossani 2014).

Promoting private capital is remarkably prominent in the AIIB's Articles of Agreement, giving the MDB responsibility for its promotion in the region. The Articles suggest that, as argued above, the practice of this China-led development financier is not much friendly to the state than the old traditional MDBs. The NDB is a little more conspicuous in its purposes, referring to 'support' for public and private projects. The similarities of purposes and inclusion of facilitating private investment demonstrates that the new MDBs aim to promote debt-based, capitalist expansion in the same way as the old ones have.

4.4 Conclusion

There are so many dimensions to the MDBs discussed in Chapters 3 and 4 that it is hard to offer simple conclusions. The chapters highlight the connections between MDB creation, geopolitics, economic theory, and debt. They demonstrate that there is a fair degree of coherence around the aims and objectives of the MDBs; almost all exhibit a Keynesian influence, which is not surprising given their logic is the Keynesian idea that markets will not always ensure adequate levels of investment. Some are more statist, others more pragmatic, and the EBRD brought in a neoliberal tone, but, in the end, they are all focussed on promoting market-based economic growth in line with banking principles. There is a remarkable consensus around the need for more and more debt to promote economic growth, despite there still being no orderly default and restructuring mechanism for states at the international level.

Many of the MDBs started out with strong regional missions but few have been able to live up to them in practice; not many governments want to be burdened by joint loans that they may not get an equal share of benefits from. This demonstrates the dominance of the state in development discourse and it permeates the analysis and lending strategies of the MDBs too. The MDBs have helped naturalise the idea that states are actual and effective units that can control development challenges at the same time as their banking and neoliberal logics lead them to want to constrain the state and promote the benefits of markets. This is the tension at the heart of the MDBs.

The durability of the MDB model and the MDBs themselves are further factors that leap out of the analysis – 'once established MDBs do not disappear, but rather transform and evolve' (Delikanli, Dimitrov, and Agolli 2018, 21). The BDEGL is the only suspended MDB we have found and even it still exists on paper. Still, as the chapter demonstrates, many MDBs have faced challenges. Nonetheless, they are substantial financial actors. The 23 MDBs studied by Delikanli, Dimitrov, and Agolli (2018, 49) had a total portfolio (loans, equity investments, and debt securities) of $1.13 trillion in 2016 or 1.6% of world GDP, which was a decline from earlier in the decade. In addition, states have turned to the idea of creating new MDBs time and again when faced with obstacles, which suggests they consider productive investment of the trillions of dollars that now float around the world is an ongoing challenge. States seem to like the influence that MDBs provide and, as Chapter 5 shows, once established MDBs are quite cheap for them. The next chapter focusses on the structure of the MDBs and it emphasises how their structure as banks has been a long-underestimated influence. Indeed, Kapur, Lewis, and Webb (1997, 1111) note that at times the World Bank's 'financial and development personas' have been 'more competitive than complementary.'

Bibliography

AFESD. 1997. *Annual Report 1997.* Safat, Kuwait: Arab Fund for Economic and Social Development.

Africa Fintech Summit. 2019. "5 Questions with Admassu Tadesse, President & Chief Executive of Trade and Development Bank (TDB)." https://africafintechsummit.com/2019/11/19/5-questions-with-admassu-tadesse-president-chief-executive-of-trade-and-development-bank-tdb/.

AIIB. 2015. Articles of Agreement. Beijing: Asian Infrastructure Investment Bank.

Amland, Bjørn H. 2018. "Nordic Donors to Discuss Strengthening Nordic Development Fund." Development Today. http://www.development-today.com/magazine/Frontpage/nordic_donors_to_discuss_strengthening_nordic_development_fund.

Amsden, Alice. 1989. *Asia's Next Giant: South Korea and Late Industrialisation.* New York: Oxford University Press.

Babb, Sarah. 2009. *Behind the Development Banks: Washington Politics, World Poverty, and the Wealth of Nations.* Chicago, IL and London: The University of Chicago Press.

Banerjee, Abhijit, Angus Deaton, Nora Lustig, Ken Rogoff, and Edward Hsu. 2006. An Evaluation of World Bank Research, 1998–2005. September 24. Washington, DC: World Bank.

Bazbauers, Adrian Robert. 2018. *The World Bank and Transferring Development: Policy Movement through Technical Assistance.* Cham: Palgrave Macmillan.

Bello, Walden. 1994. *Dark Victory: The United States, Structural Adjustment, and Global Poverty*. London: Pluto.

Bissio, Roberto. 2003. "Civil Society and the MDGs." *Development Policy Journal* 3 (April):151–60.

Bond, Patrick. 2015. "BRICS and the Sub-imperial Location." In *BRICS: An Anti-Capitalist Critique*, edited by Ana Garcia and Patrick Bond, 15–26. Chicago, IL: Haymarket Books.

Bonizzi, Bruno, Christina Laskaridis, and Jan Toporowski. 2019. "Global Liquidity, the Private Sector and Debt Sustainability in Sub-Saharan Africa." *Development and Change* 50 (5):1430–54. doi: 10.1111/dech.12507.

Booth, David. 2008. *Aid Effectiveness after Accra: How to Reform the 'Paris agenda'*. London: ODI.

Bracking, Sarah. 2009. *Money and Power: Great Predators in the Political Economy of Development*. London: Pluto Press.

Broad, Robin. 2004. "The Washington Consensus Meets the Global Backlash: Shifting Debates and Policies." *Globalizations* 1 (2):129–54.

BSTDB. 2019. Medium-Term Strategy and Business Plan 2019–2022. Black Sea Trade and Development Bank. Accessed 1 June 2020. https://www.bstdb.org/MTSBP_2019-2022.pdf

Cahill, Damien. 2014. *The End of Laissez-Faire? On the Durability of Embedded Neoliberalism*. Cheltenham: Edward Elgar.

Cammack, Paul. 2004. "What the World Bank Means by Poverty Reduction and Why it Matters." *New Political Economy* 9 (2):189–211.

Carroll, Toby. 2010. *Delusions of Development: The World Bank and the Post-Washington Consensus in Southeast Asia*. Houndmills, Basingstoke: Palgrave Macmillan.

Cevallos, Ricardo. 1996. "The Central American Bank for Economic Integration." *Tulane Journal of International and Comparative Law* 4 (2):245–74.

Chang, Ha-Joon. 2002. *Kicking Away the Ladder: Development Strategy in Historical Perspective*. London: Anthem Press.

Chossudovsky, Michel. 1997. *The Globalisation of Poverty: Impacts of IMF and World Bank Reforms*. London: Zed Books.

Delikanli, Ihsan Ugur, Todor Dimitrov, and Roena Agolli. 2018. *Multilateral Development Banks: Governance and Finance*. Cham: Palgrave Macmillan.

Dossani, Sameer. 2014. BRICS Bank: New Bottle, How's the Wine? *Bretton Woods Bulletin* (Februrary).

EBRD. 2013. Basic Documents of the European Bank for Reconstruction and Development. London: European Bank for Reconstruction and Development. Accessed 11 March 2020. https://www.ebrd.com/news/publications/institutional-documents/basic-documents-of-the-ebrd.html

Engel, Susan. 2010. *The World Bank and the Post-Washington Consensus in Vietnam and Indonesia: Inheritance of Loss*. London: Routledge.

Engel, Susan, and Adrian Robert Bazbauers. 2020. "Multilateral Development Banks: Washington Consensus, Beijing Consensus or Banking Consensus?" In *Rethinking Multilateralism in Foreign Aid: Beyond the Neoliberal Hegemony*, edited by Viktor Jakupc, Max Kelly and Jonathan Makuwira, 113–31. Abingdon, Oxon and New York: Routledge.

Fine, Ben. 2001. *Social Capital versus Social Theory: Political Economy and Social Science at the Turn of the Millennium*. London: Routledge.

Fine, Ben. 2005. "The New Development Economics." In *The New Development Economics: After the Washington Consensus*, edited by K.S. Jomo and Ben Fine, 1–20. New Delhi: Tulika Books.

Gabor, Daniela. 2018. *Understanding the Financialisation of International Development through 11 FAQs*. Washington, DC: Heinrich Böll Stiftung North America.

Gabor, Daniela. 2020. The Wall Street Consensus. SocArXiv papers.

George, Susan, and Fabrizio Sabelli. 1994. *Faith and Credit: The World Bank's Secular Empire*. London: Penguin Books.

Goldin, Ian, Mike Mariathasan, Co-Pierre Georg, and Tiffany Vogel. 2014. "The Financial Sectors." In *The Butterfly Defect: How Globalization Creates Systemic Risk, and What To Do about it*, edited by Ian Goldin and Mike Mariathasan, 36–69. Princeton, NJ and Oxford: Princeton University Press.

Gowan, Peter. 1999. *The Global Gamble: Washington's Faustian Bid for World Dominance*. London: Verso.

Greenwald, Bruce C., and Joesph Stiglitz. 1986. "Externalities in Economies with Imperfect Information and Incomplete Markets." *Quarterly Journal of Economics* 90 (2):229–64.

Harvey, David. 2010. *The Enigma of Capital: And the Crises of Capitalism*. Oxford: Oxford University Press.

Hickel, Jason. 2016. "The True Extent of Global Poverty and Hunger: Questioning the Good News Narrative of the Millennium Development Goals." *Third World Quarterly* 37 (5):749–67.

Hulme, David. 2009. The Millennium Development Goals (MDGs): A Short History of the World's Biggest Promise. University of Manchester, Brooks World Poverty Institute. BWPI Working Paper 100, Manchester.

Humphrey, Chris. 2014. "The Politics of Loan Pricing in Multilateral Development Banks." *Review of International Political Economy* 21 (3):611–39. doi: 10.1080/09692290.2013.858365.

Humphrey, Chris. 2016. "The Invisible Hand: Financial Pressures and Organisational Convergence in Multilateral Development Banks." *The Journal of Development Studies* 52 (1):92–112. doi: 10.1080/00220388.2015.1075978.

Humphrey, Chris. 2019. "'Minilateral' Development Banks: What the Rise of Africa's Trade and Development Bank Says about Multilateral Governance." *Development and Change* 50 (1):164–90. doi: 10.1111/dech.12467.

IIB. 2018. Agreement Concerning the Establishment of an International Investment Bank. New York: United Nations – Treaty Series Volume 801, 1975. Accessed 11 March 2020. https://treaties.un.org/doc/Publication/UNTS/Volume%20801/v801.pdf.

Jakupec, Viktor, and Max Kelly. 2019. *Foreign Aid in the Age of Populism: Political Economy Analysis from Washington to Beijing*. London: Routledge.

Kapur, Devesh, John P. Lewis, and Richard Webb. 1997. *The World Bank Its First Half Century, Volume 1: History*. 2 vols. Vol. 1: History. Washington, DC: Brookings Institution Press.

Kellerman, Miles. 2019. "The Proliferation of Multilateral Development Banks." *Review of International Organization* 14 (1):107–45. doi: 10.1007/s11558-018-9302-y.

Kose, M. Ayhan, Peter Nagle, Franziska Ohnsorge, and Naotaka Sugawara. 2020. *Global Waves of Debt: Causes and Consequences*. Washington, DC: World Bank.

Leiva, Fernando Ignacio. 2008. "Towards a Critique of Latin American Neostructuralism." *Latin American Politics and Society* 50 (4):1–25.

Lin, Justin Yifu, and Yan Wang. 2017. *Going Beyond Aid: Development Cooperation for Structural Transformation*. Cambridge: Cambridge University Press.

Mackenzie, Kate. 2020. *Climate Change Is a Complex Problem, But Complex Financial Products Aren't the Solution*. New York: Bloomberg Wire Service.

Mak, James, and Seiji Finch Naya. 1994. "Is There a Need for a Pacific Islands Development Bank?" *Pacific Economic Bulletin* 9 (2):35–40.

Mares, David R., and Harold A. Trinkunas. 2016. *Aspirational Power: Brazil on the Long Road to Global Influence*. Washington, DC: Brookings Institution Press.

Marshall, Katherine. 2008. *The World Bank: From Reconstruction to Development to Equity*. Abingdon: Routledge.

Mawdsley, Emma, Warwick E. Murray, John Overton, Regina Scheyvens, and Glenn Banks. 2018. "Exporting Stimulus and "Shared Prosperity": Reinventing Foreign Aid for a Retroliberal Era." *Development Policy Review* 63 (S1):O25–43. doi: 10.1111/dpr.12282.

Mistry, Percy S., and Lolette Kritzinger-van Niekerk. 1998. Development Finance and the Need for a Sub-Regional Development Financing Institution in SADC. Southern African Development Community Finance & Investment Sector Coordinating Unit Research Project.

Murray, Warwick E., and John Overton. 2016. "Retroliberalism and the New Aid Regime of the 2010s." *Progress in Development Studies* 16 (3):244–60. doi: 10.1177/1464993416641576.

NDB. 2015. Agreement on the New Development Bank. Shanghai: New Development Bank. Accessed 12 March 2020. https://www.ndb.int/data-and-documents/ndb-core-documents/

Normann, Henrik. 2019. Nordic Investment Bank – Henrik Normann – Answers to UNSW Survey 15.5.2019, edited by Adrian Robert Bazbauers: UNSW Canberra.

North, Douglass C. 1998. "The New Institutional Economics and Third World Development." In *The New Institutional Economics and Third World Development*, edited by John Harriss, Janet Hunter and Colin M. Lewis, 17–26. London: Routledge. Original edition, 1995.

OECD. 2011. "Aid Effectiveness 2005–10: Progress in Implementing the Paris Declaration." OECD Publishing. Accessed 15 January 2013. http://www.oecd.org/dac/aideffectiveness/48742718.pdf.

Ortiz, Isabel, Matthew Cummins, Jeronim Capaldo, and Kalaivani Karunanethy. 2020. *The Decade of Adjustment: A Review of Austerity Trends 2010–2020 in 187 Countries*. Geneva: International Labour Office.

Park, Susan. 2014. "Institutional Isomorphism and the Asian Development Bank's Accountability Mechanism: Something Old, Something New, Something Borrowed, Something Blue?" *The Pacific Review* 27 (2):217–39.

Park, Susan. 2017. "Accountability as Justice for the Multilateral Development Banks? Borrower Opposition and Bank Avoidance to US Power and Influence." *Review of International Political Economy* 24 (5):776–801. doi: 10.1080/09692290.2017.1363798.

Pérez, Pedro Páez. 2009–10. "The Ecuadorian Proposal for a New Regional Financial Architecture." *Journal of Post Keynesian Economic* 32 (2):163–72.

Rich, Bruce. 1994. *Mortgaging the Earth: The World Bank, Environmental Impoverishment, and the Crisis of Development*. Boston, MA: Beacon Press.

Robinson, William. 2015. "The Transnational State and the BRICS: A Global Capitalism Perspective." *Third World Quarterly* 36 (1):1–21.

Rosales, Antulio. 2013. "The Banco del Sur and the Return to Development." *Latin American Perspectives* 40 (5):27–43.

Saith, Ashwani. 2006. "From Universal Values to Millennium Development Goals: Lost in Translation." *Development and Change* 37 (6):1167–99.

Stiglitz, Joesph. 2000. "The Insider: What I Learned at the World Economic Crisis." *New Republic* 222 (16/17):57–60.

Stiglitz, Joesph. 2002. *Globalization and Its Discontents*. London: Penguin Books.

Szasz, Paul C. 1999. "Establishment of the International Fund for Agricultural Development." *Studies in Transnational Legal Policy* 31–32:32–43.

The New Times. 2009. CEPGL Mulls Reopening Bank. Accessed 1 June 2020. https://www.newtimes.co.rw/section/read/80411/

Thurbon, Elizabeth. 2016. *Developmental Mindset: The Revival of Financial Activism in South Korea*. Ithaca, NY: Cornell University Press.

Toye, John. 1993. *Dilemmas of Development*, 2nd ed. Oxford: Blackwell Publishers.

Uhlin, Anders. 2016. "Civil Society and Policy Reforms in the Asian Development Bank." In *Global Economic Governance and the Practices of the Multilateral Development Banks*, edited by Susan Park and Jonathan R. Strand, 60–79. London: Routledge.

Wade, Robert. 1996. "Japan, the World Bank, and the Art of Paradigm Maintenance: *The East Asian Miracle* in Political Perspective." *New Left Review* 217:3–36.

Wade, Robert. 2001. "Showdown at the World Bank." *New Left Review* 7:124–37.

Wade, Robert. 2018. "The Developmental State: Dead or Alive?" *Development and Change* 49 (2):518–46. doi: 10.1111/dech.12381.

Wihtol, Robert. 2013. "NDF and the Case for Niche Development Funds." Development Today. http://www.development-today.com/magazine/2013/dt_14-15/opinion/ndf_and_the_case_for_niche_development_funds.

Williamson, John. 1990. "What Washington Means by Policy Reform." In *Latin American Readjustment: How Much Has Happened*, edited by John Williamson, 7–20. Washington, DC: Peterson Institute for International Economics.

Willis, Katie. 2005. *Theories and Practices of Development*. New York: Routledge.

Woods, Ngaire. 2006. *The Globalizers: The IMF, the World Bank, and Their Borrowers*. Ithaca, NY and London: Cornell University Press.

World Bank. 1993. *The East Asian Miracle: Economic Growth and Public Policy*. Oxford: Oxford University Press.

World Bank. 2019. *Annual Report 2019: Ending Poverty. Investing in Opportunity*. Washington, DC: World Bank.

Yağcı, Mustafa. 2016. "A Beijing Consensus in the Making: The Rise of Chinese Initiatives in the International Political Economy and Implications for Developing Countries." *Perceptions* XXI (2):29–56.

5 The structure of multilateral development banks

This chapter analyses the structure of the MDBs, positioning the World Bank as the archetype and exploring how the other MDBs are similar or different. The chapter starts with voting systems and capital subscriptions and how these have shaped Bank operations. Next, the Bank's governance structure is outlined, analysing the relative influence of its Governors, Directors, and senior management. The chapter then turns to the Bank's lending system – types of loans, conditionality, procurement, and interest rates. Table 5.2 systematically compares the Bank's structures to those of other MDBs, highlighting organisational convergences and divergences.

5.1 The structure of the World Bank

The MDBs are all structured like private banks, following the model established by the IBRD. They have shareholders, predominantly states, contributing capital in return for shares and voting rights. An analysis of vote allocations, capitalisation, governance structures, and lending capacity may seem quite technical, but it is critical to understand the MDBs as organisations to comprehend their strengths and limitations and thus their role in development finance.

5.1.1 Voting rights

The negotiators at the 1944 Bretton Woods conference did not spend much time debating the IBRD's organisational structure – Article V of the Bank's establishing agreement is 'nearly an exact copy of the [IMF's] Articles XII and XIII' (Mason and Asher 1973, 29). Article V outlines the Bank's organisation and management, including its governance structure, system of voting rights, and location of offices. The voting rights were the 'realist' heart at the centre of post-war international economic organisation building at Bretton Woods. Closely following Harry Dexter White's 1942 draft (Oliver 1971), IBRD voting rights were linked to the number of shares held – each member had 250 basic votes plus one additional vote for each share of stock held. The size of each country's capital subscription was originally based on relative economy size and later subscriptions to IDA were added to encourage donations to the Bank's concessional arm. Further, there is little incentive for developing countries to have large subscriptions because they are independent of borrowing rights; this is in contrast to the IMF, where subscriptions are linked to drawing rights (Mason and Asher 1973). This means that many borrowing members have little influence over the Bank, an issue identified as a severe democratic deficit in the MDB.

Basic votes are a compromise between equal representation and power-based voting, and some MDBs have more basic votes per member than others. In the IBRD's case, capital increases were not matched by an expansion of basic votes, so their value has significantly declined (Leech and Leech 2006). Basic votes were later capped at a low 5.55% of total votes but generally have been below that. In some of the other MDBs, basic votes were set as a percentage of total votes from the outset. For example, basic votes are 20% of total votes in the AsDB, while they are 12% in the AIIB, with founding AIIB members getting an additional 600 votes giving them greater weight, though the value of these will decline as the capital stock increases. Several MDBs also have different formulas for regional and non-regional members, generally with the aim of increasing the power of developing regional member countries.

The largest shareholders in the IBRD – those countries that provide the main guarantee behind the Bank's bond issues and loans on capital markets – were originally those from the Global North, namely the US and Western European countries. With the refusal of the Soviet Union to ratify the Bretton Woods agreement, the US had 35.07% of votes in 1946 and the US and European countries combined controlled 74% (Mason and Asher 1973, 800–02). Even with an influx of new members in the 1960s, the US and Europeans still held 61% in June 1971. Japan pushed to increase its shareholding in the early 1970s (Kapur, Lewis, and Webb 1997). After the creation of the IDA add-on in 1960, adjustments to Bank shareholding reflected not just the member's economic weight but also contributions to the Bank's concessional arm. In practice, however, political factors have always weighed in too.

China and other emerging economies began campaigns in the 1990s to gain more influence in the Bretton Woods institutions and other international organisations, to better reflect geopolitical changes. The Bank undertook what was described as major 'voice' reforms after a call from the UN International Conference on Financing for Development held in Monterrey in 2002. The revised quota framework was said to be 75% based on the size of state's GDP, IDA contributions were given 20% weighting, and 5% weighting was given to country's borrowings. The formulas were never formally published however, and countries did not have to agree to reductions, so the basis of decision-making remains unclear (Vestergaard 2010). Shareholding changes introduced in 2008 and 2010 produced only a 4.5% transfer from the Global North to developing and transition countries and much less for low-income countries (Vestergaard 2010)! By 2020, the top six shareholders in the IBRD were the US, whose 15.44% shareholding grants it veto power over certain key decisions, followed by Japan (7.75%), China (4.78%), Germany (4.08%), France (3.8%), and the UK (3.8%). Resolving over- and under-representation is difficult for the Bank and the rapid growth of emerging economies exacerbates this. Nevertheless, it can be said that: (i) high-income countries as a group remain over-represented; (ii) China is significantly under-represented, as is India; and (iii) low-income countries are over-represented relative to their GDP but still have just a tiny fraction of voting power (Vestergaard 2010).

The IBRD's governing structure is made up of a Board of Governors, with representatives appointed from each member country, a Board of Directors, and a President nominally elected by the Executive Directors. Almost all MDBs follow this structure, or a close variant thereof, e.g., the EADB has a Director General in lieu of a President, although the role is analogous. Governors are generally appointed by ministries of finance, though sometimes by Treasury or state departments or central banks – they rarely come from national aid agencies. The World Bank's Board of Governors is the supreme decision-making body, but its formal responsibilities are limited to admitting and suspending members, adjudicating appeals from the Directors on interpretations of the Bank's Articles, and increasing and decreasing the capital stock. Most formal power including setting strategic directions and approving lending operations is vested in the Directors, but in practice the President and senior management have substantial control. Directors are elected for two-year terms and are paid by the Bank, not member governments. There were originally 12 Directors, but this grew to 24 in 1992 following an expansion of country membership, and in 2010 an additional Director for sub-Saharan Africa was added, bringing the total to 25. Larger boards can lead to better representation but can also complicate decision-making and coordination (Babb 2009).

The largest shareholders get to appoint Directors. For many decades, this meant the US, the UK, Germany, France, and Japan, but today also includes China. Other countries generally pool their votes in relatively stable constituencies, with directorships usually held by the largest constituency members. These elections do not precisely follow the IBRD's Articles (Strand and Retzl 2016). Directors cast the number of votes that they control or have obtained at their election and voting for all IBRD decisions is 50% of votes cast, with a few key exceptions. The first is that capital increases require 75% of voting power, but the specification that members have the right to an equal subscription when there is a capital increase means that no country can have its shareholdings reduced without agreeing, so capital increases effectively require unanimous approval (Vestergaard 2010). Second, amending the Articles of Agreement requires three-fifths of members and 85% of voting power, increased from 80% in 1989, allowing the US to retain its veto. Finally, unanimous agreement is required to modify clauses on the right to withdraw from the IBRD, rights to subscribe to increases in the authorised capital stock, and limitations on liability.

Earlier Executive Director constituencies were sometimes based on historical or colonial relationships and there were often groups with a member from the Global North who dominated. Australia is an interesting example, as it formed a group in 1953 with the Union of South Africa, Vietnam joined in 1957, and New Zealand in 1965. By 1971, the group was without Vietnam. Then, in 2003, Australia was paired with New Zealand, Cambodia, the Republic of Korea, Mongolia,

Palau, and seven Pacific Island nations. In 2020, the group was almost the same, except the seven Pacific states had expanded to ten and the group's 3.45% voting power expanded to 3.99%. *Contra* the Australian example, most groups rarely change composition (Strand and Retzl 2016). The Russian Federation has a Director elected based on their shareholding, though Syria joined their constituency. Equally, Saudi Arabia is a single-member constituency. These two single-seat groups 'mean that the remaining voting groups are larger than they otherwise would be, thus potentially reducing the formal voice of members represented by elected' Directors (Strand and Retzl 2016, 420). Most other Directors are elected based on geographical groupings, though there are mixed constituencies, including the Philippines with several Latin American states and Switzerland with Eastern European and Central Asian states. Sub-Saharan Africa is represented by three groups, one with Angola, Nigeria, and South Africa and two others with over 20 states in each, which remain by far the largest groupings despite reforms enacted to address inequitable representation (Strand and Retzl 2016, 429). The Board is the same for the IBRD, IDA, and IFC though voting power differs, for example, the US holds only 10.06% shareholding in the IDA.

Almost all other MDBs operate along similar structures, with voting power linked to shareholding and allocated relative to their economic size. They can have higher or lower percentages of basic votes and some grant regional membership voting privileges over non-regional ones. The newly created NDB is the only MDB with equal voting power in 2020, but this may change when and if other countries are admitted. Further, some MDBs have financial institutions as shareholders in addition to countries. For example, the BOAD has eight regional member countries, the Central Bank of West African States, the AfDB and the EIB, three non-regional member states, and three financial institutions acting on behalf of Germany, India, and China. The admission of such eclectic members enabled BOAD to raise funds on bond markets, which it was previously unable to do due to capital and credit rating limitations of its regional member countries.

The shareholding system reflects a corporate governance model and is subject to similar vagaries with many MDBs having a dominant shareholder or group of shareholders, which creates problems around hegemonic power. Voting is usually pursued by consensus, but this often means appointed Directors set outcomes for their constituencies (Leech and Leech 2006). As Strand and Retzl (2016, 419) note, this is an expression of the power of major shareholders and weighted voting casts 'long shadows over negotiations.' There are no rules about whose interests elected Directors represent, which becomes particularly tricky in large constituencies (Leech and Leech 2006, Woods 2006), and quality control can be problematic in the absence of an independent evaluation office that reports to the Board (Ben-Artzi 2016).

5.1.2 Capital subscriptions

As shareholder banks, four factors shape MDB lending capacity: first, their size or total capitalisation; second, the amount of capital that is paid-in and the amount callable; third, the creditworthiness – or perceptions thereof – of the largest shareholders; and, fourth, their debt-to-lending ratios. When first established, the IBRD held $10 billion capital stock, which was not enough to meet Europe's post-war reconstruction needs; hence, it was quickly superseded by the Marshall Plan. The cash-strapped British successfully argued to reduce the amount of paid-in capital from the 50% of total capital that White proposed to 20% (Gardner 1980, Mason and Asher 1973). Of the paid-in capital, only 2% had to be paid in US dollars or gold with the remainder in the member's currency. This meant in the early years, when the US dollar was the only convertible currency, the Bank's loanable funds were limited to contributions in dollars or gold (Mason and Asher 1973). As Engel (2010, 29) argued, the 'small initial capital stock and even smaller paid-in component made the Bank reliant on financial markets for capital, which profoundly shaped its subsequent operations.' Add to this a conservative debt-to-lending ratio adopted by IBRD management and clearly the Bank established a cautious business model that prioritised banking principles (Kapur, Lewis, and Webb 1997). This model was emulated in the regional, sub-regional, and specialised development banks, many of which function more as banks than development agencies (Ben-Artzi 2016), with their loan policies, financial management, and country risk assessment designed to ensure bond market approvals (Humphrey 2016).

For the IBRD in its early years, support from financial markets meant gaining allies on Wall Street (Caufield 1998). The preference for bankers as IBRD President (see Chapters 3 and 4) and in other key management roles was meant to gain investor trust. The corollary was that very few staff had development backgrounds (Kapur, Lewis, and Webb 1997). Still, in the post-war years, caution around international bonds persisted, thus raising capital was difficult for the Bank. When established in the mid-2010s, the NDB and AIIB followed the pattern of the early MDBs, with senior staff often coming across from finance sector firms like Goldman Sachs (Engel and Bazbauers 2018).

Credit rating agencies (CRAs) were a major influence on the MDBs from the outset because the ranking of MDB bonds were a major factor in their saleability. There are four key elements to CRA ratings of MDBs (Ben-Artzi 2016, Delikanli, Dimitrov, and Agolli 2018, Humphrey 2014, Kapur, Lewis, and Webb 1997). First, they examine if the MDB has preferred creditor status. Second, CRAs assess the soundness of the countries and projects that MDBs lend to and for. In terms of the countries lent to, this encourages the MDBs to have a substantial share of their loan portfolio with credit-worthy middle-income countries. The World Bank has come under criticism for its lending to high middle-income countries, particularly its lending to China (see Behar 2012). In terms of the soundness of individual loans, this led the IBRD to prioritise project lending in its early years, despite a mandate to finance programme lending (Kapur, Lewis, and Webb 1997). As early Bank staffer Victor Urquidi (1996, 48) said, the 'Bank's "bottom line" in judging a project was the "times earned column" on a spreadsheet.' However, it has always been perceptions of project quality rather than reality that matters because of the substantial gap between when projects are approved and when they are completed and their outcomes are evaluated (Kapur, Lewis, and Webb 1997).

The third way CRAs judge MDBs is the stability of their major shareholders. In other words: do they have rich industrialised member states? This is because they are the ones that would realistically be able to contribute callable capital should an MDB ever need it. The consequence is that MDBs with fewer wealthy member states have reduced access to financial markets. The AfDB, for example, admitted non-African shareholders to improve its capital base (English and Mule 1996). Fourth, CRAs use a range of financial ratios to determine MDB risk ratings, particularly equity-to-loan ratios to determine capital adequacy. Almost all MDBs have capital adequacy well above those of commercial banks and there are not many reasons for this, apart from protecting wealthy members from capital call-ins (Humphrey 2014). The IBRD gained its AAA credit rating from the major US CRAs in 1959 and kept it ever since. As Table 5.1 shows, other MDBs have not been able to achieve this, which often reflects who their major shareholders are as much as their soundness as banks.

After the 2007–8 GFC, CRAs enacted new evaluation methodologies equating the MDBs to commercial banks, even though they are effectively non-profit organisations. Consequently, Humphrey (2017, 283) argues, 'to retain their AAA bond rating, major MDBs are (i) restricting their overall capacity to make use of their balance sheet for development projects and (ii) limiting lending to some borrowing countries facing economic difficulties.' This impacts the poorest countries that already have difficulty accessing credit the most because the MDBs are powerful signallers to private finance. Such limits could prove problematic when the next financial crisis arrives, particularly as grant finance was hollowed out over the 2010s. Former MDB staffers note how the CRAs are 'strategy makers and even regulators' despite having 'very little depth of comprehension' about MDBs (Delikanli, Dimitrov, and Agolli 2018, 58). CRAs regularly put demands on the MDBs, including reducing their portfolio risk and sector and country diversification. As a result of their inordinate impact, the BRICS started talks in 2015 about

Table 5.1 Multilateral Development Bank credit ratings 2019 and outlook

AAA	*AA+ to AA –*	*A+ to A–*	*BBB+ to BBB–*	*BB+ to B–*	*No rating*
AfDB (=) AIIB (=) AsDB (=) CEB (=) EBRD (=) EIB (=) IADB (=) IBRD/IDA (=) IsDB (=) NDB (=) NIB (=)	CABEI AA (=) CDB AA+ (=)	BSTDB A– (+) CAF A+ (–) FONPLATA A– (+) IBEC A– (=) IIB A– (=)	BOAD BBB+ (=) EADB BBB– (=) EDB BBB (=)	EBID B+ (=) TDB BBB (=)	AFESD BADEA BDEAC ETDB IFAD OFID PIDB

Source: Annual Reports and MDB Websites.

Note: Outlook positive (+), stable (=), negative (–).

establishing alternatives to the US-based CRAs, but with little success. The reliance on international banking and money markets has thus created a system that priorities banking norms over development ideals.

The World Bank has increased its lending capacity in two ways over the years: first, by increasing its capital reserves and, second, by increasing its capital base. The first general capital increase (GCI) was 14 years after the Bank was established in 1959, which doubled its capitalisation; it was to ensure that increased lending did not result in too great a deterioration of its equity-to-loan ratio and was strongly supported by the US. Other shareholders have also bargained intensely to increase their capital share, as Japan did in the 1980s in the pursuit of becoming the second largest IBRD shareholder (Kapur, Lewis, and Webb 1997).

Changes to relative IBRD shareholdings are done through Selective Capital Increases (SCIs). These generally follow IMF quota reviews and see countries offered additional shares to reflect their changed international positions, although political factors are always in the mix. This was the case in 1976 when OPEC members, whose economic influence increased after the 1973 oil shock, were offered larger shareholdings than their economies warranted as then President McNamara saw them as a potential source of new funds (Kapur, Lewis, and Webb 1997). The second oil shock of 1979 reduced US resistance to a new GCI, which was agreed at $40 billion. Following US resistance to capital increases during the mid-1980s, there was a large $78.9 billion GCI in 1988 that shored up the Bank's equity-to-loan ratio for quite some time. An influx of new members including Switzerland and former Soviet states led to further capital increases so that by 1995 the IBRD's capital was $184 billion.

It took over two decades for the next GCI because, after the 1997 Asian Financial Crisis, there was a long period of relative global economic growth and stability with private financial flows on the rise. The GFC brought that to an end, and led to a $58 billion GCI under President Zoellick. This 2010 GCI was dependent on World Bank governance reforms, as were the large 2018 GCI and SCI President Kim oversaw shortly before stepping down. The 2018 capital increase was for both the IBRD's paid-in ($7.5 billion) and callable ($52.6 billion) capital, with paid-in increases always harder to obtain. The Trump administration was critical of the Bank's ongoing lending to China and, in return for supporting the capital increase, obtained commitments to operational reforms and loan pricing changes designed to reduce loans to China, but resulted in higher interest rate charges to all wealthier IBRD borrowers (Mayeda and Shankleman 2018).

Delikanli, Dimitrov, and Agolli (2018, 38–9) examined 25 MDBs calculating their subscribed capital increased by an average of 5.7% per annum between 2007 and 2016 reaching $1.4 trillion, which in 2016 was equal to 1.8% of world GDP. Further, almost all MDBs retain earnings and this on average equalled 30.7% of total subscribed capital by 2016 (Delikanli, Dimitrov, and Agolli 2018, 41). The very low costs of gaining influence by creating an MDB is likely, we think, a key reason that there are now 30 MDBs. With all the discussion about the recent establishment of the AIIB and NDB, this factor was overlooked.

5.1.3 Governance

The IBRD's Articles of Agreement state that the Executive Directors select the Bank President. In practice, however, an informal agreement between the US and European countries means that the US proposes a presidential candidate for the Directors to approve and the Europeans propose the IMF Managing Director. A major campaign by several states, NGOs, and others started in the early 2000s pushed for a more merit-based selection process, this was epitomised by the 2012 Open Letter to all World Bank Governors signed by 59 leading development NGOs and published by the Bretton Woods Project, an NGO which critically monitors World Bank and IMF activities. But it remains the case that 'at the end of the day he' – and Bank Presidents have only even been men – 'is only accountable to the President of the United States and the US Congress' (Vestergaard 2010, 11).

All World Bank Presidents have been US citizens, though two were born overseas: James Wolfensohn in Australia and Jim Yong Kim in South Korea. The US has tended to select appointees without development backgrounds and, up to Wolfensohn, the majority were bankers, demonstrating again that it is a bank as much as, if not more so than, a development agency. Since Wolfensohn, Republican administrations have adopted a more partisan approach, with the three Republican appointees – Paul Wolfowitz, Robert Zoellick, and David Malpass – all having previously served as Republican political appointees. The last two Democratic appointees did not, however; Wolfensohn was a banker and Kim a public health specialist. This suggests that Republicans have taken a far more politicised approach to the Bank than Democrats. Still, it is not uncommon for MDB presidents to come from the political world and strong political ties may help in negotiating capital increases and replenishments (Ben-Artzi 2016).

The World Bank President guides day-to-day decisions, 'under the direction of the Executive Directors' (World Bank 2012). Bank Presidents are a key influence in shaping its strategic direction, as was shown in Chapters 3 and 4; they 'were not only the source of power in the institution; they were also the ones the staff looked to for signals that would indicate the Bank's primary mission and its operational priorities in a changing world' (Kraske 1996, vii). Still, as with all MDBs, there are tensions between the Boards of Governors and Directors and senior management and staff, which can arise from different priorities around politics, development, and bank finances and who prioritises what can change over time (Ben-Artzi 2016).

The location of an MDB's headquarters is political too. In the case of the IMF and World Bank, they were to 'be located in the territory of the member holding the greatest number of shares' (World Bank 2012). The US chose to headquarter the IBRD in Washington, DC, so it would be under close governmental influence. Subsequent MDBs mostly show a similar pattern of politicking, with head office locations being a decision by major shareholders or a backlash against them.

As examples, the IADB is in Washington DC, while the AsDB is in Manila, the Philippines, to reduce member concerns about Japanese influence.

Debates about reform to World Bank governance have arisen at least once a decade both within and outside the MDB, leading to a never-ending cycle of restructuring. In terms of reform, many commentators have made the important point that MDB governance should be as sound as the MDBs expect the governance of their borrowers to be. Some outside the organisation call for reform (see inter alia Ahluwalia et al. 2016, Stiglitz 2006, Woods 2006), while others call for a more radical rethinking of international economic governance (Amin 2014, Bello, Kinley, and Elinson 1982, Cammack 2002, George and Sabelli 1994). And, yet, at the end of the day, despite regular restructuring, the Bank's governance as delineated by its Articles of Agreement remains largely unchanged since the 1940s, a template emulated by almost all other MDBs and clearly evident in both the NDB and AIIB.

5.1.4 Loans

The World Bank offers three main loan types: investment project finance, development policy loans (DPLs), and programme-for-results lending. Investment project finance for physical and social infrastructure is the Bank's staple lending instrument and can be approved as an IBRD loan, IDA credit, or as a guarantee. Investments can be in any sector and can only be financed by the Bank or co-financed with other development agencies either as loans or grants. DPLs provide budget support to governments based on commitment to a set of policy or institutional reforms. These originated from what was called non-project and programme lending, which comprised an average of 6% of Bank lending up until the late 1970s (Kapur, Lewis, and Webb 1997, 487). In the 1980s, the Bank launched structural adjustment loans (SALs) and sectoral adjustment loans (SECALs), which were conditional on macroeconomic changes. Adjustment lending peaked at around 30% of loans in the 1980s then declined in the 1990s. DPLs replaced SALs and SECALs in 2004 and made up roughly one-quarter of financing between 2005 and 2015, largely due to a spike in overall lending and emergency responses to the GFC (World Bank 2020). This is the most controversial lending instrument as it involves the Bank interfering in a country's macroeconomic policies. Compared to the coercive reputation of SALs and SECALs, DPLs are meant to be borrower-owned and -led, but the degree to which this is the case is questionable. Programme-for-results lending, previously known as programme lending, focusses investment on specific sectors. Funding is disbursed when pre-agreed results are achieved. This third instrument is focussed on lending to 'high-performing' countries. In addition, the Bank offers tailored loan programmes, but the three above loan types receive the bulk of annual approvals. The Bank also has several trust funds and grant facilities with different donors and these finances are often allocated along with a Bank loan. To develop loans, the Bank offers extensive technical assistance services (see Bazbauers 2018 for a detailed history).

Harry Dexter White's first IBRD draft went into detail about lending operations (Oliver 1971), which likely reflected his concern to ensure the exploitative lending of the inter-war years was not repeated. Further, White judged that the below-market interest rates on offer would produce a good demand for loans, which has not in fact generally been the case for the IBRD. The IDA, however, tends to be oversubscribed because of its highly concessional terms. Many of White's ideas are inscribed in the Bank's Articles of Agreement and into those of subsequent MDBs. Loan conditions are specified in Article III, Section 4 and they start with the requirement that states guarantee loan repayments made in their territory regardless of who it is to. Next, to make sure Bank funds did not compete with private banks, the IBRD had to be satisfied that the loan could not be secured from the market. Section 4 continues in outlining that loans and guarantees, except in special circumstances, must 'be for the purpose of specific projects of reconstruction and development' (World Bank 2012). Further, interest rates must be 'reasonable' and, to ensure the productive use of loans, a 'competent committee' must study each proposal and complete a written report on it (Mason and Asher 1973). Debt was also a major concern of post-war planners, so the IBRD was tasked with making prudent assessments of the borrower's capacity to repay. And, so, the aim was to create a cautious lending programme based on market ideals and framed by (Western) experts (Engel 2010).

Article 4, Point 10 of the IBRD's establishing agreement on political non-interference gives 'complete discretion' for terms and conditions, meaning that an action is non-political if the Bank says it is (Mason and Asher 1973, 27). The artificial distinction between politics and economics in Point 10 has allowed the Bank to promote clearly political economic policies and prescriptions. Even loan conditions have been political, given that they grew with the rise of neoliberal SALs and SECALs in the 1980s and then declined in part because of their lack of efficacy.

Conditionality is the product of a three-way interaction between the Bank, shareholders, and borrowers, with more powerful borrowing countries being less subject to conditionality; influential shareholders only come into play if they have particular support for, or concerns about, loans to a borrower (Hernandez 2017). The availability of finance from other sources – the private sector and other donors – is also a factor shaping the level and impact of conditionality. Focussing on the availability from other states, Hernandez (2017) found that increased lending from China was associated with a decline in Bank conditionality on loans in 54 African states. While Hernandez (2017) regards conditions positively as a way of increasing aid effectiveness and protecting resources, progressive scholars and NGOs have argued that they often undermine the state and harm the well-being of the poor (Bello 1994, Cammack 2002, Carroll 2010, SAPRIN 2004).

The World Bank's terminology for loan conditions has changed over the decades, thus if you are reading loan documents available from the Bank's project database, you might see terms like 'pre-requisites,' 'policy action,' 'triggers,' and 'challenges.' Conditions can be targeted at the macro- and mid-levels and the project level. DPLs focus on macro- and mid-level conditionality. In investment loans, conditions relate to the sector the loan is in. For example, the West Bengal Major Irrigation and Flood Management Project approved in 2019 called some of its conditions its 'theory of change' and included a condition of outsourcing operations and maintenance 'to irrigation contractors on a performance basis' (World Bank 2019, 7). This demonstrates the Bank's commitment to private sector provision of public services funded by its loans. Investment loan conditions can have even broader implications for a sector, for example, a loan for a power plant in Vietnam required not only a private provider to build and operate the plant, but also legislation to promote the expansion of private providers in the sector, despite decades of problems in privatised electricity (Engel 2010).

Projects are evaluated by their expected rates of return, though the country's overall creditworthiness is also a factor (Kapur, Lewis, and Webb 1997, Urquidi 1996). As early as 1949, due in part to the low level and poor quality of loan applications, the Bank established a system of technical assistance to develop, assess, and supervise projects (Bazbauers 2018). It also assisted with broader state macroeconomic planning and management. Both were done with the assistance of 'fly-in, fly-out' Western experts. Within two decades, the Bank had built four technical assistance pillars, a structure emulated by several other MDBs. These pillars included technical assistance embedded within projects to support implementation, stand-alone technical assistance project that often guided capacity development, survey missions that reviewed a recipient's development status to propose future lending schedules, and professional training institutes delivering courses and seminars to senior public servants (Bazbauers 2018).

The World Bank requires projects to be managed in accordance with Bank-set accounting, auditing, and other standards, though in some 'high-performing' countries the Bank allows the use of local project management systems. All Bank loans are subject to social and environmental safeguards, though the efficacy of these has long been a matter of debate, with NGOs and academics pointing to limitations. The Bank also has policies around anti-corruption in project management and procurement. And, under pressure from the US, the Bank established an Inspection Panel in 1993 to allow people negatively affected by its projects a means of redress. As Park (2017) outlines, institutional isomorphism saw most of the other RDBs follow suit over the next decade.

In terms of procurement, the Articles of Agreement were ahead of their time in specifying that loans must be untied; tied aid requires recipients to spend aid in the donor country. Bilateral Western donors have made commitments since at least the late 1980s to progress the untying of their aid particularly for the least developed countries and low-income countries but have not yet fully achieved this. Still, formal untying of procurement from donor states can be misleading, as Bracking (2009) notes there is an expectation that the largest shareholders will be the largest beneficiaries of contracts from MDBs and other development finance institutions (DFIs). In the 1990s, the US, UK, Germany, Japan, and France were the largest beneficiaries of procurement in the World Bank (51.5% of total), AsDB (98.6%), and IADB (86.3%), though they only accounted for 20% of AfDB procurement (Bracking 2009, 119). By the mid-2000s, China and India had risen dramatically up the World Bank list, dominating in civil works contracts, and they were followed by Brazil as the next largest beneficiary. In consultancy contracts, Indonesia and the Russian Federation have joined the US, the UK, and France in the top five. Of course, the beneficiaries of winning contractors are not always clear in today's globalised marketplace; contracts won by the Indonesian office of a global consultancy firm likely flow through tax havens to top income earners in the Global North.

The World Bank provides the framework for how project procurement should be undertaken and requires all Bank-financed work to be done by contractors and not the state. In terms of contracting out, in a small number of cases the Bank allows direct selection, essentially where there is only one suitable firm to provide the work or where there is a strong reason for a preferred firm. Most of the work, however, is put through open, competitive procurement. For small contracts, this may be limited to contractors in the borrower state, but the preferred mechanism is international competition. This requirement dates to loan agreements approved in 1951 (Mason and Asher 1973, 26). Competition for these contracts is complex and requires high-level technical and legal skills, access to technology and finance, and there is often a preference for larger companies that have the scale to complete complex projects (Bracking 2009). Many Western governments have long had special programmes to help their firms bid for projects and they utilise their in-country networks with government officials to benefit their companies; in other words, they adopt crony practices and North firms are not adverse to paying bribes to win projects. In practice, the lowest cost bid is not necessarily the best quality and once a company has won a contract through a low-cost bid, they can often negotiate further funding to complete it. International procurement also means that Global South countries are largely buying goods and services from places that are more developed than they are, either from the Global North or from a handful of large emerging economies like China, Brazil, and India. Thus, their debt repayments embody the labour costs – either directly in technical assistance or indirectly through the price of goods – of people paid more, often much more, than most workers in the poorest countries. In other words, MDB loans promote what Marxists label unequal exchange (Amin 2014).

Loan rates and charges vary in the World Bank dependent on the recipient country's gross national income (GNI) per capita. Low-income countries (set as GNI below $1,025 in 2020) are eligible for IDA loans, which are highly concessional. Lower-middle income countries (GNI between $1,026 and $3,995 in 2010) can receive a blend of IBRD and IDA loans. Upper-middle income countries (GNI between $3,996 and $12,375) are eligible for IBRD loans only, which are on harder terms. As of April 2020, regular IDA loans had a maturity of 38 years, a six-year grace period where no repayments are made, and an interest rate of 3.125%; terms for small economies are slightly more generous, while for somewhat wealthier states eligible for a blend of IBRD and IDA loans, they are harder. The commitment charge for loans was zero. IBRD rates are a lot more variable depending on the term of the loan (8–20 years), the currency borrowed in, whether the loan was fixed or variable, and GNI per capita of the country. Interest rates are set in relation to the London Inter-Bank Offered Rate (LIBOR), which is an interest rate average determined from estimates given by major London banks. In April 2020, they ranged between LIBOR +0.65% and +2.05% and the loans had a front-end fee and commitment fee each of 0.25%.

Earlier in the chapter, we outlined the key factors shaping assessments of MDB creditworthiness, which determine how cheaply they can borrow and, in turn, on-lend for. Examining the IBRD, IADB, and CAF, Humphrey (2014) demonstrated that the IBRD can borrow most cheaply, followed by the IADB, which has a large US shareholding, while the CAF faces higher costs because its shareholders are regional states. But the different institutions have also taken different positions on net income, decisions about how much is used to build up reserves and equity (in lieu of increases in paid-in capital), and allocation of net income to alternate financing streams, in particular to technical assistance, trust funds, and concessional arms. CAF has focussed on minimising costs to borrowers, so its loans are not as expensive as would be expected given their cost of borrowing, while the IADB is closer to the World Bank in terms of interest rates (Humphrey 2014). The IBRD could lend more cheaply if it were not for these decisions.

5.1.5 *Comparing the IBRD and other MDBs*

Each of the above sections – voting rights, capital subscriptions, governance, and loans – has made some comparisons to other MDBs, demonstrating that many key features are shared among them. Delikanli, Dimitrov, and Agolli (2018, 112) regard the MDBs as 'a family of peer cross-referenced institutions adhering to common norms and standards, with large MDBs often acting as role models.' Table 5.2, however, provides a more systematic comparison of the IBRD to the regional, sub-regional, and specialised development banks.

5.2 Conclusion

This chapter has outlined the key structural features of the World Bank, revealing it to be the standard template for an MDB. It explored voting systems, capital subscriptions, governance structures, and loan types, terms, and conditions. Overall, the clear picture is that the World Bank is a bank-like development institution, disciplined by financial markets and focussed on a development as economic growth mentality. Delikanli, Dimitrov, and Agolli (2018, 26) argue that the MDBs are not banks because they do not take deposits and that they are not licensed or supervised, operating only according to their establishing agreements

Table 5.2 Key features of the structure of IBRD and variations in other MDBs

Issue	*IBRD*	*Variations in other MDBs*
Organisational Structure	• Structured like a company. • For-profit. • Largest shareholders are non-borrowers.	• Structured like the IBRD. • Can be non-profit, e.g., the EIB; specific profits must be re-invested, e.g., the CABEI; or, have a special class of institutional shares that generate dividends, e.g., the TDB. • Can be led by borrowers, non-borrowers, or some balance between them.
Membership	• 189 member states that must be IMF shareholders.	• Can have non-IMF member states, other MDBs, and other financial institutions as members. • Smallest membership is five for the NDB.
Management	• Board of Governors representing all member states is supreme governing authority. They control decisions requiring more than a majority vote and elect appointees to the Board of Directors. • Board of Directors is responsible for strategic direction and lending operation approval but, in practice, Bank management has a lot of power. Originally 12 Executive Directors, now 25.	• All MDBs have the same basic structure. • The AfDB, AsDB, CABEI, CDB, EBRD, and IADB have resident Executive Directors, most others have non-resident ones. • Only the EIB has a larger number of Executive Directors than the World Bank; the average is around 14 and the smallest five: the ETDB and NDB. • The AIIB, CAF, and TDB have greater delegations to management for loan approvals than the major MDBs. AIIB delegates decisions up to $300 million to management, meaning little Board oversight. • The EIB has a Management Committee that comprised the President and Vice Presidents.
Shareholding and Voting	• Originally, shareholdings were to reflect relative size of economy globally, later contributions to IDA became part of formula. There are still misalignments. • Shareholders get one vote for each share of stock held plus their basic votes; originally 250 basic votes but this was changed to 5.55% of all votes, though in practice it is less. • Executive Directors have the number of votes of the shareholders they represent and cannot split their votes. • Largest shareholder is the US with 15.76% of votes.	The MDBs can have: • Higher or lower portions of basic votes, e.g., the AsDB has 20% basic votes. • Only votes per share, e.g. the NDB and EBRD. • Additional votes for founding members, e.g., the AIIB founding members get an additional 600 votes each. • Voting power linked to whether countries are regional or non-regional members; regional members generally must have the dominant shareholding, e.g., the AsDB regional membership must be 60% minimum; the AfDB has the lowest voting share of regional members at 59%. • Shareholders may be limited to borrowing states; split between borrowing and non-borrowing members (e.g., the BDEAC has 2% non-borrowing members, while the IADB's Articles specify equal split between borrowing and non-borrowing shareholdings); fully owned by non-borrowers, e.g., the BADEA and OFID.

Issue	*IBRD*	*Variations in other MDBs*
		• Equal shareholdings and votes for each member, the NDB has this and the CABEI originally had this. • Groups of countries with equal votes, e.g., the IFAD has DAC, OPEC, and G77 groupings with equal votes. • Limits on all members maximum shareholding, e.g., the TDB has a 15% limit. • One vote per Executive Director regardless of shareholding, e.g., the NIB. • Executive Directors can split votes in the AsDB, EBRD, and IsDB.
Voting Majorities	• Majority of weighted votes is required for most decisions. In practice, most votes are by consensus but voting power shapes negotiations. • Double majority (majority of votes cast by member majority) for: suspension of members or operations and distributions. • Super majority (75% of total voting power) for: increases in capital stock; currencies of lending; approving securities that the Bank can purchase. • Super majority (60% of members with 85% of voting power) for: amendments to the Articles. • Unanimous agreement to modify clauses on the right to withdraw from Bank, rights to subscribe to increases in authorised capital stock, and limits on liability.	• Most MDBs have simple majority votes for regular decisions, though there are quite a few exceptions where more than 51% is required (the AfDB, CAF, ETDB, and IIB), while the NIB requires unanimity. Like the IBRD, practice tends to be by consensus. • Special majority is required for similar decisions as per the IBRD Articles, with most just having one set of special majorities not the IBRD's three. They generally require 66% of Governors having 75% of voting power but there are variations.
President and Staff	• Meant to be elected by the Executive Directors, but by informal agreement is selected by the US. Reforms to create a more merit-based selection process have had limited impact. • President is legal representative and chief executive officer with a five-year term and a maximum of two terms. • Largest MDB with over 11,000 staff with around 60% in Washington, DC, headquarters and 40% in resident missions.	• Presidents are generally elected by Board of Governors and are often citizens of regional member states. • Senior appointments tend to be political in most MDBs. • Five-year terms are common; second terms often allowed. • Largest staffing after the IBRD is the AsDB with just over 3,000. It also has a relatively high percentage of its staff based at headquarters, whereas the AfDB have over 40% of staff decentralised.
Location of Headquarters	• In territory of largest member state. The US insisted on Washington, DC.	• Headquarters is often linked to the distribution of regional institutions across member states. • At least six located in non-borrowing countries. • The OFID is the only MDB with headquarters in a non-member state.

(Continued)

Issue	*IBRD*	*Variations in other MDBs*
Capitalisation	• The IBRD originally capitalised at $100 million, increased through GCIs and SCIs approved by Board of Governors. • In 2018, capitalised at $274.7 billion. 2018 Annual Meetings agreed to a further $60.1 billion increase, making it again the largest MDB. • Originally 20% of IBRD capital was paid-in with the rest callable, of the paid-in 2% had to be gold or hard currency like US dollars; now 6–7% of capital is paid-in. • The IFC has 100% paid-in capital and the IDA around 75%.	• Three other MDBs have subscribed capital over $100 billion – the EIB, IADB, and AsDB. The AIIB is just below $100 billion. • Mid-tier MDBs have around $50 billion – the AsDB, IsDB, and NDB. The EBRD has $30 billion. • Smaller MDBs have less than $10 billion. The smallest – the PIDB – has just over $8 million. • MDBs often start with higher paid-in capital and it reduces over time as they gain creditworthiness, e.g., the AIIB has 20% paid-in capital, RDBs had an average of 10% in 2016, and SRDBs had an average of 44% in 2016; this high level increases their lending capacity – the CAF had 68% paid-in capital and a high level of reserves.
Concessional Arm	• The IDA was established in 1961, requires regular replenishments which are very political • The IBRD has transferred a share of profits to the IDA as did the IFC, but they stopped in 2018. • From 2018, the IDA will raise funds on private markets.	• The AfDB has the AfDF and NTF. • The AsDB has the AsDF, which merged its balance sheet into Ordinary Capital Resources in 2015. • The IADB has the FSO, which also merged in 2016. • The IFAD is mostly funded by replenishments. • The IsDB has the IsDF.
Focus on Lending	• No political interference. • Finances projects that the private sector will not. • Instruments: investment and policy loans, credits, technical assistance, guarantees, and equity investments. • Social and economic conditions. • Social and environmental safeguards supported by an independent evaluation office and an Inspection Panel. • Outstanding loan portfolio in 2019: IBRD $192.8 billion; IDA $151.9 billion; Total $344.7 billion. • Loans average 2017–19: • IBRD: commitments $22.9 billion, gross disbursements $18.5 billion, and net disbursements $8.2 billion; IDA: commitments $21.8 billion, gross disbursements $14.9 billion, and net disbursements $9.9 billion.	• The EBRD promotes democracy. • Many MDBs promote regional integration. • Instruments: many have only investment and no policy lending, most offer equity investments but only some offer lines of credit, grants, technical assistance, and guarantees. • Many MDBs have less or no conditionality, i.e., the IsDB has none. • Around half have some safeguards and, where they do, they tend to be similar and be supported by an independent evaluation office and inspection panel. • The EIB has the largest outstanding loan portfolio at over $500 billion 2019 and $54 billion in loan disbursements plus a further $11.5 billion for the EIF; the BSTDB as an example of small MDB had $1.4 billion portfolio and $555 million in loan disbursements in 2019. • Most MDBs have top five borrowers that account for half of their outstanding loans (see Engen & Prizzon, 2018 for comparison of loan portfolios).

Issue	*IBRD*	*Variations in other MDBs*
Lending Terms	• 2020 IBRD loans: variable depending on loan term (8–20 years), currency borrowed in, fixed or variable, and GNI per capita of the country; interest rates between LIBOR +0.65 to +2.05%, front-end fee and commitment fee each 0.25%. • IDA loans: 38 years maturity, 6 years grace period, no commitment charge, interest rate 3.125%; terms vary a little depending on borrower GNI.	• Shorter and longer repayment periods and different interest rate regimes, e.g., revisable interest rates. • Trade loans generally have shorter terms than investment loans. • SRDBs interest rates are 130–40 basis points higher than the World Bank and RDBs.
Procurement	• Non-members states are eligible unconditionally to compete for contracts • Bank specifies procurement standards as part of loans, though in some cases borrowers can utilise their own systems.	• Most MDBs allows non-members to compete but a few allow it on worse terms or not for special funds. • The CDB, IADB, and IIB do not allow non-members to compete nor do the AsDB and NDB though they have exceptions. • Smaller MDBs tend not to specify procurement procedures.
Other Arms	• The IFC for private sector lending. • The MIGA for investment guarantees. • The ICSD for dispute settlement.	• Most fund private sector (non-sovereign) operations from main entity but two have arms like the IFC – the IADB and IsDB. • The IsDB has an arm like the MIGA. • The EIB funds non-sovereign operations from its main entity but also has separate small and medium enterprise arm and another arm a bit like the MIGA.
Other Services and Funds	• Funds and services for technical advice, trust funds.	• Most MDBs provide technical assistance and see this as an area of comparative advantage. • Some have trust funds, e.g., the EIB has technical assistance trust funds plus several facilities to support private sector investment, public-private partnerships, and pre-investment studies.
Research and Training	• The IBRD has a Research Division and the World Bank Institute (formerly the Economic Development Institute), which funds research, partners with academia, and runs seminars and conferences (Bazbauers, 2018). • Engen and Prizzon (2018) calculated that the Bank produced over 22,000 research papers since 2000.	• Only the larger MDBs have research units and only a few have training units, e.g., the EIB Institute, IsDB's Islamic Research and Training Institute, and the African and Asian Development Bank Institutes.

Sources: MDB Websites and Annual Reports and Engen and Prizzon (2018), Delikanli, Dimitrov, and Agolli (2018), Griffith-Jones (2001), Humphrey (2019)

and rules agreed by their Boards of Governors and Directors. Further, as international organisations, they have important special features, including 'preferred creditor treatment, legal ex-territoriality, immunity and so on' (Delikanli, Dimitrov, and Agolli 2018, 22). And, yet, while the MDBs may not meet such formal definitions of banks, they are strongly governed by banking and financial norms, credit rating assessments, and global capital markets, as both of the IBRD's official histories have noted (see Kapur, Lewis, and Webb 1997, Mason and Asher 1973) and Humphrey's (2014, 2016, 2019) excellent recent analysis has demonstrated.

Bibliography

Ahluwalia, Montek Singh, Lawrence Summers, Andrés Velasco, Nancy Birdsall, and Scott Morris. 2016. *Multilateral Development Banking for This Century's Development Challenges: Five Recommendations to Shareholders of the Old and New Multilateral Development Banks*. Washington, DC: Centre for Global Development.

Amin, Samir. 2014. *Capitalism in the Age of Globalization: The Management of Contemporary Society*. London and New York: Zed Books.

Babb, Sarah. 2009. *Behind the Development Banks: Washington Politics, World Poverty, and the Wealth of Nations*. Chicago, IL and London: The University of Chicago Press.

Bazbauers, Adrian Robert. 2018. *The World Bank and Transferring Development: Policy Movement through Technical Assistance*. Cham: Palgrave Macmillan.

Behar, Richard. 2012. "Too Big to Fail: The World Bank." *Forbes*, 16 July, 86–94.

Bello, Walden. 1994. *Dark Victory: The United States, Structural Adjustment, and Global Poverty*. London: Pluto.

Bello, Walden, David Kinley, and Elaine Elinson. 1982. *Development Debacle: The World Bank in the Philippines*. San Francisco, CA: Institute for Food and Development Policy and Philippine Solidarity Network.

Ben-Artzi, Ruth. 2016. *Regional Development Banks in Comparison: Banking Strategies versus Development Goals*. Cambridge: Cambridge University Press.

Bracking, Sarah. 2009. *Money and Power: Great Predators in the Political Economy of Development*. London: Pluto Press.

Cammack, Paul. 2002. "Attacking the Poor." *New Left Review* 13:125–34.

Carroll, Toby. 2010. *Delusions of Development: The World Bank and the Post-Washington Consensus in Southeast Asia*. Houndmills, Basingstoke: Palgrave Macmillan.

Caufield, Catherine. 1998. *Masters of Illusion: The World Bank and the Poverty of Nations*. London: Macmillan. Original edition, 1996.

Delikanli, Ihsan Ugur, Todor Dimitrov, and Roena Agolli. 2018. *Multilateral Development Banks: Governance and Finance*. Cham: Palgrave Macmillan.

Engel, Susan. 2010. *The World Bank and the Post-Washington Consensus in Vietnam and Indonesia: Inheritance of Loss*. London: Routledge.

Engel, Susan, and Adrian Robert Bazbauers. 2018. "Old and New Development Banks and the Future of Development Finance." FLASCO-ISA Joint International Conference, Quito, Ecuador.

Engen, Lars, and Annalisa Prizzon. 2018. *A Guide to Multilateral Development Banks*. London: ODI.

English, E. Phillip, and Harris M. Mule. 1996. *The African Development Bank*. London: Lynne Rienner.

Gardner, Richard N. 1980. *Sterling-dollar Diplomacy in Current Perspective: The Origins and the Prospects of our International Economic Order*, 3rd ed. New York: Columbia University Press.

George, Susan, and Fabrizio Sabelli. 1994. *Faith and Credit: The World Bank's Secular Empire*. London: Penguin Books.

Griffith-Jones, Stephany. 2001. *Governance of the World Bank*. UK: Department for International Development.

Hernandez, Diego. 2017. "Are "New" Donors Challenging World Bank Conditionality?" *World Development* 96 (August):529–49. doi: 10.1016/j.worlddev.2017.03.035.

Humphrey, Chris. 2014. "The Politics of Loan Pricing in Multilateral Development Banks." *Review of International Political Economy* 21 (3):611–39. doi: 10.1080/09692290.2013.858365.

Humphrey, Chris. 2016. "The Invisible Hand: Financial Pressures and Organisational Convergence in Multilateral Development Banks." *The Journal of Development Studies* 52 (1):92–112. doi: 10.1080/00220388.2015.1075978.

Humphrey, Chris. 2017. "He Who Pays the Piper Calls the Tune: Credit Rating Agencies and Multilateral Development Banks." *The Review of International Organizations* 12 (2):281–306. doi: 10.1007/s11558-017-9271-6.

Humphrey, Chris. 2019. "'Minilateral' Development Banks: What the Rise of Africa's Trade and Development Bank says about Multilateral Governance." *Development and Change* 50 (1):164–90. doi: 10.1111/dech.12467.

Kapur, Devesh, John P. Lewis, and Richard Webb. 1997. *The World Bank Its First Half Century, Volume 1: History*, 2 vols. Vol. 1: History. Washington, DC: Brookings Institution Press.

Kraske, Jochen. 1996. *Bankers with a Mission: The Presidents of the World Bank, 1946–91*. Oxford: Oxford University Press.

Leech, Dennis, and Robert Leech. 2006. "Voting Power in the Bretton Woods Institutions." In *The IMF, World Bank and Policy Reform*, edited by Alberto Paloni and Maurizio Zanardi, 27–43. London and New York: Routledge.

Mason, Edward S., and Robert E. Asher. 1973. *The World Bank Since Bretton Woods*. Washington, DC: The Brookings Institution.

Mayeda, Andrew, and Jessica Shankleman. 2018. "World Bank Edges Near Capital Boost as U.S. Drops Objection." *Bloomberg*, 22 April.

Oliver, Robert W. 1971. *Early Plans for a World Bank, Princeton Studies in International Finance No. 29*. Princeton, NJ: Department of Economics, Princeton University.

Park, Susan. 2017. "Accountability as Justice for the Multilateral Development Banks? Borrower Opposition and Bank Avoidance to US Power and Influence." *Review of International Political Economy* 24 (5):776–801. doi: 10.1080/09692290.2017.1363798.

SAPRIN. 2004. The Policy Roots of Economic Crisis and Poverty: A Multi-Country Participatory Assessment of Structural Adjustment. Structural Adjustment Participatory Review Initiative Network.

Stiglitz, Joesph. 2006. *Making Globalization Work*. London: Allen Lane.

Strand, Jonathan R., and Kenneth J. Retzl. 2016. "Did Recent Voice Reforms Improve Good Governance within the World Bank?" *Development and Change* 47 (3):415–45.

Urquidi, Victor L. 1996. "Reconstruction vs. Development: The IMF and the World Bank." In *The Bretton Woods – GATT System: Retrospect and Prospect After Fifty Years*, edited by Orin Kirshner, 30–51. Armonk, NY: M.E. Sharp.

Vestergaard, Jakob. 2010. Voice Reform in the World Bank. Danish Institute of International Studies. Accessed 24 November 2020. https://um.dk/~/media/UM/English-site/

Documents/Danida/Partners/Research-Org/Research-studies/Voice%20Reform%20in%20the%20World%20Bank%202010.pdf

Woods, Ngaire. 2006. *The Globalizers: The IMF, the World Bank, and Their Borrowers*. Ithaca, NY and London: Cornell University Press.

World Bank. 2012. World Bank. 2012. International Bank of Reconstruction and Development Articles of Agreement. Washington, DC: World Bank. Accessed 24 November 2020. https://www.worldbank.org/en/about/articles-of-agreement/ibrd-articles-of-agreement.

World Bank. 2019. West Bengal Major Irrigation and Flood Management Project (P162679), Combined Project Information Documents / Integrated Safeguards Datasheet (PID/ISDS). Washington, DC: World Bank.

World Bank. 2020. "2015 Development Policy Financing Retrospective – Results and Sustainability." Washington, DC. Accessed 3 April. https://www.worldbank.org/en/projects-operations/products-and-services/publication/dpfretrospective2015.

6 The regional development banks

The regional expansion of the multilateral development bank (MDB) system entrenched multilateral development finance (MDF) in the emerging global governance architecture, leading the regional development banks (RDBs) to become 'the titans of the emerging post-war world of development' (Culpeper 1997, 164). As Table 6.1 shows, there are five RDBs: European Investment Bank (EIB), Inter-American Development Bank (IADB), African Development Bank (AfDB), Asian Development Bank (AsDB), and European Bank for Reconstruction and Development (EBRD). They largely emerged between 1958 and 1966, with the EBRD as an outlier established in 1991. The RDBs closely resemble the IBRD in structure but differ in purpose and function, particularly their mandates on regional development, collaboration, and integration. Common among the RDBs is the pursuit of regional economic development, with support either for the growth of common markets (as in the case of the EIB) or for individual and collective economic and social development (as in the IADB, AfDB, and AsDB).

Over their histories, the RDBs have evolved greatly, to the point of straining their establishing agreements. Their memberships and capital bases have also grown significantly, and their lending operations have diversified to both address a broader range of development issues and become more interventionist through prescriptive legislative, policy, and institutional reforms. Despite two operating in the Global North and the other three in the Global South, the RDBs are similar in that their creation coincided with, and reflected, the mainstreaming of development economics and the increasing formalisation of development theory and practice. Further, they all promote regional integration (English and Mule 1996, Kappagoda 1995, Tussie 1995).

After briefly comparing the governance structures of and main challenges faced by the RDBs, this chapter provides an analytical overview of the five RDBs, presented in order of their establishment.

Table 6.1 Regional Development Banks Overview

Year	*Regional Development Banks*	*Region*	*Membership*	*Subscribed Capital*	*Annual Approvals (2018)*	*Credit Rating*	*Headquarters*
1958	European Investment Bank	Europe+	27	$275 billion	$69 billion	AAA	Luxembourg
1959	Inter-American Development Bank	Latin America and the Caribbean	48	$170.9 billion	$14.3 billion	AAA	Washington, DC, United States
1964	African Development Bank	Africa	80	$97 billion	$10 billion	AAA	Abidjan, Côte d'Ivoire (Tunis, Tunisia from 2003 to 2014)
1966	Asian Development Bank	Asia and the Pacific	67	$153 billion	$21.6 billion	AAA	Manila, Philippines
1991	European Bank for Reconstruction and Development	Europe+	66	$33.7 billion	$10.5 billion	AAA	London, United Kingdom

Source: Annual Reports.

6.1 Governance compared

The RDBs have similar organisational and managerial structures, mirroring the International Bank for Reconstruction and Development's (IBRD) corporate makeup almost identically. Although different titles are used, the IBRD and RDBs are comprised broadly of Boards of Governors and Directors and senior management teams led by Presidents and Vice Presidents, under which are professional staff, loan officers, economists, and other employees necessary to run large public organisations. Whereas the IBRD employs more than 10,000 people operating in over 120 offices worldwide, the EIB has 2,900 staff (up from 66 in 1958), IADB and AfDB employ 2,000 staff each (the African RDB began in 1966 with ten staff members), and AsDB and EBRD each employ over 3,000 staff members. For the EBRD, this includes non-staff contracted employees. Like the IBRD, the RDBs employ external contractors and consultants to supervise projects. Although the RDBs have fewer offices worldwide than the World Bank, they do have country offices, resident offices, and regional hubs throughout their working areas. The EIB has 23 country offices in the European Union (EU) and 27 offices in Africa, Latin America, and Asia, as well as Australia and the US. Similarly, the IADB, AfDB, and AsDB have country offices throughout their regions with the AfDB also having regional hubs in Africa, while the EBRD has resident offices in all countries of operation. Their regional offices mean they are generally better linked into local events than the World Bank (Anonymous 2019a, 2019b).

As with the IBRD, the Board of Governors is the supreme governing authority of the RDBs, with control over capital increases, appointing and dismissing members, and approving annual reports. Each RDB member is represented on the Board by a Governor, with voting power determined by weighted capital share subscriptions. As outlined in Chapter 5, this structure enables large vote holders to exercise considerable influence over the RDBs, comparable to US influence over the IBRD.

Much formal authority in the RDBs is delegated by the Board of Governors to the Board of Directors, again mirroring the IBRD and, like it, the Directors are responsible for the strategic direction of the RDBs and approving lending operations. Some have large executive boards, for example, the AfDB has 20 elected Executive Directors and the EIB has 29 Directors, one appointed by each member country and one by the European Commission; the World Bank has 26 Directors. Other RDBs have smaller executive boards. The IADB has 14 Executive Directors – one for the US and ten regional and three non-regional Directors. The AsDB has 12 Directors – eight representing regional member countries and four non-regionals. Distinguishing regional and non-regional shareholdings and Directors was an innovation introduced by the IADB.

Day-to-day operations in the RDBs are led by Presidents and Vice Presidents, just like the IBRD. Reflecting their membership, the EIB and EBRD Presidents are European and likely their selection reflects the EU's rotation of leadership positions among member states. The IADB and AfDB Presidents have been Latin American and African respectively, reflecting their regional missions despite having members from outside the region. However, in 2020, the US against all convention proposed a US citizen as IADB President (Vigdor 2020). The outlier is the AsDB, whose President has always been Japanese, just as IBRD's Presidents have always been US citizens. Notably, the IADB's Executive Vice President – its second-in-command – has always been from the US, with an exceptional appointee being Nancy Birdsall during the 1990s. This highlights one of the key challenges for the RDBs: balancing shareholder influence.

6.2 Key challenges

Four of the most significant challenges faced by the RDBs are (i) establishing and retaining financial credibility in a context reliant on private international money markets, (ii) maintaining their regional character, (iii) ensuring legitimacy in a changing global environment, and (iv) balancing shareholder influence.

6.2.1 Financial realities

The RDBs fundamentally exist to provide financial assistance to borrowers that otherwise could not receive enough financing from private sources. This necessarily means that the RDBs, as with other MDBs, are constrained by the exigencies of money markets. As Humphrey (2016, 93) outlines at length, the 'financial realities' of global and regional money markets shape how the RDBs operate as much as shareholder influence, professional norms, and institutional structures. The MDBs, Humphrey continues, must 'be run in a way that ensure access to capital markets,' for potential investors routinely are less concerned with development outcomes than with ensuring adequate rates of return. As outlined in Chapter 5, credit rating agencies (CRAs) have a tremendous influence on MDBs too. Changes to credit ratings after the 2008 Global Financial Crisis (GFC) hit smaller MDBs particularly strongly and undoubtedly the AsDB and IADB's decisions to merge the balance sheets of their concessional arms into their ordinary capital resources (OCR) in 2015 and 2016 respectively was one avenue for overcoming the impact of these changes. For the AsDB, this move tripled their equity and hence lending capacity. However, concessional arms have long faced political attack, and difficulty with replenishments was the norm since the 1990s (Ben-Artzi 2016). These sometimes came from donor states but at other times from non-concessional borrowers they argued that concessional arms too often see them providing development assistance to low-income states. This is because concessional funding comes from transferring profits from non-concessional resources.

Ben-Artzi's (2016, 236) study of four of the five RDBs in this chapter – not including the EIB – concluded that overall they 'function more like banks' than development agencies, not really meeting the goals set out in their Articles of Agreement. Much of their lending is 'strategic,' preferencing borrowers that are unlikely to default and states with mid to high per capita incomes in their respective regions (Ben-Artzi 2016, 240). Still, the RDBs remain an appealing – and, at times, the only – avenue for borrowers because they 'offer loans at very attractive financial terms compared to what borrowing countries could generally get themselves from other sources' (Humphrey 2014, 612). Further, they generally offer borrowing member states somewhat more voice than the World Bank does, though that varies.

6.2.2 Regional character

The RDBs are mandated to promote regional development and they have decades of close engagement with regional borrowing countries. They promote regionalisation through common market integration (EIB), individual and collective economic and social development (IADB, AfDB, and AsDB), and economic transition to facilitate regional assimilation (EBRD). The 'region' is at the core of the RDBs, flowing normatively over into each MDB being instilled with a strong 'regional character.' The EIB and EBRD promote a European identity, the IADB sponsors a common Latin American and Caribbean community, the AfDB advocates pan-Africanism, and the AsDB markets itself as an organisation working for the people of the Asia-Pacific. The challenge for the RDBs is how to balance this regional character amidst changing memberships, mission creep as they engage with and are influenced by non-regional stakeholders, and the fluidity of their regions as social constructs.

As an illustration, the AfDB was compelled to admit non-regional member countries in the 1980s, a turn it had resisted in the 1960s and 1970s as its founders desired it to be apart from the colonial legacy that shaped the African continent over several centuries (English and Mule 1996). Yet, as a decolonising region with limited capital reserves, the 'financial realities' of global and regional money markets had their impact on the MDB (Humphrey 2016, 93). Its ability to provide capital to support regional economic and social growth was restricted, and its chance of acquiring a AAA credit rating were significantly boosted by having Western member states (Humphrey 2014). During its first ten years, the AfDB approved projects totalling $451 million, whereas the AsDB – established two years after the African MDB with several wealthy Global North countries – approved $3.36 billion over its first decade. After non-regional members joined, its authorised capital increased from $6.3 billion in 1983 to $22.3 billion in 1987 (Babb 2009), but this came at the cost of constraining its autonomy. In the 1990s, as the AfDB's balance sheet deteriorated due to accumulating bad debts as borrowers entered arrears, non-regional members bailed the AfDB out on the condition that its Articles of Agreement were revised to grant non-regional stakeholders greater voice over the organisation. The US became its second largest shareholder (Coburn, Restivo, and Shandra 2015). The decision to expand the AfDB's membership made the RDB better able to serve its region but at the cost of constraining its autonomous African identity and approach to development.

A different challenge to regional identity has been created for the AsDB by the establishment of the Asian Infrastructure Investment Bank (AIIB) in 2015. Japan and China demonstrate different understandings of 'Asia,' which Cook (2015) explained as reflecting each country's geographical position; China is a land power with an inland capital and 'an East-West continental understanding of Asia.' The AIIB members have a strong representation from Central and South Asia and the Middle East, and of note there are eight Middle Eastern countries in the AIIB that are not in the AsDB, though several Middle Eastern states expressed early interest in the AsDB. Russia is a regional member in the AIIB but not a member of the AsDB, while Turkey is a regional member in the AIIB and a non-regional AsDB member. Japan, as 'an archipelagic power on the North Pacific periphery of the Eurasian landmass, has a North-South maritime understanding of Asia' (Cook 2015). The AsDB includes 14 Pacific Island states that were not AIIB prospective founding members, though a couple have since joined. Here we see a battle for leadership in Asia being played out in how MDBs are structured and how 'region' is constructed by regional powers.

6.2.3 *Legitimacy*

To maintain legitimacy, the RDBs have revised their approach to development assistance, introduced new agencies and affiliates, and updated their establishing agreements to respond to the changing global environment. Legitimacy is a significant factor for all MDBs, for donors must regard concessional arms as viable for replenishment, money markets must see them as creditworthy, and borrowers as preferable lenders to other funding sources and to accept their lending schedules and reform proposals. Many of the poorest and smallest countries are severely limited in pursuing alternative financing options other than MDBs, but the RDBs, as banks, need a broad borrower base and large borrowers to provide adequate profits, which fund their staff and other costs. Recent changes responding to demand and legitimacy challenges include the EIB integrating the European Investment Fund (EIF) and European Fund for Strategic Investments (EFSI) in 2000 and 2014 respectively to better engage with private investment flows and the AsDB and IADB merging their concessional loan windows with their OCR to increase equity. These expansions were likely a response to threats perceived by the creation of the AIIB and NDB but also reflect the push from the Global North to shift from grant to loan financing, the so-called 'beyond aid' or retroliberal agenda.

6.2.4 Shareholder influence

Shareholder influence is a perennial issue for the MDBs. They are public organisations owned by their members, but RDBs have unequal shareholder structures with the distribution of voting rights based on purchased capital shares. With inequality the norm, how do the RDBs balance the interests of both small and large shareholders? Commonly, leading shareholders exercise considerable influence over strategic directions and the appointment of presidents and for the IBRD this still means the US. While the US does not play a formal role in the EIB, it is the largest shareholder in the IADB and EBRD, the equal largest shareholder in the AsDB alongside Japan, and the second largest in the AfDB, behind Nigeria, though the AfDB does not effectively have a dominant shareholder. Further, in both the EIB and EBRD, the dominant shareholders are a group of core EU states – Germany, France, and Italy (and formerly the UK, which left the EIB due to Brexit).

The significant influence of the US is felt formally via political appointees in staffing – the IADB's Executive Vice President has always been an American – and informally by refusing loans to countries in opposition to the US, for example, the IADB was pressured during Antonio Ortiz Mena's presidency (1971–88) to refuse loans to Sandinista-led Nicaragua and the AsDB did not lend to Vietnam for many years following the end of the Vietnam War (Babb 2009, 29). The US served as 'the writer, producer, and main actor of the script' (Shaw 1991, 537) in establishing the Bretton Woods baseline, a condition maintained in most of the RDBs.

Of the seven presidents leading the EIB, only one – Philippe Maystadt of Belgium – has not been from one of the four largest shareholders. Similarly, the AsDB's President has always been Japanese. The exception is the AfDB, with each of its nine presidents coming from nine different countries: Sudan, Tunisia, Ghana, Malawi, Zambia, Senegal, Morocco, Rwanda, and Nigeria. Block voting by the AfDB's regional member countries – that today control over 59% voting power – has played a central role in electing its presidents. For example, Kwame Donko Fordwor of Ghana (May 1976–July 1979) was elected President with 50.66% of the vote after several months of political manoeuvrings by various African nations (Mingst 1990, 20). Further, shareholder influence emerges in project approvals and lending practices. Of 5,087 projects by the EIB between 1958 and 2016, Germany France, and Italy – the largest shareholders – were among the top four recipients, totalling 33% of all loans approved to its 28 members. Shareholder dominance impacts operations and borrower ownership; the EBRD and AsDB have little borrower influence, while the IADB has more, and the AfDB the most (Ben-Artzi 2016).

6.3 European Investment Bank

The EIB was established on 1 January 1958 by the Treaty of Rome as an organ of the European Economic Community (EEC), the latter also being founded by the same treaty. As per Article 2 of the Treaty, the EEC and EIB were created to establish 'a common market and… to promote… a harmonious development of economic activities, a continuous and balanced expansion, an increase in stability, an accelerated raising of the standard of living and closer relations between the [member states]' (cited in Griffith-Jones and Tyson 2013, 2). Gutner (2002, 68 and 219n80) outlined one unique feature of the EIB that distinguishes it from the other RDBs – in addition to having the lowest profile of the RDBs, 'It prefers not to think of itself as a "development" institution,' with Gutner repeatedly reminded in interviews with EIB staff 'that "development" is not in the Bank's name.' This point of distinction was recently repeated by Gavas (2019), Co-Director of Development Cooperation in Europe, who compared the EIB with the EBRD: 'In a nutshell, the EIB is the EU's bank but not a development bank, while the EBRD is a development bank but not the EU's bank.' While avoiding development nomenclature, the EIB's mandate includes financing projects for developing less developed regions, undertakings that cannot be entirely financed by other sources, and activities of common interest to its members. Further, it has the structure of an MDB and participates in several MDB cooperation forums and sectoral efforts like the 2016 MDB platform to coordinate on economic migration and forced displacement. In other words, it does not just have all the hallmarks of an MDB, it is one.

The EIB is the EU's bank – its aims are to further the objectives of the EU – and it has been the world's largest multilateral lender and borrower. While the World Bank Group committed $60 billion in 2015, the EIB Group approved €92 billion. Capital increases agreed in 2018 for the World Bank Group, however, will see its capital base expand beyond the EIB. The European RDB's historical mandate and current lending practices detailed in Article 309 of the Treaty on the Functioning of the EU reveal influences from the IBRD and a focus on loans and guarantees from its own resources and capital markets. The EIB set precedents for later RDBs with its focus on regional development and its purposes specify that it is not-for-profit. Later RDBs followed the EIB's commitment to cooperate with other investment programmes and funds.

Since the EIB's establishment, it has had two main goals, first, reducing income differentials in the EEC (later EU) and, second, allocating financial resources to facilitate a functioning integrated market (Griffith-Jones and Tyson 2013). It initially only lent within the European region and its first loan was approved jointly with the IBRD in April 1959, demonstrating that the inter-organisational relationship between MDBs was established from their outset. The EIB authorised project financing outside of the EEC in 1962, slowly expanding activities to Asia, Africa, and Latin America. Still, 90% of financing is allocated to EU member countries, with the remaining 10% in 2017 divided between Asia and Latin America (3%), the Mediterranean (3%), Africa, the Caribbean, and the Pacific (2%), Eastern Europe, Southern Caucus, and Russia (1%), and members of the European Free Trade Association: Switzerland, Iceland, Norway, and Lichtenstein (1%). Non-EU developing countries do sometimes request financial assistance from the EIB, supposedly due to its 'trusted partner' reputation and focus on project-based lending (Anonymous 2019b) – in the crowded MDF field, the EIB's clearly defined mandate to support the EU have resulted in limited interest. The 2019 Wise Persons Report's investigations into the EIB found it 'to have little or no experience working with low income countries and countries with fragilities,' exposing weaknesses in activities outside the EU (Wieser 2019, 23).

On 5 June 2000, the EIB became the EIB Group when it became the majority shareholder of the EIF. The EIF commenced operations in 1994 as a public-private partnership to finance trans-European network infrastructure and promote small and medium enterprises (SMEs). Since 2000, the EIF has acted as EIB's specialist arm for risk capital for SMEs, indicative of a growth in MDB focus on private sector financing. On 26 November 2014, the EIB Group grew to include the EFSI, which mobilises private capital in projects of strategic importance for the EU and was designed to help the EU's investment gap. EFSI's activities are supported by a €16 billion guarantee from the EU and a €5 billion from EIB capital. EIF and EFSI operations broadly parallel those of the International Finance Corporation (IFC) and Multilateral Investment Guarantee Agency (MIGA) in the World Bank Group.

There are 27 member countries in the EIB, with membership limited to EU members. Germany, France, and Italy each own 16.1% shareholding. Combined with Spain's 9.7%, the top four shareholders control 58% of the RDB. In contrast, the smallest five shareholders – Luxembourg, Cyprus, Latvia, Estonia, and Malta – each control less than 0.11%. Capital shares are determined by a member's economic weighting in the EU in terms of relative size of GDP at the time of accession. The weighting is capped, however, so that France, Germany, and Italy retain the same share level. Due to Brexit, the UK's former 16.1% shareholding was to be sold to other member countries and it will be interesting to see how that process is managed and how relative shareholdings are altered. Brexit has restricted lending targets by 15% to mitigate risks (Anonymous 2019b) and there is speculation that mid-tier shareholders may absorb shares of the UK. Current President Werner Hoyer has noted the damage Brexit could have on the EIB's ability to lend, creating uncertainty for an otherwise stable MDB (Giles and Pickard 2018). However, Brexit may not have a drastic impact on capital, since capital invested is small compared to callable capital and other European states should be able to take up the capital relatively easily.

Day-to-day activities are overseen by a Management Committee led by the EIB President and eight Vice Presidents. Seven Presidents have led the EIB since 1958, all of whom except one have been citizens of the four largest shareholders – see Table 6.2, which also provides an indication of key priorities and issues under each President. Incumbent President Hoyer, who assumed office in January 2012,

Table 6.2 European Investment Bank Presidents

President	*Nationality*	*Tenure*	*Details*
Pietro Campilli	Italian	Feb 1958– May 1959	Oversaw administrative establishment of the EIB and approval of the first loan on 21 April 1959. Campilli served as Minister of several different Italian ministries following the 1943 overthrow of Fascism.
Paride Formentini	Italian	Jun 1959– Sep 1970	First full-term President, Formentini authorised the first borrowing operation in 1961 and project financing outside the European Community in 1962. Before becoming President, he served first as Deputy Director General and then Director General of the Bank of Italy between 1947 and 1959.
Yves Le Portz	French	Sep 1970– Jul 1984	Supervised admission of new members including Denmark, Greece, Ireland, and the UK, issued first borrowing operation in *eurco* (a proto version of the Euro), and developed activities in support of the common market. Previously worked in the French finance ministry and the UN Economic and Social Council.
Ernst-Günther Bröder	German	Aug 1984– Mar 1993	Encouraged integration of former Soviet states at the end of the Cold War, agreed to finance projects to Poland and Hungary in 1989 and the Czech and Slovak Federal Republic, Bulgaria, and Romania in 1991. Extended activities to Latin America and Asia and supported private sector development. He later became the first Chair of the World Bank Inspection Panel.
Sir Brian Unwin	British	Apr 1993– Dec 1999	Oversaw extension of EIB's activities to the Baltic States – Estonia, Latvia, and Lithuania – in 1993, membership admission of Austria, Finland, and Sweden in 1995, and first borrowing operation in Euros on 12 February 1997. He held many roles in the British public service, including Treasury and Customs and Excise.
Philippe Maystadt	Belgian	Mar 2000– Dec 2011	EIB Group was founded following the inclusion of the EIF in June 2000. Poverty alleviation and sustainable growth became operational cornerstones, culminating in the adoption of EIB's Environmental and Social Handbook in September 2010. Served as EIB Governor for ten years before becoming President and chaired the Interim Committee of the IMF after leaving the EIB.
Werner Hoyer	German	Jan 2012– Present	Pursued a special capital increase in January 2013 in response to the ongoing shocks of the global and Eurozone financial crises, launched the EFSI in November 2014 and the Economic Resilience Initiative in 2016, which was designed to support regions outside of Europe affected by the refugee crisis.

Source: Annual Reports and EIB Website.

has commented on the need for the European Commission and EIB to clearly demarcate responsibilities; 'As long as… we do not try to become policymakers and the European Commission does not try to play bank, we are prepared for more impact' (cited in Salinger 2018). This comment demonstrates a significant difference between the EIB and the IADB, AfDB, and AsDB: the EIB is an organ within a larger regional organisation, whereas the Global South RDBs are stand-alone entities. Notably, many of the sub-regional development banks (SRDBs) have similar origins to the EIB, starting with the Central American Bank for Economic Integration (CABEI) in 1960 (see Chapter 7). Given its association with the EU, Robinson (2009) argues that the EIB is not just a regional bank but an actor within multi-level governance networks enabling the EU to operate as a regional organisation.

The EIB's investments impact EU policymaking and are said to have a '"catalytic effect", leveraging greater [EU] expenditure than would otherwise occur' (Robinson 2009, 652). This is because, in addition to financing loans, guarantees, microfinance, and equity investments, the EIB unlocks financing from other sources, including the EU budget. Further, its contribution to project costs is limited to half of the amount established during appraisal, differentiating it from the IBRD which can fund full project costs. EIB loans last between four and 20 years, with loan rates varying from project to project (Faure, Prizzon, and Rogerson 2015). Due to its confidential relationship with partners, mirroring the EBRD's 'merchant bank' model, the EIB does not publish details of financing terms and conditions. This lack of transparency is concerning given that the EIB invests taxpayer funds, which is a growing challenge as MDBs engage more extensively with the private sector and is another way MDBs are contributing to financialisation.

Over €1.1 trillion has been invested by the EIB in over 11,800 projects in more than 60 countries since commencing lending operations in 1959. Between 2000 and 2017, its annual approvals more than doubled, from €41.4 billion in 2000 to €83.8 billion in 2017. Its lending peaked in 2009 – €103.9 billion – during the 2008 GFC indicating some commitments to Keynesian counter-cyclical financing, which the World Bank has only infrequently achieved despite the commitments to this in its Articles of Agreement. Of new loans in 2016, €33.7 billion were for SMEs, €19.7 billion for infrastructure, €16.9 for climate change, and €13.5 billion for innovation and skills. Historically, transportation and credit were the sectors that received the most funding, totalling just over 50% of cumulative lending. Recent EIB projects include the Intesa San Paolo Midcap Loan IV, a €300 million line of credit project to finance eligible investments promoted by mid-cap companies in Italy – such financial intermediary loans further increase concerns around loan transparency. There was also the Aeroporto Di Roma Fiumicino Sud, a €500 million transportation project increasing capacity and operational efficiency of Fiumicino Airport in Italy. These indicative examples demonstrate that the EIB is a conservative MDB favouring investment projects, with an agenda of 'smart' and 'inclusive' growth focussed on 'building a high-value, high-employment economy with innovation in multiple fields leading to new commercial activity and employment' (Griffith-Jones and Tyson 2013, 5).

Gutner (2002, 68) noted close to two decades ago that the EIB does not have a 'policy voice' like the other RDBs, for its members

> have little incentive to create an institution that tells them what to do. As a result, the EIB has no separate policy research arm or country lending strategies, and it does not directly promote a particular set of its own policy ideas or innovative types of loan conditionality.

For several decades, the EIB often did 'not even design or develop the projects it lends money to. Project promoters present project ideas to the Bank, and the Bank will evaluate projects of interest through an appraisal procedure' (Gutner 2002, 123). In contrast, the World Bank was deeply engaged in project design from the outset, but this has led to questions about whether borrowers have ownership of their projects. The EIB changed during the 2000s and 2010s with the establishment of several advisory and trust fund facilities supporting private sector investment, public-private partnerships, and pre-investment studies. The EIB Group also coordinates the EIB Institute, an in-house teaching and learning institute that funds research, partners with academia, runs seminars and conferences, and functions as a social and cultural hub. It is comparable to the IBRD's Economic Development Institute (EDI) and World Bank Institute (WBI), demonstrating again organisational convergence at play in the MDB system, and the way that MDBs aim to educate or socialise people around its world view.

In summary, the EIB is a very large bank annually approving cumulative loan amounts far exceeding the other RDBs combined. Its large capital base lends support to Humphrey's (2014) argument that raising the capital base is easier for MDBs that have shareholders as borrowers, than for those where the major stakeholders are non-borrowers. Members as borrowers also seem to have ensured limited conditionality and more borrower ownership of projects. While mirroring the MDB template of the IBRD, it has become as much a financial investor in European SMEs, infrastructure, and climate projects as a development bank, though it is not the only MDB that operates along this model and the World Bank's Maximising Finance for Development (MFD) agenda seems to take inspiration from the EIB. Still, it funds technical assistance to get regional cooperation projects going and for projects in Europe's less developed regions, so there it operates more like a standard development bank, mobilising finance for public goods and where the private sector under-invests (Anonymous 2019b). The EIB's organisational priorities are clear: financing loans that balance and stabilise the EU's internal market and are of common interest to EU members. Griffith-Jones and Tyson (2013, 17) list the 'critical enablers' of the EIB as a successful MDB as: its AAA rating paired with a non-profit rationale enabling long-dated, low-cost, and large-scale financing, coupled with its intertwined position within the EU enabling support for the high-level strategy for European integration. It is the model of what other regional integration-based MDBs wanted to become, though in most cases the regional integration projects have collapsed.

6.4 Inter-American Development Bank

The background history of the IADB is the product of complicated efforts to foster Latin American regionalism dating back to the late 1800s (Barria and Roper 2004), as discussed in Chapter 2. There was a further push to create a body for the region from 1939 which again proved unsuccessful, in part because the proposed body was far broader than just a development bank and because the US withdrew its support. The Organisation of American States (OAS), founded in April 1948, organised the 1957 Economic Conference of OAS in Buenos Aires, Argentina, which (again) proposed that the Inter-American Economic and Social Council form a specialised committee to investigate the feasibility of an inter-American financial organisation. The US supported the proposal in 1958, in part because of Vice President Richard Nixon's hostile reception on a tour of Latin America and of the increasing success of Cuban revolutionaries (Barria and Roper 2004, 623, Tussie 1995, 18–19). Interestingly, one other trigger for the IADB's formation was as a 'counterweight' to the IBRD's monopolistic position as a 'market player rather than a market maker or facilitator' (Phillips 2009, 17). Even investors on Wall Street were concerned by the unrivalled presence of the World Bank. Further, countries in the region 'felt that the World Bank was not paying enough attention to Latin America, was uninterested in regional integration projects, and was too concerned with past defaults' (Krasner 1981, 305). To illustrate, the IBRD approved $170.9 million to Latin America and the Caribbean in 1957 and 1958, while Asia and the Middle East received $516.9 million. IBRD loans of the time to Latin America also focussed on electric power and transportation, not domestic industry and social projects as were wanted by countries from the region (Humphrey 2016, 98).

Many Latin American and Caribbean countries during the 1950s felt their region lacked suitable investment to meet development financing needs. The IADB emerged from talks favouring the state-led development model of Raúl Prebisch and the UN Economic Commission for Latin America (UN-ECLA). The IADB was seen as a crucial link in resource transfers to overcome market failures, weak private sectors, and insufficient capital investment (Tussie 1995). That the US accepted these arguments confirms Rapley's (2002, 1) position that, '[i]n the early post-war period, development thought like conventional economic wisdom, was really neither left nor right. There existed a broad consensus that economies need more state intervention than they have been given in the past.' The IADB was finally established in 1959, when the OAS approved its Articles of Agreement, which is quite like the IBRD's.

The IADB was mandated to foster economic and social development in the developing member countries of the region by promoting both individual country growth and collective regional integration. The concept of a 'Latin American and Caribbean region' is relatively less contested and more geographically determined compared to the far more contentious and fluidly constructed 'Asian' or 'Asia-Pacific' region (Bull and Bøås 2003, 250). The US suggested including a concessional lending arm in the establishing agreement – the Fund for Special Operations (FSO) – as a parallel to the International Development Association (IDA), which was only established in 1960. Further, the establishing agreement 'permitted more flexibility than the World Bank to make loans directly to private industry without requiring a government guarantee, an important demand of Latin American countries intent on developing their domestic industrial base' (Humphrey 2016, 99), a territory the World Bank was, in fact, not willing to traverse. Still, in its early years, it actually lent mostly to sovereign states for housing, education, and sanitation (Ben-Artzi 2016). Technical assistance has an explicit place in the IADB's functions, which was not the case in the earlier MDBs.

There are now 48 member countries in the IADB: 26 regional developing member countries, 20 non-regional member countries, and the US and Canada. As per its Articles, each member country holds 135 votes plus one for each share of ordinary capital stock held. The US is the largest shareholder with 30% voting power (enabling it to veto FSO decisions, though not ordinary capital loans), while regional developing countries collectively hold over 50% voting power. However, the US exercises considerable influence due to the RDB's headquarters being in Washington, DC, its Executive Vice President always being an American citizen (Babb 2009, 27–28), and it employs a 'large percentage of American citizens' (Ben-Artzi 2016, 92). If the US does not support a proposal, it is unlikely to get to the voting stage (Ben-Artzi 2016).

The Board has 14 members and they meet weekly and are fairly active (Ben-Artzi 2016). This may be part of the way that it keeps it distinct regional characteristics. Regional states as collective majority shareholders perceive themselves as decisive in decisions, leaders in development finance and donor coordination, and the IADB President has evolved into a 'regional statesperson' (Nelson 2000, 407). Of the regional member states, Argentina and Brazil dominate with close to 11.4% of voting power each, followed by Mexico with 7.3%. Most remaining regional member countries own less than half a per cent each. Although not greatly influential during its early decades, the IADB – just like the AfDB and AsDB – has become a powerful regional actor (Bull and Bøås 2003).

Four Presidents have led the IADB (see Table 6.3). Elected for five-year terms and able to be re-elected, the President is supported by an Executive Vice President and three Vice Presidents: for Countries, for Sectors and Knowledge, and for Finance and Administration. The President has always been chosen from a regional member country, unlike the IBRD and AsDB's appointment of American and Japanese leaders. In practice, the US, Argentina, and Brazil have informally picked the presidents (Lopes 2019). Reflecting the World Bank's MFD agenda, incumbent President Luis Alberto Moreno argued in 2017 that the IADB must become 'bigger' in its annual financial approvals and more flexible to respond to its heterogeneous region. A new president is scheduled to be elected in September 2020 and in June the US broke protocol by nominating an American, Mauricio Claver-Carone, a Trump Administration appointee in the National

Table 6.3 Inter-American Development Bank Presidents

President	*Nationality*	*Tenure*	*Details*
Felipe Herrera	Chilean	1960–1970	Economist, lawyer, academic, and political socialist, Herrera built a 'bank of ideas' accepting both structuralist and monetarist economists.
Antonio Ortiz Mena	Mexican	1971–1988	Mexico's former Minister of Finance and Public Credit, Mena increased lending tenfold and focused on infrastructure and heavy industry. He resigned before his term ended amid suspicions US President Ronald Reagan was intervening in the IADB's internal affairs through Secretary of State George P. Schultz's attempt to block of a $58 million loan to Sandinista Nicaragua.
Enrique Valentín Iglesias García	Uruguayan / Spanish	1988–2005	Focused on sustainable development, poverty reduction, competitiveness, state modernisation, social development, and equity. He also responded to antagonistic US demands for an organisational restructuring and established the IIC and MIF.
Luis Alberto Moreno	Colombian / American	2005–Present	A former Colombian Ambassador to the US, Moreno commenced an organisational transformation and generational change. He spearheaded a record increase of women in leadership positions and improved transparency and accountability.

Source: Annual Reports and IADB Website.

Security Council and 'anti-Castro warrior' who seems have little expertise on the region outside Cuba (Waldron 2020). But the US has Brazilian backing so may yet prevail.

The World Bank Group, AfDB, and AsDB all have concessional lending facilities created after their establishment and operating as separate legal entities. The IADB's soft loan window, the FSO, was built in and began operations when the Bank was founded in 1959, making it the first concessional lending body of the MDBs (Babb 2009, 27, Tussie 1995, 5). The purpose of the FSO is rather vague: 'the making of loans on terms and conditions appropriate for dealing with special circumstances arising in specific countries or with respect to specific projects' (IaDB 1996, Article IV, Section 1). The IDA is clearer in providing concessional terms to less developed member states but both organisations probably took the idea of replenishments from SUNFED (see Chapter 3). The Articles allow for financing

FSO operations from the income derived from IADB operations, though it has only made minimal allocations over the years (Humphrey 2014). This is because borrowing states oppose the reallocation as a transfer from some borrowers to others. Transfers to the IDA are not in the IBRD Articles; they occur but have been opposed by many IBRD borrowers. This is a case of ideas flowing from an RDB to the World Bank rather than the reverse as generally highlighted in this chapter. In 2016, the IADB agreed to effectively close the FSO, transferring its resources to ordinary capital, though it did create a new blended loan instrument that five member countries have access to. This followed a similar AsDB decision in 2015 and, as noted earlier, is part of a donor push to limit grants, expand loans, and achieve harder financing terms for Global South countries.

Like the World Bank and EIB, there is an IADB Group, which comprises the IADB, Inter-American Investment Corporation (IIC), and Multilateral Investment Fund (MIF). The IIC commenced work in 1989, though the establishing agreement became effective in March 1986. It finances private sector investment projects without government guarantees, and so it is comparable to the World Bank's IFC. The IIC approved 162 projects totalling $2.24 billion in 2016, with sectoral approvals divided into financial markets (41.3%), energy (31.2%), science and technology (7.5%), transport (6.9%), agriculture and rural development (3.9%), and other (9.2%). In 'other,' the IIC mostly funds projects supporting private sector financing partnerships, securitisation, trusts, and development banks. This growth in IFC-equivalents funding financial intermediaries is a contemporary trend in the MDBs. The MIF was launched in 1993 to provide technical assistance for private sector growth. It approved $86 million in 2016, with an active portfolio of over 500 projects supporting micro and small private business development.

The IADB was a marginal development financier up until the 1980s under President Antonio Ortiz Mena. The vast increase in petrodollars after the 1973 and 1979 oil price shocks saw large commercial loan flows into the region, made possible by the removal of restrictions on finance ministers to offer government guarantees on commercial loans (Scheman 1997, 86). However, the 1982 debt crisis ended private capital flows to the region, and public lending was supported by structural adjustment. Compelled by a changing political climate and the impact of US President Ronald Reagan's neoliberal turn, the IADB moved away from social sector lending and became 'closely identified with the World Bank's economic liberalisation and integration agenda' (Nelson 2000, 407). Robin Broad, as an international economist working on the World Bank and IADB at the US Treasury Department, 'was struck by the certainty of political appointees at Treasury about the unquestioned correctness of [structural adjustment] policies' (Broad and Cavanagh 2009, 7). This situation was heightened by the close proximity of the IBRD and IADB headquarters in Washington, DC (Culpeper 1997, 115), and the centrality of the World Bank and IADB to the Baker Plan for debt relief proposed in 1985 (Babb 2009, 128). Further, Tussie (1995, 96) notes that President Iglesias (1988–2005) 'warned against "counterproductive dichotomies" and promoted a pragmatic convergence of ideas' under the Washington Consensus. During the

1980s, the IADB's annual lending increased to help with its role in debt and averaged $2.3 billion (the IBRD's average per annum was $12.3 billion). A large capital increase in 1988, likely a reward for its support in implementing structural adjustment, further enhanced lending capacity. The 1988 increase was overseen by newly elected President Enrique Valentín Iglesias García and was $26 billion, followed by an additional $40 billion in 1994, meaning its capital base reached $101 billion (Scheman 1997, 87). Further, like the IBRD, it has been consistently building up its reserves, another key determinant of capacity to borrow on financial markets.

Thus, the IADB's fortunes changed in the 1990s. Lending dramatically increased in 1991 and since 1994 it has been Latin America and the Caribbean's main source of development financing, only recently rivalled by the Development Bank of Latin America (CAF) (see Chapter 7). From 1994 to 2008, the IADB approved over $108.6 billion in loans to the region, totalling 50% of all multilateral lending. Notably too, from 1998 to 2009, the IADB was able to loan at a slightly lower interest rate than the IBRD, despite not having the backing of as many Northern states (Humphrey 2014). This may have been because of growing competition from a range of private and public financiers; on the public side, Chinese and Brazilian development finance increased substantially in the region and the CAF became more of a competitor.

Like the IBRD, the IADB sought a capital increase after the 2008 GFC, but it obtained quite a bit less than it sought, with the US and Europeans reportedly opposed to higher contributions, while borrowers sought a greater increase. As with the World Bank, the reluctance to increase paid-in capital has resulted in pressure to increase earnings to build up reserves, as a substitute for capital. The transfer of FSO resources to OCR also increased its capitalisation. As of the end of 2018, IADB's subscribed capital reached $176.8 billion, while its paid-in capital was $11.9 billion. With many wealthy non-borrowing countries reinforcing its AAA credit rating, the IADB is comparable to the IBRD 'in relation to capitalisation ratios and the use of reserves to build equity as opposed to paid-in capital' (Humphrey 2014, 634).

Between 1961 and 2017, IADB OCR and FSO approvals totalled $266.8 billion, with FSO loans making up just $20 billion. The four largest recipients of OCR loans were Brazil (21%), Mexico (16%), Argentina (16%), and Colombia (9%). Approvals per annum increased significantly during the GFC, with $5.3 billion approved in 2000 while $15.5 billion was approved in 2009 (IADB 2010). In 1999, they started using country groupings to organise loans. Originally, they had four, but it is now two, with 'Group I' comprising the higher per capita income states that get 65% of loans, while 'Group II' gets 35%. In 2017, approvals included 90 sovereign-guaranteed loans totalling $11.4 billion, divided into 73 investment projects ($7.9 billion) and 17 policy-based loans ($3.4 billion) (IADB 2017). The 90 sovereign-guaranteed loans focussed on infrastructure and the environment (51%), institutions for development (38%), the social sector (8%), and trade and regional integration (2%). Thus, its portfolio appears to have matched the general shift back to infrastructure that has been happening across the sector.

Beyond financial assistance, the IADB Group manages several advisory facilities for project preparation. These facilities include the Project Preparation Facility that provides up to $1.5 million in project preparation financing, an Infrastructure Fund that assists public, private, and mixed entities develop and prepare infrastructure projects, and the Regional Infrastructure Integration Fund that provides technical assistance for the preparation of strategic integration projects. Project preparation has long been a challenging issue for the World Bank (Bazbauers 2018), and the number of trust funds on this topic demonstrates that IADB faces the same challenge.

In summary, the IADB was the first Global South MDB, whereas the EIB emerged from the Global North. While the US is the leading shareholder controlling nearly 20% voting power more than the next largest shareholder, the RDB has legitimacy in the region and helped set groundwork for structures and institutional approaches adopted by the AfDB and AsDB.

6.5 African Development Bank

The AfDB is Africa's leading development finance organisation. As per its Articles of Agreement, its mandate is to 'contribute to the sustainable economic development and social progress of its regional members individually and jointly' (AfDB 2016) and it follows the purposes and functions model established by the IBRD, although notably it does not mention guarantees only direct financing. Like the IADB, it promotes regional integration and individual country growth. It pursues its mandate through project and programme lending, resource mobilisation, technical assistance, and private investment promotion in Africa and has become a beacon of pan-Africanism (Babb 2009, 30).

The RDB's origins can be traced to a report published in 1957 by the Council of Europe Study Group for the Development of Africa, which recommended the formation of a Bank for African Development. The Tubman-Nkrumah-Touré Conference of 1958, named for the then Presidents of Liberia, Ghana, and Guinea, held in Saniquelle, Liberia, announced a commitment to building bodies for regional integration and solidarity. These proclamations took place amid the decolonisation of most of the African continent during the mid- to late 1950s and 1960s; it was a point of significance to establish an 'African bank' independent from former colonial powers. Robert Kwaku Gardiner, the former Ghanaian Minister of Economic Planning, commented that the AfDB 'is one of a number of continental institutions that African governments have set up to provide assistance to indigenous organs to enable member countries to free themselves from the grip of colonial dependence' (cited in Fordwor 1981, ix).

After several conferences in 1960, including the All-African Peoples Conference and the Second Conference of Independent African States, the UN Economic Commission for Africa (UN-ECA) – at the request of African nations – coordinated studies for an African development bank. The in-principle decision to create such a bank was made in March 1962. Concurrently, the Committee of Nine – a thinktank made up of financial experts and economists from Cameroon,

Ethiopia, Guinea, Liberia, Nigeria, Sudan, Tanganyika, and Zanzibar – engaged with African and non-African states to propose recommendations on its financial and administrative structure (Ajomo 1976). Thus, despite the early involvement of the Council of Europe, the AfDB was largely an African initiative. The Agreement Establishing the AfDB was signed on 14 August 1963 in Khartoum, Sudan, after two years of consultation and preparation; it became effective on 10 September 1964. The first Board of Governors meeting was held in November 1964 and it commenced operations on 1 July 1966.

There are 80 member countries in the AfDB: 54 regional and 26 non-regional shareholders. The regional shareholders include every recognised African mainland and island state, whereas the non-regionals are far more disparate, including the US and wealthy European, Asian, Middle Eastern, and Latin American countries. Regional members control roughly 59% of voting power, while non-regionals control 41%. As of December 2019, regional voting power was led by Nigeria (9.4%), Egypt (5.7%), South Africa (5.1%), and Algeria (4.3%). Non-regional voting power was led by the US (6.7%), Japan (5.6%), Germany (4.2%), and Canada (3.9%). China is also a member, but with only 1.2% voting power. Unlike in the IADB, the US is only the second largest shareholder, behind Nigeria. To become an AfDB member, non-regionals must first become members of the Bank's concessional arm: the African Development Fund (AfDF). Compared to the World Bank and other RDBs, AfDB voting power is more diffuse, meaning that no one country can effectively dominate formal decision-making.

The AfDB has always advocated a regional 'African identity,' much more so than the IADB or AsDB. Up until the 1950s, except for Liberia, Ethiopia, and Egypt, the African continent was either under European colonial rule or, as in South Africa, living under apartheid. Its recent history of oppression led the fledgling organisation to initially restrict membership to independent African states, prohibiting non-regional entrants. At the outset, it was proposed

> that the Board of Governors, the Board of Directors, the President, and the top management of the Bank would be wholly African. The memory of colonial domination was too recent, and for many too bitter, to countenance new ties to the North.
>
> (English and Mule 1996, 20)

This approach made the AfDB unique. Its 'African identity,' however, was tempered during the 1960s and 1970s by a split between francophone African states and other African countries, with the smaller francophone states determined to maintain their diplomatic relationship with France, while mitigating the influence of larger members like Nigeria (English and Mule 1996, 20). While an exemplar of pan-Africanism, ideological and strategic differences between African leaders and countries translated into emerging tensions: 'Beneath the alleged unity of the [Organisation of African Unity] were acute ideological differences between African countries' (Biney 2019, 182).

The AfDB's governance structure has 'produced a particularly active role for the Board of Directors. With no one country claiming the right to nominate the President, his or her re-election depends to a large extent on satisfying as many' Directors as possible (English and Mule 1996, 2). Given the diffusion of voting power between AfDB's members, presidential elections have been contentious, with competing regional states alleging 'favouritism' and efforts to undermine consensus leadership (English and Mule 1996, 22–24). AfDB's governance has thus tended to shift between consensus decision-making and political bargaining by coalitions, far more so than the other RDBs (Shaw 1991, 542). There is an informal understanding the Presidents will rotate between the three broad linguistic and geographical groupings of the continent: Arabic, Anglophone, and Francophone (Ben-Artzi 2016). There have been nine Presidents to date, all from regional member states and Table 6.4 outlines their priorities and achievements. The incumbent President is Akinwumi Ayodeji Adesina of Nigeria, who assumed duties in September 2015.

Paralleling the expansion of the World Bank, within its first decade the AfDB grew to become a Group through the launch of the AfDF and Nigeria Trust Fund (NTF). The AfDF is AfDB's concessional lending arm. It was agreed to in 1972 and established by President Abdelwahad Labidi in November 1974. Between 1974 and 2014, it invested $45 billion using finances replenished every three years by donor countries. It arose because AfDB loans at commercial interest rates (though lower than most states could access on their own) requiring on-time repayment were not viable for a number of African nations and many of the poorest African members did not qualify for OCR loans (Coburn, Restivo, and Shandra 2015, 277). In its functions and operations, it was copying the trend set by the IDA and FSO. The NTF was built in 1976 by an agreement between the AfDB and Nigeria to provide concessional financing to eligible low-income members. It began operations with $80 million and that increased to $253 million by 2012, prioritising agricultural loans. The AfDF and NTF were useful to the AfDB, increasing financial approvals during its early decades when it was strongly constrained by its limited capital reserves and many of its member countries did not qualify for non-concessional financing.

By the late 1970s, in the wake of the oil price shocks, the constraints of AfDB's limited capital base became too great and it began efforts to invite non-regional countries to become members (Culpeper 1997, 31, Mingst 1990, 13). Its initial authorised capital stock was only $370 million and annual approvals averaged $21 million in the early 1970s, compared to the IADB approving an annual average of $685 million and AsDB approving $272 million (English and Mule 1996, 10). As Babb (2009, 30) remarks, the 'AfDB's members came to the conclusion that it was better to sacrifice some measure of autonomy in order to build a bigger and more influential bank.' To build the AfDB's reputation and role as a leading regional lender, its Board of Governors approved in-principle the admission of non-regional members in 1977 and amended its Articles in 1982. Non-regional members were first admitted in 1987 and this saw AfDB's authorised capital

Table 6.4 African Development Bank Presidents

President	*Nationality*	*Tenure*	*Details*
Mamoun Beheiry	Sudanese	Nov 1964–Aug 1970	Governor of the Central Bank of Sudan and member of the Committee of Nine, Beheiry strove to establish the AfDB as an efficient and well-governed bank, while attempting to address growing regional political pressures.
Abdelwahad Labidi	Tunisian	Aug 1970–May 1976	Set and met a $25 million lending target per year over three years and intensified AfDB's contacts with, and search for, business connections. Special focus directed to Sahelian countries, humanitarian assistance, and long-term food security financing.
Kwame Donko Fordwor	Ghanaian	May 1976–Jul 1979	Highly controversial, he was challenged by the Executive Directors as acting as an influential AfDB 'player' taking unilateral action and 'not a neutral participant envisaged by economic technocrats' (Mingst, 1990, p. 21). Tensions escalated, leading to his forced resignation.
Goodall Gondwe	Malawian	1979–1980	A 'caretaker' presidency in the fallout of Fordwor's resignation.
Wila D. Mung-omba	Zambian	Jun 1980–May 1985	Increased the AfDB's capital position from $1 billion to $8 billion, net income from $2 million to $75 million, and achieved a AAA credit rating.
Babacar N'diaye	Senegalese	May 1985–Aug 1995	Noted pan-Africanist, oversaw a large capital increase to $23.3 billion, established the first private sector development unit, advocated policy-based, structural adjustment lending over project lending, and appointed AfDB's first female Vice President for Operations.
Omar Kabbaj	Moroccan	Aug 1995–Aug 2005	Oversaw major organisational reforms in 1996 and 2002 to re-establish the AfDB's credibility after the problems of structural adjustment. Restricted the number of times a president could be re-elected; reformed procedures for staff selection; improved loan oversight, monitoring, and evaluation; emphasised country-led programs; and, strengthened country studies, reports, and analytical work.
Donald Kaberuka	Rwandan	Sep 2005–Aug 2015	Emphasised private sector and infrastructure development and regional integration. During his tenure, the AfDB became Africa's premier financial institution. He also improved accountability and transparency mechanisms and emphasised selectivity and focus in lending operations.
Akinwumi Ayodeji Adesina	Nigerian	Sep 2015–Present	Adesina adopted a new Development and Business Model in April 2016 to align the AfDB with its Ten-Year Strategy 2013–22 for achieving inclusive and green growth and the High 5s priorities: Light Up and Power Africa, Feed Africa, Industrialise Africa, Integrate Africa, and Improve the Quality of Life for the People of Africa. He faced an official probe in 2020 regarding whistle blower allegations of nepotism and mismanagement; initial review cleared him, but an international review was appointed in July.

Source: Annual Reports and AfDB Website.

increase from $6.3 billion in 1983 to $22.3 billion in 1987. AfDB and AfDF loan approvals consequently increased, from $1.7 billion approved between 1979 and 1981 to $8.8 billion between 1991 and 1993 (Babb 2009, 31). As its credit rating rallied, the AfDB began to invest in and borrow from international capital markets. This pragmatic move by the Governors demonstrates the financial power of the Global North and its finance markets, and the limited capacity of a development banking model to challenge it. Indeed, a neo-Gramscian analysis says it shows the disciplinary financial power of the Global North.

Like the AsDB, in its early decades the African RDB mostly lent for agriculture and infrastructure. It reluctantly introduced structural adjustment loans in the 1980s after pressure imposed by newly admitted non-regional members, specifically the US (Pandolfelli and Shandra 2013, 340). The AfDB was concerned with being 'IMF-ised' and rather than attach policy conditionalities to loans, it preferred to inform potential borrowers that failure to implement reforms would make future loan approvals more difficult (Mingst 1990, 74). Nonetheless, lending increased significantly from 1985 and close to half of loan approvals were policy-based in 1987, up from negligible levels in preceding years and they resembled IMF and World Bank structural adjustment packages. A lack of in-house expertise in adjustment lending led the AfDB to follow the Bretton Woods siblings, along with pressure by the US, to coordinate more closely with the IBRD (Pandolfelli and Shandra 2013, 341–2).

In the 1990s, the AfDB fell into difficult times due to accumulating bad debts as its borrowers entered arrears and regional economic stagnation limited new loans (Coburn, Restivo, and Shandra 2015, 278). Lending declined from 1993 and the Bank's recently acquired AAA credit rating was downgraded to AA+. Grant and subsidised loans from non-regional members prevented default on AfDB loans (Bulow and Rogoff 2005), on the condition that the AfDB commit more resources to structural adjustment lending, alter voting shares to increase non-regional voting power from 23% to 40%, and modify voting rules to require a 70% majority on decisions, granting non-regional states an effective veto (Babb 2009, 31). This forcefully demonstrates how Global South initiatives can be overwhelmed by Northern financial discipline. Further, it was long regarded as having problems with inadequate country offices, lack of technical expertise, in particular project preparation, and inefficiency and corruption (Ben-Artzi 2016).

Following an attempted coup d'état in Côte d'Ivoire in 2002 and a rapid deterioration in the country's stability, the AfDB's headquarters were relocated from Abidjan to Tunis, Tunisia, where it remained between 2003 and 2014, before returning to its original host country. Interestingly, this transition period coincided with a rapid improvement in the strength of the AfDB as an MDB. It resumed operations within just three months of moving 'over a thousand personnel and several tons of vital documents' (Akin-Olugbade 2003, 738) and managed to exceed the previous few years annual lending commitments, restore its AAA credit rating not held since 1995, and launch its first $1 billion global bond (Akin-Olugbade 2003, 738). Though, rather than the move, the Bank's revived fortunes need to be understood in relation to the global commodities boom and its positive impact on African growth as well as growing Chinese investment in the continent and organisational reforms initiated by President Omar Kabbaj (1995–2005) and continued by Donald Kaberuka (2005–15).

The AfDB returned from an uncertain future to become in the 2000s and 2010s Africa's leading financial institution. Under incumbent President Akinwumi Adesina, who assumed office in September 2015, the African RDB has pursued the High 5s agenda, outlining five operational priorities: Light Up and Power Africa, Feed Africa, Industrialise Africa, Integrate Africa, and Improve the Quality of Life for the People of Africa (AfDB 2018). Aligned with the Sustainable Development Goals (SDGs), the Higher 5s agenda promotes green growth, infrastructural development, and regional integration, underpinned by the central message that African development requires greater private sector mobilisation, which the AfDB argues it is positioned to catalyse. Note the emergence of a strong emphasis on the private sector for MDB investments, while the infrastructure agenda can be linked to Chinese influence on the subsequent re-focussing of the World Bank and other MDBs.

Like the World Bank, AfDB Group assistance is divided into three categories of eligibility depending on income levels: AfDB-eligible only, AfDF-eligible only, and a blend of AfDB and AfDF resources. Morocco, Tunisia, Nigeria, South Africa, and Egypt have historically been the largest recipients of AfDB project approvals, receiving 55% of all loans and grants. Cumulative Group lending highlights that it is still a small RDB approving $121 billion between 1967 and 2016. In contrast, the IADB committed $267 billion from 1961 to 2017. The African RDB approved 5,279 projects between 1967 and 2016, which means the average loan size has also been quite small at just over $50 million. The IBRD's average loan size was $100 million up until the mid-1990s and their size involved a 'trade-off between the quantity and quality of lending' (Ranis 1997, 86). For the AfDB, given the politics around its lending programme, the small size of loans is unlikely to indicate a greater focus on quality. It does reflect the Bank's small capital base, the relatively small economies of many borrowers, and the history of default by some states.

Like the IBRD and IADB, the AfDB Group offers a range of technical and advisory services and has developed several trust funds, such as the South-South Cooperation Trust Fund, which is a technical assistance initiative the AfDB and Brazil signed in March 2011 to build partnerships for knowledge exchange. It launched the African Development Institute (AfDI) in 1973 to enhance lending operations. Through knowledge exchange, the AfDI builds policy dialogue and development management in Africa. In 2010, the AfDI was reoriented to become the AfDB's capacity building point-of-contact, delivering face-to-face and e-learning courses and seminars, research, and capacity and strategic cooperation seminars. It is broadly equivalent to the World Bank's WBI.

In summary, the AfDB was the first Global South-controlled MDB, but because of several factors – including regional member financial situations, global economic changes, and isomorphic pressures – it had to embrace more of the global MDB order and resultantly became more influenced by the Global North, directly – in the case of the US – and indirectly – in the case of broader MDF approaches. Yet, the AfDB has grown from a minor and uncertain MDB to become Africa's leading multilateral financial organisation, setting standards on regional development both practically and intellectually.

6.6 Asian Development Bank

As the IADB and AfDB were founded, calls came from Asia-Pacific countries – including Japan, Thailand, Sri Lanka, and India – that an Asian RDB should be formed to transfer financial resources and support regional cooperation and integration (Nakao 2017). There was growing dismay from Asia-Pacific countries that the World Bank's share of lending to the region was inadequate to meet its needs and that its procedures were cumbersome. Japan in particular was concerned about the IBRD's political dominance by the US and Europe and that this curtailed the capacity of the region to effectively provide a voice in the institution (Kellerman 2019). Japan was interested in establishing an Asian RDB in 1962, as it viewed states in the Asia-Pacific as a vital source of raw material, food, and markets for exports and foreign investment (Kappagoda 1995, 14); an MDB was a more neutral channel for investment for a country that had only two decades before attempted to occupy much of the region through force. While the US originally opposed the AsDB's formation, it came to support it – as usual Cold War geopolitics overcame its concern that an Asian RDB would undermine its influence in the region, much like the IADB (Kappagoda 1995, 14). Deepening US involvement in the Vietnam War led to the position that an economically strong Asia-Pacific would be better able to resist perceived Soviet and Chinese expansionism (Nakao 2017).

In March 1963, the UN Economic Commission for Asia and the Far East (UN-ECAFE) proposed a resolution to establish an Asia-Pacific development bank. The Agreement Establishing the AsDB, referred to as its Charter, sets its purpose as fostering 'economic growth and co-operation in the region of Asia and the Far East... and to contribute to the acceleration of the process of economic development of the developing member countries in the region, collectively and individually' (AsDB 1967). The AsDB mirrored earlier MDBs closely from its inception, with the first President Takeshi Watanabe attending meetings held by the IBRD and IADB 'to gather information about how they were run' before the Asian RDB began operations (McCawley 2012, 51). The AsDB opened its doors on 19 December 1966 with 19 regional and 12 non-regional members, a significant difference from the AfDB's initial regional-only membership, and its initial focus – given the region's agricultural orientation – was food production and rural development (McCawley 2012, 75), though it quickly turned to infrastructure too.

The 'most obvious factor distinguishing' the AsDB from other RDBs 'is its strong Japanese influence' (Babb 2009, 29). It's history and governance structure are interwoven with Japan's organisational and regional leadership, from the appointment of Japanese nationals to positions of importance to Japan's initial financial contributions (Rathus 2008). From senior management to voting capacity, Japan is the AsDB's most influential regional member. In fact, studies have argued that all AsDB projects 'require Japanese support; otherwise, they do not even proceed to the Board of Directors for approval' (Lim and Vreeland 2013, 44). However, the US has equal shareholdings and Ben-Artzi (2016) noted the strong tensions between the two, in particular over visions for economic development.

There are 67 member countries in the AsDB: 48 regional shareholders and 19 non-regional. Regional members control over 65% voting power and non-regionals close to 35%. As of 2019, Japan and the US are the equal largest shareholders, with 15.6% voting power each, which is an increase from 2015 when they both had around 12.7%. This power structure is unique with two hegemons and little borrower influence (Ben-Artzi 2016). China only joined the AsDB in 1986 but by 2016 was its third largest borrower behind India and Indonesia. China also has the third largest voting share, which jumped from 5.5% in 2016 to 6.4% in 2019, with India a close fourth at 6.3%. Both China and India are active in AsDB governance (O'Keeffe, Pryke, and Wurf 2017), which is a change from the traditional deficit in borrower influence. With China's establishment of the AIIB and the One Belt, One Road initiative (Jakupec and Kelly 2015, Kajimoto 2017), the Japan-led AsDB may struggle to maintain its key role in the region.

Like the IBRD and other RDBs, daily operations are managed by the AsDB President and six Vice Presidents, overseeing a permanent staff of over 3,000 personnel. There have been ten Presidents, all of whom have been Japanese, paralleling US control over the World Bank. Table 6.5 highlights their tenures, priorities, and challenges. Prior to the appointment of Masatsugu Asakawa in January 2020, President Takehiko Nakao led the AsDB from 2013 to 2020 and emphasised the importance of climate change, infrastructural growth, and private investment to the future of the Asian RDB (Anonymous 2019a).

The AsDB is supported by the AsDF. It was founded in 1974 and is AsDB's concessional lending arm and the largest of the AsDB's Special Funds. During the AsDB's first decade, numerous Special Funds delivered concessional funding; President Watanabe described their multitude as a 'nightmare,' creating unnecessary overlap and confusion (McCawley 2012, 10). The AsDF reduced the overlap, becoming the focal delivery point for concessional lending. During the upheavals of the 1973 and 1979 oil price shocks, many low-income countries accessed AsDF loans instead of AsDB OCR. AsDF operations were at first denominated in US dollars but after 1982 were linked to Special Drawing Rights (SDRs) to improve currency stability. Between 1973 and 2016, the AsDF was replenished 11 times to a value of $31.7 billion, but, as with the IDA, each replenishment led to disputes between leading donors over its activities (Erquiaga 2016, 10).

Grant lending was introduced in 2005 and the AsDF became a grant-only affiliate in 2017 because, in May 2015, the Governors approved an initiative to combine AsDB OCR with AsDF concessional resources, merging the balance sheet of both. OCR equity tripled from $18 billion to $53 billion; the consolidation was proposed to increase annual financing capacity to $20 billion by 2020 with co-financing meant to double that (O'Keeffe, Pryke, and Wurf 2017). In other words, this was a way for the Bank to increase its capital base without having to negotiate the politics of a capital increase with key shareholders. It was also likely

Table 6.5 Asian Development Bank Presidents

President	*Tenure*	*Details*
Takeshi Watanabe	Nov 1966– Nov 1972	Watanabe likened the AsDB to 'a family doctor' learning about the health of their patients. Regional surveys were conducted to develop a fuller understanding of needs.
Shiro Inoue	Nov 1972– Nov 1976	Annual lending commitments increased from $316 million in 1972 to $776 million in 1976. The AsDF was established in 1974 to finance concessional loans.
Taroichi Yoshida	Nov 1976– Nov 1981	Introduced multi-project loans and restructured operations to be country focused. Sector lending was introduced in 1980.
Masao Fujioka	Nov 1981– Nov 1989	Promoted greater coordination of operations and increased co-financing and equity investments to the private sector.
Kimimasa Tarumizu	Nov 1989– Nov 1993	Annual lending commitments increased to $5 billion. By 1991, cumulative lending reached $37.6 billion for 1,039 projects since 1966.
Mitsuo Sato	Nov 1993– Jan 1999	Began an organisational restructuring to shift to a more country-focused approach and was active in responding to the 1997 Asian Financial Crisis.
Tadao Chino	Jan 1999– Jan 2005	Introduced several new initiatives, including the Poverty Reduction and Private Sector Development Strategies, and took a lead role in post-conflict reconstruction.
Haruhiko Kuroda	Feb 2005– Mar 2013	Set out Strategy 2020 and carried out several internal reforms. He also led the first general capital increase in 14 years, tripling AsDB's capital base to $165 billion.
Takehiko Nakao	Apr 2013– Jan 2020	Announced plans in May 2014 to combine OCR lending with AsDF's resources, a reform designed to increase annual lending and grant approvals by 50%.
Masatsugu Asakawa	Jan 2020–Present	Began term emphasising the future role of the AsDB as the 'partner of choice' in the Asia-Pacific (a response to the creation of the AIIB), but COVID-19 has since reframed immediate priorities.

Source: Annual Reports and AsDB Website.

a response to the establishment of the AIIB and the World Bank's MFD agenda. AsDF-eligible countries continue to receive concessional assistance, even though operations are approved through AsDB OCR.

The AsDB began as a conservative project lender with a strong focus on agriculture and its lending grew quite slowly until the 1990s. It later diversified into infrastructure so much that it was sometimes referred to as the 'Asian Dams and Bridges' bank. By the late 1970s, it had introduced a diverse range of lending products including policy-based lending in 1978. The 1979 oil shock expedited these changes, as policymakers in developing Asian countries became intensely concerned about food and energy security, and AsDF concessional approvals grew. Besides project loans, the AsDB began to prove programme loans (quick-disbursing loans designed to increase productive capacity in high-priority areas), multi-project loans (financial products that draw together projects considered too small for normal operations), and sector loans (projects financing capital requirements in specific sectors) (McCawley 2012, 126). It started lending to the private sector in 1983 but this lending remained small for decades (Ben-Artzi 2016). The IBRD, IADB, AfDB, and AsDB followed a similar path in introducing lending instruments, demonstrating isomorphic alignment.

During its early years, the AsDB's comparative advantages over the larger World Bank were its strong networks in the region, greater flexibility, and a less bureaucratic approach to lending but, as Bank staff acknowledged in interviews, this has reduced over time. These networks meant they had a focus on sub-regional integration initiatives like the Greater Mekong Subregion, which are part of its strategy to 2030. The AsDB was a little less hostile to the state than the World Bank (see Chapter 4), though some analysts have questioned whether they in fact offered a unique model (Komori 2016).

In the early 1990s, the AsDB undertook an internal review like the World Bank's Wapenhans review, prompted by concerns over project quality. As with the World Bank, the review found that there was an 'approval culture' (cited in Komori 2016, 30). The report and pressure from the US led to it become a broader MDB, funding social sector projects. The 1997 Asian Financial Crisis also impacted the AsDB greatly, with much of the optimism surrounding the 'East Asian Miracle' evaporating (Bello 1999). Significantly, the Crisis saw the AsDB move beyond project and programme lending to reflect more an IMF-style role as an emergency liquidity provider, although the AsDB addressed more social sector support while the IMF's principal focus was balance-of-payments stability (McCawley 2012, 219). Following the Asian Crisis, and in part because of critiques of its approach to the crisis, the AsDB became the first RDB to have a Board-approved governance policy ensuring its portfolio benefits the poor. In November 1999, it adopted poverty alleviation as its main mission, reassessing Asia's development path following exposed vulnerability. Notably, this change preceded the World Bank, which introduced its policy on 31 December 1999. Still, as Sims (2015) argues, its poverty alleviation objectives tend to be constrained by its neoliberal agenda.

AsDB's poverty-alleviation mission saw it support the Millennium Development Goals (MDGs) unveiled in 2000, alongside the IADB and AfDB. In 2001, its lending dramatically increased and continued to increase across the rest of the decade (Ben-Artzi 2016). The poverty focus shaped its response to the 2003 outbreak of severe acute respiratory syndrome when it focussed on developing health systems and to increased natural disasters in the region such as the December 2004 Asian tsunami. The Bank also dramatically increased its lending to the private sector, going from 1% of lending in 2001 to 16% in 2015 (O'Keeffe, Pryke, and Wurf 2017, 63), with plans to get to one third of lending by 2024 with $2.50 in co-financing for every dollar invested (AsDB 2018). With the AsDB supporting the innovative financing agenda, following the trend of the World Bank's MFD, relations with the US have improved (O'Keeffe, Pryke, and Wurf 2017).

Historically, most of the AsDB Group's lending came from its OCR, while AsDF projects made up a third a total lending. Between 2008 and 2017, OCR annual approvals averaged $11.35 billion, while AsDF approvals averaged $2.93 billion. Illustrating its growth trajectory, the AsDB approved $3.4 billion between 1967 and 1976 and $140.3 billion between 2007 and 2016. Of $17.46 billion total approvals in 2016, the sectoral division of activities was energy (26%), transport (22%), public sector management (13%), finance (11%), urban infrastructure and services (9%), industry and trade (6%), agriculture, natural resources, and rural development (6%), education (5%), health (1%), and communications (0.3%) (AsDB 2016). It no longer lends much for agriculture but a lot for energy and transport and a significant amount of policy-based lending for public sector reform. The largest recipients of AsDB Group finance in 2016 were India (17%), China (12%), and Azerbaijan and Indonesia (10%). India and China have also been large borrowers in the World Bank, which is not surprising since their development challenges and number of people living in poverty are still large. Despite that, the US has been pushing for China to graduate to developed country status (and thus stop borrowing) from the AsDB and World Bank.

Like the World Bank and most RDBs, the AsDB maintains a technical assistance portfolio, although relative funding declined significantly for it in the mid-1990s (O'Keeffe, Pryke, and Wurf 2017). As with the IADB and AfDB, advisory services are mandated in its Charter. Its technical assistance has been consolidated into 'transaction technical assistance' and 'knowledge and support technical assistance.' The former covers services directly benefitting projects financed by the AsDB, while the latter includes other advisory services, such as general institutional capacity building and policy advice. It also coordinates several technical assistance grants and funds. Finally, like the IBRD and AfDB, it manages a training institute: the AsDB Institute (AsDBI). Established in 1996, it conducts research and delivers face-to-face and online training to mid- and senior-level country officials. Its work in the knowledge terrain is not regarded internally or externally as being of the quality found at the World Bank (O'Keeffe, Pryke, and Wurf 2017). But, still, it has a fairly strong commitment to the production of developmental 'common sense' and in 2018 it produced 7,102 knowledge outputs (Sims 2020).

In summary, the AsDB has similar organisational structures and operational mandates to the IBRD, IADB, and AfDB. It has always been led by a Japanese President, just as IBRD's President has always been an American. Shareholder power in the AsDB is divided between Japan as the leading regional member and the US as the leading non-regional member, like Nigeria and the US in the AfDB, but Chinese influence has grown. Its region has gone from one of the poorest in the world when the MDB was formed to one of the fastest growing; inequality and pockets of persistent poverty remain key challenges. One question is whether it has kept up with the times – up to the 1990s, it was regarded as close to its members, very flexible, and the most state-friendly MDB, but this reputation waned after the 1997 Asian Financial Crisis. It now faces competition from the China-led AIIB (see Chapter 8), which challenges its regional construction of 'Asia' and its development of more complex loan procedures reflecting institutional isomorphism. Still the symbiosis between MDBs reduces competition, with the AsDB having signed memoranda of understanding with both the AIIB and NDB and already co-financing projects with the AIIB.

6.7 European Bank for Reconstruction and Development

The EBRD was proposed to facilitate the post-Soviet transition of Central and Eastern Europe following the end of the Cold War. As per the Agreement Establishing the EBRD, signed in Paris, France, on 29 May 1990, its mandate is to 'foster the transition towards open market-oriented economies and to promote private and entrepreneurial initiative in the Central and Eastern European countries committed to and applying the principles of multiparty democracy, pluralism and market economics' (EBRD 2013). The EBRD is unique among the RDBs in that, first, it was created decades after the other regional banks and, second, its mandate focusses explicitly on private sector development and democratic reform, while most other MDBs specifically exclude any interference in the political affairs of member countries (Korfker 2013, 86). Indeed, its purposes and functions have nothing of the Keynesian tone of the IBRD and other RDBs. Rather, the language around 'structural and sectoral economic reforms, including demonopolisation, decentralisation, and privatisation' (EBRD 2013) speaks to the Washington Consensus agenda. Nevertheless, its establishment at the height of this era signifies that the 'public sector still had an investment role in transitional economies' (Phillips 2009, 9).

Unlike most other RDBs, it does not have a concessional lending arm and its Articles limit the amount it can lend to states (Ben-Artzi 2016). As Babb (2009, 31) said, 'because it lends heavily to private investors, in many respects it looks more like the World Bank's IFC, or even a private bank, than it does a development bank.' But many SRDBs, especially the trade and development banks, look similar and the larger MDBs have been expanding their non-sovereign operations. The EBRD's Establishing Agreement entered into force on 28 March 1991 and it began operations on 15 April. Between 1991 and 2017, it approved over 5,300 projects totalling €290 billion.

French President François Mitterrand proposed the establishment of a post-Soviet transition bank in 1989, which was endorsed by the European Council in December 1989 as it was clear that the Soviet bloc was in the throes of collapse. After a meeting between OECD member countries and representatives from Malta, Cyprus, Central and Eastern European countries, the EEC, and EIB in January 1990, negotiations for the EBRD concluded in May 1990, 'barely four months after the initial meeting – perhaps the speediest creation of a new multilateral institution in history' (Culpeper 1997, 29). The rapid turnaround from proposal to establishment is explained by the speed of the Soviet bloc's collapse and the capacity of the states backing the proposal.

There were initial disputes over whether a new European RDB was necessary, with the US claiming that the World Bank and IFC already encompassed the EBRD's mandate. Further, some Western European states claimed that the EIB could be expanded to focus on post-Soviet transition, rather than establish an entirely new MDB (Gutner 2002, 59–60). Calls to expand the EIB were immediately shut down by the EIB itself, which 'was distinctly uninterested in accepting responsibility to lead a Western aid initiative' in Central and Eastern Europe (Gutner 2002, 60). In the end, it was the uniqueness of the EBRD's mandate – the interplay between economic liberalisation and the promotion of democratic polities – that facilitated the creation of the new RDB. However, its operational overlap with commercial banks has led to a new set of critics who continue to question its need for existence. Further, the EBRD promoted 'big bang' privatisation and liberalisation in Central and Eastern Europe, which was largely a failure. Output declined rapidly while the number of people living in poverty increased. Privatisation often resulted in the enrichment of a new authoritarian oligarchy. Thus, it is not surprising that the EBRD was often mired in scandal (see Table 6.6) and came under critical scrutiny (Ben-Artzi 2016).

The EBRD has 66 shareholder countries from five continents plus the EU and EIB. The US joined and took the largest capital subscription of 10% while France, Germany, Italy, the UK, and Japan each have 8.52%, totalling close to 53% of votes. The EIB and EU own 3% each. No other RDB has a regional organisation or RDB as a shareholder, however many of the SRDBs do, which often serve as important sources of capital and security.

In the EBRD's case, the EU and EIB are important capital sources; the EU has contributed 36% of all grant financing since the EBRD's establishment and it aims to align the EBRD's operational priorities with EU policy – a distinctive disciplinary approach to development. The EBRD's Board is very large, which Strand (2003) attributes to its political mandate resulting in many state's wanting their voices heard. It has more donors than borrowers on its Board; borrowers have almost no influence and the major shareholders have even more power than their shareholdings suggest (Strand 2003). The 2019 Wise Persons Report concluded that the EBRD is 'generally responsive to EU policies,' though member states do not always coordinate because of their different interests and this could increase after Brexit (Wieser 2019, 22).

The EBRD President serves as chief of staff and legal representative, just like the other RDBs. Six Presidents have led it, all European nationals. Table 6.6 provides highlights of each presidency and demonstrates that the EBRD has had ongoing challenges with scandals, poor lending practices, and profligacy. While other RDBs have had frequent challenges with project quality, the number of scandals and level of profligacy seems more in keeping with poorly run state banks in some developing countries or a few of the SRDBs than it does an RDB. The most recent President was Sir Suma Chakrabarti, who was born in India but is a British national; he stepped down in July 2020 and, due to COVID-19, there has been a delay in appointing his successor. Upon joining the EBRD, President Chakrabarti emphasised two priorities: first, the economic situation in Eastern Europe and, second, supporting the Southern and Eastern Mediterranean after the Arab Spring (EBRD 2012). EBRD staffing is more dominated by bankers than the other RDBs, with few development experts, and thus 'bankers and bureaucrats carry out the EBRD's political goals' (Ben-Artzi 2016, 93).

Table 6.6 European Bank for Reconstruction and Development Presidents

President	*Nationality*	*Tenure*	*Details*
Jacques Attali	French	Apr 1991– Jun 1993	Proposed the idea of the EBRD in June 1989 and chaired the Paris Conference that led to its creation. His tenure was mired by scandal, including uncontested and shocking mismanagement and profligacy.
Jacques de Larosière	French	Sep 1993– Jan 1998	Restored EBRD's reputation and credibility following predecessor's controversies and scandals.
Horst Köhler	German	Sep 1998– Apr 2000	Addressed EBRD's annual $305 million loses by reforming its notoriously lax investment policies and opulent trimmings.
Jean Lemierre	French	Jul 2000– Jul 2008	Before joining EBRD, Lemierre was head of France's Treasury. He later served as a key negotiator in the Greek debt restructuring.
Thomas Mirow	French	Jul 2008– Jul 2012	Previously served as Chairperson of Germany's Social Democrat Party and Alternate Governor at the World Bank. Advocated a strong neoliberal response to the 2008 GFC, though adjustment and restructuring.
Sir Suma Chakrabarti	Indian / British	Jul 2012– Jul 2020	Came from extensive experience in international development economics and policymaking. Responsible for the Green Economy Transition (GET), engagement with the Sustainable Development Goals (SDGs) and 2015 Paris Agreement, and emphasised private sector and market growth. Due to COVID-19, the election of his successor was postponed until October 2020.

Source: Annual Reports and EBRD Website.

EBRD finance is divided into three categories: loans, equity investments, and guarantees to promote trade. Its loans have a maturity period of one to 15 years, no grace period, although project-specific grace periods may be incorporated, and are offered at either fixed or floated interest rates (Faure, Prizzon, and Rogerson 2015). Thus, its standard terms are much harder than the other RDBs, especially given the absence of a concessional lending arm. Loan repayments are normally in equal, semi-annual instalments. Annual investments averaged $9.1 billion between 2010 and 2017. Loan disbursements steadily grew since its establishment, with a jump in loans from around 2006; Russia has been its major borrower (Ben-Artzi 2016). Since commencing lending operations, its main sectoral focusses have been financial institutions (€44 billion cumulative 1991 to 2007), industry, commerce, and agribusiness (€33.5 billion), infrastructure (€22.3 billion), and energy (€19.6 billion). Its interest rates are similar or only slightly lower than commercial banks, though maturities are generally longer (Ben-Artzi 2016). These foci are reflective of its commercial bank persona and are similar to the IFC, with the 2019 Wise Persons Report stating that the EBRD's 'expertise is strong in relation to the development of the private sector, even if it does not have comprehensive sector coverage and is weak in, especially, social sectors such as health care and education' (Wieser 2019, 22). Lending to financial intermediaries has been coming under increasing scrutiny in recent years due to a lack of transparency and environmental impact. Its private sector projects generally range from €4 million to €218 million, but average investments are a relatively small at €22 million. In contrast to the IADB, AfDB, and AsDB, the EBRD is far more aligned to project-based lending and equity investments, revealing again it is more like a commercial bank than a traditional RDB.

EBRD lending is supported by technical assistance, divided into policy reform dialogue services and advisory services. Policy reform dialogue services focus on coordinating the strategies, policies, and related initiatives that support the EBRD's transition mandate and advisory services help SMEs access business advice just like the technical assistance portfolio of the IFC. The EBRD also sponsors the Central European Initiative (CEI), a regional forum founded in 1989 comprised of 18 member countries mainly from Central and Eastern Europe that promotes collaboration and consultation.

In summary, reflecting its persona as a commercial bank with a development agenda, the EBRD is less transparent than the other RDBs. It also has several unique features vis-à-vis other MDBs. First, it does not provide concessional finance and focusses on private investment and, second, it promotes a political agenda by encouraging democratic reform. Despite being established much later than the other RDBs, its founding is reminiscent of the other regional banks, in the sense that the AfDB responded to the integration and development of post-colonial Africa. The major difference is that the EBRD emerged at the height of the Washington Consensus, which it presents as 'common sense,' in contrast to the Keynesian/New Deal tone of the earlier RDBs. Thus, the EBRD aims 'to offer structural coherence in post-communist transition' (Shields 2015, 180).

Bibliography

AfDB. 2016. *Agreement Establishing the African Development Bank*. Abidjan, Côte d'Ivoire: African Development Bank.

AfDB. 2018. "The High 5s for Transforming Africa." https://www.afdb.org/en/the-high-5/.

Ajomo, M.A. 1976. "Regional Economic Organisations: The African Experience." *The International and Comparative Law Quarterly* 25 (1):58–101.

Akin-Olugbade, Adesegun A. 2003. "Managing Development in a Time of Crisis: The Legal Framework for the Temporary Relocation of the African Development Bank." *The International Lawyer* 38 (3):725–39.

Anonymous. 2019a. Asian Development Bank Interview #1. edited by Adrian Robert Bazbauers: UNSW Canberra.

Anonymous. 2019b. European Investment Bank Interview #1. edited by Adrian Robert Bazbauers: UNSW Canberra.

AsDB. 1967. Agreement Establishing the Asian Development Bank.

AsDB. 2016. Annual Report 2016. Manila: Asian Development Bank.

AsDB. 2018. *Strategy 2030: Achieving a Prosperous, Inclusive, Resilient, and Sustainable Asia and the Pacific*. Manila: Asian Development Bank.

Babb, Sarah. 2009. *Behind the Development Banks: Washington Politics, World Poverty, and the Wealth of Nations*. Chicago, IL and London: The University of Chicago Press.

Barria, Lilian A., and Steven D. Roper. 2004. "Economic Transition in Latin American and Post-Communist Countries: A Comparison of Multilateral Development Banks." *International Journal of Politics, Culture, and Society* 17 (4):619–38. doi: 10.1023/B:IJPS.0000031235.74193.a4.

Bazbauers, Adrian Robert. 2018. The World Bank and Transferring Development: Policy Movement through Technical Assistance, International Political Economy Series. Cham: Palgrave Macmillan.

Bello, Walden. 1999. "The Asian Financial Crisis: Causes, Dynamics, Prospects." *Journal of the Asia Pacific Economy* 4 (1):33–55. doi: 10.1080/13547869908724669.

Ben-Artzi, Ruth. 2016. *Regional Development Banks in Comparison: Banking Strategies versus Development Goals*. Cambridge: Cambridge University Press.

Biney, Ama. 2019. "Pan-Africanism: A History." In *Routledge Handbook of South-South Relations*, edited by Elena Fiddian-Qasmiyeh and Patricia Daley, 177–87. London: Routledge.

Broad, Robin, and John Cavanagh. 2009. *Development Redefined: How the Market Met Its Match*. Boulder, CO: Paradigm Publishers.

Bull, Benedicte, and Morten Bøås. 2003. "Multilateral Development Banks as Regionalising Actors: The Asian Development Bank and the Inter-American Development Bank." *New Political Economy* 8 (2):245–61. doi: 10.1080/13563460307176.

Bulow, Jeremy, and Kenneth Rogoff. 2005. "Grants versus Loans for Development Banks." *American Economic Review* 95 (2):393–7.

Coburn, Carolyn, Michael Restivo, and John M. Shandra. 2015. "The African Development Bank and Infant Mortality: A Cross-national Analysis of Structural Adjustment and Investment Lending from 1990 to 2006." *International Journal of Comparative Sociology* 56 (3–4):275–96. doi: 10.1177/0020715215610799.

Cook, Malcolm. 2015. "Two Asias: AIIB v ADB." *The Straits Times*, 5 June. Accessed 20 June 2016. http://www.straitstimes.com/opinion/two-asias-aiib-v-adb.

Culpeper, Roy. 1997. *Titans or Behemoths?* London: Lynne Rienner.

EBRD. 2012. "Speech Transcript: Suma Chakrabarti at a Press Conference on 1 October 2012 in London." European Bank for Reconstruction and Development. https://www.ebrd.com/cs/Satellite?c=Content&cid=1395238673972&d=Mobile&pagename=EBRD%2FContent%2FContentLayout.

EBRD. 2013. Agreement Establishing the European Bank for Reconstruction and Development. London: European Bank for Reconstruction and Development

English, E. Phillip, and Harris M. Mule. 1996. *The African Development Bank*. London: Lynne Rienner.

Erquiaga, Philip. 2016. *A History of Financial Management at the Asian Development Bank: Engineering Financial Innovation and Impact on an Emerging Asia*. Manila: Asian Development Bank.

Faure, Raphaëlle, Annalisa Prizzon, and Andrew Rogerson. 2015. *Multilateral Development Banks: A Short Guide*. London: Overseas Development Institute.

Fordwor, Kwame Donkoh. 1981. *The African Development Bank: Problems of International Cooperation*. New York: Pergamon Press.

Gavas, Mikaela. 2019. The Wise Persons Group Report on Europe's Development Finance Architecture: Merger, Acquisition, or Reinvention?: Centre for Global Development.

Giles, Chris, and Jim Pickard. 2018. "European Investment Bank wants UK to Remain a Member." *Financial Times*. https://www.ft.com/content/24a5c5c0-8441-11e8-96dd-fa565ec55929.

Griffith-Jones, Stephany, and Judith Tyson. 2013. The European Investment Bank: Lessons for Developing Countries. In *WIDER Working Paper*.

Gutner, Tamar L. 2002. *Banking on the Environment: Multilateral Development Banks and Their Environmental Performance in Central and Eastern Europe*. Cambridge, MA: The MIT Press.

Humphrey, Chris. 2014. "The Politics of Loan Pricing in Multilateral Development Banks." *Review of International Political Economy* 21 (3):611–39. doi: 10.1080/09692290.2013.858365.

Humphrey, Chris. 2016. "The Invisible Hand: Financial Pressures and Organisational Convergence in Multilateral Development Banks." *The Journal of Development Studies* 52 (1):92–112. doi: 10.1080/00220388.2015.1075978.

IADB. 1996. Agreement Establishing the Inter-American Development Bank. Washington, DC: Inter-American Development Bank

IADB. 2010. Annual Report 2010. Washington, DC: Inter-American Development Bank.

IADB. 2017. Annual Report 2017. Washington, DC: Inter-American Development Bank.

Jakupec, Victor, and Max Kelly. 2015. "The Relevance of Asian Development Bank: Existing in the Shadow of the Asian Infrastructure Investment Bank." *Journal of Regional Socio-Economic Issues* 5 (3):31–46.

Kajimoto, Tetsushi. 2017. "As Japan Adapts to China's Rise, AsDB Wrestles with Relevance." https://www.reuters.com/article/uk-adb-asia/as-japan-adapts-to-chinas-rise-adb-wrestles-with-relevance-idUKKBN17Z18V.

Kappagoda, Nihal. 1995. *The Asian Development Bank*. London: Lynne Rienner.

Kellerman, Miles. 2019. "The Proliferation of Multilateral Development Banks." *The Review of International Organizations* 14 (1):107–45. doi: 10.1007/s11558-018-9302-y.

Komori, Yasumasa. 2016. "The Asian Development Bank: Joining the Fight against Corruption?" In *Global Economic Governance and the Practices of the Multilateral Development Banks*, edited by Susan Park and Jonathan R. Strand, 21–38. London: Routledge.

Korfker, Fredrik. 2013. "Reflections on Private-sector Evaluation in the European Bank for Reconstruction and Development: 1991–2010." *Evaluation* 19 (1):85–96. doi: 10.1177/1356389012472267.

Krasner, Stephen D. 1981. "Power Structures and Regional Development Banks." *International Organization* 35 (2):303–28.

Lim, Daniel Yew Mao, and James Raymond Vreeland. 2013. "Regional Organizations and International Politics: Japanese Influence over the Asian Development Bank and the UN Security Council." *World Politics* 65 (1):34–72. doi: 10.1017/S004388711200024X.

Lopes, Mark. 2019. "Latin America's Other Election: The Next IDB President." Accessed 2 July. https://www.americasquarterly.org/article/latin-americas-other-election-the-next-idb-president/.

McCawley, Peter. 2012. *Banking on the Future of Asia and the Pacific: 50 Years of the Asian Development Bank*. Manila: Asian Development Bank.

Mingst, Karen. 1990. *Politics & the African Development Bank*. Lexington: The University of Kentucky Press.

Nakao, Takehiko. 2017. "Economic Outlook for Asia and the Role of the Asian Development Bank." *Asia-Pacific Review* 24 (1):37–57. doi: 10.1080/13439006.2017.1321295.

Nelson, Paul. 2000. "Whose Civil Society? Whose Governance? Decision Making and Practice in the New Agenda at the Inter-American Development Bank and the World Bank." 6 (4):405. doi: 10.1163/19426720-00604003.

O'Keeffe, Annmaree, Jonathan Pryke, and Hannah Wurf. 2017. *Strengthening the Asian Development Bank in 21st Century Asia*. Sydney: Lowy Institute for International Policy.

Pandolfelli, Lauren E., and John M. Shandra. 2013. "The African Development Bank, Structural Adjustment, and Child Mortality: A Cross-National Analysis of Sub-Saharan Africa." *International Journal of Health Services* 43 (2):337–61. doi: 10.2190/HS.43.2.i.

Phillips, David A. 2009. *Reforming the World Bank: Twenty Years of Trial – and Error.* Cambridge: Cambridge University Press.

Ranis, Gustav. 1997. "The World Bank Near the Turn of the Century." In *Global Development Fifty Years After Bretton Woods: Essays in Honour of Gerald K. Helleiner*, edited by Roy Culpeper, Albert Berry and Frances Stewart, 72–89. London: North South Institute / Macmillan Press.

Rapley, John. 2002. *Understanding Development: Theory and Practice in the Third World.* Boulder, CO: Lynne Reinner Publishers Inc.

Rathus, Joel. 2008. "China, Japan and Regional Organisations: The Case of the Asian Development Bank." *Japanese Studies* 28 (1):87–99. doi: 10.1080/10371390801939112.

Robinson, Nick. 2009. "The European Investment Bank: The EU's Neglected Institution*." *JCMS: Journal of Common Market Studies* 47 (3):651–73. doi: 10.1111/j.1468–5965.2009.01818.x.

Salinger, Adva. 2018. "Q&A: EIB President Werner Hoyer on European Aid Turf War, Iran, and More." Devex. https://www.devex.com/news/q-a-eib-president-werner-hoyer-on-european-aid-turf-war-iran-and-more-93566.

Scheman, L. Ronald. 1997. "Banking on Growth: The Role of the Inter-American Development Bank." *Journal of Interamerican Studies and World Affairs* 39 (1):85–100. doi: 10.2307/166498.

Shaw, Christopher L. 1991. "Par Inter Paribus: The Nature of Power in Cooperation: Lessons (For the United States) From the African Development Bank." *African Affairs* 90 (361):537–58. doi: 10.1093/oxfordjournals.afraf.a098468.

Shields, Stuart. 2015. "The European Bank for Reconstruction and Development as Organic Intellectual of Neoliberal Common Sense in Post-Communist Transition." In *Global Economic Governance and the Development Practices of the Multilateral Development Banks*, edited by Susan Park and Jonathan R. Strand, 167–86. Abingdon: Routledge.

Sims, Kearrin. 2015. "The Asian Development Bank and the Production of Poverty: Neoliberalism, Technocratic Modernization and Land Dispossession in the Greater Mekong Subregion." *Singapore Journal of Tropical Geography* 36 (1):112–26. doi: 10.1111/sjtg.12093.

Sims, Kearrin. 2020. "The ADB and AIIB: Cooperation, Competition, and Contestation." In *Rethinking Multilateralism in Foreign Aid: Beyond the Neoliberal Hegemony*, edited by Viktor Jakupec, Max Kelly and Jonathan Makuwira, 145–159. London: Routledge.

Strand, Jonathan R. 2003. "Power Relations in an Embedded Institution: The European Bank for Reconstruction and Development." *European Integration* 25 (2):115–29.

Tussie, Dianne. 1995. *The Inter-American Development Bank.* London: Lynne Rienner.

Vigdor, Neil. 2020. "Trump Administration's Nominee for Development Bank Chief Breaks with Protocol." *New York Times*, June 17. https://www.nytimes.com/2020/06/17/business/Mauricio-claver-Carone-inter-american-bank.html.

Waldron, Travis. 2020. "The Man (And The Mission) Behind Trump's Clash with Venezuela." HuffPost, accessed 2 July.

Wieser, Thomas. 2019. Europe in the World: The Future of the European Financial Architecture for Development: An Independent Report by the High-Level Group of Wise Persons on the European Financial Architecture for Development Council of the European Union (General Secretariat). In *Secretariat of the Wise Persons Group*: General Secretariat of the Council of the EU: Economic and Financial Affairs.

7 The sub-regional development banks

The increasing sophistication of multilateral development finance (MDF) and the growing needs of the Global South during the 1960s led to the sub-regional expansion of the multilateral development banks (MDBs). Encompassing 1960–2006, this phase in the growth of MDF saw the staggered emergence of 15 relatively small banks attempting to fill capital needs unmet by the World Bank and regional development banks (RDBs) and to promote sub-regional integration (Wihtol 2014). Labelled the sub-regional development banks (SRDBs), they 'serve a group of borrowers that share borders or geographical or other characteristics and that stand apart from their neighbours in other ways' (Culpeper 1997, 54). Put simply, the SRDBs serve regions-within-regions, such as East Africa or the Caribbean. Compared to the World Bank and RDBs, the SRDBs are more varied in operation and organisational stability, with a few sub-regionals today rivalling their regional counterparts and others almost collapsing due to mismanagement.

There are 15 functional SRDBs (see Table 7.1); we are not including the Development Bank of the States of Great Lakes (BDEGL), which collapsed in 1993 due to regional conflict, though it still exists on paper. In order of their establishment, the SRDBs are the Central American Bank for Economic Integration (CABEI), International Bank for Economic Cooperation (IBEC), East African Development Bank (EADB), Caribbean Development Bank (CDB), Development Bank of Latin America (CAF), International Investment Bank (IIB), West African Development Bank (BOAD), FONPLATA Development Bank, ECOWAS Bank for Investment and Development (EBID), Development Bank of Central African States (BDEAC), Eastern and Southern African Trade and Development Bank (TDB), Pacific Islands Development Bank (PIDB), Black Sea Trade and Development Bank (BSTDB), ECO Trade and Development Bank (ETDB), and Eurasian Development Bank (EDB). Geographically, geopolitically, and historically diverse, the SRDBs comprise a significant and under-researched stratum of the MDBs, all of which have inherited their basic structures from the World Bank and RDBs.

The first SRDB – CABEI – was established in 1960 and the most recent – EDB – commenced operations in 2006. Over those five decades, the sub-regional banks came into being due to varied factors. Some were founded to address insufficient financing from existing MDBs, as in the case of the CABEI, CDB, and PIDB.

Table 7.1 Sub-Regional Development Banks overview

Year	*Sub-regional development banks*	*Region*	*Membership*	*Authorised capital*	*Annual approvals (2018)*	*Credit rating*	*Headquarters*
1960	Central American Bank for Economic Integration	Central America	15	$7 billion	$2.44 billion	AA	Tegucigalpa, Honduras
1963	International Bank for Economic Cooperation	Soviet States	8	$457 million	$148 million	A-	Moscow, Russia
1967	East African Development Bank	East Africa	4 (Class A) 9 (Class B)	$2.174 billion	$26.3 million	BBB-	Kampala, Uganda
1970	Caribbean Development Bank	Caribbean	28	$1.764 billion	$352 million	AA+	Wildey, St. Michael, Barbados
1970	Development Bank of Latin America	Latin America	20	$15 billion	$13.7 billion	A+	Caracas, Venezuela
1970	International Investment Bank	Soviet States	9	$2 billion	$802.5 million (net)	A-	Budapest, Hungary
1973	West African Development Bank	West Africa	17	$1.9 billion	$709.3 million	BBB+	Lomé, Togo
1974	FONPLATA Development Bank	River Plate Basin	5	$3 billion	$425.1 million	A-	Santa Cruz, Bolivia
1975	ECOWAS Bank for Investment and Development	West Africa	15	$2 billion	$141.8 million (2017)	B+	Lomé, Togo
1975	Development Bank of Central African States	Central Africa	12	$2 billion	$185.0 million (2016)	No rating	Brazzaville, Republic of Congo
1985	Eastern and Southern African Trade and Development Bank	Eastern and Southern Africa	36	$3 billion	$1.965 billion (2017)	BBB	Bujumbura, Burundi
1989	Pacific Islands Development Bank	Pacific Islands	9	$9.3 million	$6.6 million	No rating	Hagatna, Guam
1997	Black Sea Trade and Development Bank	Black Sea Region	11	$3.78 billion	$624 million	A-	Thessaloniki, Greece
2005	ECO Trade and Development Bank	ECO Member States	6	$1.5 billion	$80 million (2017)	No rating	Istanbul, Turkey
2006	Eurasian Development Bank	Eurasia	6	$7 billion	$1.4 billion	BBB	Almaty, Kazakhstan

Source: Annual Reports.

Others emerged as organisations formalising sub-regional communities, such as the EADB within the East African Community, BOAD within the West African Monetary Union (WAMU), and TDB – when known as the Preferential Trade Area (PTA) Bank – as the financial arm of the Common Market for Eastern and Southern Africa (COMESA). Notably, most of these SRDBs are more functional than the communities they were designed to support. In addition, many SRDBs have changed their mandates over time, with the IIB – founded as a Soviet alternative to the World Bank in 1970 – losing its purpose after the Cold War but being restructured in 2012. Further, while many sub-regionals are small annual financiers, such as the EADB which approved $26.3 million in 2018, others – notably the CAF, authorised $13.7 billion in 2017 – have expanded greatly to rival the World Bank and RDBs in annual commitments to their regions. Humphrey (2019, 166) classifies the SRDBs as 'minilateral development banks,' or those 'MDBs that were created and are still run by developing countries themselves, and are generally smaller in size compared to the World Bank and major regional MDBs.' They are significant because of their number and because they are borrower-led and yet remain under-researched and cloaked in obscurity compared to the larger MDBs.

The SRDBs face challenges in common with the other MDBs, as well as unique problems given their smaller size, scope, and operational capacity. In broad terms, the SRDBs are like other MDBs. As Chapter 5 demonstrated, the MDBs follow the same plan established by the World Bank, which is a strong reason for looking at them together. They are created and owned by groups of states that make an initial capital subscription and they seek to borrow funds from markets, which they on-lend. And yet there are considerable differences between the sub-regional banks and the larger MDBs. Existing below the 'mezzanine level' of the RDBs, the SRDBs excel most where a specialisation defines their mandate and operations (Banda 2015, 4). Attempting to comparatively analyse 15 organisations is problematic, but broad trends emerge from the SRDBs that make possible indicative understandings.

Starting with the positive aspects, many Global South SRDBs have achieved good credit ratings without capital from the Global North and have opted for alternative approaches to conditionality that make them attractive to borrowing countries (United Nations 2005, xiv). In addition, several SRDBs provide non-traditional assistance – for example, the PIDB offers residential and consumer loans – and almost all are owned and operated by Global South borrowing countries, a great contrast to the influence of the Global North, especially the US, in the World Bank and RDBs. They have also facilitated sub-regionalisation (Zappile 2016). There seems to be a greater sense of borrowing country ownership than in the World Bank; as Gutner (2002, 33) highlights, the World Bank's 'executive directors represent over 180 countries and have no real control over the Bank's projects and policies.' Given the tension between higher-level governance and senior management, this reveals an interesting line of thought about MDBs with smaller memberships; it may lead to more control and influence by higher-level governance, thus the political and developmental goals of member states may be more apparent. The SRDBs can also provide more specialised financial assistance on better terms than private banks and invest in countries the World Bank regards as risky (United Nations 2005, 125–6). Simply put, the SRDBs can perform functions that global and regional MDBs cannot, this is their comparative advantage (Ocampo 2002, Prada 2012, Sagasti and Prada 2006). Humphrey (2017) highlights that while member countries invest relatively small amounts each in SRDBs, that amount is compounded by their collective efforts and borrowings on international capital markets. While this may not be a significant benefit for very wealthy countries, it is very significant for relatively poorer countries that are able to pool their resources to achieve more than they would otherwise. In this way, SRDBs can be justified on several grounds: they are better able to accommodate borrower circumstances than the World Bank; country members eligible for loans are the main shareholders; and, countries with poor credit grades individually can improve their financial standing collectively (Banda 2015).

Despite these positive aspects, there are many obstacles to effective SRDB operations, including low capital bases compared to the larger MDBs and capability limitations as the more prestigious RDBs often attract higher quality staff applicants than the sub-regional banks (Zappile 2016). Further, SRBDs face great difficulties during regional debt crises. As illustrations, the EADB and BDEAC in Southern Africa suffered greatly during the extended debt crisis of 1980s and 1990s due to failed member integration, lack of political commitment to regional actions, non-repayments, worsening portfolio performance, reluctance to borrow from foreign donors, and deteriorating economic conditions (Mistry and Kritzinger-van Niekerk 1998). In addition, many SRDBs lack robust accountability and transparency mechanisms compared to the World Bank and RDBs (Park 2014). For example, the CABEI demonstrates medium levels of accountability through a Compliance Office, Institutional Responsibility Plan, and Environment and Social Policy, while the BOAD only provides financial audits and the BSTDB only has an Internal Audit Department for complaint contacts (Zappile 2016). Also, only a few SRDBs maintain operational transparency, with the CDB being an exemplar with an Information Services Centre and Official Information Disclosure policy (Zappile 2016). Poor accountability and transparency derive from several factors, including limited resources and personnel capacity, as well as the political motivations of leading shareholders and whether accountability and transparency are an important concern for borrowing members. They have also had relatively little academic and civil society attention, again iterating that their operations are mired in obscurity.

The remainder of this chapter provides an analytical overview of the 15 functional SRDBs, beginning chronologically with the CABEI and concluding with the EDB.

7.1 Central American Bank for economic integration

The General Treaty on Central American Economic Integration – signed on 13 December 1960 by Guatemala, El Salvador, Honduras, and Nicaragua – sought to develop a Central American common market and free trade area to promote sub-regional integration and joint development. Among other provisions, the Treaty established the CABEI, which began operations as the first SRDB on 31 May 1961. Costa Rica joined in September 1963 as the fifth founding member. Proposed as the financial arm of Central American integration and development, the CABEI's Constitutive Agreement prioritises infrastructural, industrial, agricultural, economic, social, and environmental programmes and projects that develop individual countries and promote regional integration, thus resembling the RDBs established before it. Today, the SRDB is part of the Central American Integration System (SICA, in Spanish: *Sistema de la Integración Centroamericana*), the economic and political organisation of Central American states established in December 1991.

CABEI's five founding members achieved independence from Spanish colonial rule in 1821, prior to which they were organised as a single administrative unit (Simmonds 1967). Cevallos (1996, 246) notes that 'integration and unionism are not new terms to Central Americans. The nations of Costa Rica, Guatemala, Honduras, El Salvador, and Nicaragua established the Federation of Central American States immediately after their independence from Spain in 1821.' After the Second World War, regional integration was formalised through the Central American Common Market (CACM, or *Mercomun*) of 1961, which sought to create a customs union, adopt common external tariffs, eliminate intra-regional tariffs, and develop joint industrial planning. Both the CACM and CABEI were created through several years of slow progress towards regional integration beginning in 1952 and continued throughout the 1960s (Cochrane 1965, Duvall 1964). CABEI emerged from within the CACM framework and 'is considered by some to be the only part of the integration effort that has remained functional' (Cevallos 1996, 248).

While the 1960s saw CABEI grow due to global conditions favourable to international market borrowing, regional integration was stymied by emerging conflict between Honduras and El Salvador in 1969, which undermined CACM. This was compounded by the 1973 oil price shock that revealed Central America significantly over-extended in debt; this came to a head with the 1982 debt crisis, as well as violent conflicts in Nicaragua and El Salvador (Cevallos 1996). These difficulties motivated CABEI to open membership to non-regional shareholders in 1989; the SRDB lost the capacity to effectively support Central America during the 1980s and sought help from international sources, which routinely came with significant conditions attached (Cevallos 1996). In the 1990s, with an expanded membership, CABEI once again became a meaningful sub-regional organisation by improving its administrative governance, punctually servicing its debt obligations, and promoting sub-regional trade liberalisation as part of SICA (Cevallos 1996).

The CABEI's 2015–19 Institutional Strategy focussed on sustainable development and competitiveness and its priority sectors were competitiveness services, financial intermediation, development finance, energy, rural development and the environment, human development, and productive and social infrastructure (CABEI 2015). Such a development plan would not be out-of-place in the World

Bank or the Global South RDBs and the focus on financial intermediation is particularly telling in terms of the influence of the World Bank. Its current 2020–24 Strategic Framework focusses on internal organisational changes: strengthening its governance transparency and accountability, as well as fiscal austerity; improving project efficiency; promoting regional integration effectively; and, consolidating and strengthening its financial capacity (CABEI 2020). Both the 2015–19 Strategy and 2020–24 Framework prioritise climate action, long recognised as a leading sub-regional issue.

Headquartered in Tegucigalpa, Honduras, with regional offices in Guatemala, El Salvador, Nicaragua, and Costa Rica, along with its five regional founding members, CABEI has three regional and seven non-regional non-founding members. The regional founding members are the largest shareholders, each holding 12.17% of shares. This reveals a trend in most SRDBs, a shareholder base primarily controlled by regional members. When CABEI opened membership to non-regional members in September 1989, the first new entrants were Taiwan (rare for an MDB given tensions this would cause with China) and Mexico in 1992, followed by Argentina and Colombia in 1995 and 1997. South Korea is the most recent member, joining in 2019, just after Cuba in 2018. Taiwan is the second largest shareholder with 9.18% share participation. The regional founding members control 60.86% of shareholdings while the non-regional members control 30.72%, with Taiwan and South Korea holding over half of that. Interestingly, Argentina and Colombia – as non-regional members – are permitted to request loans and guarantees, rare in the SRDBs.

An Executive President and Executive Vice President lead CABEI, like the other MDBs, though there are caveats about prospective candidates. As per Article 20 of CABEI's Constitutive Agreement, the Executive President's term is five years and may be re-elected once only and they must be a national of the regional founding states and of 'recognised capacity and broad experience in economic, financial, or banking affairs.' The Executive Vice President, as per Article 21, must be a different nationality from the Executive President; a device to balance shareholder influence. Fifteen Executive Presidents have led the CABEI; for an MDB, this is a large number.

CABEI is the largest MDB operating in the Central American region. Over its first two decades, over three quarters of loans focussed on project lending for physical infrastructure, electricity and water, housing, and manufacturing (Cáceres 1985). Between 2005 and 2016, CABEI loans totalled 47% of disbursements to the region, compared to 33% by the Inter-American Development Bank (IADB) and 20% by the World Bank (CABEI 2016). The five founding member countries have received 95% of all loan approvals. Between 2011 and 2017, annual loan approvals averaged $1.7 billion. Given that CABEI approved 25 projects in 2017, the average loan size was $68 million. Over 90% of all loans have been approved to the public sector. This lack of a shift towards private sector engagement is quite different from the lending activities of the World Bank Group and RDBs.

In summary, CABEI was the first SRDB and preceded the founding of the African and Asian MDBs in the 1960s. In organisational structure, it closely resembles the IADB, which preceded it, including a mandate to promote individual country and regional development. Many later SRDBs, notably Latin American and African sub-regional banks, mirror its form closely. CABEI is an important example of the role envisaged for financial arms in sub-regional integration.

7.2 International Bank for Economic Cooperation

The IBEC was established on 22 October 1963 as the first multilateral bank of the former USSR. It preceded the IIB by several years. Its initial aims were to build economic and trade cooperation between Council of Mutual Economic Assistance (CMEA) countries, also known as COMECON, by means of multilateral settlements in transferable rubles and convertible currency. Just like the IIB, IBEC would revise its operational approach following the collapse of the Soviet Union and the end of the Cold War. As per its current Establishing Agreement, the former Soviet MDB's aims in the 21st century include promoting the development of foreign economic ties between member countries and facilitating the transition of interested member countries from command- to market-based economics (IBEC 2019).

From its establishment, IBEC was created as a Soviet alternative to the Global North-led international financial institutions (IFIs), just like the IIB, although its original role was envisaged as an early IMF-like clearing or settlements house. However, it also included an MDB element as it provided credits for expanding exports and industrial investment and other productive investments (Francuz 1969). It originally used transferable rubles as its currency and subscriptions were relative to the size of exports in intra-CMEA trade (Francuz 1969). Of an initial capital of 300 million transferable rubles, 20% was initially to be paid-in but this quickly increased to 30%. Interestingly for a Soviet MDB, it began purchasing and selling securities in 1986 to develop its capital base and operational reach. With the end of the Cold War, it discarded the ruble on 1 January 1991 and replaced it with the ECU, the currency predecessor to the Euro. At the time, its authorised capital was ECU 400 million. On 1 January 1999, the Euro became its currency of balance.

Beginning in 2002, IBEC undertook several institutional and organisational restructurings in order to better reflect a 'modern MDB' (IBEC 2018). In 2015, the IBEC Council approved the 2016–20 Strategy to develop the MDB's role in the former CMEA region, prioritising foreign trade operations in IBEC member countries. In 2018, its mission was revised to focus on lending financial support to foreign trade operations conducted by companies in member states and facilitating integration into global value chains and boosting competitiveness with priorities on social and economic development in member states (IBEC 2018). At the same time, the IBEC in 2017 received its first international credit rating: BBB-.

IBEC now has eight member countries: Bulgaria, Czech Republic, Mongolia, Poland, Romania, Russian Federation, Slovak Republic, and Vietnam. Cuba was a member country, joining in 1974, but mutual financial relations were settled in 2013, meaning that Cuba formally cut ties with the MDB. Vietnam joined in

1977, at the formal end of the Vietnam War. The Russian Federation is the largest shareholder with 51.6% shareholding, followed by the Czech Republic (13.3%) and Poland (12%). This trend is reflective of the other Russian-led MDBs, whereby IBEC could be argued to be an extension of Russian foreign and economic policy.

The Council of the Bank is IBEC's highest administrative body and its representatives must come from Ministries of Finance or Central Banks. Denis Ivanov, a Russian national, is the incumbent Chairperson of the Board. He was in the Russian Ministry of Foreign Affairs (1997–2004) and head of the London office of the Vnesheconombank (2004–13), the Russian state development corporation. In 2013, Ivanov was made Deputy Chairperson of the Board of the IIB and was appointed Chairperson of the Board of IBEC in April 2018. Ivanov's predecessor was Vladimir Bely, also a Russian national, who assumed office in 2007.

Like other MDBs, the IBEC partners with non-financial institutions in IBEC member countries, international institutions, development banks, and export credit agencies, and private commercial banks. Such relationships are necessary for a modern MDB operating in global financial markets, as well as demonstrating the interconnectedness of MDF as an institutional field. IBEC's lending portfolio includes loans to banks issued for trade finance, syndicated loans to banks to support the economies of member countries, loans to the customers of non-banking organisations, and loans and investment securities (IBEC 2019). Its main activities include trade finance operations and finance to support export and import operations – it is thus focussed on intra-regional trade and financial integration. In this sense, it is like the trade and development banks that started with the PTA Bank in 1985. In addition to its main activities, IBEC also provides commercial loans (short-term credits) and extends credit lines to private corporations (IBEC 2020). In 2017, its working loan portfolio was €21.8 million. This increased considerably to €129.6 million in 2018: €83.3 million for loans to non-banking institutions, €36.8 million in trade finance loans to banks, and €9.5 million syndicated loans to banks (IBEC 2019). The significant increase in the loan portfolio between 2017 and 2018 was the result of initiatives begun in 2016 to improve IBEC's operational structure to better resemble a 'modern MDB,' so while it was not founded as an MDB, we think it now qualifies as such.

7.3 East African Development Bank

The EADB was established in 1967 as one of the main institutions of the East African Community. The Community had existed in various forms since the 1940s: the East African High Commission (1948–61 under colonial administration), East African Common Services Organisation (1961–67 during the decolonising transition), and East African Community (1967–77). The EADB became operational very quickly after its three founding members gained independence from colonial rule: Tanzania (1961), Uganda (1962), and Kenya (1963). This is a very different situation from CABEI; its founding members achieved independence in the early 1800s. EADB resembles the African Development Bank (AfDB) in demonstrating from the outset a strong desire to resist the lingering influences of colonial rule and to be an East African organisation. As per the EADB's Charter, its mandate is to promote sustainable socioeconomic development in East Africa through development finance and advisory services, with an emphasis on projects that 'generally promote the development of the region.'

In 1977, the East African Community was dissolved. Several factors led to the collapse, including significant tensions growing between member countries due to their conflicting economic systems – at the time, Kenya was pushing capitalist private sector expansion while Tanzania was maintaining Julius Nyerere's 'African socialist' economic model. Following the dissolution of the Community in 1977, the EADB was re-established as an independent organisation under its own Charter in 1980. As part of its re-establishment, its role and mandate were revised, its operational scope broadened to include financial services targeting socioeconomic development and regional integration, its membership opened to non-regional actors, its administration decentralised to country offices in Kenya, Tanzania, and Uganda, and it introduced advisory and consultancy services. The re-establishment significantly restructured the SRDB, aligning it with structures and practices of earlier MDBs. In July 2000, the treaty establishing the new East African Community (EAC) entered into force and the EADB once again became the financial pillar of the sub-regional community.

EADB shareholding is divided into Class A and Class B shareholders. Class A shareholders are the current four East African member countries – Kenya, Tanzania, Uganda, and Rwanda – that hold over 87% of shares. Class B shareholders hold 13% of shares and include three development finance institutions (DFIs) – the AfDB, Netherlands Development Company, and German Investment and Development Company – and six commercial banks: Nordea Bank (Stockholm), SBIC Africa Holdings (Johannesburg), Barclays Bank (London), Standard Chartered Bank (London), Consortium of Yugoslav Institutions, and Commercial Bank of Africa (Nairobi). The AfDB, Barclays Bank, and Consortium of Yugoslav Institutions joined in 1970, demonstrating the early need for additional stakeholders to supplement early limited capital; it was the first MDB with such a diverse shareholding. With the BDEGL non-functional, Rwanda and Burundi joined the modern EAC in 2008; Rwanda joined the EADB in 2008 too, while Burundi is currently undergoing admission. South Sudan joined the EAC in 2016, so there is a possibility it could join the EADB in the future. Rwanda's shareholding increased from 1% when it first joined to 9.51% in 2018, reflecting its rapidly growing economy. In 2015, EADB's Governing Council agreed to increase the authorised capital 100% from $1.08 billion to $2.16 billion (following an increase from $270 million to $1.08 billion in 2003) to cater for Burundi's future admission and an increase in Class B shareholdings, while maintaining the EADB Charter's requirements that Class B shareholders are limited to 10% of total authorised shares – although, in 2018, Class B shares were 12.67% following a Governing Council resolution authorising the increase in 2013. Notably, in 2015, the EADB was the first East African organisation to achieve a BBB- credit rating, a consequence of its expanded capital base as well as organisational reforms instituted by incumbent Director General Vivienne Yeda.

A Director General leads the EADB. Tracing the history of the East African SRDB reveals considerable turmoil, including financial mismanagement, as well as success. The first Director General Iddi Simba recounts that, at the time of establishing the EADB,

> globally, development banking was a new industry and in East Africa we had absolutely no development bank anywhere. Needless to say, there was no expertise in the region that could guide and advise on how to start and run a development bank.
>
> (cited in EADB 2017, 16)

In fact, when Simba received the Charter and $2 million in initial capital contributions, a headquarters had not yet been established. To seek advice, Simba 'travelled to Scandinavian countries to recruit expatriate experts who came to Kampala to join the Bank' (EADB 2017, 17).

The EADB's early (mis)fortunes were deeply shaped by its founding EAC member countries. Uganda was especially a source of concern, starting with Idi Amin's dictatorial regime, the uncertainty that followed his deposition, and then the 1981–86 Ugandan Civil War. Such instability led the EADB to effectively lose one founding member country. Coupled with the collapse of the EAC in 1977, the EADB had two consecutive Acting Director Generals: Henry Kajura (1978–79) and David Mulira (1979–81).

As part of EADB's restructuring under its own Charter in 1980, the East Africa SRDB appointed two non-African Director Generals in the 1980s: Lars Ekengren of Sweden and Per Aasmundrud of Norway. They were chosen because the 'political situation was tense at the time and the Presidents could not agree on the nationality of the new Director General' (Ekengren cited in EADB 2017, 20). As a result, Acting Director General Mulira turned to the Swedish International Development Cooperation Agency (SIDA), which had existing relations with the EADB since signing a line of credit in 1972, for advice. SIDA then approached the Nordic Investment Bank (NIB), where Ekengren worked as a Senior Advisor (Ekengren cited in EADB 2017, 20). Aasmundrud was similarly drawn from Nordic development banks.

The SRDB was 'in a deep crisis' during the 1980s with 'hardly any resources in foreign exchange' and 'was practically in default with the World Bank' (Ekengren cited in EADB 2017, 20). Further, it 'experienced more or less continuous delays in transfer of payments… straining the Bank's liquidity' (Aasmundrud cited in EADB 2012). In other words, the EADB was close to collapse. In response, Ekengren established an Advisory Panel in 1981 to improve the SRDB's reputation as a stable financial entity for global financial markets and Aasmundrud oversaw a doubling of shareholder capital in 1986 from SDR 40 million to SDR 80 million.

Despite the progress of the 1980s, a 1997 quantitative study found that the EADB had 'not lived up to the expectations of those who were instrumental in its establishment,' with problems undermining the identification, financing, and post-evaluation of projects (Murinde and Kariisa-Kasa 1997, 100). While it became the first entity to issue corporate bonds in East Africa, in 1996 to the

Kenyan capital market and in 1997 in Uganda and 1999 in Tanzania, its non-performing loan portfolio reached 30% in the early 2000s.

The 2000s saw the expulsion of several leading EADB officials, including Director General Godfrey Tumusiime in 2008 – the Board of Governors cancelled his contract due to financial mismanagement. The Bank posted losses in the millions. Incumbent Director General Vivienne Yeda, who assumed office in January 2009 and who previously served as the AfDB's Resident Representative and Country Manager for Zambia, resuscitated the spiralling SRDB. In 2013, the EADB was ranked the Best Performing DFI in Africa by the Association of African DFIs and, in 2014, Yeda received the *African Banker* magazine's African Banker of the Year Award, the Africa-America Institute's Business Leader Award, and the Centre for Economic and Leadership Development's Africa Female Economic Champion Award for her successful revitalisation of the EADB through a significant organisational restructuring and the recovery of outstanding loans.

The EADB's activities are diverse and include financing operations (capital, lines of credit, bond issuance, and co-financing arrangements), products and services (real estate and property development, asset finance, trade finance, equity, and venture capital), and advisory and consulting services. Its primary lending instruments are short-, medium-, and long-term loans. Between 2004 and 2015, the annual average approved investments totalled $73.3 million. This, however, does not adequately reflect the difficult period faced during the final years of Director General Tumusiime's term when approvals dropped from $108.6 million in 2006 to $31.5 million in 2008. Under Director General Yeda, annual approvals increased to $78 million in 2012 and $184 million in 2015 before declining to $22 million in 2017 and $26 million in 2018. The considerable fluctuations in annual approvals over the 2010s are a consequence of Yeda's reforms to ensure reliable projects capable of repayment are approved as well as recipient demand for projects.

In summary, the EADB reveals the potential significance of well-managed SRDBs in supporting their borrowing member countries and the considerable obstacles posed by a small capital base and membership. It demonstrates the narrow margins between success and failure for a Global South-led MDB.

7.4 Caribbean Development Bank

Following the 1966 Canada/Commonwealth Caribbean Conference, a recommendation was made to investigate the feasibility of a financial institution to serve the Commonwealth Caribbean countries and territories. In July 1967, a UNDP report recommended the creation of a Caribbean development bank with $50 million capital; such an institution was justified given that during the 1950s and 1960s 'the smaller colonial territories of the Eastern Caribbean did not have access to the major international lending institutions' and concerns that 'without economic and social development, political unrest could spread from one island to another' (Ingham and Figueroa 2009, 4). The UNDP report was accepted by a meeting of officials in Georgetown, Guyana, in August 1967, where a committee formed to draft the CDB's Establishing Agreement. The draft Agreement was submitted in 1968, signed in Kingston, Jamaica, on 18 October 1969, and entered into force on 26 January 1970. The CDB began operations in January 1970 and later became an associate institution of the Caribbean Community (CARICOM), which was established in 1973. In CARICOM, the CDB serves a role comparable to the EADB in the EAC, as the financial arm of a sub-regional organisation.

The Agreement Establishing the CDB states its purposes as contributing 'to the harmonious economic growth and development of the member countries of the Caribbean' and promoting 'economic cooperation and integration among them, having special and urgent regard to the needs of the less developed members of the region.' The International Bank for Reconstruction and Development (IBRD) includes an explicit reference to less developed members but the 'special and urgent regards' is new and reflects growing concerns about developing countries expressed in documents like the New International Economic Order (NIEO). In pursuing its purposes, the CDB's functions include financing projects, providing technical assistance, supporting regional financial institutions, stimulating regional capital market development, and mobilising financial resources from within and outside of the Caribbean. The CDB began operations with $25 million in paid-in capital. By 2018, its callable capital reached $1.375 billion and paid-in capital was $388.5 million. As a result, the CDB has been regarded as playing 'an important role in the mobilisation of resources for investment in parts of the Caribbean' (Hardy 1995, 1).

There are 28 regional, other regional, and non-regional member countries in the CDB. There are 19 regional Caribbean members that control 55% of shareholding, with Jamaica and Trinidad and Tobago controlling over 17% each, while most other regional members each control less than 1%. Regional members are the only shareholders eligible to borrow. The remaining shareholders are the other regional members – Brazil, Colombia, Mexico, and Venezuela holding close to 9.5% collectively – and non-regional members – Canada, China, Germany, Italy, and the UK together controlling 35%. Although other regional and non-regional members are not eligible to borrow funds, they have voting rights. This is significant as the five non-regional members individually control larger shareholdings than most regional borrowing members, except for Jamaica and Trinidad and Tobago. So, in 2018, Anguilla, Virgin Islands, Cayman Islands, Montserrat, and Turks and Caicos Islands shared one Governor and Alternate Governor, while the non-regional members have one Governor and Alternate Governor each. This is a common trait among many SRDBs, where the influence of non-regional members has grown thanks to small MDBs attempting to expand their capital base through the admission of strong, non-regional shareholders.

The CDB President is Chairperson of the Board of Directors and Chief Executive Officer. Five Presidents have led the CDB, all appointed from the borrowing member countries as outlined in Table 7.2. Hardy (1995, 4) comments that the CDB 'has been very fortunate in its presidents, who have imparted a strong sense of purpose and stability in the institution'; many have come from academic backgrounds with specialised knowledge in development economics, a trait rare in the leadership of the MDBs as most come from commercial finance and banking backgrounds.

Table 7.2 Caribbean Development Bank Presidents

President	*Country and Tenure*	*Tenure*	*Details*
Sir William Arthur Lewis	St Nevis	1970–73	Nobel Prize winning economist making significant contributions to economic development, industrial structure, and the history of world economics. Lewis 'laid the foundation for the Bank as a sound project-lending and financial institution. He also drew attention to the structural problems (low savings, low productivity, and overvalued exchange rates) that have long constrained the region's economic growth' (Hardy, 1995, 4).
William G. Demas	Trinidad and Tobago	1974–88	Distinguished economic scholar and Caribbean leader. Serving three terms, Demas 'guided the Bank through a period of steady expansion up to the early 1980s and the subsequent period of austerity for the borrowers and the Bank. During his tenure, he emphasised the need for increasing food production, improving the operations of the DFCs, supporting regional projects, and coordinating aid and national development strategies' (Hardy, 1995, 4).
Sir Neville Vernon Nicholls	Barbados	1988–2001	A Barbadian scholar, Nicholls served as CDB Vice President (Operations) at the time of his election to President. He saw 'the CDB through a difficult transition period, with the departure of four senior officials and several project analysts and economists in 1988–1989. He also inherited the problem of widespread arrears on CDB loans, which the Bank addressed by refusing the approve new loans (or disburse existing ones) until arrears were cleared' (Hardy, 1995, 4).
Dr Compton Bourne	Guyana	2001–11	Academic economist focused on public policy and institutional management. In 2010, Bourne reflected on the role of the CDB: 'For the Caribbean, economic integration is another essential plank in the development architecture. The CDB, in keeping with its Charter mandate, diligently pursues this objective, contributing actively to the establishment of critical institutions for economic integration and seeking to ensure balanced development among the members of the Caribbean Community' (Bourne, 2010).
Dr William Warren Smith	Jamaica	2011–Present	Smith also served as CDB Vice President (Operations) at the time of his election to President. In 2018, he outlined his vision of the CDB: 'The events of last year's hurricane season led to the adoption of the slogan "Build back better". It underscores the determination of the people of our Region to triumph over our vulnerabilities. We have a long and proud history of triumphing over adversity. We hail from small and relatively poor countries, yet we compete and perform with distinction, on the world stage, in varied fields of endeavour, be it business, sports, the creative arts or politics' (Smith, 2018).

Source: Annual Reports and CDB Website.

The CDB manages the Special Development Fund (SDF) and United Special Development Fund (SDFU). The SDF, established in 1970, provides concessional loans for high development priority projects. Like those from the International Development Association (IDA), SDF loans have longer maturities and grace periods and lower interest rates than OCR loans. The SDFU was launched in 1982 to streamline SDF operations, which suffered problems like approvals with differing terms and conditions creating funding inefficiencies. Thus, it provided fixed concessional lending arrangements. Contributions to the SDFU are provided in four-year replenishments from regional and non-regional shareholders. Historically, concessional financing comprises a significant portion of cumulative CDB lending.

Between 1970 and 2018, the CDB approved $3.3 billion in OCR financing and $1.9 billion in SDF/SDFU financing. Annual OCR and concessional approvals are small, reflecting the relatively small size of the Bank and its member countries. Between 2007 and 2016, average annual OCR approvals were $143.5 million and average annual SDF approvals were $59.2 million. In 2018, OCR approvals by sector were general budget support ($139.9 million), transportation and communication ($87.3 million), environmental sustainability and disaster risk reduction ($38 million), energy ($14.5 million), water and sanitation ($10.5 million), and social infrastructure and services ($4.9 million). Thus, CDB provides a remarkable high level of budgetary support and it would be interesting to examine if there is much conditionality attached.

The CDB also manages a robust portfolio of project-related and non-project-related technical assistance. Project-related technical assistance includes pre-investment studies, project preparation and loan appraisal support, training, and remedial assistance to correct project operations. Non-project-related technical assistance is broader in scope and can involve consultancies, institutional support to national and regional bodies, and training programmes for government departments. The Technical Cooperation Division (TCD) coordinates the CDB's technical assistance portfolio and its mission statement is 'To lead the [CDB's] efforts to build capacity, transfer knowledge and skills, and strengthen institutions in Borrowing Member Countries (BMCs) by working closely with other Divisions, BMCs, and development partners.' The TCD is not unique to the CDB; most MDBs recognise the importance of advisory services to effective project implementation and have established departments to manage service delivery.

In summary, the CDB has a reputation as a stable and effective if relatively small SRDB. While illustrating the difficulties many Global South-led MDBs face, including the practical need to admit non-regional shareholders thereby potentially eroding sub-regional autonomy, it nonetheless demonstrates that with strong leadership, regional support, and the cultivation of a developmental niche, the SRDBs can be effective in pursuing their mandates.

7.5 Development Bank of Latin America

The Agreement Establishing the Andean Development Corporation (CAF, in Spanish: *Corporación Andina de Fomento*) was signed on 7 February 1968 by Bolivia,

Chile, Colombia, Ecuador, Peru, and Venezuela. In May 1969, the Cartagena Agreement was signed, creating the political framework for the Andean Community. The CAF was designed to serve a significant financial role in the Community, and it formally commenced operations on 8 June 1970. Bolivia and Ecuador received CAF's first loans in 1971, investment projects financing rice storage networks and fisheries complexes. While initially a very small MDB, the CAF is a rare example of an SRDB that has grown over the decades to come to rival the annual approvals of the World Bank and RDBs (specifically, the IADB) operating in its region.

Between 2006 and 2015, the CAF redefined its mission and transformed itself from a sub-regional Andean financial entity into a Latin American institution. In 2010, CAF adopted a new name: Development Bank of Latin America (in Spanish: *Banco de Desarrollo de América Latina*). Despite the name change, the acronym CAF continues to be used. The new name reflects the growth of CAF into a Latin American – and no longer just an Andean – MDB, as well as the admission of new members beyond the Andean Community from a diverse grouping of Latin American shareholders.

As per its revised Establishing Agreement, CAF promotes sustainable development and regional integration in the public and private sectors of shareholder countries through credit operations, non-reimbursable services, and support in the technical and financial structuring of projects. While reflective of the Articles of the RDBs and other SRDBs, CAF's mandate to finance projects in all shareholder countries is unique – its project financing is not restricted to certain members and its geographical focus of operations includes its Latin American stakeholders and loans to banks in Spain and Portugal. This means CAF is a powerful example of a DFI challenging the traditional North-South model, indeed in this respect it is more innovative than the New Development Bank (NDB) and Asian Infrastructure Investment Bank (AIIB), which replicate the donor-recipient MDB model rather than the financial cooperative model.

CAF commenced operations in 1970 with five shareholder countries from the Andean region: Bolivia, Colombia, Ecuador, Peru, and Venezuela. The five founding members today control over 64% of voting power. Beginning in 1990, it gradually expanded its membership to include 12 other countries from Latin America and the Caribbean as well as Spain and Portugal. Of the non-founding members, Argentina – which joined in 2001 – controls the largest shareholding: 8.9%. In addition, 13 private commercial banks from the Latin American and Caribbean region are also shareholders, although collectively they control only 0.05% shareholding and are regarded as one shareholder. So, CAF expanded from five shareholders prior to 1990–20 in 2015. The expansion of membership not only enabled it to increase its capital base significantly – important to its dramatic growth in annual approvals over the 2000s and 2010s – but also to become better representative of Latin America and the Caribbean and not just the Andean Community; with the admission of Uruguay in 2001, all members of MERCOSUR are shareholders.

The shareholder expansion from 1990 was a practical necessity, since the CAF commenced operations with little start-up capital – $25 million paid over several years – and, by '1981, the CAF's finances were in a precarious state, with only US$15 million in loans committed that year' (Humphrey 2016, 104). After L. Enrique García Rodríguez became Executive President in 1991, the CAF underwent a significant restructuring to make it resemble more the corporate model of the World Bank and IADB, hiring consultants 'from Coopers and Lybrand and a former World Bank vice president to review the CAF's operations and make recommendations for overhauling internal process' (Humphrey 2016, 106), geared towards improve the MDB's reputation and obtaining its first credit rating. This demonstrates the conditioning influence of global capital markets and credit ratings to the effective operation of MDBs.

The CAF has tiered share types: 'A' shares are more influential in key issues such as corporate or capital structure changes, while 'B' and 'C' have less power and are represented by four directors of the 21. Despite the tiered structure, the CAF's shareholding 'gives all members representation on the Board and a strong influence on operations, as the Board votes by majority of members present (with no reference to capital contributions)' (Humphrey 2015a, 9). Compared to other MDBs, the CAF's shareholding structure allows the wealthy countries of Chile, Colombia, Peru, and Venezuela to supply higher levels of capital while still offering the poorer member countries 'significant voting power' (Humphrey 2016, 103).

An Executive President leads the CAF and it has only had two. From December 1991 to April 2017, Bolivian L. Enrique García Rodríguez led CAF, a very long tenure rare among the MDBs. The orientation of CAF as a Latin American MDB today is largely the consequence of García's leadership, including several credit rating upgrades, expansion of country membership, and increasing annual approvals from $400 million in the early 1990s to over $12 billion annually since 2015 (García 2006). One of the final accomplishments of García's presidency was a general capital increase of $4.5 billion in 2015; huge considering it commenced operations with just $25 million in total capital. Prior to the CAF, García worked for 17 years in the IADB, including serving as Treasurer. Peruvian Luis Carranza Ugarte succeeded García in April 2017. Ugarte is a renowned economist and has experience working in the IMF and was chief economist for Latin America and Emerging Markets of the *Banco Bilbao Vizcaya Argentaria* (BBVA) in Spain.

During the 2010s, CAF came to exceed the World Bank's Latin American annual commitments and rival those of the IADB. In 2017, the World Bank approved $5.9 billion to Latin America and the Caribbean and the IADB approved $13.4 billion, while the CAF approved $12.3 billion. To demonstrate the rapid expansion of CAF lending, consider the following: in 2000, CAF approved $2.3 billion in new loans, in 2005, the figure was $4.8 billion, and, in 2010, it was $10.5 billion. Of $13.7 billion approved in 2018, the largest sectoral allocations were transport (27.3%), energy (23%), and publication administration (17.2%), demonstrating a more traditional infrastructural focus for the Bank. Such a rapid expansion in annual lending commitments while maintaining a strong capital base and expanding its credit rating is an achievement unmatched by the other MDBs.

The CAF's main lending instruments are medium- and long-term loans, credit lines, equity investments, syndicated loans, guarantees, trade finance, and grants. The focus on medium- to long-term rather than short- to medium-term loans is another sign of its strength, as smaller MDBs prefer instruments with quicker maturities. It provides technical assistance through its Fund for Technical Cooperation, which approved $30 million in 2016 representing 45% of annual advisory services. In contrast to other MDBs, CAF

> loans are approved very rapidly, usually under three months, and face only two major review levels' and the MDB itself 'is highly decentralised, with local staff able to lead project development without needing to refer to HQ for many decisions.
>
> (Humphrey 2015b, 17)

While 'this model of MDB is very attractive to many borrowers,' there are trade-offs, including that 'project quality has been questioned at times, with inadequate preparation and design leading to delays and problems during implementation' (Humphrey 2015b, 17). Given the increasing size, scope, and therefore influence of CAF, problems of inadequate project quality will become more serious. Indeed, CAF's credit rating was downgraded by S&P Global Ratings (2019) to A+ with a negative outlook; it was the only MDB in 2019 with a negative outlook, though 2020 may see more join this category.

In summary, CAF is an anomaly as a SRDB. The expansion of its shareholder membership, revision of mandate to address Latin American and not just Andean development issues, and considerable growth of its loan portfolio arguably has made the CAF resemble more an RDB over the 2010s. Nonetheless, CAF is not without limitations. Ray and Kamal (2019, 194) conclude that it cannot be deemed a 'potential substitute' for the World Bank and RDBs yet, given that the more established MDBs 'can boast decades of successful operations, the development of "knowledge banks" and the establishment and maintenance of global standards in environmentally and socially responsible lending.' Instead, the CAF complements existing MDBs without yet replacing them.

7.6 International Investment Bank

The IIB was proposed as an initiative to promote socialist economic integration between Soviet bloc countries and allies during the Cold War (Baran 1979/1980). It was associated with the CMEA, which facilitated multilateral economic interactions between members between 1949 and 1991 (Stone 2008). The Soviet RDB was an attempt to build regional connections and economic and industrial growth and modernise member countries; as a Soviet alternative to the World Bank, it was a 'hybrid of state socialism and capitalist finance' (Stone 2008, 48). Its establishing agreement was signed on 10 July 1970 and it began operations on 1 January 1971.

The IIB's founding members were the People's Republic of Bulgaria, People's Republic of Hungary, German Democratic Republic, Mongolian Democratic Republic, People's Republic of Poland, Czechoslovak Socialist Republic, and the USSR. Membership was expanded to include the Socialist Republic of Romania (1971), Cuba (1974), and the Socialist Republic of Vietnam (1977). Its original charter stated on paper that all member countries had 'an equal voice in its decisions,' while in practice 'the Soviet Union's overwhelming economic and political weight spurred the IIB's other members to defer to it' (Stone 2008, 61). During the Cold War, the IIB financed loans exceeding €7 billion, focussing on joint investment programmes.

With the end of the Cold War, the relevance of the IIB was called into question; it lost its purpose and stagnated for two decades, comparable to the experiences of IBEC. The reunification of Germany and dissolution of Czechoslovakia led to their withdrawal in 1990 and 1993, with Poland following in 2000 as it sought to join the European Union (EU). Not only were member countries leaving but the IIB's original purpose was to integrate socialist countries, a redundant task given that shareholders were transitioning from command- to market-based economies. Further, the IIB reflected the rigid economic flaws of the Soviet bloc. As Stone (2008, 48–9) comments at length,

> the IIB failed in its overall mission to invigorate the stagnating economies of the Soviet bloc. The reasons for its failure, intimately tied to the rigidities of the Soviet command economy, highlight the obstacles to reform of the late Soviet system. The bank's efforts foundered not only because of the Soviet economy's dependence on raw material exports but also, more profoundly, because of the Soviet Communist Party's insistence on maintaining administratively determined prices, central planning, and tight links with the East European satellites. Those fundamental principles of the Soviet system constrained what the IIB could accomplish. From Moscow's perspective, abandoning these core principles would mean abandoning the Soviet experiment altogether. In that sense, the IIB's experience suggests that the late Soviet economic system was fundamentally not reformable.

In 2012, new management took control of the stalled SRDB with a mandate from the remaining shareholders to start a complex reformation. The IIB's 2013–17 Strategy 'was of marked anti-crisis nature,' but the relaunch struggled due to financial, economic, and geopolitical shocks affecting its shareholders (IIB 2017, 4). Despite challenges, the IIB entered debt capital markets in 2014, the first time in its history, and began issuing bonds in Russia, Slovakia, and Romania. Its 2018–22 Development Strategy revised the mission of the MDB again, moving from providing loans on commercial principles to execute joint investment projects to 'facilitating connectivity and integration between the economies of the Bank's member states in order to ensure sustainable and inclusive growth, competitiveness of national economies, backed by the existing historical ties' (IIB 2017, 5). As part of the Strategy, the IIB intends to build its capabilities and increase paid-in capital to expand annual financial commitments. In 2018, it signed a cooperation agreement with CABEI and became a member of the International Development Finance Club, which has five SRDBs as members perhaps with the aim of shoring up their legitimacy but also demonstrating that there are complex networks between the MDBs.

The IIB's shareholders today include EU and non-EU member countries, nine in total. The Russian Federation is the overall largest shareholder as well as the largest non-EU shareholder, controlling over 44% of voting power. Cuba, Vietnam, and Mongolia are the three other non-EU shareholders, collectively owning just over 1.6%. The five EU shareholders – Bulgaria, Hungary, Czech Republic, Romania, and Slovak Republic – together control nearly 48% voting power, with Bulgaria being the second overall largest shareholder holding 12.43%. With $2 billion authorised capital, the paid-in capital of the nine countries was just above $400 million in 2020.

Since 1970, the IIB has been headquartered in Moscow, Russia. In 2019, however, its headquarters moved to Budapest, Hungary – a move designed to more effectively engage with EU and Western capital markets, a necessary precursor to the small SRDB expanding its influence; the credit rating agencies Fitch, Moody's, and S&P all responded favourably to the change. The relocation has not been without controversy, however, with tensions between shareholders. In addition to Hungarian taxpayers being responsible for the rent, refurbishing, and security of the new headquarters (as per the revised establishing agreement), diplomatic immunity means that the Hungarian state would not be able to enter the building without prior authorisation; the IIB is endowed with the capacity to bring non-EU persons into the EU without EU consent (Marianna and Zoltán 2019).

The IIB Council, comprised of member representatives, leads the IIB. It is managed by a Board, appointed by the Council. The current Chairperson of the Board is Nikolay Kosov, a Russian national, appointed in September 2012. Between 1977 and 1992, Kosov served in the USSR Ministry of Foreign Affairs and, between 1998 and 2007, was the First Deputy to the Chairperson of Vnesheconombank, a Russian state development corporation; Denis Ivanov, the incumbent IBEC Chairperson, served the same corporation. IIB Chairperson Kosov is supported by five Deputy Chairpersons and over 160 staff members.

The IIB primarily finances loans through national financial institutions, development banks, and export-import banks. It also co-finances projects with other MDBs and national financial institutions. In 2018, net projects approvals were largely for financial services (26%), power generation and transmission (24.1%), and rent and leasing (16.2%) (IIB 2018). Between 1970 and 2019, the IIB financed over 280 investment projects totalling €9 billion. Given that the IIB financed $7 billion during its Cold War era, this demonstrates that the IIB has quickly rebuilt its portfolio since restructuring in 2012.

In summary, the IIB demonstrates the centrality of geopolitics to the role and functioning of MDBs. While all MDBs position themselves as financial institutions promoting economic growth through investments, they are also geopolitical actors representing the interests of their member countries. The IIB nearly dissolved during the 1990s and 2000s as its relevance in promoting socialist integration collapsed. Still, like most MDBs, it did not disappear, and it has been able to reinvent itself with strong leadership. It is now an active and interesting DFI worthy of further research.

7.7 West African Development Bank

A study submitted to the WAMU Council of Ministers in December 1970 recommended that part of the income generated by the Central Bank of West African States (BCEAO), inaugurated in 1959, should be directed to initiatives promoting West African regional integration. During a March 1973 WAMU Council meeting, the chairperson responsible for reforming WAMU introduced a draft agreement for establishing a West African development bank. Like many MDBs, the agreement was signed quickly and on 14 November 1973 BOAD (in French: Banque Ouest Africaine de Développement) was founded, but it only became operational in 1976. When first established, it operated as the MDB of WAMU. On 1 August 1994, BOAD became a specialised and autonomous body of the West African Economic and Monetary Union (WAEMU), comparable to the EADB operating as the financial pillar of the EAC. Its current mission is to promote the balanced development of WAEMU member countries and contribute to the economic integration of West Africa, which mirrors the mission of other SRDBs.

There are several sub-regional organisations pursuing West African regional integration, a history dating back to French colonial rule (Quah 2016). After the Second World War, 'former French colonies and France set up a monetary arrangement in the form of the CFAF zone. The CFAF zone comprises… countries grouped into two monetary unions, WAEMU and' the Central African Economic and Monetary Community (CEMAC) (Tsangarides and Qureshi 2008, 1262). The CFAF (in French: Communauté Financière d'Afrique Franc) is the currency issued by the BCEAO, with the West African Bank performing functions similar to a central bank since November 1962 (Bhatia 1985). While West Africa is like East Africa in that sub-regional organisations soon followed decolonisation, the region is unique due to the relationship maintained with its former colonial power, France (Ouedraogo 2013).

The BOAD originally only had regional member countries, but today has 17 shareholders. From WAEMU, BOAD's members are Benin, Burkina Faso, Côte d'Ivoire, Guinea Bissau, Mali, Niger, Senegal, and Togo. The BCEAO is also a shareholder, demonstrating the BOAD's position as part of a sub-regional arrangement. WAEMU members hold over 93% shareholding. The other shareholders are an eclectic mix of MDBs (the AfDB and European Investment Bank (EIB)), national governments (France, Belgium, and Morocco), and the People's Bank of China, Eximbank of India, German state-owned development bank KfW, together holding over 60% shareholding. The non-regional shareholders reveal the continued influence of former European colonial powers, notably France, since decolonisation, as well as the need for smaller Global South-led MDBs to build their capital and creditworthiness via the admission of wealthier non-regional countries and banks. When BOAD's membership was restricted to regional members, it had limited capacity to raise funds on bond markets. But, since admitting non-regional shareholders, it has grown. In 2016, BOAD made one of the largest American dollar bond debuts of a West African organisation with a $750 million five-year trade, made possible by the inclusion of non-regional shareholders.

Christian Adovelande of Benin is BOAD's incumbent President. Before taking office in February 2011, he served as Vice President of Ecobank Transnational Incorporated Group (a pan-African regional banking group operating in West and Central Africa) between 2009 and 2011 and President of the EBID from 2002 to 2011; indeed, his resume reveals a leadership history in West African integration. As of December 2018, BOAD employed 295 employees, revealing it is a relatively small SRDB. President Adovelande was preceded by Abdoulaye Bio-Tchané of Benin from 2008 to 2010, who led the IMF's African Division between 2002 and 2007, illustrating the common trend of senior staff movement between international organisations.

The BOAD initially lent only to regional member governments but since 2002 it has provided loans to the private sector for development projects of regional significance, as well as lines of credit to small and medium enterprises (SMEs). In other words, it is following trends set by the World Bank. It has also funded debt-relief programmes on the basis that funds saved are diverted to health programmes, education, and infrastructure improvements. Between 1976 and 2018, it approved $8.82 billion through 1,149 operations. Annual approvals fluctuated from $500 to $900 million between 2008 and 2016 with an average of 40 operations approved each year. This reveals average loan sizes to be quite small for an MDB, between $10 and $20 million. In 2018, over 92% of financing was for direct loans, with the remaining 8% for refinancing and equity investments, and there was a 58% to 42% split between non-commercial and commercial loans.

In promoting regional integration and solidarity, the BOAD focusses on three priorities: infrastructure (communications, hydraulic equipment, and electricity), rural and industrial sector productive improvements, and project preparation studies. In 2016, its strategic areas included accelerating regional integration through sustained infrastructure financing, support for inclusive growth, food security, and sustainable development, and support for businesses and governments (BOAD 2016).

In summary, the BOAD is embedded within a larger sub-regional architecture and, while this is common among SRDBs, few of those systems are still functioning; West Africa is the positive exception. Despite being small in size, it has played an influential role in promoting West African regional integration (Ouedraogo 2013). Its size and scope are not insubstantial when understood as relative to its region and the 2016 US dollar bond debut revealed it to be a leading financial organisation in West Africa. Still like many of the other small MDBs, the BOAD has suffered from personnel constraints, issues related to borrower creditworthiness, and project problems like a long lag-time between project assignment and implementation.

7.8 FONPLATA Development Bank

The River Plate Basin Treaty dates to the February 1967 Joint Declaration of Buenos Aires, when the five River Plate countries – Argentina, Bolivia, Brazil, Paraguay, and Uruguay – proposed to better coordinate their regional interactions. In April 1969, the Treaty was formalised with the overarching purpose of organising studies, programmes, and works to better manage water resources, industries, and financial actions along shared borders and areas of common interest. The Plate Basin Financial Development Fund was established by the River Plate countries on 12 June 1974 when its Articles of Agreement were signed; the Articles entered into force on 14 October 1976 and the Fund commenced operations in 1977, becoming the third Latin American SRDB after the CABEI and CAF. An extension of the River Plate Basin Treaty, the Fund served sub-regional integration, acting as the Treaty's financial mechanism (Ocampo and Titelman 2009, 2012).

In November 2018, the Fund renamed itself the FONPLATA Development Bank through revisions to its Constitutive Agreement, which were an attempt to better reflect its growth into a fully fledged MDB over the 2010s. This growth was achieved by creating the office of Executive President in 2010, significantly increasing subscribed capital in 2013 and 2016, and quadrupling annual loan approvals. Over its history, the World Bank, IADB, and CAF have co-financed Fund projects (Ocampo and Titelman 2009) and, during the 2010s, it explored new relationships, including signing a memorandum of strategic cooperation with the NDB in April 2017 (Shelepov and Andronova 2018). In addition, while previously regarded as among the 'less transparent funding bodies' (Pieck 2011, 195), it has recently followed more established MDBs in creating robust transparency and accountability mechanisms. The FONPLATA Bank of the 2010s is a stable and influential MDB, whereas previously it operated as an opaque funding window.

As per its new Constitutive Agreement, the 'purpose of FONPLATA shall be to support the integration and harmonious and inclusive development of the member countries for their better integration within the region and the global market by funding studies, projects, programs, assistance, and technical advice' (FONPLATA 2018b). Broadly reflecting the mandates of other SRDBs, it is unique in stating that its purpose is both regional and global market integration.

FONPLATA has five member countries. The two largest shareholders are Argentina and Brazil, with 33.3% voting power each, followed by Bolivia, Paraguay, and Uruguay with 11.1% each. The SRDB is thus wholly owned by borrowing member countries (Humphrey 2019). Despite this, its Constitutive Agreement allows non-founding members and agencies to join, although none have so far. With a stable A- credit rating and $3 billion authorised capital, it is uncertain what additional shareholders could offer the SRDB, as well as what the MDB could offer new entrants, a dilemma reflected in the current membership of the NDB.

Juan E. Notaro Fraga is FONPLATA's incumbent Executive President. A Uruguayan economist and agricultural engineer, Notaro was elected in 2012 and re-elected in 2017; he will vacate office in 2022, as per term limits. Prior to his appointment, Notaro was Deputy Secretary of the IADB from 2008 to 2012 and before that Executive Director for Uruguay on the Boards of Directors of the World Bank and IADB. Uncharacteristically for an MDB, the position of Executive President was only created in 2010, with Fotaro being the first appointee; the creation of the presidency was an attempt to revitalise the SRDB. In a June 2019 editorial, Notaro (2019) detailed key issues affecting the River Plate Basin, including the population doubling since the 1970s and challenges related to literacy, infant mortality, poverty, and economic growth, commenting that FONPLATA,

> with its renewed strategy and the support of its member countries, is focused on becoming increasingly important by supporting the development agendas of our countries. In the last six years, we have approved more projects than in the previous 39 years, totalling a higher amount than all funding granted by this institution since 1974. We have also formed alliances with other development banks and opened our institution to new partners.

This statement highlights that the SRDB is following standard banking norms to renew its legitimacy in a crowded field of public and private development finance, through specialisation as an MDB focussed on sub-regional integration.

FONPLATA's first capital replenishment was approved in 2013, which more than doubled its authorised capital to $1.2 billion; it commenced operations with $160 million in initial contributions and in 2006 had $415 million in authorised capital (Ocampo and Titelman 2009). A second capital replenishment approved in 2016 increased its authorised capital to $3 billion, six times what was available in 2012, and paid-in capital was a high $866 million in 2019. The growth in capital led to a corresponding increase in annual approvals, from an average of $50 million prior to 2012 to $425 million in 2018.

Between 2012 and 2018, it approved $1.9 billion in new loans, more than double the amount approved from when it commenced operations (FONPLATA 2018a). Still, the average size of loans remained relatively static. To illustrate, $94.8 million in new loans was approved in 2013, with significant increases in 2016 ($315.7 million) and 2018 ($415.1 million), whereas average loans size remained between $25 and $32 million. This suggests that the number of loans approved annually increased significantly. Also, despite increasing loan numbers, sectoral priorities remained stable; for much of the 2010s, logistics and transportation accounted for 63% of new loans (FONPLATA 2018a, 2019).

As part of the 2013 and 2016 capital replenishments, FONPLATA's operational strategy shifted to focus on four development axes: national and regional integration, with an emphasis on border areas; improving the competitiveness of productive sectors; building co-financing arrangements with other development institutions; and, promoting social and economic infrastructure (FONPLATA 2019). This operational strategy reveals the SRDB to be a project-based investment bank prioritising regional integration through infrastructural development.

In summary, FONPLATA's growth during the 2010s resembles CAF's, albeit remaining a much smaller SRDB. Through organisational restructuring and an expansion of its capital base, as well as myriad other reforms, the River Plate SRDB grew from a small funding window to an influential MDB. This demonstrates the potential influence of the smaller MDBs, given requisite support and strong leadership, a recurring trend emerging from the case studies in this chapter.

7.9 ECOWAS Bank for Investment and Development

EBID is the financial arm of the Economic Community of West African States (ECOWAS). It was originally established in 1975 as the Fund for Cooperation, Compensation, and Development of the Economic Community of West African States (ECOWAS Fund) and commenced operations in 1979. In January 2004, the Fund was reorganised into EBID, which created two specialised agencies: the ECOWAS Regional Development Fund (ERDF) for financing public sector projects and the ECOWAS Regional Investment Bank (ERIB) for financing private sector projects. In June 2006, a further restructuring was approved merging ERDF and ERIB into a single organisation, so EBID has operated in its current form since January 2007. Despite the complex history of reorganisation and restructuring, EBID has many traits of the other SRDBs, including a growing significance as a sub-regional intermediary over the past two decades, a focus on public and private investment, and adaptation to mitigate limited capital availability and a poor credit rating.

The objective of EBID is to approve loans and guarantees for investment projects and programmes for the economic and social development of member states, mobilise resources inside and outside ECOWAS, provide technical assistance, and manage ECOWAS resources and special funds (EBID 2020). These objectives are very similar to the RDBs and other SRDBs and recognise that it operates as the financial arm of a formal sub-regional organisation.

There are three notable sub-regional organisations operating in West Africa: ECOWAS, WAEMU, and the West African Monetary Zone (WAMZ). Tsangarides and Qureshi (2008, 1274) identify that in addition to problematic overlap and resource duplication between the three sub-regional organisations, there are 'considerable dissimilarities in the economic characteristics of the countries in West Africa, leading to difficulties in intra-regional coordination between member countries.' ECOWAS was founded in 1975 in Lagos, Nigeria, and today has 15 member countries, eight of which are also members of WAEMU and five non-WAEMU members of ECOWAS are part of WAMZ (Robert 2004, Tsangarides and Qureshi 2008). When first established, ECOWAS' objective was 'to promote economic cooperation and integration among West African states through monetary and economic union' (Gupta 2015, 5). After a push in the mid-1980s to boost investments in industrial enterprises and other areas, the ECOWAS Treaty was revised in July 1993, an attempt to further formalise the sub-regional grouping and accelerate integration; the 'revised document was far more detailed than its predecessor and clearly listed the powers of officials. More than just a statement, it was a descriptive and regulating treaty' (Gupta 2015, 8).

Nigeria was the driving force behind the economic and political expansion of ECOWAS and proposed sending soldiers under the authority of the sub-regional organisation to restore peace in Liberia, Sierra Leone, and Guinea Bissau (Yabi 2010). The influence of Nigeria over ECOWAS is large, even if it is not always successful in its political manoeuvres (Momodu 2018). Given a population 'estimated to be 300 million in 2015, representing 35% of the total population of sub-Saharan Africa' (Aglina, Agbejule, and Nyamuame 2016, 333), and three quarters of its member countries 'identified among the world's least developed countries' (Robert 2004, 5), ECOWAS is not an insignificant institutional arrangement and EBID is its financial arm.

The EBID has 15 member countries. The largest shareholder by far is Nigeria, with 31.34% shareholding, followed by Ghana (15.71%) and Côte d'Ivoire (14.76%). Together, these three member countries hold almost 62% shareholding, meaning they effectively control the SRDB. The remaining shareholders hold from just over 6% (as in the case of Liberia) to less than 1% (as held by Cabo Verde). While entirely controlled by borrowing member states, there is great disparity in corporate influence. In 2016, EBID's Board representation was divided into an ECOWAS Commission Observer and individual representatives for Nigeria, Ghana, and Côte d'Ivoire, while the remaining countries were clustered into Group I, II, and III representative groups with four countries represented in each group.

Following the June 2006 reorganisation of its current structure, EBID doubled its authorised capital from $800 million to $1.5 billion in 2011, enabling it to expand its lending operations – still, this is half of FONPLATA with a much larger population covered. Despite the capital increase, however, EBID had not received an international credit rating until 2018 when Moody's (2018) assigned a first-time foreign currency issuer rating, allocating the SRDB a B+ credit rating with a negative outlook.

EBID's incumbent President is Ghanaian Dr. George Agyekum Nana Donkor, who took office in February 2020. Prior to his appointment, President Donkor served as EBID Vice President of Finance, Administration, and Corporate Services for several years. He was preceded by Nigerian Bashir Mamman Ifo (2011–20), who held several senior positions in EBID from 1995, including Acting Managing Director of ERIB. These two appointments suggest a recent preference for internal promotion as opposed to external recruitment.

In 2017, EBID approved 12 projects for $141.8 million, nine of which were private sector loans and the remaining three public sector. Infrastructure is the largest sector financed by the SRDB, with it having 'contributed to the funding of most of the West African highway network, linking Nouakchott in Mauritania and Lagos in Nigeria, and linking Dakar in Senegal and N'Djamena in Chad, providing the interconnecting roads between the two highways' (EBID 2008, 8). Between 1979 and 2017, it approved 266 projects totalling $2.33 billion, revealing it to be a small SRDB comparable to the BDEAC, with both originally established in 1975, currently comprised of 12–15 member countries, and $2 billion or less in authorised capital. Eligibility to receive financial assistance requires the applicant to be an ECOWAS member and its largest borrowers (in order) are Benin, Senegal, Togo, Mali, and Guinea.

In summary, EBID follows the trend of several other SRDBs in acting as the financial arm of a sub-regional organisation. It was a minor MDB for many decades due to shareholder conflict and limited access to capital markets. Like many other SRDBs, however, economic growth in its region has renewed its relevance.

7.10 Development Bank of Central African States

The BDEAC (in French: *Banque de Développement des États de l'Afrique Centrale*) is a small SRDB operating in Central Africa, comparable to EBID. It was established through an agreement signed in December 1975 and commenced operations in January 1977. The SRDB finances development projects in CEMAC member states and prioritises regional integration, transport and energy infrastructure, and education, health, and social development. Given its position as a leading Central African financial organisation, it has close relations with the Bank of Central African States (BEAC), which is a leading BDEAC shareholder. The BEAC was founded in 1972, its official currency is the Central African CFAF, and its responsibilities include conducting CEMAC monetary and exchange rate policy. A 2019 audit by the Central African Banking Commission (COBAC) revealed concerns about BEAC's large exposure to BDEAC and recommended that the central bank refrain from providing additional financing to the SRDB until substantive reforms were implemented (IMF 2019). This demonstrates concerns about the financial health of the Central African community.

The Central African SRDB's shareholders are diverse. There are six regional member states – Cameroon, Central African Republic, Republic of Congo, Gabon, Chad, and Equatorial Guinea – that each hold 8.48% voting share, totalling close to 51%. Like the West African SRDBs, BDEAC's regional members are francophone African states. The BEAC is also a regional shareholder, holding 33.43% voting power, which means that BDEAC is largely owned by a sub-regional central bank, which is rare for an MDB and reveals that BDEAC is part of a larger sub-regional grouping. In addition, BDEAC has five non-regional shareholders: the AfDB and the governments of France, Kuwait, Libya, and Morocco. The non-regional members hold around 2% shareholding collectively. Unusual for an MDB, 14% of shares are not yet subscribed.

The Chairperson of the Board of Directors leads BDEAC. The incumbent Chairperson is Fortunato Ofa Mbo Nchama of Equatorial Guinea who took office in March 2017 and who previously served as the Second Deputy Secretary of the Democratic Party of Equatorial Guinea. His predecessor was Abbas Mahamat Tolli of Chad, who assumed office in 2015 but left two years later to become BEAC Governor. Tolli had the difficult task of restoring BDEAC's reputation in the aftermath of his predecessor Michaël Adandé's turbulent tenure. Adandé became Chairperson in 2011 and led the MDB into significant failures and personal scandal, calling into question BDEAC's capacity to operate. In 2014 and 2015, two successive bond issues totalling €107 million by Adandé failed to meet their targets, damaging BDEAC's fragile reputation. After these failures, Adandé dismissed the financial management team, two days before it was announced that the Board had asked him to resign (Mbadi 2015). In addition, Adandé had public conflict with BDEAC Vice President André Nzapayéké, 'with reciprocal accusations of mismanagement, the two men no longer speak to each other and criticise each other' (Soudan 2013). While the larger MDBs have not been without scandal, such problems can severely undermine smaller SRDBs. Ben-Artzi (2016) argued that MDBs need one key shareholder that takes a key interest in operations to ensure they are well governed. In BDEAC's case, however, BEAC – as its largest shareholder – has also been mired in corruption scandals, including in 2010 when 'top-ranking Gabonese officials in the BEAC were found to have embezzled millions, giving much of the money to members of France's two main political parties' (Ryan 2010); they were said to have embezzled $36 million over a five-year period.

Between 1977 and 2017, BDEAC approved 194 loans totalling $1.8 billion, as well as 44 studies and four equity investments (BDEAC 2018). It is a small MDB in terms of annual approvals, reflecting its small borrowing membership and capital base. BOAD, which is similar in size, structure, and membership, has been far more effective – BDEAC financed 170 projects between 1976 and 2013 while BOAD approved 697 over the same period (Mbadi 2015). In 2016, BDEAC approved five lending operations – four projects and one renewal of guarantee, totalling $185 million, disbursed as agriculture, transportation, and agro-industry investments. In 2017, most lending operations in progress were BBB to CCC credit rated, with only a couple reaching A- and some D rated; this demonstrates the loan portfolio to be vulnerable, making it difficult for the MDB itself to acquire a credit rating.

In summary, BDEAC demonstrates the difficulties smaller SRDBs can face when operating in low resource environments, including problems of leadership and financial stability and credibility. While other SRDBs have been able to address such difficulties and improve their standing, BDEAC remains troubled.

7.11 Eastern and Southern African Trade and Development Bank

The PTA Bank was formed in November 1985 following the 1981 Treaty Establishing the Preferential Trade Area (PTA), which became the COMESA in December 1994. It is the first of a sub-set of SRDBs that focus on trade finance as much as (and sometimes more than) development and regional integration. Trade finance, with short maturities assisting profitability, offers small SRDBs a useful niche. As COMESA's financial arm, the SRDB operated under its legal name – the Eastern and Southern Trade and Development Bank – and had two trading names: the PTA Bank in English and *Banque de la ZEP* in French. A 'modest' SRDB for its first two decades, by 1999 it 'had a small portfolio, a very high stock of non-performing loans… and substantial difficulties in finding projects to fund due to the moribund state of regional trade and lack of interest by borrowers' (Humphrey 2019, 169). After 2000, however, it began to institute organisational reforms, expand membership to include additional regional as well as non-regional members, and rally its credit rating. In May 2016, the SRDB's Board of Governors approved rebranding the MDB as the TDB and developed a new logo, which became effective in 2017; the name change, as with CAF, can be interpreted as a 'soft reboot' to reflect new priorities. The TDB is today the second largest MDB operating in Africa behind the AfDB and the largest borrower-led 'minilateral development bank' (Humphrey 2019, 166).

The TDB's current mission is to 'be at the forefront of extending reliable financial & non-financial services to advance trade, development, and regional economic integration through customer-focused and innovative instruments' (TDB 2018, ix). The focus on regional integration is comparable to the RDBs and other SRDBs, while the prioritisation on innovative financial instruments reflects the World Bank agenda but is notable given that it remains a small SRDB with an uncertain capital base and credit rating. Indeed, the TDB has long struggled to strengthen its credit rating, given the major shareholders providing its callable capital have low ratings with many dependent on foreign aid to support their foreign currency needs (Humphrey 2019, 171–2).

Membership in TDB is open to COMESA and non-COMESA countries, non-regional countries, and institutional and banking shareholders. When it first commenced operations, it had nine regional members, whereas today it has 36 shareholders: 22 regional, two non-regional, and 12 institutional members. With membership expanding since 2000, it added several regional members in the mid-2010s, most recently Madagascar in 2018. The non-regional members are the National Bank of Belarus and People's Bank of China, the latter joining in 2000. The institutional members are a diverse mix of banking and financial institutions, including the AfDB, Arab Bank for Economic Development in Africa (BADEA), and OPEC Fund for International Development (OFID), as well as African insurance, pension, and social security funds. Humphrey (2019, 175) argues that the expansion of membership was

> (1) to strengthen the bank's capital base and hence lending capacity; (2) to bring in new borrowing countries to diversify and de-risk the loan portfolio; and (3) to bring in shareholders with higher sovereign ratings to strengthen TDB's own credit rating.

TDB's capital stock subscriptions are divided into Class A and Class B shares. Class A shares are owned by regional member countries and the AfDB, while Class B shares are owned by non-regional and institutional members, as well as the AfDB, which holds shares in both classes. Class A shares have a par value of $22,667 and Class B $4,533.40. In 2018, Class A authorised capital was $2 billion, Class B was $1 billion, and paid-up capital was $357 million (Class A) and $105 million (Class B). The largest Class A shareholders are Egypt, Ethiopia, and Kenya holding 8.61% each, while China is the largest Class B shareholder with 15.39%. The two classes were the consequence of share structure reforms enacted in December 2012, designed to draw in new capital. As a result, Humphrey (2019, 169) argues,

> no member even comes close to veto power in the boards of governors or directors, which generally require a simple majority – or, in special cases, a two-thirds majority – for decision-making. This has led to a relatively harmonious environment on the boards where, according to senior management, most issues are decided by consensus.

Adamassu Tadesse of Ethiopia is the current TDB President, assuming office in April 2012. Building on the legacy of his predecessor Michael Gondwe of Zambia who began the expansion of membership and escalation of annual trade finance approvals as well as reducing non-performing loans from over 20% in 2005 to 5% when he left office (Humphrey 2019, 179), President Tadesse further reformed TDB's organisation and operations. In recognition of his achievements, Tadesse was awarded the 2019 African Banker of the Year Award at the African Banker Awards. Tadesse's achievements include growing equity capital and annual profits four-fold and assets five-fold between 2012 and 2019 and, in 2017, TDB received its first investment grade ratings from Moody's and Global Credit Ratings, Africa's largest ratings agency. In addition, TDB attracted 15 new shareholders, both regional countries and pension and insurance funds. As Tadesse comments, 'It is fair to say the Bank has shot out the lights in terms of its strategy and corporate plan targets' (cited in Africa Fintech Summit 2019).

TDB provides two main lending instruments. First, Project and Infrastructure Finance, a long-term lending window that finances projects with a tenor of up to 15 years and, second, Trade Finance, a short-term lending window financing projects up to three years. Over the past two decades, Trade Finance has by far become the lead lending stream. Project and Infrastructure Finance grew from $176 million in annual approvals in 2008 to $323 million in 2016. In contrast, Trade Finance grew from $118 million in 2006 to $3.27 billion in 2012 and has maintained an annual average of over $3 billion since 2012. Humphrey (2019) argues that the expansion of Trade Finance is because it is safer than project finance in terms of repayment and it is easier to structure transactions. Trade Finance also capitalises on TDB's new relationships with commercial banks in OECD countries. This innovation in lending is indicative of the most successful SRDBs, particularly those with lower credit ratings and capital bases.

In summary, the expansion of TDB during the 2010s resembles that of CAF, although the Latin American SRDB is greater in size and influence. Both saw a considerable expansion in membership, growth in annual approvals, and development in regional stature to rival the more established RDBs in their regions, although TDB lags behind AfDB while CAF's lending trajectory may lead it to outperform IADB over the coming decade. Still, TDB is a model of what small a SRBD in Africa can achieve with the right membership and leadership.

7.12 Pacific Islands Development Bank

The PIDB was established in July 1989 by the Association of Pacific Island Legislatures, following a proposal to create a Pacific Islands MDB unanimously endorsed by the Association in May 1987. The Association and hence the SRDB represent most US associated states in the Micronesian region of the Pacific worried that the US was going to end aid (Mak and Naya 1994). Notably, it does not cover any of the Polynesian or Melanesian Pacific Island states. PIDB was founded to address insufficient financial assistance to the region from existing MDBs and private investors and to specialise in addressing the needs and challenges of the Pacific Islands. Mirroring other SRDBs, the 'mission and purpose of the Bank is to contribute to the acceleration of the process of economic and social development of the member states and nation, individually and collectively, and to promote economic cooperation among them' (PIDB 2019b).

The SRDB is wholly owned by nine Micronesian borrowing members: Marshall Islands (21.41%), Yap (15.47%), Pohnpei (13.97%), Commonwealth of the Northern Mariana Islands (10.75%), Guam (10.75%), Palau (10.75%), Kosrae (8.81%), Kwajalein Atoll (5.37%), and Chuuk (2.71%). Its shareholders do not include all Association members; Hawaii, Nauru, and Kiribati are not part of the PIDB. While regional membership ensures a 'Pacific Islands identity,' the shareholding includes many of world's least developed countries that suffer problems associated with small island developing states (Tisdell 2002). This is reflected in the SRDB's relatively microscopic capital of $9.3 million, which limits the PIDB's reach and impact. It is by a far margin the smallest MDB in terms of capital structure and annual loan approvals.

A Board of Governors, Board of Executive Directors, and senior management govern PIDB, like the other MDBs. Each shareholder appoints two representatives to the Board of Governors, with most responsibility delegated to the nine-member Board of Directors. The PIDB President manages day-to-day operations supported by managers of administration and of loans, both of whom are appointed by the President and respectively oversee corporate administration and the lending portfolio. The incumbent President is Christopher A. Cruz, who assumed office on 16 December 2019. He succeeded Aren Palik, who led PIDB for two decades. President Cruz previously worked in the Bank of Guam, beginning as a management trainee in 2007 before being promoted to credit officer in 2008. In 2012, he was promoted to assistant vice president and branch manager of the Bank of Guam's Pohnpei branch, before being promoted to vice president and relationship banking manager in 2014, a post he held until joining the PIDB as president. Cruz's professional resume is a notable exception from other MDB presidents, who mostly come from political or senior government roles or from senior roles in large commercial banks.

The PIDB is a unique MDB in that it approves residential home and consumer loans, as well as private sector commercial loans. While consumer loans are small in financial amount (usually $500–$25,000), they are the bulk of its portfolio. In 2013, 93 of 129 approved projects were consumer loans, totalling just over $1 million of the $4.8 million commitments that year (PIDB 2014). Commercial loans are the largest loans approved in size, with 69% of loans approved in 2016 being commercial loans (PIDB 2017). The minimum commercial loan size is $20,000, with the maximum determined by equity capital allocated by country. In 2016, outstanding loans by sector divided into commercial loans ($8 million), residential home loans ($2.3 million), and consumer loans ($1.34 million). The year 2018 saw a large increase in new loans: 67 loans totalling $6.6 million. This is considerably larger than the 38 loans totalling $2.9 million approved in 2017 (PIDB 2019a). The difference between the two years derives from a doubling of residential home loans (in number and total financing amount), as well as an increase in commercial tourism loans from $9,000 to $3.4 million, which may turn out to be a problem for the PIDB given the impact of COVID-19 on tourism.

In summary, the PIDB is a very small SRDB, with significant resource and geographical limitations. Despite these challenges, it is an important organisation for member states that, like other Pacific Islands and small island developing states more generally, are poorly represented in MDBs, both in terms of shareholding and annual lending allocations. The PIDB is also a good illustration of the innovation often demonstrated in other SRDBs in response to the needs of their region; in this case, providing consumer and residential loans. In 1994, Mak and Naya (1994, 40) commented that the:

> constraint on the development of the Pacific Islands is not funding alone but lies in each country's (in)ability to use aid efficiently, promote private sector development, implement appropriate policy reforms, [and] develop human resources to build the capacity for policy analysis and development management.'

There is some truth in this. However, it also demonstrates a major limitation of MDBs; they are based on the idea that capitalist-led development is the only path and the limits of this view become clear when looking at sustainable paths for most small island developing nations.

7.13 Black Sea Trade and Development Bank

The BSTDB was established by the 11 member countries of the Black Sea Economic Cooperation (BSEC) sub-regional community as BSEC's financial pillar. Its Establishing Agreement was signed in 1994 and entered into force in 1997. The SRDB commenced operations in June 1999. Both BSEC and BSTDB are post-Cold War entities, emerging from attempts to build economic and political connections while avoiding regional antagonisms during post-Soviet transition (Manoli 2013). Following the collapse of the Soviet bloc, many Black Sea countries

> found themselves in an unprecedented situation to the extent that their existing economic structures became inappropriate virtually overnight for the open and competitive business environment to which they were now exposed. This has constituted a challenge for the Black Sea region, while at the same time providing it with ample opportunities to become part of an economically integrated global playing field.
>
> (Imre 2006, 243)

As per the BSTDB's (2011) Establishing Agreement, its purpose is

> to effectively contribute to the transition process of the Member States towards the economic prosperity of the people of the region and to finance and promote regional projects and provide other banking services to projects of the public and private sectors in the Member States and trade activities among the Member States.

Thus, it reflects the SRDBs and SRDBs in promoting regional integration, but the language also suggests a commercial bank focus, like the IIB and EDB.

BSEC was created with the signing of the Istanbul Summit Declaration and Bosphorus Statement in June 1992 and its Charter entered into force on 1 May 1999, one month before the BSTDB began operations. In addition to the BSTDB, BSEC has developed other sub-regional bodies, including its Parliamentary Assembly, Business Council, and International Centre for Black Sea Studies. Despite this, BSEC is an 'unassertive' sub-regional body and does not

> seem to be actively tackling the key problems for its aims, neither has it built up its own capacity for action, increased the coherence or unity among the BSEC family, or given substance to the idea of Black Sea integration.
>
> (Hajizada 2014, 117)

This is problematic given regional conflicts, ongoing economic crises, political instability in Ukraine, and the Russian annexation of Crimea (Vladova and Knieling 2014) but perhaps also reflects these constraints.

There are 11 BSTDB shareholders, including EU and non-EU member countries (Imre 2006). Russia, Turkey, and Greece are the largest shareholders, each holding 16.6% of voting power, followed by Romania (14.1%) and Bulgaria and Ukraine (13.6% each). The remaining shareholders – Azerbaijan, Albania, Armenia, Georgia, and Moldova – collectively hold the residual capital share. In addition, BSTDB has a dozen observer institutions that can attend and communicate in annual meetings and are involved in loan co-financing. These institutions include the AsDB, EBRD, EIB, IFC, IIB, and NIB, as well as national development banks such as the Development Bank of Austria and Russian Development Bank. Many of these observers hold AAA credit ratings, which is beneficial to BSTDB when approving co-financed loans. It also demonstrates that BSTDB has been very active in building networks with other MDBs.

Notably, while BSTDB's authorised capital remained the same between 2008 and 2019 (€3.45 billion), the proportion of subscribed, callable, and paid-in capital increased. In 2008, subscribed capital was €1.1 billion, callable capital was €805 million, and paid-in capital €345 million. By 2019, subscribed capital increased to €2.29 billion, callable to €1.6 billion, and paid-in to €687 million. As a result, its financial standing improved over the 2010s, with the capital increases coinciding with its credit rating rallying from BBB+ to A-.

Six Presidents have led the BSTDB, all of whom have served single four-year terms. All Presidents have been either Turkish or Russian, suggesting that Turkey and Russia are the leading influencers in the SRDB, despite Greece holding equal shareholding. This is reinforced by the fact that Turkey and Russia have been the two largest recipients of BSTDB financial assistance, receiving over 22% and 18% respectively between 1999 and 2018.

Between 1999 and 2009, BSTDB financed 161 operations in its member countries totalling $2 billion. In contrast, between 2009 and 2018, it financed 238 operations totalling over $3.8 billion. This demonstrates not only an increase in operations but an increase in the average size of approved projects. Between 1999 and 2018, the financial sector cumulatively received the largest percentage of loan approvals (42.8%), revealing BSTDB's persona as a 'commercial' MDB. Its products and services include short- and long-term loans, trade finance, credit lines to SMEs, equity investments, guarantees, and co-financing.

In summary, BSTDB greatly resembles the IIB and EDB, all three of which are greatly influenced by Russia. The main similarities between the three SRDBs are that they are a mix between a commercial bank and an MDB and they are post-Soviet regional integration initiatives.

7.14 ECO Trade and Development Bank

The Economic Cooperation Organisation (ECO) is a formal regional body founded by Iran, Pakistan, and Turkey in 1985. It is the successor to the Regional Cooperation for Development that operated from 1964 to 1979, which ceased to function following the 1979 Iranian Revolution. Despite being established in 1985, ECO was non-functional until 1991, when its foundational treaty was altered, leading it to become a fully fledged organisation. In 1992, following the end of the Cold War and dissolution of the Soviet Union, ECO admitted several new members, including Afghanistan, Azerbaijan, Kazakhstan, Kyrgyzstan, Tajikistan, Turkmenistan, and Uzbekistan (Javaid and Siahmardy 2017); there are now ten ECO member countries. An important aspect of ECO has been the gradual dismantling of tariff barriers 'to promote intra-regional trade and gradual integration of the region with global markets' (Ali and Khalid 2015, 14033). After the 1992 expansion of membership, the founding ECO members – Iran, Pakistan, and Turkey – signed Articles of Agreement to establish the ETDB in March 1995. However, it would not be until August 2005 that the Articles were ratified. The ETDB commenced operations in 2008.

As per the ETDB's (2005) Articles of Agreement, the 'Bank shall mobilise resources for the purposes of initiating, promoting, and providing financial facilities to expand intra-regional trade and accelerate economic development of ECO member countries.' These purposes are pursued through project financing, cooperation with other financial institutions, special funds, and related banking activities. It is notable that technical assistance is not explicitly stated, with the functions prioritising banking activities. The SRDB's vision is to 'become the financial pillar of economic cooperation among ECO member states by fostering sustainable economic development and integration' (ETDB 2018, 6), and its mission is to promote private and public sector investment, foster intra-regional trade, contribute to economic and social development for the welfare of people in the ECO region, and promote good governance and environmental consciousness, a mission transferrable with most of the other MDBs.

There are six ETDB shareholders – membership eligibility is restricted to ECO member countries and the Bank has encouraged the four remaining ECO members to join. Iran, Pakistan, and Turkey are the main shareholders, each controlling 30.6% of voting power. The remaining 8% is divided between Afghanistan (4.59%), Azerbaijan (2.98%), and Kyrgyzstan (0.61%). The ECO's three founding members clearly dominate the SRDB, reflected further in that ETDB is headquartered in Istanbul, Turkey, and has two representative offices: one in Iran and one in Pakistan. As small SRDB, it employed just 38 staff in December 2017.

The incumbent ETDB President is Yalçın Yüksel, a Turkish national, who assumed office in November 2019, his previous position being Acting Director General of Public Finance at the Turkish Ministry of Treasury and Finance. President Yüksel succeeded President Javaid Aslam, a Pakistani national, who was appointed in 2015 and who previously served as Secretary to the Prime Minister of Pakistan. President Aslam was preceded by Iranian Hossein Ghazavi, who took office in 2011 and who was previously First Vice Governor of the Iran Central Bank. The three main ETDB members have rotated their presidential leadership. As per the ETDB's Articles, the term of the first president was five years while each subsequent president is appointed for four-year terms.

Between 2008 and 2017, ETDB approved $1.3 billion in loans to its member countries; but disbursements totalled $507 million, meaning that a large portion of approved loans are awaiting disbursement. The SRDB offers project, corporate, trade, and SME finance and co-financing and soft loans. Priority sectors are transportation, agricultural infrastructure, and energy, with a focus on intra-regional integration. Over its first decade, the geographical focus of operations disproportionately focussed on the three main shareholders: Turkey (58.2%), Iran (18.8%), and Pakistan (18.6%); over 95% of all approvals (Engen and Prizzon 2018).

In summary, the ETDB reflects the traits of other small-scale MDBs, notably its narrow membership, capital base, annual approvals, and absent credit rating. It is part of a sub-regional organisation but largely serves the three main shareholders. Given its reliance on these states, its continuing operations are largely contingent on the capacity of Turkey, Iran, and Pakistan to coordinate.

7.15 Eurasian Development Bank

Eurasian regional integration has progressed gradually since the collapse of the Soviet Union. While initiatives were stalled during the 1990s, due to successive banking and financial crises impacting transitioning economies, important strides were made late in the decade and throughout the 2000s and 2010s. In 1999, a treaty was signed by several Eurasian countries to establish in future the Eurasian Customs Union and Single Economic Space, followed in 2000 with the founding of the Eurasian Economic Community (EURASEC), which was based on the EEC (Vinokurov 2018). The Eurasian Customs Union became effective in January 2010, conceived as a mechanism to integrate former Soviet states. In January 2012, the Eurasian Economic Space became effective. Both were followed by the Eurasian Economic Union (EAEU), signed in May 2014 and effective in January 2015. As part of the complex emergent architecture of Eurasian integration, the EDB became an important financial pillar, acting as part of a 'new wave' of integration tools offering institutional support to economic ties (Vinokurov 2018, 5).

The EDB was established in 2006 with a $1.5 billion capital base at the initiative of Russian President Vladimir Putin and Kazakh President Nursultan Nazarbayev. Its Articles outline the SRDB's purposes as to 'foster the strengthening and development of market economy in the member states… and to enhance trade and economic integration among them by engaging in investment activities' (EDB 2006). Its responsibilities are largely the promotion of financial and economic cooperation, very much following the IIB and BSTDB conservative investment bank format.

There are six EDB member countries. In addition to founding shareholders Russia and Kazakhstan, Armenia, Belarus, Kyrgyzstan, and Tajikistan joined between 2009 and 2011. In practice, Russia and Kazakhstan effectively control the Bank, not surprising given that Russia holds 65.97% capital share and Kazakhstan 32.99%. The remaining shareholders own just over 1% collectively. Alongside the IIB and BSTDB, the EDB is the third SRDB operating as an extension of Russian foreign and economic policy.

A Chairperson leads the EDB. To date, three Chairpersons have led it, all of whom have been Russian. The first was Igor Finogenov, in office from 2006 to 2015, who prior to his appointment was a commercial banker. Dmitry Pankin succeeded Finogenov in 2015 but remained in office only for two years before being appointed the incumbent BSTDB President. Andrey Belyaninov succeeded Pankin in December 2017 (Vinokurov 2018).

In 2018, EDB's cumulative lending portfolio held 85 projects: 84 projects in its member countries and one direct investment fund participation project. By 2020, its cumulative loan portfolio totalled $8.2 billion. Electric power, finance, transport, and mining have been the main sectors financed (Vinokurov 2019). In 2018, EDB approved 29 new projects totalling $1.4 billion, highlighting that despite being a new MDB it has the capital to approve considerably larger annual commitments than most other SRDBs. Russia and Kazakhstan are historically the largest recipients of EDB finances, with 47.1% of approvals to Russia and 36.4% to Kazakhstan in 2018.

The Eurasian Fund for Stabilisation and Development (EFSD), previously known as the EURASEC Fund, was established in 2009 'as a response to the challenges of the global economic crisis' (Vinokurov 2018, 5). EDB administers EFSD's staffing, administration, and financial modelling, but final decision-making is vested in the Council of the Fund. EFSD offers financial assistance to its member countries with priority focus on anti-crisis, balance of payments, and stabilisation programmes (Vinokurov 2018, 62). It thus resembles the IMF to a degree, although its operations go beyond the IMF's mandate (Fritz and Mühlich 2019). The Fund's capital resources are $9.1 billion, with its capital drawn from contributions and not raised in capital markets. In 2019, its portfolio comprised 15 projects with $5.5 billion accumulated financial commitments, 90% of which were for budgetary support (Vinokurov, Efimov, and Levenkov 2019).

The EDB established a Technical Assistance Fund (TAF) in 2008 to provide financial support for pre-investment and innovation research, build regional integration, strengthen market infrastructures, and ensure sustainable growth. As of 2017, TAF's cumulative portfolio included 63 projects totalling $7.2 million, with the majority approved as part of investment projects (49%) and regional integration studies (34%) (EDB 2018). In addition, illustrating its focus on regional integration, EDB has developed the Integration Barometer 'to study the attitudes of citizens in member states towards the creation of the EAEU, as well as the opinions of citizens of other countries regarding the possibility of them joining the Union' (Vinokurov 2018, 57).

In summary, the EDB is a mid-tier SRDB promoting Eurasian regional integration. Comparable to the IIB and BSTDB, however, it is also a foreign policy extension of its leading shareholder – Russia – and thus mirrors the US in the World Bank and China in the AIIB. Yet, in this case, Russia is a borrowing member country and not just an organisational and decision-making hegemon. It demonstrates that playing a leading role in an MDB is an item on the checklist of many major powers and the financial resources MDBs control are politically useful.

Bibliography

Africa Fintech Summit. 2019. "5 Questions with Admassu Tadesse, President & Chief Executive of Trade and Development Bank (TDB)." https://africafintechsummit.com/2019/11/19/5-questions-with-admassu-tadesse-president-chief-executive-of-trade-and-development-bank-tdb/.

Aglina, Moses Kwame, Adebayo Agbejule, and Godwin Yao Nyamuame. 2016. "Policy Framework on Energy Access and Key Development Indicators: ECOWAS Interventions and the Case of Ghana." *Energy Policy* 97:332–42. doi: 10.1016/j.enpol.2016.07.012.

Ali, Muhammad, and Nooreen Khalid. 2015. An Analytical Study of Economic Cooperation Organization (ECO): Challenges and Perspectives. *European Academic Research* 2 (11): 14031–14045.

Banda, Lufeyo. 2015. Report on the Assessment of African Sub-Regional Development Banks' Contribution to Infrastructure Development. The Infrastructure Consortium for Africa.

Baran, Alois. 1979/1980. "Origin and Development of the International Investment Bank." *Soviet and Eastern European Foreign Trade* 15 (4):79–104.

BDEAC. 2018. Annual Report 2017. Brazzaville, Republic of Congo: Development Bank of Central African States.

Ben-Artzi, Ruth. 2016. *Regional Development Banks in Comparison: Banking Strategies versus Development Goals*. Cambridge: Cambridge University Press.

Bhatia, Rattan. 1985. The West African Monetary Union: An Analytical Review. In *Occassional Papers*: International Monetary Fund.

BOAD. 2016. Annual Report 2016. Lomé, Togo: West African Development Bank.
Bourne, C. March 22, 2010. The Global Economic Crisis: Developing Economies and the Role of Multilateral Development Banks. Address by Professor Compton Bourne to the International Labour Office. Caribbean Development Bank. https://www.caribank.org/sites/default/files/publication-resources/THE%20GLOBAL%20ECONOMIC%20CRISIS_%20Geneva_March22.pdf
BSTDB. 2011. Agreement Establishing the Black Sea Trade and Development Bank. Black Sea Trade and Development Bank.
CABEI. 2015. 2015–2019 Institutional Strategy: Integrating Sustainable Development and Competitiveness. Tegucigalpa, Honduras: Central American Bank for Economic Integration.
CABEI. 2016. Annual Report 2016. Tegucigalpa, Honduras: Central American Bank for Economic Integration.
CABEI. 2020. 2020–2024 Strategic Framework: The Region's Sustainable Development Pillar. Tegucigalpa, Honduras: Central American Bank for Economic Integration.
Cáceres, Luis René. 1985. "Domestic Savings and Investment in Central American and the Role of the Central American Bank for Economic Integration." *Savings and Development* 9 (3):265–96.
Cevallos, Ricardo. 1996. "The Central American Bank for Economic Integration." *Tulane Journal of International and Comparative Law* 4 (2):245–74.
Cochrane, James D. 1965. "The Central American Bank for Economic Integration: A Descriptive Note." *Caribbean Studies* 5 (2):64–73.
Culpeper, Roy. 1997. *Titans or Behemoths?* London: Lynne Rienner.
Duvall, Donald K. 1964. "Latin American Economic Integration Developments." *International and Comparative Law Bulletin* 9 (1):34–42.
EADB. 2012. The East African Development Bank 1967–2012: 45 Years Strong, Your Partner in Development. Kampala, Uganda: East African Development Bank.
EADB. 2017. Annual Report 2017. Kampala, Uganda: East African Development Bank.
EBID. 2008. ECOWAS Zone Guide for Investors. Lomé, Togo: ECOWAS Bank for Investment and Development.
EBID. 2020. Annual Report 2019. Lomé, Togo: ECOWAS Bank for Investment and Development.
EDB. 2006. Articles of Agreement. Almaty: Eurasian Development Bank.
EDB. 2018. Annual Report 2017. Eurasian Development Bank.
Engen, Lars, and Annalisa Prizzon. 2018. A Guide to the Multilateral Development Banks. London: Overseas Development Institute.
ETDB. 2005. Articles of Agreement. Şişli: ECO Trade and Development Bank.
ETDB. 2018. Annual Report 2017. ECO Trade and Development Bank.
FONPLATA. 2018a. Annual Report 2018. Santa Cruz, Bolivia: FONPLATA Development Bank.
FONPLATA. 2018b. Financial Fund for the Development of the River Plate Basin Articles of Agreement.
FONPLATA. 2019. Annual Report 2019. Santa Cruz, Bolivia: FONPLATA Development Bank.
Francuz, Henryk. 1969. "The International Bank for Economic Cooperation." *Staff Papers (International Monetary Fund)* 16 (3):489–503.
Fritz, Barbara, and Laurissa Mühlich. 2019. "Regional Financial Arrangements in the Global Financial Safety Net: The Arab Monetary Fund and the Eurasian Fund for Stabilization and Development." *Development and Change* 50 (1):96–121. doi: 10.1111/dech.12466.

García, Enrique. 2006. "IGO Development Financing in the Andean Region." *The Brown Journal of World Affairs* 12 (2):177–89.

Gupta, Arushi. 2015. Regional Integration in West Africa: The Evolution of ECOWAS. In *Occasional Papers*: Observer Research Foundation.

Gutner, Tamar L. 2002. *Banking on the Environment: Multilateral Development Banks and Their Environmental Performance in Central and Eastern Europe*. Cambridge, MA: The MIT Press.

Hajizada, Mukhtar. 2014. "Patterns of Regional Collaboration and Institutional Cooperation Around the Black Sea." *Perceptions* XIX (3):101–21.

Hardy, Chandra. 1995. *The Caribbean Development Bank*. London: Lynne Rienner Publishers.

Humphrey, Chris. 2015a. Developmental Revolution or Bretton Woods Revisited? The Prospects of the BRICS New Development Bank and the Asian Infrastructure Investment Bank. London: Overseas Development Institute.

Humphrey, Chris. 2015b. Infrastructure Finance in the Developing World: Challenges and Opportunities for Multilateral Development Banks in 21st Century Infrastructure Finance. Seoul: The Global Green Growth Institute.

Humphrey, Chris. 2016. "The Invisible Hand: Financial Pressures and Organisational Convergence in Multilateral Development Banks." *The Journal of Development Studies* 52 (1):92–112. doi: 10.1080/00220388.2015.1075978.

Humphrey, Chris. 2017. "He Who Pays the Piper Calls the Tune: Credit Rating Agencies and Multilateral Development Banks." *The Review of International Organizations* 12 (2):281–306. doi: 10.1007/s11558-017-9271–6.

Humphrey, Chris. 2019. "'Minilateral' Development Banks: What the Rise of Africa's Trade and Development Bank Says about Multilateral Governance." *Development and Change* 50 (1):164–90. doi: 10.1111/dech.12467.

IBEC. 2018. The Updated Strategy of the International Bank for Economic Cooperation. Moscow, Russia: International Bank for Economic Cooperation.

IBEC. 2019. Annual Report 2018. Moscow, Russia: International Bank for Economic Cooperation.

IBEC. 2020. Financial Statements 2019. Moscow, Russia: International Bank for Economic Cooperation.

IIB. 2017. Development Strategy of the International Investment Bank for 2018–2022: Growing for Greater Development Impact. Moscow, Russia: International Investment Bank.

IIB. 2018. Annual Report 2018. Budapest, Hungary: International Investment Bank.

IMF. 2019. Central African Economic and Monetary Community (CEMAC). In *IMF Country Reports*. Washington, DC: International Monetary Fund.

Imre, Ahmet. 2006. "Financial Cooperation within the Black Sea Region: The Experience of the Black Sea Trade and Development Bank." *Southeast European and Black Sea Studies* 6 (2):243–55. doi: 10.1080/14683850600694312.

Ingham, Barbara, and Mark Figueroa. 2009. "W. Arthur Lewis and the Legacy of the Caribbean Development Bank." *Journal of Eastern Caribbean Studies* 34 (4):1–20.

Javaid, Umbreen, and Habibollah Javan Siahmardy. 2017. "Globalization, Interdependence and Economic Cooperation Organization (ECO)." *South Asian Studies* 32 (1):27–28.

Mak, James, and Seiji Finch Naya. 1994. "Is There a Need for a Pacific Islands Development Bank?" *Pacific Economic Bulletin* 9 (2):35–40.

Manoli, Panagiota. 2013. "Black Sea Cooperation: A Difficult Path to Overcoming Divisions and Marginalization." *Plural* 1 (1–2):210–16.

Marianna, Biró, and Kovács Zoltán. 2019. "Putin's Bank Moves to Budapest, Gets All Conceivable Privileges and Immunities." Index. https://index.hu/english/2019/02/20/international_investment_bank_russia_hungary_putin_orban_immunity/.

Mbadi, Omer. 2015. "After the Adandé era, How the BDEAC Can Revive." Jeune Afrique. https://www.jeuneafrique.com/mag/241372/economie/apres-lere-adande-comment-la-bdeac-peut-se-relancer/.

Mistry, Percy S., and Lolette Kritzinger-van Niekerk. 1998. Development Finance and the Need for a Sub-Regional Development Financing Institution in SADC. Southern African Development Community Finance & Investment Sector Coordinating Unit Research Project.

Momodu, Raheemat. 2018. "Nationalism Underpinned by Pan-Regionalism: African Foreign Policies in ECOWAS in an Era of Anti-Globalization." In *African Foreign Policies in International Institutions*, edited by Jason Warner and Timothy M. Shaw, 95–112. New York: Palgrave Macmillan. doi: 10.1057/978-1-137-57574-6

Moody's. 2018. "Moody's Assigns First-time B1 Issuer Rating to EBID; Negative Outlook." Moody's Investors Service. https://www.moodys.com/research/Moodys-assigns-first-time-B1-issuer-rating-to-EBID-negative--PR_381970.

Murinde, Victor, and Joram Kariisa-Kasa. 1997. "The Financial Performance of the East African Development Bank: A Retrospective Analysis." *Accounting, Business & Financial History* 7 (1):81–104. doi: 10.1080/095852097330775.

Notaro, Juan E. 2019. "FONPLATA, 45 Years Bringing Development Closer to the People." FONPLATA https://www.fonplata.org/en/news/30-06-2019/fonplata-45-years-bringing-development-closer-people.

Ocampo, José Antonio. 2002. "Recasting the International Financial Agenda." In *International Capital Markets in Transition*, edited by John Eatwell and Lance Taylor, 19–22. New York: Oxford University Press.

Ocampo, José Antonio, and Daniel Titelman. 2009. "Subregional Financial Cooperation: The South American Experience." *Journal of Post Keynesian Economics* 32 (2):249–68. doi: 10.2753/PKE0160-3477320208.

Ocampo, José Antonio, and Daniel Titelman. 2012. Regional Monetary Cooperation in Latin America. In *ADBI Working Paper*. Tokyo: Asian Development Bank Institute.

Ouedraogo, Nosseyamba Benjamin. 2013. "Stock Market Development and Economic Growth in West African Economic and Monetary Union." *African Journal of Economic and Sustainable Development* 2 (2):172–88.

Park, Susan. 2014. "Institutional Isomorphism and the Asian Development Bank's Accountability Mechanism: Something Old, Something New, Something Borrowed, Something Blue?" *The Pacific Review* 27 (2):217–39.

PIDB. 2014. Annual Report 2013. Pacific Islands Development Bank.

PIDB. 2017. Annual Report 2016. Pacific Islands Development Bank.

PIDB. 2019a. Annual Report 2018. Pacific Islands Development Bank.

PIDB. 2019b. "Mission & Purpose." Pacific Islands Development Bank. https://pacificidb.com/mission-purpose/.

Pieck, Sonja K. 2011. "Beyond Postdevelopment: Civic Responses to Regional Integration in the Amazon." *Journal of Cultural Geography* 28 (1):179–202. doi: 10.1080/08873631.2011.548497.

Prada, Fernando. 2012. World Bank, Inter-American Development Bank, and Sub-Regional Development Banks in Latin America: Dynamics of a System of Multilateral Development Banks. In *AsDBI Working Paper Series No. 380:13*. Tokyo: Asian Development Bank Institute.

Quah, Chee-Heong. 2016. "A Diagnostic on the West African Monetary Union." *South African Journal of Economics* 84 (1):129–48. doi: 10.1111/saje.12089.

Ray, Rebecca, and Rohini Kamal. 2019. "Can South–South Cooperation Compete? The Development Bank of Latin America and the Islamic Development Bank." *Development and Change* 50 (1):191–220. doi: 10.1111/dech.12468.

Robert, René. 2004. The Social Dimension of Regional Integration in ECOWAS. In *Working Paper Series*: International Labour Organisation.

Ryan, Yasmine. 2010. "Gabon 'Siphoned Funds' to France." Al Jazeera. https://www.aljazeera.com/news/africa/2010/12/2010122984115531832.html.

S&P Global Ratings. 2019. Introduction To Supranationals Special Edition 2019.

Sagasti, Francisco, and Fernando Prada. 2006. "Regional Development Banks: A Comparative Perspective." In *Regional Financial Cooperation*, edited by José Antonio Ocampo, 68–106. Maryland: Brookings Institution Press.

Shelepov, Andrei, and Inna Andronova. 2018. "Engagement between the New Development Bank and Other Development Banks: A Formal Basis for Future Cooperation." *International Organisations Research Journal* 13 (1):99–113.

Simmonds, K. R. 1967. "The Central American Common Market: An Experiment in Regional Integration." *International and Comparative Law Quarterly* 16 (4):911–30. doi: 10.1093/iclqaj/16.4.911.

Smith, W. W. May 30, 2018. President's Remarks: 48th Annual Meeting of the Board of Governors: Opening Ceremony. St. George's, Grenada: Caribbean Development Bank.

Soudan, François. 2013. "BDEAC: Between Michaël Adandé and André Nzapayéké, the Tea Towel Is Burning." Jeune Afrique. https://www.jeuneafrique.com/136971/politique/bdeac-entre-micha-l-adand-et-andr-nzapay-k-le-torchon-br-le/.

Stone, David R. 2008. "CMEA's International Investment Bank and the Crisis of Developed Socialism." *Journal of Cold War Studies* 10 (3):48–77. doi: 10.1162/jcws.2008.10.3.48.

TDB. 2018. *Annual Report 2018*. Bujumburu: Trade and Development Bank.

Tisdell, Clem. 2002. "Globalisation, Development and Poverty in the Pacific Islands: The Situation of the Least Developed Nations." *International Journal of Social Economics* 29 (12):902–22. doi: 10.1108/03068290210447969.

Tsangarides, Charalambos G., and Mahvash Saeed Qureshi. 2008. "Monetary Union Membership in West Africa: A Cluster Analysis." *World Development* 36 (7):1261–79. doi: https://doi.org/10.1016/j.worlddev.2007.06.019.

United Nations. 2005. World Economic and Social Survey 2005: Financing for Development. New York: United Nations.

Vinokurov, Evgeny. 2018. *Introduction to the Eurasian Economic Union*. New York: Palgrave Macmillan.

Vinokurov, Evgeny. 2019. *Interaction of Eurasian and International Financial Institutions*. Almaty: Eurasian Development Bank.

Vinokurov, Evgeny, Alexander Efimov, and Artem Levenkov. 2019. "The Eurasian Fund for Stabilization and Development: A Regional Financing Arrangement and Its Place in the Global Financial Safety Net." Almaty: Eurasian Development Bank.

Vladova, Galya, and Jörg Knieling. 2014. "Potential and Challenges for the Black Sea Regional Cooperation." *Eastern Journal of European Studies* 5 (1).

Wihtol, Robert. 2014. Whither Multilateral Development Finance? In *AsDBI Working Paper Series*. Tokyo: Asian Development Bank Institute.

Yabi, Gilles Olakounlé. 2010. The Role of ECOWAS in Managing Political Crisis and Conflict: The Cases of Guinea and Guinea-Bissau. Abuja, Nigeria: Friedrich-Ebert-Stiftung.

Zappile, Tina M. 2016. "Sub-Regional Development Banks: Development as Usual?" In *Global Economic Governance and the Development Practices of the Multilateral Development Banks*, edited by Susan Park and Jonathan R. Strand, 187–211. Oxon: Routledge.

8 The specialised development banks

The specialised development banks are the fourth and final multilateral development bank (MDB) grouping we explore in this book. Compared to the relative typological cohesion of the World Bank Group, regional development banks (RDBs), and sub-regional development banks (SRDBs), the specialised development banks are far more disparate in mandate and operation; they are specialised as niche development financiers. Adding to the typological confusion, a few of the specialised banks could arguably be classified as regional or sub-regional actors, with their operations occurring in discrete geographical areas. Still, the mandate of the specialised banks sets them apart, often being focussed on narrower objectives compared to the other MDBs. Emerging in response to changes in the global political economy, including post-Second World War reconstruction, the 1973 oil price shock, and the 21st-century rise of emerging powers, the specialised banks first arrived in 1956 when the Council of Europe Development Bank (CEB) – the first MDB after the International Bank for Reconstruction and Development (IBRD) – was founded. They continue to appear through to the 2015 launch of the China-led Asian Infrastructure Investment Bank (AIIB), though most were established in the decade between 1968 and 1977.

There are nine specialised development banks, as outlined in Table 8.1. Two, the CEB and International Fund for Agricultural Development (IFAD), work as stand-alone actors, while the remaining seven can be viewed as three strategic blocs: an Arab-led grouping, a Nordic one, and the BRICS: Brazil, Russia, India, China, and South Africa.

The Arab-led group of MDBs include the Arab Fund for Economic and Social Development (AFESD), Arab Bank for Economic Development in Africa (BADEA), Islamic Development Bank (IsDB), and OPEC Fund for International Development (OFID). They are closely associated and emerged within several years of each other between 1968 and 1976, in large part catalysed by rapid capital accumulation in oil exporting Arab countries. It is not an Arab-only grouping, comprising Islamic and oil-exporting elements, but Arab countries are at their heart. The Nordic group evolved from the Nordic Investment Bank (NIB) established in 1975 and was later joined by affiliated Nordic multilateral institutions. It is positioned within Nordic development cooperation arrangements and is led by Denmark, Finland, Iceland, Norway, and Sweden with support from

Table 8.1 Specialised development banks overview

Year	*Specialised development banks*	*Region*	*Membership*	*Subscribed capital*	*Annual approvals (2018)*	*Credit rating*	*Headquarters*
1956	Council of Europe Development Bank	Europe	42	\$6.22 billion	\$4.4 billion	AAA	Paris, France
1968	Arab Fund for Economic and Social Development	Arabic States	22	\$9.87 billion	\$1.5 billion	No rating	Kuwait City, Kuwait
1974	Arab Bank for Economic Development in Africa	Africa	18	\$4 billion	\$565 million	No rating	Khartoum, Sudan
1974	Islamic Development Bank	Islamic States	57	\$70 billion	\$1.1 billion	AAA	Jeddah, Saudi Arabia
1975	Nordic Investment Bank	Nordic and Baltic States+	8	\$6.9 billion	\$4.9 billion	AAA	Helsinki, Finland
1976	OPEC Fund for International Development	Global	12	\$4.26 billion	\$1.5 billion	No rating	Vienna, Austria
1977	International Fund for Agricultural Development	Global	177	\$8.05 billion (paid-in only)	\$3.3 billion (2016–18)	No rating	Rome, Italy
2014	New Development Bank	BRICS	5	\$50 billion	\$4.6 billion	AA+	Shanghai, China
2015	Asian Infrastructure Investment Bank	Asia and Oceania	97	\$96.7 billion	\$7.5 billion	AAA	Beijing, China

Source: Annual Reports.

the Baltic states: Latvia, Lithuania, and Estonia. It promotes development in the Nordic-Baltic region and globally. The third group comprises the BRICS-led New Development Bank (NDB) and China-led AIIB, established in 2014 and 2015. They are expressions of the burgeoning influence of emerging economies in the 21st century and have sparked an exhaustive debate about whether they reinforce or challenge the Global North-led status quo. More to the point, as Humphrey (2019, 165) contends, the 'recent creation of the' NDB and AIIB shows that 'MDBs appear to have continued relevance in global development finance.'

The specialised development banks are niche development financiers, with each of their mandates revealing much about their role. The CEB helps European countries manage the social impact of refugees and displaced persons as well as ecological disasters and IFAD mobilises concessional resources for agricultural development. IsDB supports economic and social progress in accordance with Shari'ah financial principles, the Nordic Development Fund (NDF) – an affiliate of the Nordic grouping – has since 2009 specialised in the provision of grants for climate change interventions in low-income countries, and the NDB and AIIB both support sustainable infrastructure financing. There are grey areas where some of the specialised banks could be labelled RDBs or SRDBs, for example, the NIB began from Nordic regional arrangements. Nonetheless, given their niche mandates, the nine MDBs discussed in this chapter are best positioned typologically as specialised development banks.

Apart from the CEB and IFAD, the other specialised development banks represent Nordic, Arab, and emerging economy influence, as noted above. This point is worth further elaboration, particularly since the Nordic development model is distinct from that of the US and Western Europe, the Arab-led MDBs often support Arab solidarity, and the emerging economies offer a geopolitical alternative to Global North-led finance. The following section explores these alternative sources of development finance, before the remainder of the chapter provides an analytical overview of the specialised MDBs, beginning chronologically with the CEB and concluding with the AIIB.

8.1 Alternative sources of development finance

8.1.1 Nordic development finance

The Nordic countries – Denmark, Finland, Iceland, Norway, and Sweden – have a strong reputation for their social democratic and regulatory systems, consistently high human development rankings, and eco- and climate-friendly outlook (Clement 2004). Compounded by their standing as 'honest brokers' and 'faithful implementers' of international norms and rules, they have built considerable trustworthiness in their bilateral and multilateral interactions with less developed countries (Bengtsson, Elgstrom, and Tallberg 2004, 312). Broadly defined by 'human internationalism' (Engh and Pharo 2009), the foreign aid and development assistance programmes of the Nordic countries have long promoted poverty alleviation as both a moral obligation and a benefit to aid donors as much as aid recipients (Stokke 1989). Poverty alleviation, social welfare, environmental protection, good governance, and human rights typically characterise Nordic aid, with each Nordic country delivering their own national aid programmes as well as collaborating multilaterally through the Nordic Finance Group.

Inter-Nordic cooperation has seen largely consistent progress since the end of the Second World War, encompassing finance and trade, collective security, and environment and development (Czarny 2017). There have been ebbs and flows, however, with tensions created during the Cold War and by European Union (EU) accession. Despite these, multilateral engagement within the Nordic region remains strong, with Forsberg (2013) arguing that it stems not only from institutions, like the Nordic Council (founded in 1952) and Nordic Council of Ministers (established in 1971), but also a shared 'Nordic identity'. In the context of multilateral development assistance, the Nordic Finance Group illustrates inter-Nordic cooperation.

Ørvik (1974, 88) made the prophetic claim that the 'seventies may well become a watershed in Nordic regional cooperation.' From a multilateral development finance (MDF) standpoint, this was very accurate. Following the NIB's establishment in 1975, there came the Nordic Project Fund (Nopef) in 1982, NDF in 1988, and Nordic Environment Finance Corporation (NEFCO) in 1990; collectively, they comprise Nordic Finance Group. The Nordic countries are generally more progressive than OECD and EU donors in their foreign aid, well exceeding average official development assistance (ODA) contributions and donating more than other European countries to multilateral organisations. They are also distinct from US and Western European aid models, with a reputation as 'soft donors' that rely on recipient terms rather than dictating conditions (Danielson and Wohlgemuth 2003, Elgström and Delputte 2016). Further, the Nordic countries 'publicly assumed the role of bridge-builders between developing and industrialised countries' during African decolonisation (Engh and Pharo 2009, 115). The Swedish International Development Cooperation Agency's (SIDA) engagement with African SRDBs and the appointment of two Nordic citizens to run the East African Development Bank (EADB) are examples of this trend. In addition, foreign aid served as a connecting node between African and Nordic countries and many 'diplomatic missions in African countries were only established after the [Nordic] aid agencies were located there' (Selbervik and Nygaard 2006, 22). Nordic aid has had its controversies, notably a joint Nordic development aid project established in 1968 was tangentially involved in President Julius Nyerere's *ujamaa* peasant village programme that used force and coercion to become one of Africa's largest resettlement efforts (see Paaskesen 2010). But, overall, the legacy of Nordic development cooperation is positive, standing as a viable (if smaller) alternative to other Western aid programmes.

8.1.2 *Arab development finance*

Regional integration and cooperation between Arab countries began in 1945 with the founding of the Arab League, a time when the countries of the Middle

East were ranked among the lowest levels of socioeconomic development globally (Yousef 2004). It was spurred by Arab nationalism, anti-colonial sentiment, and backed by oil wealth and institutionalised through successive initiatives in the 1950s. The intent was to strengthen the structural position of the region (Corm 2006, Worrall 2017), and development finance formed one pillar.

Since the 1970s, Arab ODA has exceeded the average among OECD countries. Although peaking in the 1970s and 1980s, Arab ODA averaged 13% of global ODA and 75% of non-OECD ODA between 1973 and 2008, with most aid being untied and without conditions (Kellerman 2019, Rouis et al. 2010, Shushan and Marcoux 2011, Tok, Calleja, and El-Ghaish 2014,). Like the Nordic countries, Arab development finance offers an alternative investment stream, particularly to countries that are not allies of OECD donors, especially the US.

Saudi Arabia, Kuwait, and the UAE-lead Arab ODA and the Arab MDBs. There is a complex network of bilateral and multilateral Arab development organisations, which is unified under the Coordination Secretariat for Arab National and Regional Development Institutions. The Coordination Secretariat was established under the auspices of the AFESD in 1975 to coordinate Arab aid and avoid resource duplication – although, in practice, its power is limited to data collection and dissemination. It comprises three national development agencies – the Kuwait Fund for Arab Economic Development (1961), Abu Dhabi Fund for Development (1971), and Saudi Fund for Development (1974) – and four MDBs – the AFESD, BADEA, IsDB, and OFID – and also the IMF-like Arab Monetary Fund (AMF) and other bodies (Fritz and Mühlich 2019, Momani and Ennis 2012, Rouis et al. 2010, Shushan and Marcoux 2011, Zimmermann and Smith 2011). While the IsDB and OFID are not Arab-only MDBs, Arab countries are among their largest shareholders (Neumayer 2003).

The emergence of so many Arab development organisations in the 1960s and 1970s was prompted by the 1967 Arab-Israeli War and 1973 oil price shock, as well as broader attempts to further Arab foreign policy, promote regional stability and solidarity, and establish an alternative to Global North-led finance (El Mallakh and Kadhim 1976, Neumayer 2003). Tudoroiu (2012, 25–6) argues that the Organisation of the Petroleum Exporting Countries (OPEC) can be understood as a mirror of the BRICS in that both groupings are heterogeneous and 'the creation of OPEC was due to Third World nationalism directed against Western economic neo-colonialism,' just as the formalisation of the BRICS was to carve out space for emerging economies. Further, both OPEC and the BRICS exercise financial and geopolitical influence. The Arab-Israeli War led to an expansion of Arab foreign aid as oil-exporters not directly participating in the conflict – Kuwait, Libya, and Saudi Arabia – offered financial support to countries such as Jordan, Egypt, and Syria that suffered heavy economic and human losses (Corm 2006, Porter 1986, Williams 1976).

The 1973 oil shock prompted a major expansion of Arab MDF. The oil-rich Arab countries used some of their vast petrodollar reserves as aid to (i) offset potential negative political fallout from oil-importing countries suffering financial decline from oil price spikes and (ii) to dissuade the Global North and South that oil reserves were being used as an economic 'weapon' (Corm 2006, El Mallakh and Kadhim 1976, Porter 1986, Shushan and Marcoux 2011). Equally, though, key Western powers encouraged many of these ventures as outlined in Chapter 4. As Corm (2006, 294) argues, Arab aid was not only political but at the time 'Arab oil-exporting countries did not have the capacity to absorb the new financial flows that were accruing to them,' a situation similar to that of China in the NDB and AIIB. The resultant petrodollars were not just used in aid but invested in Northern banks, which became a key driver of the 1982 debt crisis.

Arab countries received 62% of Arab ODA between 1970 and 2008, followed by Asian and African countries with large Muslim populations (Momani and Ennis 2012). A 'striking feature of Arab aid is its high volatility… Arab aid has had huge swings over the years, and changes in oil prices seem to be the major driving factor' (Villanger 2007, 228). Cumulative Arab ODA increased from $7.7 billion between 1970 and 1974 to $32.7 billion from 1980 to 1984, and then declined to $6.8 billion between 1995 and 1999 as oil prices fell. Next, it rapidly increased to $15.7 billion as oil prices spiked between 2000 and 2004 (Corm 2006). The four Arab MDBs are financed from capital subscriptions and loan repayments and thus are fairly sheltered from oil price fluctuations (Rouis et al. 2010).

8.1.3 BRICS development finance

The BRIC acronym was coined by Goldman Sachs Chief Economist Jim O'Neill in 2001, describing countries 'with the most potential for growth in the first half of the twenty-first century, based on demography, the size of potential markets, recent growth rates, and the embrace of globalisation' (Robinson 2015, 4). At first used as an investment strategy, the 2008 Global Financial Crisis (GFC) catalysed the formalisation of the grouping as the crisis undermined the Global North's paradigmatic credibility (Cammack 2018, Duggan 2015, Stuenkel 2015, Tudoroiu 2012). With the 2010 admission of South Africa, the BRICS built new institutional arrangements, including the NDB and Contingent Reserve Arrangement (CRA) – an IMF-style $100 billion fund that member countries can draw from in financial emergencies – and they are all members of the China-led AIIB, while India, Brazil, and South Africa comprise the IBSA Dialogue Forum. We agree with the argument that the BRICS do not intend to displace the capitalist status quo (see Harmer and Buse 2014, Nayyar 2016, Robinson 2015, Thakur 2014, Tudoroiu 2012). Instead, they 'pose a within-system challenge… they challenge its most liberal content, while becoming dependent on, and engaging with, its existing institutional structures' (Stephen 2014, 914). Nevertheless, the BRICS demonstrate an 'aspiration to be "rule makers" instead of "rule takers"' (Duggan 2015, 17).

The rise and sustainability of the BRICS have been exhaustively reviewed over the past two decades. Some economic analyses claim that the BRICS are finished because they have not been able to maintain predicted growth rates (see Sharma 2012), even though they recovered quickly after the GFC (Chen and De Lombaerde 2014). Such analyses overlook the fact that the BRICS are more than simply an investment strategy; they are a formalised grouping and they are actively changing global governance. Yet, their institutionalisation runs into difficulties given their disparate cultures, politics, and demographics. South Africa, as an example, has often been regarded an odd choice for the grouping, given its relative economic size. However, its inclusion reflects a logic of having strategic influence in sub-Saharan Africa, and South Africa has a leading role in the Southern African Development Community and African Union as well as being the only African country in the G20 (Petropoulos 2015, Tella 2017). Further, Russia has been constrained by low oil prices and Western sanctions (Stephen 2017) and Brazil under President Jair Bolsarno has created tensions by aligning closely with US President Donald Trump, hence some of their original unity has dissipated with political changes. The BRICS additionally display 'various symptoms of internal crisis and socioeconomic oppression… including severe inequality, poverty, unemployment, diseases, violence… inadequate education and prohibitions on labour organising… [and] worsening political and civil rights violations' (Bond 2013, 267).

The development agenda of the BRICS illustrates both their role as alternative sources of finance and their strategic pursuit of their own foreign policy interests, as well as some challenge to Global North donors (Chin 2014, Gu et al. 2016, Naim 2007, Tok, Calleja, and El-Ghaish 2014, 595, Woods 2008). In founding of the NDB and AIIB, it has been usefully suggested that the BRICS are not restructuring the world economy but positioning themselves more influentially within it. They do not want to supplant the existing system because they benefit from its institutions (Qobo and Soko 2015, Zavyalova 2016).

China, as the centrepiece of the BRICS, is particularly relevant to MDF. The NDB and AIIB are 'entwined with the Belt and Road Initiative (BRI) – a vast infrastructure-building, trade, and investment strategy that Beijing launched in 2013' (Kalathil 2018, 52). Notably, however, the new MDBs are but one facet of Chinese development assistance, with finance moving in larger volumes through the China Development Bank and Export-Import Bank. This finance is generally well received by many developing countries given it lacks the conditionality of Global North-led MDF (Chin and Gallagher 2019, 246). Significantly, Chinese development assistance almost exclusively focusses on infrastructure investment.

8.2 Council of Europe Development Bank

Established in 1956, the CEB is Europe's first MDB and the world's second after the IBRD. While its European geographical focus suggests it could be labelled an RDB, its social mandate situates it better as a specialised bank: the

> primary purpose of the Bank is to help in solving the social problems with which European countries are or may be faced as a result of the presence of refugees, displaced persons or migrants consequent upon movements of refugees or other forced movements of populations and as a result of the presence of victims of natural or ecological disasters.
>
> (CEB 2019)

The impetus for CEB was the movement of large numbers of refugees and displaced persons into Western Europe after the Second World War. Nonetheless, it was structured as an MDB with an initial $6.7 million capital base obtained from member subscriptions. Of that amount, 25% was immediately paid up and the remaining 75% fully paid by 1960. This high level of paid-in capital enabled CEB to borrow from capital markets (Bussière and Willaert 2006, 24). In 2017, CEB's subscribed capital base was €5.5 billion, ranking it broadly in the middle of the specialised development banks, although far smaller than the IsDB, NDB, and AIIB.

The Council of Europe was established in 1949 and today operates as Europe's leading human rights organisation. The CEB was founded several years by the then eight Council members, with CEB 'attached to the Council of Europe and administered under its supreme authority' (CEB 2019), although the MDB was financially and legally independent. The Council emerged from political cooperation after the Second World War, with the 1948 Brussels Pact countries – Britain, France, Belgium, the Netherlands, and Luxembourg – coming together with Italy, Ireland, Denmark, Norway, and Sweden in May 1949 to establish it. By 1950, the Council expanded to include Greece, Turkey, Iceland, and West Germany. Resettlement of displaced persons and refugees was prioritised by Council members, as were initiatives to promote human and social rights (Bussière and Willaert 2006).

Pierre Schneiter was appointed as the Special Council of Europe Representative for National Refugees and Over-Population in December 1953 to investigate the feasibility of establishing an organisation to manage European resettlement issues. Schneiter concluded that a socially oriented bank led by the Council would be most appropriate, financing resettlement actions and building employment opportunities (Bussière and Willaert 2006). After tensions were resolved between Council members over financial questions, the CEB was signed into effect on 16 April 1956 by West Germany, France, Belgium, Greece, Iceland, Italy, Luxembourg, and Turkey. Notably, the UK, although a Council of Europe founding member, did not join. When first established, CEB was called the Council of Europe Resettlement Fund for National Refugees and Over-Population in Europe, with the name change in 1999 to better reflect both its growth into an MDB and its revised strategic focus on development concerns beyond resettlement.

The first decade of operations addressed post-Second World War resettlement, but CEB became less relevant during the 1970s and 1980s as the inter-European movement of people stabilised. Still, it had a tenfold increase in annual approvals and diversified its loan portfolio to sectors not traditionally associated with resettlement such as housing. The end of the Cold War renewed the MDB's relevance; a focus on post-Soviet transition became a masthead in the 1990s and 2000s, with CEB's 2005–9 Development Plan prioritising its 20 new members mostly situated in Central and Eastern Europe that joined after 1991 (Bussière and Willaert 2006). Successive Council of Europe Summits revised the CEB's mandate: 1993 Vienna Summit – promoting regional collaboration; 1997 Strasbourg Summit – strengthening European social cohesion; and 2005 Warsaw Summit – building a free, democratic, and more inclusive Europe. The Bank's current priorities include sustainable and inclusive growth, job creation, public infrastructure, gender equality, the integration of refugees, displaced persons, and migrants, and climate change mitigation and adaptation. The CEB today increasingly resembles a traditional MDB.

The CEB has 42 member states, with admission eligibility contingent on membership in the Council of Europe, which has 47 members. Prior to Brexit, Austria and the UK were the only EU members not in it. All member countries are eligible to receive CEB loans, a contrast to the IBRD where lending is reserved for countries below a GNI threshold. Like the European Investment Bank (EIB), CEB is exclusively owned by regional European members; there are no non-regional shareholders. Germany, France, and Italy are the largest shareholders – each holding over 16% voting share – followed by Spain and Turkey. Over half of the remaining member countries each control less than 1% shareholding.

As per Table 8.2, five Governors have led the CEB, with appointee nationality alternating between two of the three largest shareholders: France and Germany. The first Governor, René Plas, called the Resettlement Fund an 'organisation for human solidarity on a banking basis' (cited in CEB 2016a, 1), demonstrating both Keynesian ideals and the legacy of the banking model. Rolf Wenzel is the incumbent Governor and he previously served in Germany's Federal Ministry for Finance, as Senior Advisor to Germany's IMF Executive Director, and as an Asian Development Bank (AsDB) Director, again demonstrating MDB networks. Wenzel (cited in International Banker 2017) highlighted the benefits of the banking model when he said that the

> CEB is a self-financing institution, so there are no demands on its members for capital beyond their subscribed capital contributions. The bank is financially sound, has a solid loan portfolio, and has no default or arrears on its loans. It also maintains a prudent financial strategy and an efficient risk-management framework.

Wenzel's predecessor Raphaël Alomar similarly noted in 2004 that CEB 'intends to enhance its capacity as a development bank' by strengthening its expertise and intensifying 'pre-existing close partnerships with other financial as well as non-financial international institutions' (cited in CEB 2004, 11).

Like the IBRD, CEB's main lending instruments are project and programme loans. Funds are raised on international capital markets and, in 2017, CEB issued its first social inclusion bond. The MDB finances up to 50% of project costs and programme loans are disbursed in tranches (CEB 2017). It is supported by two financing facilities: the European Co-Financing Facility, which focusses on facilitating borrower absorption of EU grants, and the Public Sector Finance Facility. CEB also provides technical and advisory services to ensure project feasibility and loan repayment, just like most other MDBs.

Between 1956 and 2017, CEB disbursed over €41 billion. From 2008 to 2017, it averaged €2.47 billion in annual loan approvals and €1.83 billion in disbursements,

Table 8.2 Council of Europe Development Bank Governors

Governor	*Nationality*	*Tenure*	*Details*
René Plas	French	1956–68	Guided the Resettlement Fund through its first decade, setting the tone of the organisation.
Charles-Henri Bonfils	French	1968–78	Supervised the admission of new member countries and the diversification of operations to prioritise social housing, vocational training, and territorial development.
Roger Vanden Branden	German	1979–93	Presided over an uneventful 1980s, noted mainly for a tenfold expansion of assets and loans achieved through the admission of new members and capital increases.
Raphaël Alomar	French	1993–2011	Oversaw a significant overhaul of the CEB, including the name change to better reflect its MDB status, and helped tackle the post-Soviet transition, the introduction of the MDGs, and the onset of the 2008 GFC and 2009 Eurozone Crisis.
Rolf Wenzel	German	2011–Present	Integrated the SDGs into CEB's operational mandate and directed significant resources to the ongoing refugee crisis, particularly through the Migrant and Refugee Fund established in October 2015.

Source: Annual Reports and CEB Website.

with both increasing substantially since 2016 – from €2.3 billion (31 projects) in 2015 to €3.45 billion (35 projects) in 2016 to €3.9 billion (41 projects) in 2017 – in response to the 2015 Syrian Refugee Crisis. Indeed, CEB's 2017–19 Development Plan was drafted in response to the Crisis, which saw the largest movement of refugees into Europe since the Second World War (CEB 2016b).

In summary, CEB is a relatively small MDB compared to the RDBs, but it is comparable to many of the larger SRDBs. Despite its social mandate, its organisational structure and operational guidelines reveal it to be an investment-oriented MDB, prioritising economic growth through small and medium enterprises (SMEs), job creation, physical infrastructure, and housing. It also collaborates extensively with financial intermediaries – an approach the large MDBs are now increasingly taking – and relies on joint-venture financing to deliver its projects. Thus, despite its specialised mandate, it sits comfortably within the standard MDB framework, reflecting many common organisational traits.

8.3 Arab Fund for Economic and Social Development

The Agreement Establishing AFESD was adopted by the Economic and Social Council of the Arab League on 16 May 1968, making it the first Arab-led MDB, although the agreement only became effective on 18 December 1971 (Rouis et al. 2010). It commenced operations in 1974. As per its original Articles of Agreement, its purposes were to participate in the 'financing of economic and social development projects in the Arab states and countries' by financing 'economic projects of an investment character' and delivering technical assistance to public and private enterprises. At the time of its establishment, it differed from the national Arab development funds and most MDBs, with the exception of CEB, in that 'social projects' were explicitly mandated (Porter 1986, Tok, Calleja, and El-Ghaish 2014). The original Articles were amended in 1997 following a study sanctioned by the Board of Governors to investigate how it could better support the Arab private sector (AFESD 1997). The revised Articles expand its mandate to finance private sector projects, establish and participate in equity capital, and establish and manage special funds. This aligned its lending operations to reflect contemporary mainstream MDBs.

Unlike IsDB and OFID but like BADEA, the AFESD is an exclusively Arab-led development bank, with shareholder eligibility contingent on Arab League membership. It has an entirely regional and borrowing membership, currently consisting of the 22 Arab League member states. Consistent with trends in Arab bilateral and multilateral development assistance, Kuwait and Saudi Arabia are the largest shareholders, with Kuwait being responsible for submitting the original proposal for AFESD to the Arab League in the late 1960s (Shushan and Marcoux 2011).

A Director General leads the AFESD and chairs the Board of Directors. There have been three Directors General. Incumbent Director General Abdlatif Al-Hamad has led AFESD since 1985, a long-term appointment rare among the MDBs, though IsDB is similar. Interviews conducted with Al-Hamad by Villanger (2007, 242) revealed the significance of AFESD: 'recipient countries facing severe conditions for receiving finance from the WB/IMF have turned to Arab donors to get the same finance without having to implement any conditions.'

The AFESD provides financing to public sector projects on concessional terms and to private sector projects promoting private sector development, as well as through a special account to fund small- and medium-sized projects, which was established in 2009 (Shushan and Marcoux 2011, 1970). In 2016, it softened its lending terms and reduced interest rates for low-income and other member countries. In addition, it provides a suite of technical and advisory services to support project feasibility.

Between 1974 and 2017, AFESD approved 663 loans totalling $32 billion, with infrastructure projects receiving close to 71% of all approvals (Engen and Prizzon 2018). As Corm (2006, 308) argues, AFESD's 'basic activities are to provide soft lending to Arab League countries for infrastructure projects,' with an emphasis on regional infrastructure projects such as those 'promoting the inter-Arab grid to connect national electricity systems.' Rouis et al. (2010, 26) expands this point, commenting that a

> landmark of AFESD's contribution to Arab regional integration is the financing of the Arab Electricity Grids Interconnection Projects. Over the past ten years, total investment from all sources in these projects has reached US$ 1 billion… AFESD has contributed over two thirds of the financing of these projects on concessional terms.

Egypt, Morocco, Tunisia, Oman, and Mauritania have been the largest recipients of AFESD disbursements. Cumulative loan approvals nearly doubled between 2007 and 2017, reflecting its capital base reaching $10 billion. Further, like many other MDBs, it has promoted co-financing to deliver its development projects. Between 1974 and 2016, over 11% of AFESD co-financing was with the World Bank, IFAD, and AfDB and over 56% with Arab national and regional development institutions.

Kuwait, Saudi Arabia, the UAE, and Qatar have not received loans from AFESD but have received grants, demonstrating that even the wealthiest oil-exporting shareholders can benefit from it. Every other member country – except for Comoros, with which it has had very limited engagement – has received both loans and grants. As of 2017, Palestine had received only five loans but 173 grants totalling over $92 million, reflecting Arab concern for the territory. Between 2001 and 2010, it allocated 10% of its yearly net income to the Palestinian Authority and, from 1974 to 2007, 19% of AFESD grants were allocated to the West Bank and Gaza (Rouis et al. 2010).

In summary, while it is a relatively small specialised development bank, reflecting the subscribed capital and annual approvals of an SRDB, the AFESD has nonetheless performed an important role as a niche financier of Arab integration, mirroring the CEB's social mandate.

8.4 Arab Bank for Economic Development in Africa

The BADEA was the second MDB established by the Arab League. It was formed on 18 February 1974 when its establishing agreement was signed, and it began operations in March 1975. It was the first inter-regional bank founded to build 'Arab and African solidarity' (Neumayer 2003, 136), emerging in part because the 1973 oil price shock severely impacted many African economies (Johnson 1983). Politically, BADEA aimed to curtail Israel's influence in Africa, with Uganda being the first country to break ties with Israel in 1972. BABEA thus represented both the expansion of Arab capital in line with the region's growing petrodollar reserves and a political tool to build Arab-African cooperation to minimise Israel's influence following the 1973 Arab-Israeli War (Johnson 1983, Porter 1986, Shushan and Marcoux 2011).

BADEA's (2009) objective 'is to foster economic, financial and technical cooperation between Africa countries and Arab World countries,' drawing Arab public and private investment into African natural resources and extractives (Johnson 1983, Porter 1986, Shushan and Marcoux 2011). The beneficiaries of BADEA operations may include African governments, public and private companies operating in African countries in which African governments or citizen have a majority capital shareholding, and mixed Arab-African companies pursuing development outcomes (BADEA 2009). BADEA encourages Arab-African trade by financing Arab exports into Africa and, in the mid-2000s, it began offering concessional loans (Shushan and Marcoux 2011). The mandate on Arab-African cooperation makes it a specialised development bank.

The BADEA's shareholders are 18 Arab League member countries. The five largest shareholders (in order) are Saudi Arabia, Kuwait, Libya, Iraq, and the UAE. Collectively, these countries hold over 77% shareholding, with Saudi Arabia controlling close one quarter. All shareholders are Arab countries, whereas African non-members are the recipients of BADEA's financial and technical assistance; the borrowers do not have any voting power – it is very much a donor led MDB.

A Director General leads the BADEA, who is appointed from the non-permanent members of the Board of Directors. The Board has eleven members, with the nine largest shareholders holding permanent seats and the smaller member countries jointly selecting two non-permanent representatives. Since 1974, five Director Generals have led BADEA, each from a different country (see Table 8.3). In line with South-South cooperation ideals, Dr Chedly Ayari, the first Director General, commented in 1975 that

> Our intention is… to put Afro-Arab cooperation on the map as a dimension of international economic cooperation which all countries, especially the rich industrial nations, must reckon with. Arab aid and cooperation efforts should be in a context of a new world economic order, based on equality and justice.
>
> (cited in Johnson 1983, 625)

Such rhetoric has been repeated in the NDB and AIIB.

Between 1975 and 2018, BADEA approved over 660 projects totalling \$4.8 billion (BADEA 2018), with infrastructure projects receiving 51.6% of total loan commitments. Compared to other MDBs, it is a small development financier: \$125 million via 16 projects in 2000, \$192 million via 23 projects in 2010, and \$320 million via 23 projects in 2018. Most projects are co-financed and its contribution to project financing is limited to 60% of total costs (Rouis et al. 2010). It also offers concessional lending terms to public sector projects.

Five-Year Plans govern BADEA's operations, with the first plan introduced in 1983 to improve resource delivery to recipient countries (Shushan and Marcoux 2011). Each plan is monitored by strict performance targets. The seventh Five-Year Plan (2015–19) allotted \$1.6 billion to loans, an increase of \$600 million over

Table 8.3 Arab Bank for economic development in Africa Director Generals

Director Generals	*Nationality*	*Tenure*	*Details*
Dr Chedly Ayari	Tunisian	1974–87	Had an academic career in economics and law. Served as: World Bank Executive Director and AfDB Board member in the 1960s; Tunisian Minister of Planning (1969–70 and 1974–5); Minister of Economy (1972–4); and Governor of the Central Bank of Tunisia (2012–18). Due to 'administrative differences,' the BADEA Board of Governors placed Ayari on leave in April 1987. These mainly concerned Ayari's promotion of increased commitments to African countries when shareholders wanted to limit funding to guarantee loan repayments. Ayari 'sought to give the Bank… a larger role in Arab development than the 19 member-states have been willing to allow' (Johnson, 1983, 625).
Ahmed Al Harti Al Wardi	Moroccan	1988–97	Appointed Director General during a tense period between the Board of Governors and senior management, leading to a redefinition of the Director General's role to be subject to greater oversight by the Governors.
Ustaz Medhat Sami Lofti	Egyptian	1997–2006	Modestly expanded annual lending approvals from $120 million in 2000 to $163 million in 2006, with the infrastructure sector receiving over half of annual commitments.
Abdel Aziz Khelef	Algerian	2006–15	Served in the Algerian Department of Industry and Energy in the 1970s and as Algerian Minister of Commerce (1980–86), Minister of Finance (1986–88), Secretary of State for Maghrebi Affair (1989–91), Secretary General of the Presidency of the Republic (1991–92), and Minister Delegate for Maghreb Cooperation and Affairs (1992–93). He also worked for IsDB (1994–2006).
Dr Sidi Ould Tah	Mauritanian	2015–Present	Prior appointments: Mauritanian Bank for Development and Commerce (1984–6); financial analyst, Food Security Commission (1986); advisor, Director General and Director, Internal Auditing Department, Nouakchott Port Authority (1988–96); Investment Promotion Officer then Technical Assistant to IsDB President (1999–2006); advisor, Mauritanian President and Prime Minister (2006–8); and Minister of Economy and Finance (2008–15), representing Mauritania in the World Bank and several RDBs, SRDBs, and specialised banks.

Source: Annual Reports and BADEA Website.

the previous plan (BADEA 2015). Of that, $1.1 billion was earmarked for public sector projects, $450 million for private sector projects, and $50 million for technical assistance operations. Three pillars underpinned the seventh Plan: support for African development through (i) public and private sector project financing, (ii) technical assistance to build human and institutional capacity, and (iii) Arab exports to African states; the pillars reiterate BADEA's Arab-African cooperation mandate as a specialised development bank.

8.5 Islamic Development Bank

An international Islamic financial institution, IsDB's Articles of Agreement were ratified in 1974 pursuant to the Declaration of Intent issued by the 1973 Conference of Finance Ministers of Muslim Countries held in Jeddah, Saudi Arabia (Ray and Kamal 2019). The Board of Governors held their inaugural meeting in July 1975 and the MDB formally began operations in October. It is unique even among Arab-led specialised banks because it aims to foster 'economic development and social progress [in] member countries and Muslim communities individually as well as jointly in accordance with the principles of the Shari'ah' (IsDB 2019 emphasis added). Thus, it 'strictly bans the practice of interest on financial transactions' (Tok, Calleja, and El-Ghaish 2014, 597). Like the RDBs and SRDBs, it promotes national and regional development, participates in equity capital, undertakes public and private project investment, manages special funds, promotes trade, and conducts research (IsDB 2019). Still, its focus on lending to people from one religion and conformance to its religious principles mean it is best understood as a specialised development bank.

IsDB emerged as a response to the Organisation of Islamic Cooperation (OIC) discussing the role of a multilateral organisation delivering Shari'ah-compliant financial resources to member countries. The idea was initially debated during the 1970 Second Islamic Conference of Foreign Ministers and was endorsed by King Faisal Bin Abdulaziz of Saudi Arabia (Hernandez and Vadlamannati 2017, Kuhn 1982). It 'was specifically created to bridge the gap between rich and poor Muslim countries' (Wilson 1989, 444), promoting Islam and building Arab solidarity (Villanger 2007). The focus on Shari'ah principles means IsDB has never instituted policy-based lending, nor engaged significantly – compared to other MDBs – in financial sector lending given the Shari'ah prohibition on excessive speculation (Kellerman 2019, Rouis et al. 2010).

Conformance to Shari'ah principles has not prevented IsDB from becoming an influential MDB. It has developed a suite of innovative lending instruments. During its first decade, it introduced short-term trade credits delivered under a service charge, machinery leasing, and private sector equity investment arrangements (Porter 1986). Its current modalities include: interest-free loans with a service fee to recoup administrative costs of no more than 2.5% per annum; profit-sharing schemes; leasing of capital goods; and, receipt of rent from borrowers (Corm 2006, Lessambo 2015, Rouis et al. 2010, Shushan and Marcoux 2011). It is worth noting that IsDB has been able to pursue these approaches in large part because of the petrodollar surpluses of its leading shareholders, notably Saudi Arabia. Yet, in the current low interest rate environment, its products are not as competitive as they were.

The IsDB has 57 member countries, including Arab and non-Arab shareholders, with membership eligibility contingent on being an OIC member. Arab countries are a minority numerically, with non-Arab members from Africa, Asia, and Latin America, but they are the largest capital subscribers (Shushan and Marcoux 2011). The largest ten shareholders are: Saudi Arabia (23.5%), Libya (9.43%), Iran (8.25%), Nigeria (7.66%), the UAE (7.51%), Qatar (7.18%), Egypt (7.07%), Kuwait (6.92%), Turkey (6.25%), and Algeria (2.54%). These shareholders hold over 85% of capital subscriptions. Saudi Arabia has exercised considerable influence through its large shareholding as well as ISDB's headquarters being in Jeddah and the only two Presidents both being Saudi nationals. As Hernandez and Vadlamannati (2017, 913–4) comment, 'fulfilling and maintaining its role as a leader in Islamic societies is a foreign policy priority for Saudi Arabia and it perceives itself as the principal responsible for the development, cooperation and support of the region.' This foreign policy priority echoes that of the US in the World Bank.

The small number of presidents is unusual for an MDB. The first President, Dr Ahmad Mohamed Ali Al Madani, led IsDB from 1975 to 2016; he was re-elected several times. Thus, much of IsDB's history was written by Dr Ali's leadership. From Saudi Arabia, Dr Ali previously served as Director of the Scientific and Islamic Institute in Yemen (1958–9) and Acting Rector of King Abdulaziz University (1967–72). Dr Bandar Hajjar succeeded Dr Ali in October 2016. Among other roles, Dr Hajjar once served as Saudi Arabia's Hajj Minister. His IsDB nomination caused discontent due to his alleged mismanagement of the annual Hajj Pilgrimage and the 2015 'Hajj Stampede' (Taylor 2015). At the time of his appointment, Dr Hajjar said that IsDB 'needs to shift away from providing individual, small-scale intervention to value chain solutions' (cited in Zuvela 2017). This shift became part of an ongoing transformation of IsDB, decentralising its organisational structure and altering how it engages with borrowers. Interestingly, as Ray and Kamal (2019, 204 and 206) comment at length, day-to-day decisions are overseen by a

> larger than usual number of engineers and other technical members. The bank more or less relies on the judgment of these teams, and thus avoids the need for the Board's involvement for every project approval. Indeed the… IsDB does not have a resident Board. The Directorial Board only gets involved in the approval process for projects deemed sensitive.

Over its history, the IsDB evolved into the IsDB Group, comparable to the expansion of the IBRD into the World Bank Group. Outlined in Table 8.4, there are five IsDB Group organisations other than the IsDB. Each organisation in the IsDB Group maintains and emphasises its conformance to Shari'ah principles.

Table 8.4 The Islamic Development Bank Group

Agency	*Established*	*Details*
Islamic Research and Training Institute (IRTI)	1981	The primary organisational unit for the delivery of Islamic finance research, training, information, and advisory and technical assistance. Its priority research areas are innovation and stability, human development, and sustainable development.
Islamic Corporation for the Insurance of Investment and Export Credit (ICIEC)	1994	Provides investment and export credit insurance to Islamic countries, with the aim of boosting trade between OIC members. In 2017, 36 member countries benefitted from its insurance products, resulting in $11.27 billion in facilitation.
Islamic Corporation for the Development of the Private Sector (ICD)	1999	Provides finance for private sector projects, promotes competition and entrepreneurship, and encourages cross border investments. It has an authorised capital of $4 billion and its shareholders are IsDB, 53 Islamic countries, and five public financial institutions.
Solidarity Fund for Development (IFSD)	2007	Seeks to reduce poverty by promoting pro-poor growth, human development, health care, education, and productive and sustainable income and employment. It is designed as a Waqf, or an Islamic trust under which all income earned from investments is used to finance future actions. Cumulative approvals between 2008 and 2016 totalled $2.8 billion through 106 operations in 33 member countries.
International Islamic Trade Finance Corporation (ITFC)	2008	ITFC has consolidated all trade finance business of the IsDB Group, approving $4.48 billion in 2016.

Source: Annual Reports and IsDB Group Website.

Cumulative IsDB Group net lending approvals between 1976 and 2018 were $131.3 billion. Whereas IsDB Group approved $4.8 billion during its first decade (1976–85), it approved $84.1 billion between 2008 and 2018, revealing considerable growth. Notably, annual ITFC approvals have overtaken annual IsDB OCR approvals, a rare occurrence in an MDB. ITFC approvals increased from $2.2 billion in 2010 to $5.2 billion in 2018 compared to a decline in OCR approvals from $5.1 billion in 2014 to $1.1 billion in 2018. The IsDB (2018) offers two reasons for these changes. First, between 2017 and 2018 IsDB focussed on project implementation and the delivery of previously approved projects with less emphasis on new approvals. Second, ITFC consolidated all IsDB Group trade finance and IsDB has advocated for greater trade connections between Islamic countries.

An additional explanation is that trade financing with its fast turnover is more lucrative for smaller MDBs. Co-financing is a large part of IsDB operations. In 2019, OCR approvals were $1.04 billion, with $2.94 billion in co-financing; the largest co-financiers were the World Bank Group and AsDB (IsDB 2020). This demonstrates that despite the Shari'ah focus, IsDB is well networked with other MDBs. Indeed, it is quite active in several MDB coordination networks.

In summary, IsDB has become an influential and well-respected Arab-led specialised development bank. While annual OCR commitments have recently been rivalled by AFESD and OFID, for several decades it was the largest of the Arab-led MDBs. Its conformance to Shari'ah principles is unique but the rapid growth of trade finance via ITFC demonstrates that traditional banking demands of turnover and income (perhaps even profits) are not absent.

8.6 Nordic Investment Bank

Denmark, Finland, Iceland, Norway, and Sweden agreed to establish the NIB in 1975 to promote economic growth and cooperation between the five Nordic countries. It began operations in 1977. As per its Establishing Agreement, NIB prioritises investment projects, with financing available based on sound banking principles and socioeconomic considerations. Like the EIB, it regards itself more an investment bank than a development bank (Normann 2019), though its sectoral focuses resemble the other MDBs (Engen and Prizzon 2018). Operations were initially restricted to the Nordic region, but the NIB approved its first investment loan outside of its membership area in 1983 and in 1992 participated in the Baltic Investment Programme designed to help build the private sectors of Latvia, Lithuania, and Estonia following independence from Soviet rule (Hellén and Eriksson 2011). NIB's broad mandate today is a prosperous and sustainable Nordic-Baltic region, with project finance directed to improving Nordic and Baltic competitiveness and environmental sustainability, and is part of an institutionalised 'Nordic voice,' underpinned by the 'common values of a democratic tradition, pluralism, environmentalism, and a common sense of solidarity' (Rūse 2014, 235). In 2016, Finland's then Prime Minister Juha Sipilä described the NIB as 'not only a child of Nordic co-operation; today, it is also the most tangible institution of Nordic-Baltic co-operation' (cited in NIB 2016).

Attempts to establish a Nordic investment bank had been made in the 1950s, alongside efforts to create a customs union. New attempts were made during the 1960s. It was not until the third attempt made in late 1974 and early 1975 that success followed, formalising Nordic integration (Normann 2019, Wiklund and Sundelius 1979). The NIB, as it would become, came to be favourably regarded by the Nordic governments as being able to effectively coordinate major investment projects and stave off pressures from high oil prices and deteriorating current account balances (Dennis 2015, Normann 2019). This is not to suggest that support was uniform; Iceland demonstrated unequivocal support, Finland and Sweden broadly supported it, but there was significant resistance from Denmark and Norway and from large Nordic business organisations. Tensions focussed on weighted membership representation – given economic and population size disparities between the Nordic countries – and loan eligibility conditions, i.e., the factors considered when approving projects (Dennis 2015). In the end, several factors came together to explain why this proposal succeeded, including the political costs of failing a third time to establish a Nordic bank, a compressed timetable for negotiations, and the proposal not being attached to a complex customs union (Dennis 2015).

The five Nordic countries are the NIB's founding members, while the three Baltic states – Latvia, Lithuania, and Estonia – joined in January 2005. The Baltic states expressed interest in joining after receiving loans in the early 1990s (Hellén and Eriksson 2011). In contrast to other MDBs, member shareholdings are based on economy size and not share purchases. Sweden is thus the largest shareholder with 34.6% capital share, followed by Norway (21.5%) and Denmark (21.1%). Iceland and Estonia are the smallest shareholders, holding 0.9% each. Its authorised capital is €6.1 billion and paid-in capital is €418.6 million, which is significant given that the NIB can grant loans and guarantees up to 250% of capital reserves (Lessambo 2015).

As per Table 8.5, five Presidents have led the Bank, one from each of the Nordic states. The incumbent President is Henrik Normann, who took office in April 2012. The Office of President is supported by the Executive Committee, Asset and Liability Committee, Credit Committee, Finance Committee, and Business and Technology Committee – a governance structure resembling more an investment bank than an MDB. As of December 2018, the NIB employed 199 people in permanent positions, comparable in size to most SRDBs, with the average employment length being 12.2 years.

Since commencing lending operations, NIB has financed over 2,200 investment projects inside and outside its membership area, with most approvals being to the Nordic-Baltic region. While it lends outside its membership, approvals are in relatively small amounts. Non-member projects are required to be of mutual interest to member and non-member countries. In 2018, non-member states received just 5% of annual approvals, some €200 million. To build its non-member lending portfolio, NIB has established cooperation agreements with the BSTDB, CABEI, and CAF and with countries in Africa, Asia, Eurasia, Latin America, and the Middle East. Notably, in comparison to the 'flexible' and 'rapid' project approval process of the NDB and AIIB, the NIB opts for more rigorous and lengthy processes: 'NIB considers its thorough credit and mandate reviewing processes as adding a quality stamp to our customers' project' (Normann 2019).

Over the past two decades, annual loan approvals doubled from €2.1 billion in 1997 to €4.3 billion in 2018. It offers long-term loans and guarantees on competitive market terms to the public and private sectors and normal total project costs are €20 million and above, with NIB financing generally not exceeding 50% of total project costs (Normann 2019). Illustrating again that it regards itself more as an investment bank than a development bank, Normann (2019) says that the 'NIB does not offer development finance as such, but provides long-term loans and guarantees… to projects contributing to our mandate, based on sound

Table 8.5 Nordic Investment Bank Presidents

President	*Nationality*	*Tenure*	*Details*
Bert Lindström	Swedish	1975–86	Oversaw NIB's establishment, its growth from Nordic-only to non-member lending, secured its AAA credit rating, and supervised the doubling of its authorised capital from SDR 400 to 800 million.
Jannik Lindbæk	Norwegian	1986–94	Oversaw the expansion of NIB operations into the Baltic region following the collapse of the Soviet Union. After his presidential appointment, Lindbæk served as Executive Vice President of the IFC from 1994–9. Lindbæk (2010) articulated the necessity of organisations like NIB: 'There will be a constant and growing need in both the public and private sector for long-term financing. That the [EIB] has grown to become the world's biggest bank is indicative of how useful and important IFIs like NIB and EIB are. They may be less glamorous than the commercial banks, but they are crucial for economic and social development.'
Jón Sigurðsson	Icelandic	1994–2005	Oversaw the establishment of a new facility for environmental investment loans in 1997 and supervised an increase of NIB's authorised capital to €4 billion in 1999.
Johnny Åkerholm	Finnish	2005–12	Oversaw a strengthened prioritisation of environmental issues and supervised the 2011 issuing of the NIB's first Green Bond. Previously, Åkerholm served as Under-Secretary of State for Economic Affairs, Ministry of Finance, Finland (1995–2003) and Secretary General of EBRD.
Henrik Normann	Danish	2012–Present	Oversaw issue of NIB's inaugural benchmark environmental bond in 2014 and established an Arctic lending facility in 2015 and a special lending facility to invest in green bonds issued by companies and municipalities in member countries in 2016. Prior to NIB, he served as Managing Director, Danske Markets, the investment banking arm of the Danske Bank Group. In 2012, Normann (2012), echoing Lindbæk's 2010 comments, said, 'Commercial banks cannot maintain long-term funding... Therefore, organisations such as NIB are crucial to complete some of the region's big communication, infrastructure, and pollution-fighting projects.'

Source: Annual Reports and NIB Website.

banking principles.' In 2018, NIB's sectoral approvals were industries and services (31%), infrastructure, transportation, and telecommunications (27%), energy and environment (22%), and financial institutions and SMEs (20%); such sectoral approvals denote its investment project portfolio.

The NIB has an explicit environmental mandate, translated into climate project financing and green bond issuances. Between 2011 and 2018, the Nordic MDB issued €3.5 billion in environmental bonds, and the Nordic share of cumulative green bond issuances between 2007 and 2018 was an estimated 7%, meaning the Nordic countries are at the forefront of this area of climate action. Further, all loans are assessed on their environmental benefits – ranging from pollution prevention to climate change mitigation and adaptation – and, in 2018, NIB updated its Environmental Bond Framework 'to more widely finance investments that benefit the environment' (Normann 2019).

Like the World Bank Group and IsDB Group, the NIB is part of the Nordic Finance Group made up of four international financial institutions (IFIs) headquartered in Finland: the NIB, NDF, NEFCO, and Nopef. While relatively small, the Nordic Finance Group reveals a complex network of complementary financing arrangements oriented to the approval and disbursal of climate finance. Nopef was the first part of the group formed in 1982. Today, it is managed by NEFCO and offers financing to Nordic private sector SMEs to prepare (notably green) investments outside the EU area; it approved some 3,000 projects totalling €104 million between 1982 and 2018. Compared to other MDBs, the Nordic Finance Group IFIs were early adopters of climate and environmental action, with rhetoric supported by their loan portfolios and mainstreaming initiatives.

The NDF was established in 1988 and began operations in 1989 originally as a concessional lending window for social and economic development in developing countries globally. After acting as a minor MDB for its first fifteen years, the Nordic Development Cooperation Ministers in 2005 recommended disbanding it after the member countries, notably Denmark, failed to agree on a fifth capital replenishment and suspended financing. In 2009, following a review supported by Finland and the Nordic Council endorsing that the NDF continue its activities, the member countries approved a new mandate, to shift from soft loans for social and economic development to grants for climate change interventions in low-income countries (Amland 2018, Normann 2019). Its head office is in the NIB's Helsinki headquarters, with the Nordic fund acquiring services at self-cost price from NIB – office premises, administration, ICT services, and accounting – while remaining legally independent. The NIB has an appointed observer on the NDF's Board of Directors. Thus, it seems to operate a bit more separately than the IDA does from the IBRD.

The Nordic fund's capital stock has increased steadily since commencing operations: 1991 €4 million; 1994 €60 million; 2000 €360 million; and 2008 €691 million. As of 2015, its subscribed capital was €1 billion, with capital drawn from the development cooperation budgets of the five Nordic member countries: Sweden (37%), Denmark (23%), Norway (21%), Finland (18%), and Iceland (1%). Yet, as Amland (2018) highlights,

> If the Nordic donors do not inject more capital, the fund's resources will slowly be depleted… Several sources confirm that there is disagreement about the way forward among Nordic donors. Denmark remains opposed to new replenishments, Norway and Sweden have a wait-and-see approach while Finland and Iceland favour an expansion of NDF. Since Nordic donors cannot agree upon a joint replenishment of NDF, voluntary donor contributions have been raised as an alternative way of providing more resources to NDF.

Wihtol (2013) argues that the niche fund should be strengthened due to its strong track record as nimble, respected, and efficient. It has a client-friendly reputation that focusses on co-financing, promotion of 'progressive' Nordic values such as equality, and on the most vulnerable. Its innovative project portfolio has been emulated in Latin America.

Since adopting its new mandate in 2009, the NDF has been led by three Managing Directors: Helge Semb, Pasi Hellman, and Karin Isaksson, whose history demonstrates links to MDBs and development players. Iterating its relevance as a niche MDB, Hellman said that the Nordic fund

> has its own narrow pigeonhole in the field of climate finance… One of our greatest strengths is the fact that we are a small and agile fund. We can even focus on small and micro-enterprise projects for which the World Bank, for instance, is too big.
>
> (cited in Toivanen ND)

Between 1989 and 2008, the Nordic fund approved 188 concessional credits valued at €940 million, with sectoral priorities being infrastructure, education, agriculture, and environment. Since 2009, annual climate intervention grants have been few and small in cost: an average of 12 projects totalling €40 million annually. In 2018, it approved nine projects totalling €47.2 million (48% to Africa, 22% to Latin America, 20% to Asia, and 10% to multiple regions) (NDF 2018). It regularly co-finances projects with other MDBs and the Nordic bilateral development organisations. The NDF also finances and manages the Nordic Climate Facility (NCF), which targets private and public partnerships between Nordic and NDF-partner organisations with the aim of building innovative climate change projects. Twenty-one countries in Africa, Asia, and Latin America are eligible for NCF financing.

In 1989, concurrent to the NDF commencing operations, NIB formed NEFCO as a special unit. NEFCO and NIB became independent organisations in 1993, with NEFCO mandated to facilitate investments in green growth and climate change action. It 'focuses on small and medium-sized projects with demonstrable value. The IFI also offers bankability through risk capital, grants, and environmental verification' (Normann 2019). NEFCO in 2018 was the first Nordic institution to receive a Green Climate Fund (GCF) accreditation. In that same year, it approved 124 new projects for €64.6 million.

In summary, the NIB is like other specialised development banks in that it could be classified as a regional, sub-regional, or specialised bank. Its distinctly

Nordic political and economic values as well as its weight on environmental and climate action, however, makes it a specialised bank, as does its role at the centre of the Nordic Finance Group. Similarly, the NDF is 'an important addition to the Nordic toolbox' (Wihtol 2013); it is small and its future depends upon Nordic capital replenishments but it is innovative and demonstrates that debt is not always the answer.

8.7 OPEC Fund for International Development

OFID was the fourth and final Arab-led MDB to emerge between 1968 and 1976. While not an Arab-only MDB, Saudi Arabia is the largest shareholder and Arab countries hold close to 65% of capital subscriptions (Tok, Calleja, and El-Ghaish 2014). Established in January 1976, it was proposed at the March 1975 Conference of the Sovereign and Heads of State of OPEC to channel aid to developing countries. It was an instrument to strengthen financial cooperation and solidarity between Global South oil-exporters and importers (Shushan and Marcoux 2011). As Ibrahim Shihata (1979, 31), OFID's first Director General, commented, the

> adjustment of the price of oil and the financial surplus it generated, coupled with the growing scarcity of this strategic commodity, have all given the oil producing countries of the South a new bargaining position, placing them, at least temporarily, in the vanguard of developing countries in their quest for a new world economic order.

Put simply, OFID arose from the 1973 oil price shock as both an expression of South-South solidarity and the growing geopolitical influence of oil-exporting emerging economies. While the global importance of OPEC foreign aid has declined in recent decades, 'OPEC aid was a major player in international development,' contributing 'on average 13.5% of all aid between 1974 and 1994,' and its aid was 'heavily driven by geopolitics' (Kragelund 2008, 565).

As per its Establishing Agreement, OFID provides concessional financing for balance of payments support and the implementation of development projects in non-OPEC developing countries as well as loans to international development agencies with developing countries as beneficiaries. OPEC countries are not eligible to receive OFID finance. OFID was originally called the OPEC Special Fund and had a different charter but its mandate was similar, especially the strengthening of financial cooperation between OPEC members and other developing countries by providing concessional finance (Shihata 1976). The major distinction between the Special Fund and OFID concerns their organisational autonomy and formalised status. The Special Fund was 'a collective aid facility of OPEC member countries, in the form of an international account jointly owned by these countries and jointly administered by a "Governing Committee" of which they were all members' (Shihata 1980, 879). In other words, the Fund was a temporary 'clearinghouse for aid that oil-producing states were well-placed to give as a result of sharply increased revenues from oil exports' (Shushan and Marcoux 2011, 1970). OFID, however, is an MDB. The Special Fund commenced operations in August

1976 with an initial endowment of $800 million. Saudi Arabia and Iran contributed 25% each of the initial capital contribution and Venezuela, the third largest contributor, contributed 14% (Zamora 1980). Following a revision of its charter in May 1980, the Special Fund became OFID, transitioning from a short-term facility 'into a multilateral agency with its own legal personality' (Porter 1986, 53) in another demonstration of the staying power of international organisations.

There are now twelve OFID member countries. Saudi Arabia is the largest shareholder with over 33% of shares, mirroring its position in the AFESD, BADEA, and IsDB. Venezuela is the second largest shareholder with 15% and Kuwait, Nigeria, and Iran round out the five major shareholders, with these five countries controlling over 76% of shares (Tok, Calleja, and El-Ghaish 2014, Zimmermann and Smith 2011). The other member countries are Algeria, Ecuador, Gabon, Indonesia, Iraq, Libya, and the UAE. Ecuador reactivated its membership in June 2014 after a 22-year absence and Qatar terminated its membership in July 2019. By December 2016, member pledged capital contributions totalled $4.4 billion of which $3.5 billion were direct contributions.

As Table 8.6 details, the OFID has been led by four Director Generals since 1976, who have been from Egypt, Nigeria, and Saudi Arabia. As of December 2018, cumulative OFID lending included $14.5 billion in public sector lending, $3.8 billion in Trade Finance Facility lending, $3.4 billion in Private Sector

Table 8.6 OPEC Fund for International Development Director Generals

Director-General	*Nationality*	*Tenure*	*Details*
Ibrahim F.I. Shihata	Egyptian	1976–83	Oversaw the establishment of the OPEC Special Fund and its 1980 restructuring into OFID. While at OFID, he served as an IFAD Executive Director. An expert on international development, Shihata later served as the World Bank General Counsel from 1983 to 1998, the first person from a developing country to be appointed to the position. Shihata (1981, 251), reflecting on OPEC's members, said, 'Although depicted in the media as the "new rich" countries, all of them are at an early stage of development if judged by the relevant social and economic indicators and not by false appearances of wealth. As in the rest of the developing world, the success of their development efforts is to a great extent dependent on the goodwill of the industrialised countries. They are all food-deficit countries, with some depending almost entirely on food imports. Not one of them has a powerful industrial base. With the possible exception of Indonesia, none of them has major exports other than oil. At least five of them are debtors in the international financial market… These facts make the study of the impressive external aid record of OPEC countries of particular interest, where the lessons to be drawn may differ sharply from those reflected in current opinion.'

Director-General	*Nationality*	*Tenure*	*Details*
Y. Seyyid Abdulai	Nigerian	Aug 1983–Oct 2003	Oversaw a two-decade expansion of OFID into a significant MDB, building its staff, capital base, and borrower country engagement. At the UNESCO General Conference in Paris, France, on 8 November 1983, Abdulai (1990, 9) noted, 'Of immediate significance to us is the drastic reduction in economic assistance of the developed countries to the Third World. This has steadily taken place on grounds that one should not send resources outside when one has not been able to do everything at home. The fallacy of this thinking is becoming increasingly clear. The world cannot be divided into outside and inside. Global interdependence makes nonsense of such a classification.'
Suleiman Jasir Al-Herbish	Saudi	Nov 2003–Oct 2018	Oversaw an institutional rebranding of OFID including a new vision focused on sustainable development and poverty alleviation and a mission to foster South-South partnerships. He pursued a campaign to eradicate energy poverty, labelling energy poverty as the 'missing ninth' MDG; access to energy became the seventh SDG. Prior to his appointment at OFID, Al-Herbish served for thirteen years as the Governor of Saudi Arabia at OPEC.
Abdulhamid Alkhalifa	Saudi	Nov 2018–Present	Prior to his appointment, he served as Deputy Secretary General of the Saudi Arabian Public Investment Fund and held leadership positions at the World Bank Group.

Source: Annual Reports and OFID Website.

Facility lending, and $1.7 billion for IFAD, IMF Trust Fund, and grant assistance. Over the past two decades, new annual approvals increased considerably, from $284 million in 2000 to $1.5 billion in 2018. OFID's Trade Financial Facility, established in 2006 to provide trade finance to public and private enterprises, shaped this increase in annual approvals (Rouis et al. 2010). Of the $284 million in new approvals in 2000, $257 million was public sector lending. In contrast, of the $1.5 billion approved in 2018, $732 million was public sector lending while close to $540 million was trade finance (OFID 2018). Its priority sectors are energy, transportation, finance, agriculture, water and sanitation, telecommunications, health, industry, and education, mostly delivered as project investments (Ramady and Mahdi 2015).

8.8 International Fund for Agricultural Development

The IFAD is a specialised agency of the United Nations founded in 1977. Its mandate is to 'mobilise additional resources to be made available on concessional terms for agricultural development in developing Member States' (IFAD 2019). Of the MDBs outlined in this chapter, IFAD is arguably the most specialised, with its projects and programmes aimed at expanding rural food production and improving the nutrition of the poor (King 1985). As Tasie (2013, 187) notes, unlike other IFIs,

> which have a broad range of objectives, the Fund has a very specific mandate to combat hunger and rural poverty in developing countries… [It] is generally accepted that the Fund has a distinct and catalytic role in improving the livelihood of both subsistence and market-oriented small-holder farmers and producers.

IFAD began operations in 1978 with $1.05 billion and led 60 country surveys in 1979 to build its initial project pipeline.

The origins of IFAD date back to the early 1970s and the sub-Sahelian food crisis (Wihtol 2014). Global food insecurity and a sudden decline in agricultural investment created extreme food shortages in developing countries, aggravated by the 1973 oil shock, which drastically curtailed agricultural production. In response, the UN General Assembly convened the November 1974 World Food Conference that, among other achievements, endorsed Resolution XIII to establish IFAD, addressing a gap in MDF other MDBs were not adequately closing (Kamau and Colaiacomo 2012, King 1985, Talbot 1980). While there 'was little open opposition to the fund proposal,' with the US and Soviet Union publicly supporting it, the US opposed it behind the scenes, perceived IFAD as challenging the World Bank's role in agriculture. It changed its position after 'it became reasonably clear that OPEC would give substantial financial support to the fund' (Talbot 1980, 263–4). Indeed, Szasz (1999) reports there was a challenge between OECD DAC donors and OPEC states in 1974 to each put up around $600m for agricultural development in developing states and it was the desire of Arab states for a new institution where they would have more influence that was decisive in IFAD's establishment. Kamau and Colaiacomo (2012, 473) equally contend that, while there was a financing gap, IFAD 'was more of a political consideration than a functional one,' with OPEC 'preferring the establishment of an independent organization which they could control by exercising their swing vote.' Like the Arab-led MDBs, OPEC's support for IFAD was also in part to restore its reputation in oil-importing developing countries following the 1973 oil shock. The OFID directed $861 million from OPEC to the IFAD's initial capital and first replenishment round.

There are 177 IFAD shareholders. Membership is open to all UN member countries and shareholders are divided into List A (primarily OECD members), List B (primarily OPEC states), and List C (developing countries). List C is subdivided into C1 (Africa), C2 (Europe, Asia, and the Pacific), and C3 (Latin America and the Caribbean). List A members hold 49% of shares, List B 11%, and List C 39%. Each IFAD shareholder is represented on the Governing Council, with representation made up of Original Votes and Replenishment Votes. Below the Governing Council, the Executive Board has 18 representatives elected from member countries.

IFAD's ten largest shareholders are the US (6.99%), Japan (4.18%), Germany (4.24%), the UK (3.12%), Italy (3.74%), the Netherlands (3.88%), Sweden (4.07%), France (3.1%), Canada (3.47%), and Saudi Arabia (3.14%). Collectively, they control almost 40% of shareholdings and they are some of the biggest providers of agricultural subsidies, which distort global food markets. Further, like the World Bank, those countries which benefit most from IFAD interventions are the smallest shareholders, with the majority holding less than 0.25% each. Like the IDA and other concessional financiers, but rare among stand-alone MDBs, IFAD relies on capital replenishments drawn from member states, which gives large donor countries strong influence over IFAD's operational priorities and budgets.

The IFAD is led by a President, who serves as Chairperson of the Executive Board. Since 1977, six Presidents have led the MDB and as they have come from a diverse range of countries: Saudi Arabia, Algeria, Kuwait, Sweden, Nigeria, and Togo. The incumbent President is Gilbert Houngbo, who took office in April 2017.

Between 1978 and 2016, IFAD approved over one thousand loans and debt-relief grants totalling $17.1 billion and over 2,700 grants totalling $1.1 billion (IFAD 2016). It mobilised $10.4 billion in co-financing, with its largest multilateral co-financing partners being OFID (21.2%), AfDB (17.7%), IBRD (8.1%), and AFESD (7.4%) (IFAD 2017). Given that the Arab-led MDBs were central to establishing IFAD, it is relevant that two of its largest co-financiers are OFID and AFESD. IFAD's main work areas include climate and environment, crops, fisheries and aquaculture, gender, indigenous people, land, livestock and rangeland, market access, nutrition, farmer organisations, rural finance, water, and youth. These priority areas iterate the IFAD's specialised focus on rural poverty alleviation and smallholder agricultural development.

Like many MDBs, IFAD has an independent evaluations office reviewing project performance. In 2002, the office published its first Annual Report on Results and Impact of IFAD Operations. This revealed that between 2002 and 2016, IFAD's project performance in agricultural and rural development was comparable to the World Bank but significantly better than the AfDB (70% moderately satisfactory or better compared to 48%) and AsDB (86% compared to 62%) (IFAD IEO 2018).

In summary, IFAD is a small organisation with an annual lending capacity a quarter the size of the AfDB., Yet, it plays a significant, specialised role in the agricultural and rural sectors, with a project portfolio that is far more pro-poor than the large MDBs.

8.9 New Development Bank

The *Agreement on the New Development Bank* was signed in July 2014 by Brazil, Russia, India, China, and South Africa at the BRICS Fortaleza Summit. The Agreement entered into force in July 2015 and the NDB commenced operations the same month. An NDB-like organisation was first proposed by Indian Prime Minister Manmohan Singh after the 2008 GFC, as an alternative to the Global North-led MDBs. Nicholas Stern and Joseph Stiglitz – both former World Bank chief economists – played a role in its development, presenting on it when it was circulated in 2011 among BRICS countries. Stern claimed at a 2013 conference in London that their ideas were as much about ensuring BRICS governments were tied-up in partnerships with big business in order to guarantee their contractual reliability as it was to increase focus on sustainability and climate finance (see Bond 2020). The March 2012 Delhi Summit discussed the feasibility of forming a BRICS-led MDB, a discussion that led to the formal agreement to establish the NDB at the March 2013 Durban Summit. The Durban Summit Declaration (BRICS 2013) argued that the

> prevailing global governance architecture is regulated by institutions which were conceived in circumstances when the international landscape in all its aspects was characterised by very different challenges and opportunities… We aim at progressively developing BRICS into a full-fledged mechanism of current and long-term coordination on a wide range of key issues on the world economy and politics.

China was initially sceptical of the utility of the proposed MDB, but agreed to it after 'India's proposal received support from all the other members' (Wang 2019, 224).

NDB's (2015) mission is to 'mobilise resources for infrastructure and sustainable development projects in BRICS and other emerging economies and developing countries, complementing the existing efforts of multilateral and regional financial institutions for global growth and development.' It earns its title as a specialised bank due to its focus on infrastructure and sustainable development as well as being currently limited to financing projects in BRICS countries; there appears to be little interest from other states to receive NDB project financing (Wang 2019).

The formal rationale for the NDB is like the AIIB, that emerging economies and developing countries need infrastructure investment, MDBs can finance long-term projects that private investors tend to avoid, and are able to offer technical and advisory support (Lingxiao, Yao, and Zexian 2015, Wang 2017). Infrastructure projects have always been the bread-and-butter of the MDBs, as discussed in Chapter 9, though they are often difficult terrain too. Qobo and Soko (2015, 279) link the neglect in infrastructure investments in emerging markets and developing countries to, narrowly, signs of market failure and, more broadly, historical neglect and power imbalances in the global economic system.

Beyond the formal rationale, however, the BRICS-led MDB serves other purposes. One important catalyst, as Stuenkel (2015, 108) outlines, is that the BRICS 'have large foreign exchange reserves and the question is whether these reserves can be beneficially pooled so that more of the savings can be invested rather than hoarded.' Thus, the NDB, particularly for China, is a means of circulating excess capital and transforming that capital into political currency. Further, Chin (2014, 370) outlines at length the respective national interests motivating the BRICS to form NDB:

- Brazil: a source of finance for infrastructure development needs and a tool to raise the profile of Brazil's National Development Bank.
- Russia: a means to encourage intra-BRICS trade and investment and a geostrategic tool to connect with the Global South.
- India: a source of finance for infrastructure, given its ineligibility to receive aid from certain donors, including the IDA.
- China: a means of opening new avenues for its construction companies and stimulating job creation, as well as a vehicle for its global leadership, particularly in the context of its stewardship of the AIIB.
- South Africa: a source of development finance for Africa and a tool for South African leadership in its region.

The NDB is thus both an expression of BRICS formalisation and a political instrument, particularly in the context of their limited voice in other MDBs (Reisen 2015, 302, Wang 2017, 4).

The five BRICS countries are currently the only members of the MDB. They hold an equal number of shares and voting rights and no one member has veto power, a significant departure from the World Bank's structure. Each NDB shareholder is currently allocated 100,000 shares, with a further 500,000 shares unallocated. Authorised capital is $100 billion but subscribed capital is a modest $50 billion, with each of the BRICS contributing $10 billion, only 20% of which is paid in. Non-BRICS countries are eligible to join the NDB, although to date none have. The AIIB had 37 members in its first year of operations, but the NDB is yet to expand. If new states join, the Establishing Agreement prevents the voting power of the founding BRICS to drop below 55% of total voting power (NDB 2015), meaning they would always hold a veto provided they acted in unison, which has not always been the case (Serrano Oswald 2019). Indeed, political differences between members have increased. The prominence of the BRICS is further enshrined in the Establishing Agreement by the condition that the NDB President must be appointed on a rotational basis from one of the founding members.

KV Kamath was the NDB's first President and he contended at a UN South-South Roundtable in 2015 that

> the NDB believes that we are amongst the first development lending institutions to be set up at the initiative of the South. We would also like to believe that the setting up of the NDB, in a way, is a coming of age of the countries of the South.
>
> (Kamath 2015)

Although a misleading statement, given the number of MDBs owned and operated by Global South countries, it reveals that NDB is not only a financial institution but a political actor focussed on the global balance of power between the North and South. Further, examining NDB's management team highlights the embeddedness of the financial status quo. Kamath served in the AsDB's Private Sector Department and came from a career in the Indian private banking sector and Leslie Maasdorp, NDB Vice President and Chief Financial Officer, 'was the main privatiser of South Africa's state assets and also worked in the local leadership of Bank of America and Barclays'; the appointment of such individuals suggests a 're-legitimisation of world financial order' as opposed to a rejection of it (Bond 2013, 615). Indeed, President Kamath, although championing the NDB as a Global South MDB, said that 'Our objective is not to challenge the existing system as it is but to improve and complement the system in our own way' (cited in Tejas 2015). This result is not surprising given the structural implication of setting up the NDB as a traditional development bank.

President Kamath was replaced in July 2020 by an appointee from right-wing populist Brazilian President Jair Bolsonaro: Marcos Troyjo. Bolsonaro, though nationalist and conservative, started espousing liberal economic policies during his 2018 presidential campaign, which is where Troyjo fits in. He was a Deputy Economy Minister and Special Secretary for Foreign Trade and International Affairs under Bolsonaro and represented the Brazilian Government on the boards of multilateral development institutions. Prior to that he had been a diplomat and an academic economist at Columbia University. Troyjo (2017) is a critic of deglobalisation and of neostructuralism in Latin America (discussed in Chapter 4) and a fan of free trade. Indeed, he said to have played a key role in the 2019 deal between the South American MERCOSUR trading bloc and the EU, which had been under negotiation for 20 years. It seems likely he will align the NDB in neoliberal directions, with a greater focus on infrastructure and less on the environment.

The NDB approved its first projects between April and June 2016, renewable and clean energy projects to Brazil, India, China, and South Africa, which was at least in part about virtue signalling with its first loans. However, a close examination reveals NDB investments involved questionable co-financing and execution through local intermediaries. Bond (2020) outlines how the loans to South African parastatals, including the power utility Eskom and to financial intermediaries, are very problematically caught up in South Africa's unsustainable and crony-based regime of accumulation. Further, most of these loans were issued in US dollars not South African rand, as were the bulk of NDB loans in its first five years, increasing foreign currency exposure for borrowers. Corruption and procurement fraud are also major concerns in most of the BRICS and the NDB does not appear to have adequately addressed this, but the same is true of most MDBs.

The NDB has signed partnership agreements with several MDBs, including the AfDB, AsDB, AIIB, EBRD, EIB, and World Bank, as well as national development banks: Brazil's BNDES, the China Development Bank, and Development Bank of Southern Africa. Between 2016 and May 2020, the NDB approved 55 projects worth $16.6 billion. In 2017, its lending portfolio grew to include projects to the transportation, water management, urban development, environmental efficiency, and social infrastructure sectors (NDB 2017). In addition, it established a Project Preparation Fund in January 2017, mirroring the older MDBs in demonstrating the need for adequate advisory and technical assistance to draft sound investments, which suggest too that an adequate project pipeline and project quality will be ongoing challenges. The NDB's strong capitalisation and prudential rules resulted in S&P's awarding it an AA+ rating in 2018, which it has maintained since, again demonstrating it fits the standard MDB model.

In summary, alongside the China-led AIIB, the BRICS-led NDB is significant because it is the first specialised bank established in over two decades and the first new MDB in close to a decade. The creation of more MDBs either demonstrates the continued relevance of the model or the lack of imagination across the global community in development thinking. Either way, the NDB is not a rejection of the MDF status quo. As Reisen (2015, 297) argues, the NDB and AIIB, with their focus on infrastructure, 'introduce choice for potential borrowers in terms of funding cost and modalities,' but do not break with established norms.

8.10 Asian Infrastructure Investment Bank

The idea for the AIIB came about in 2009 when the China Centre for International Economic Exchange considered the feasibility of a China-led MDB. Chinese President Xi Jinping publicly proposed the AIIB with President of the State Council Li Keqiang in October 2013 (Shelepov 2016, Wang 2019). With support gained from Southeast Asian countries through multilateral consultations, a memorandum of understanding on establishing the AIIB was signed in October 2014 between China and twenty Asian countries (Wang 2019). Following several negotiation rounds, its Articles of Agreement were signed by fifty countries on 29 June 2015 and entered into force on 25 December (Shelepov 2016). The AIIB officially commenced operations on 16 January 2016, approving its first projects on 24 June.

As per AIIB's Articles of Agreement, its purposes are to 'foster sustainable economic development, create wealth and improve infrastructure connectivity in Asia by investing in infrastructure and other productive sectors' and 'promote regional cooperation and partnership' in Asia and Oceania (AIIB 2015). Its functions include promoting public and private investment, financing development projects and programmes, and encouraging private co-financing. It is very similar to the NDB, with both being specialised banks investing in sustainable economic development and infrastructure (Humphrey 2015, Wang 2019, Wihtol 2014). The AIIB serves 'China's need to export its production overcapacity in order to arrest its domestic economic slowdown' and is a response to China's limited influence over major MDBs (Chan 2017, 569), after a decade or so of expanding its influence in a number of them.

The AIIB has been interpreted as a financial arm of China's BRI (Callaghan and Hubbard 2016, Chan 2017, Hameiri and Jones 2018), which is interlinked as part of 'a grand economic and diplomatic strategy' to 'promote Chinese influence' and minimise 'the effects of Washington's Asia-Pacific policy' (Cai 2018, 841). President Xi proposed the Silk Road economic belt in September 2013 while touring Kazakhstan and the 21st-century maritime Silk Road in October 2013 while in Indonesia, matching the October 2013 proposal for the AIIB (Callaghan and Hubbard 2016, Chan 2017). Pairing an MDB with a strategic initiative is not new; many SRDBs and specialised banks were established as part of formal regional arrangements. While clearly a projection of China's geostrategic influence, the AIIB – just like NDB – is not a rejection of the MDF status quo, indeed it is very similar to the AsDB (Engel and Bazbauers 2018, Hameiri and Jones 2018). In fact, it has been said that one reason why AIIB conforms to established norms and standards – from governance structures to lending terms – is to legitimise by association the BRI (Callaghan and Hubbard 2016). Certainly, this has paid off for AIIB credit ratings; it received a AAA rating from S&Ps and equivalents from Moody's and Fitch in 2017 and has maintained that since.

As of mid-2020, there were 45 regional member countries and 37 non-regionals in the AIIB, as well as five prospective regional members and 15 prospective non-regionals. The 45 regional members hold 76.35% of capital subscriptions and the 37 non-regionals hold 23.65%. China is the largest shareholder with 30.78%, followed by regional members India (8.65%) and Russia (6.76%). Germany (4.64%), France (3.49%), and the UK (3.16%) are the largest three non-regional members. This means that three of the BRICS countries hold the largest total capital subscriptions, with the other two – Brazil and South Africa – currently listed as prospective founding members. Thus, while AIIB is positioning itself as a broad multilateral body with a large membership, NDB's shareholding is very small, suggesting that it is more focussed on reinforcing and localising the BRICS grouping whereas AIIB is more focussed on China-centric regional leadership (Cooper 2017, Grabel 2019, Wang 2019). Further, as Humphrey (2015, iv) argues, while

> bringing in a mix of industrialised and developing countries will give the AIIB strong standing in the international arena as well as capital markets, it also means that it will face the same pressures as many existing major MDBs to impose stringent requirements on its operations.

Thus, the AIIB could be more accountable and norm-conformist than the NDB. Further, key decisions require a 75% supermajority, meaning that China could be vetoed by groupings of member countries (Hameiri and Jones 2018, Serrano Oswald 2019). However, the AIIB Board is not resident and has delegated a large degree of authority to management to approve loans (to the value of $300 million), which limits oversight and gives staff and management remarkable authority over the MDB.

Headquartered in Beijing, the influence of China over the AIIB is clear, particularly with the appointment of Jin Liqun as the MDB's first and incumbent President. Jin was appointed by consensus at the sixth Meeting of Chief Negotiators held on 24 August 2015. A former Vice Minister of Finance in China, Jin served as a Vice President of AsDB (Gabusi 2017), further demonstrating that the AIIB is likely to conform to established MDB standards and is enmeshed in the MDB system. In a telling commentary by an anonymous high-level Chinese official, Serrano Oswald (2019, 208) records that

> AIIB is not doing something new or different. It is trying to fill the gap that the existing MDBs have failed to do so. The demand in infrastructure is huge but the existing MDBs are not able to fund. AIIB is taking the best parts from the MDBs and trying to make improvements on those shortcomings… The Operational Policy on Financing was drafted by experts from ADB, EIB, EBRD, WB.

The US actively campaigned against the AIIB's establishment, far more forcefully than it had in attempting to prevent the formation of many other MDBs, which is not surprising as the only other banks established by a hegemonic competitor – the USSR with the International Bank for Economic Cooperation (IBEC) and International Investment Bank (IIB) – were small and not organisations that the US could influence. The US claimed that the China-led MDB would 'fail to meet environmental standards, procurement requirements, and other safeguards adopted by the World Bank' (Reisen 2015, 302). It also claimed that it was unnecessary given the work of the AsDB. It even went so far as to pressure its allies not to join (Chin and Gallagher 2019, 246), which ended up embarrassing the Obama administration as allies including Australia, Canada, France, Germany, and the UK became members. Former US Treasury Secretary Lawrence Summers referred in April 2015 to the considerable number of countries joining the AIIB as 'the moment the United States lost its role as the underwriter of the global economic system' (cited in Wang 2019, 222). It appears that opposing the AIIB was less about norms and standards and more about the fact that China was leading it.

By the end of 2018, the AIIB had approved 35 projects. Fourteen projects were stand-alone financed by the AIIB and 21 were co-financed. Only $7.5 billion was invested between 2016 and 2018 though the aim was $10 to $15 billion per annum; the slow start is not surprising as the history of MDBs demonstrates that project pipelines take time to develop. Indeed, it established a Project Preparation Special Fund in June 2016 to support eligible members, particularly low-income countries, to prepare infrastructure projects through feasibility studies and advisory services. By the end of 2017, three countries had contributed $108 million to the Special Fund: China, South Korea, and the UK. The AIIB's thematic priorities are sustainable infrastructure, cross-border connectivity, and private capital mobilisation. During its first two years, $716 million in private capital was mobilised, reflecting the financialisation agenda and indicating the capitalist banking norms of the AIIB.

In summary, like so many other MDBs, the AIIB is not just a development bank but a political actor and an arm of a broader regional arrangement – in this case, the semi-formal BRI (Wang 2017, 4). As an MDB, however, the AIIB is not a counter-hegemonic challenge to established capitalist banking or MDF norms.

In form, function, and purpose, it is quite indistinguishable from other specialised and regional banks and would be unlikely to receive the media and academic attention it currently does if it were not led by China (Chin 2016, Serrano Oswald 2018). The NDB and AIIB thus 'herald a new era' in terms of the geopolitical influence of the Global South 'but also provide a valuable continuity with both the post-World War II era and the more recent past' by reflecting long-standing MDB and MDF norms (Griffith-Jones in Humphrey et al. 2015, 8).

Bibliography

Abdulai, Y. Seyyi. 1990. Development: The Unresolved Issues: Selected Statements by Y. Seyyid Abdulai, Director-General of the OPEC Fund for International Development. Vienna, Austria: OPEC Fund for International Development.

AFESD. 1997. *Annual Report 1997.* Safat, Kuwait: Arab Fund for Economic and Social Development.

AIIB. 2015. Articles of Agreement. Beijing: Asian Infrastructure Investment Bank.

Amland, Bjørn H. 2018. "Nordic Donors to Discuss Strengthening Nordic Development Fund." Development Today. http://www.development-today.com/magazine/Frontpage/nordic_donors_to_discuss_strengthening_nordic_development_fund.

BADEA. 2009. Agreement Establishing the Arab Bank for Economic Development in Africa. Khartoum: Arab Bank for Economic Development in Africa

BADEA. 2015. Seventh Five-Year Plan 2015–2019. Khartoum: Arab Bank for Economic Development in Africa.

BADEA. 2018. Annual Report 2018. Khartoum: Arab Bank for Economic Development in Africa.

Bengtsson, Rikard, Ole Elgstrom, and Jonas Tallberg. 2004. "Silencer or Amplifier? The European Union Presidency and the Nordic Countries." *Scandinavian Political Studies* 27 (3):311–34.

Bond, Patrick. 2013. "Sub-imperialism as Lubricant of Neoliberalism: South African 'Deputy Sheriff' Duty within Brics." *Third World Quarterly* 34 (2):251–70. doi: 10.1080/01436597.2013.775783.

Bond, Patrick. 2020. "BRICS Banking and the Demise of Alternatives to the IMF and World Bank." In *International Development Assistance and the BRICS*, edited by Jose A. Puppim de Oliveira and Yijia Jing, 189–218. London: Palgrave Macmillan.

BRICS. 2013. "BRICS and Africa: Partnership for Development, Integration and Industrialisation." 27 March. Accessed 3 April. http://brics5.co.za/about-brics/summit-declaration/fifth-summit/.

Bussière, Eric, and Emilie Willaert. 2006. *Council of Europe Development Bank: The Social Development Bank in Europe.* Paris: Council of Europe Development Bank.

Cai, Kevin G. 2018. "The One Belt One Road and the Asian Infrastructure Investment Bank: Beijing's New Strategy of Geoeconomics and Geopolitics." *Journal of Contemporary China* 27 (114):831–47. doi: 10.1080/10670564.2018.1488101.

Callaghan, Mike, and Paul Hubbard. 2016. "The Asian Infrastructure Investment Bank: Multilateralism on the Silk Road." *China Economic Journal* 9 (2):116–39. doi: 10.1080/17538963.2016.1162970.

Cammack, Paul. 2018. "Situating the Asian Infrastructure Investment Bank in the Context of Global Economic Governance." *Journal of Chinese Economic and Business Studies* 16 (3):241–58. doi: 10.1080/14765284.2018.1476082.

CEB. 2004. *Report of the Governor 2004*. Paris: Council of Europe Development Bank.

CEB. 2016a. *60 Years of European Solidarity*. Paris: Council of Europe Development Bank.

CEB. 2016b. *Development Plan 2017–2019*. Paris: Council of Europe Development Bank.

CEB. 2017. *Handbook for the Preparation and Implementation of Projects*. Paris: Council of Europe Development Bank.

CEB. 2019. "Articles of Agreement." Paris: Council of Europe Development Bank.

Chan, Lai-Ha. 2017. "Soft Balancing against the US 'Pivot to Asia': China's Geostrategic Rationale for Establishing the Asian Infrastructure Investment Bank." *Australian Journal of International Affairs* 71 (6):568–90. doi: 10.1080/10357718.2017.1357679.

Chen, Lurong, and Philippe De Lombaerde. 2014. "Testing the Relationships between Globalization, Regionalization and the Regional Hubness of the BRICs." *Journal of Policy Modeling* 36 (S1):S111–31.

Chin, Gregory. 2014. "The BRICS-Led Development Bank: Purpose and Politics Beyond the G20." *Global Policy* 5 (3):366–73.

Chin, Gregory. 2016. "Asian Infrastructure Investment Bank: Governance Innovation and Prospects." *Global Governance: A Review of Multilateralism and International Organizations* 22 (1):11. doi: 10.1163/19426720-02201002.

Chin, Gregory, and Kevin Gallagher. 2019. "Coordinated Credit Spaces: The Globalization of Chinese Development Finance." *Development and Change* 50 (1):245–74. doi: 10.1111/dech.12470.

Clement, Keith. 2004. "Structural Fund Programmes as Instruments for Sustainable Regional Development a Review of Nordic Effectiveness." *Innovation: The European Journal of Social Science Research* 17 (1):43–60. doi: 10.1080/1351161042000190736.

Cooper, Andrew F. 2017. "The BRICS' New Development Bank: Shifting from Material Leverage to Innovative Capacity." *Global Policy* 8 (3):275–84. doi: 10.1111/1758-5899.12458.

Corm, Georges. 2006. "The Arab Experience." In *Regional Financial Cooperation*, edited by José Antonio Ocampa, 291–328. Washington, DC: UN ECLA and Brookings Institution Press.

Czarny, Ryszard M. 2017. *A Modern Nordic Saga: Politics, Economy and Society*. Cham: Springer International Publishing.

Danielson, Anders, and Lennart Wohlgemuth. 2003. Swedish Development Cooperation in Perspective. Lund: Lund University, Department of Economics.

Dennis, Bengt. 2015. "Green Light at Third Attempt: How NIB Came to be Forty Years Ago." Nordic Investment Bank. https://www.nib.int/who_we_are/news_and_media/articles/1761/green_light_at_third_attempt_how_nib_came_to_be_forty_years_ago.

Duggan, Niall. 2015. "BRICS and the Evolution of a New Agenda within Global Governance." In *The European Union and the BRICS: Complex Relations in the Era of Global Governance*, edited by Marek Rewizorski, 11–25. New York: Springer.

El Mallakh, Ragaei, and Mihssen Kadhim. 1976. "Arab Instititionalised Development Aid: An Evaluation." *Middle East Journal* 30 (4):471–84.

Elgström, Ole, and Sarah Delputte. 2016. "An End to Nordic Exceptionalism? Europeanisation and Nordic Development Policies." *European Politics and Society* 17 (1):28–41. doi: 10.1080/23745118.2015.1075765.

Engel, Susan, and Adrian Bazbauers. 2018. "Old and New Development Banks and the Future of Development Finance." FLASCO-ISA Joint International Conference, Quito, Ecuador.

Engen, Lars, and Annalisa Prizzon. 2018. A Guide to the Multilateral Development Banks. London: Overseas Development Institute.

Engh, Sunniva, and Helge Pharo. 2009. "Nordic Cooperation in Providing Development Aid." In *Regional Cooperation and International Organizations: The Nordic Model in Transnational Alignment*, edited by Norbert Götz and Heidi Haggrén, 113–30. Abingdon, Oxon: Routledge.

Forsberg, Tuomas. 2013. "The Rise of Nordic Defence Cooperation: A Return to Regionalism?" *International Affairs* 89 (5):1161–81. doi: 10.1111/1468-2346.12065.

Fritz, Barbara, and Laurissa Mühlich. 2019. "Regional Financial Arrangements in the Global Financial Safety Net: The Arab Monetary Fund and the Eurasian Fund for Stabilization and Development." *Development and Change* 50 (1):96–121. doi: 10.1111/dech.12466.

Gabusi, Giuseppe. 2017. ""Crossing the River by Feeling the Gold": The Asian Infrastructure Investment Bank and the Financial Support to the Belt and Road Initiative." *China & World Economy* 25 (5):23–45. doi: 10.1111/cwe.12212.

Grabel, Ilene. 2019. "Continuity, Discontinuity and Incoherence in the Bretton Woods Order: A Hirschmanian Reading." *Development and Change* 50 (1):46–71. doi: 10.1111/dech.12469.

Gu, Jing, Richard Carey, Alex Shankland, and Anuradha Chenoy. 2016. "Introduction: International Development, South-South Cooperation and the Rising Powers." In *The BRICS in International Development*, edited by Jing Gu, Alex Shankland and Anuradha Chenoy, 1–24. New York: Palgrave Macmillan.

Hameiri, Shahar, and Lee Jones. 2018. "China Challenges Global Governance? Chinese International Development Finance and the AIIB." *International Affairs* 94 (3):573–93. doi: 10.1093/ia/iiy026.

Harmer, Andrew, and Kent Buse. 2014. "The BRICS: A Paradigm Shift in Global Health?" *Contemporary Politics* 20 (2):127–45.

Hellén, Siv, and Barbro Eriksson. 2011. "NIB 35 Years: Building Nordic Economic Cooperation." Nordic Investment Bank. https://www.nib.int/who_we_are/news_and_media/articles/1165/nib_35_years_building_nordic_economic_cooperation.

Hernandez, Diego, and Krishna Chaitanya Vadlamannati. 2017. "Politics of Religiously Motivated Lending: An Empirical Analysis of Aid Allocation by the Islamic Development Bank." *Journal of Comparative Economics* 45 (4):910–29. doi: 10.1016/j.jce.2016.09.008.

Humphrey, Chris. 2015. Developmental Revolution or Bretton Woods Revisited? The Prospects of the BRICS New Development Bank and the Asian Infrastructure Investment Bank. London: Overseas Development Institute.

Humphrey, Chris. 2019. "'Minilateral' Development Banks: What the Rise of Africa's Trade and Development Bank Says about Multilateral Governance." *Development and Change* 50 (1):164–90. doi: 10.1111/dech.12467.

Humphrey, Chris, Stephany Griffith-Jones, Richard Carey, and Annalisa Prizzon. 2015. Multilateral Development Banks in the 21st century. Three Perspectives on China and the Asian Infrastructure Investment Bank. London: Overseas Development Institute.

IFAD. 2016. Annual Report 2016. Rome, Italy: International Fund for Agricultural Development.

IFAD. 2017. Annual Report 2017. Rome, Italy: International Fund for Agricultural Development.

IFAD. 2019. Agreement Establishing the International Fund for Agricultural Development. Rome: International Fund for Agricultural Development.

IFAD IEO. 2018. 2018 Annual Report on Results and Impact of IFAD Operations. Rome, Italy: IFAD Independent Evaluation Office.

International Banker. 2017. "Interview with Dr. Rolf Wenzel, Governor of the Council of Europe Development Bank." Accessed 4 September 2019. https://internationalbanker.com/finance/interview-dr-rolf-wenzel-governor-council-europe-development-bank/.

IsDB. 2018. *Annual Report 2018*. Jeddah: Islamic Development Bank.

IsDB. 2019. Articles of Agreement. Jeddah: Islamic Development Bank.

IsDB. 2020. Annual Report 2019. Jeddah: Islamic Development Bank.

Johnson, Willard R. 1983. "The Role of the Arab Bank for Economic Development in Africa." *The Journal of Modern African Studies* 21 (4):625–44. doi: 10.1017/S0022278X00024241.

Kalathil, Shanthi. 2018. "China in Xi's "New Era": Redefining Development." *Journal of Democracy* 29 (2):52–58. doi: doi:10.1353/jod.2018.0024.

Kamath, K.V. 2015. "United Nations South-South Roundtable, New York." New Development Bank. Accessed 4 April. http://www.ndb.int/president_desk/united-nations-south-south-round-table-new-york/.

Kamau, Faith, and Marieclaire Colaiacomo. 2012. "Financing for Development: Examining the Concept of Resource Mobilization for International Organizations, a Case Study of the International Fund for Agricultural Development (IFAD)." *International Organizations Law Review* 9:467–96. doi: 10.1163/15723747-00902008.

Kellerman, Miles. 2019. "The Proliferation of Multilateral Development Banks." *The Review of International Organizations* 14 (1):107–45. doi: 10.1007/s11558-018-9302-y.

King, John Andrews. 1985. "The International Fund for Agricultural Development: The First Six Years." *Development Policy Review* 3 (1):3–20. doi: 10.1111/j.1467-7679.1985.tb00357.x.

Kragelund, Peter. 2008. "The Return of Non-DAC Donors to Africa: New Prospects for African Development?" *Development Policy Review* 26 (5):555–84. doi: 10.1111/j.1467-7679.2008.00423.x.

Kuhn, W. E. 1982. "The Islamic Development Bank: Performance and Prospects." *Nebraska Journal of Economics and Business* 21 (3):49–63.

Lessambo, Felix I. 2015. *International Financial Institutions and Their Challenges: A Global Guide for Future Methods*. New York: Palgrave Macmillan.

Lingxiao, Tang, Ouyang Yao, and Huang Zexian. 2015. "The Foundation for the Establishment of the BRICS New Development Bank: Immediate Impetus and Theoretical Rationale." *Social Sciences in China* 36 (4):40–56. doi: 10.1080/02529203.2015.1088622.

Momani, Bessma, and Crystal A. Ennis. 2012. "Between Caution and Controversy: Lessons from the Gulf Arab States as (Re-)emerging Donors." *Cambridge Review of International Affairs* 25 (4):605–27. doi: 10.1080/09557571.2012.734786.

Naim, Moises. 2007. "Rogue Aid." Foreign Policy. http://www.foreignpolicy.com/articles/2007/02/14/rogue_aid.

Nayyar, Deepak. 2016. "BRICS, Developing Countries, and Global Governance." *Third World Quarterly* 37 (4):575–91.

NDB. 2015. Agreement on the New Development Bank. Shanghai: New Development Bank.

NDB. 2017. Annual Report 2017. Shanghai, China: New Development Bank.

NDF. 2018. Annual Report 2018. Helsinki, Finland: Nordic Development Fund.

Neumayer, Eric. 2003. "What Factors Determine the Allocation of Aid by Arab Countries and Multilateral Agencies?" *The Journal of Development Studies* 39 (4):134–47. doi: 10.1080/713869429.

NIB. 2016. "NIB 40: Financing the Future Seminar." http://annualreport.nib.int/2016/in-detail/40th-anniversary/nib-40-financing-the-future-seminar/.

Normann, Henrik. 2012. "In profile: Henrik Normann, Nordic Investment Bank." emefinance https://www.emeafinance.com/live/deals-top/debt-capital-markets/2191-in-profile-henrik-normann-nordic-investment-bank-1442

Normann, Henrik. 2019. Nordic Investment Bank – Henrik Normann – Answers to UNSW Survey 15.5.2019, edited by Adrian Robert Bazbauers: UNSW Canberra.

OFID. 2018. Annual Report 2018. Vienna, Austria: OPEC Fund for International Development.

Ørvik, Nils. 1974. "Nordic Cooperation and High Politics." *International Organization* 28 (1):61–88. doi: 10.1017/S0020818300004367.

Paaskesen, Kristian Ravn. 2010. "A Bleak Chapter in Nordic Development Aid History?: The Nordic Co-operative Assistance Project in Tanzania." *Scandinavian Journal of History* 35 (4):451–70. doi: 10.1080/03468755.2010.520079.

Petropoulos, Sotiris. 2015. "Opportunities, Challenges and Prospects of South Africa in the BRICS." In *The European Union and the BRICS: Complex Relations in the Era of Global Governance*, edited by Marek Rewizorski, 161–80. Cham: Springer.

Porter, R. S. 1986. "Arab Economic Aid." *Development Policy Review* 4 (1):44–68. doi: 10.1111/j.1467-7679.1986.tb00496.x.

Qobo, Mzukisi, and Mills Soko. 2015. "The Rise of Emerging Powers in the Global Development Finance Architecture: The Case of the BRICS and the New Development Bank." *South African Journal of International Affairs* 22 (3):277–88. doi: 10.1080/10220461.2015.1089785.

Ramady, Mohamed, and Wael Mahdi. 2015. *OPEC in a Shale Oil World. Where to Next?* New York: Springer.

Ray, Rebecca, and Rohini Kamal. 2019. "Can South–South Cooperation Compete? The Development Bank of Latin America and the Islamic Development Bank." *Development and Change* 50 (1):191–220. doi: 10.1111/dech.12468.

Reisen, Helmut. 2015. "Will the AIIB and the NDB Help Reform Multilateral Development Banking?" *Global Policy* 6 (3):297–304. doi: 10.1111/1758-5899.12250.

Robinson, William. 2015. "The Transnational State and the BRICS: A Global Capitalism Perspective." *Third World Quarterly* 36 (1):1–21.

Rouis, Mustapha, Steven Tabor, Stefano Migliorisi, Eric Neumayer, and Komlan R. Kounetsron. 2010. *Arab Development Assistance: Four Decades Of Cooperation* Washington, DC: World Bank.

Rūse, Ilze. 2014. "Nordic-Baltic Interaction in European Union Negotiations: Taking Advantage of Institutionalized Cooperation." *Journal of Baltic Studies* 45 (2):229–46. doi: 10.1080/01629778.2013.846928.

Selbervik, Hilde, and Knut Nygaard. 2006. Nordic Exceptionalism in Development Assistance? Aid Policies and the Major Donors: The Nordic Countries. Bergen: Chr. Michelsen Institute (CMI Report R 2006: 8).

Serrano Oswald, Omar Ramon. 2018. "The New Architects: Brazil, China, and Innovation in Multilateral Development Lending." *Public Administration and Development* 0 (0):1–12. doi: 10.1002/pad.1837.

Serrano Oswald, Omar Ramon. 2019. "The New Architects: Brazil, China, and Innovation in Multilateral Development Lending." *Public Administration and Development* 39 (4–5):203–14. doi: 10.1002/pad.1837.

Sharma, Ruchir. 2012. "Broken BRICs: Why the Rest Stopped Rising." *Foreign Affairs* 91 (6):2–7.

Shelepov, Andrei. 2016. "Comparative Prospects of the New Development Bank and Asian Infrastructure Investment Bank." *International Organisations Research Journal* 11:132–52.

Shihata, Ibrahim F. I. 1976. "Organization of the Petroleum Exporting Countries: Agreement Establishing the OPEC Special Fund." *International Legal Materials* 15 (6):1356–63. doi: 10.1017/S0020782900035002.

Shihata, Ibrahim F. I. 1979. "The OPEC Special Fund and the North-South Dialogue." *Third World Quarterly* 1 (4):28–38.

Shihata, Ibrahim F. I. 1980. "Organization of the Petroleum Exporting Countries: Agreement Establishing the OPEC Fund for International Development." *International Legal Materials* 19 (4):879–85. doi: 10.1017/S0020782900039243.

Shihata, Ibrahim F. I. 1981. "The OPEC Fund for International Development." *Third World Quarterly*, Taylor & Francis, Ltd, 3 (2):251-268. ISSN: 01436597, 13602241.

Shushan, Debra, and Christopher Marcoux. 2011. "The Rise (and Decline?) of Arab Aid: Generosity and Allocation in the Oil Era." *World Development* 39 (11):1969–80. doi: 10.1016/j.worlddev.2011.07.025.

Stephen, Matthew. 2014. "Rising Powers, Global Capitalism, and Liberal Global Governance: A Historical Materialist Account of the BRICs Challenge." *European Journal of International Relations* 20 (4):912–38.

Stephen, Matthew. 2017. "Emerging Powers and Emerging Trends in Global Governance." *Global Governance: A Review of Multilateralism and International Organizations* 23 (3):483–502. doi: 10.1163/19426720-02303009.

Stokke, Olav. 1989. *Western Middle Powers and Global Poverty: The Determinants of the Aid Policies of Canada, Denmark, the Netherlands, Norway and Sweden*. Uppsala: Scandinavian Institute of African Studies.

Stuenkel, Oliver. 2015. *The BRICS and the Future of Global Order*. Lanham, MD: Lexington Books.

Szasz, Paul C. 1999. "Establishment of the International Fund for Agricultural Development." *Studies in Transnational Legal Policy* 31–32:32–43.

Talbot, Ross B. 1980. "The International Fund for Agricultural Development." *Political Science Quarterly* 95 (2):261–76. doi: 10.2307/2149367.

Tasie, C. M. 2013. "Effects of International Fund for Agricultural Development (IFAD) Credit Supply on Rural Farmers in Rivers State, Nigeria." *Journal of Development and Agricultural Economics* 5:186–91. doi: 10.5897/JDAE12.062.

Taylor, Adam. 2015. "A Deadly Stampede Shows the Danger of the Hajj." *New York Times*. Accessed 25 September. https://www.washingtonpost.com/news/worldviews/wp/2015/09/24/a-deadly-stampede-shows-the-danger-of-the-hajj/.

Tejas, Aditya. 2015. "BRICS Nations Open New Development Bank in Shanghai as "Alternative" to IMF, World Bank." *International Business Times*, 21 July. Accessed 21 February 2016. http://www.ibtimes.com/bricsnationsopennewdevelopmentbank shanghaialternativeimfworldbank2017592.

Tella, Oluwaseun. 2017. "South Africa in BRICS: The Regional Power's Soft Power and Soft Balancing." *Politikon* 44 (3):387–403. doi: 10.1080/02589346.2017.1295620.

Thakur, Ramesh. 2014. "How Representative are BRICS?" *Third World Quarterly* 35 (10):1791–808.

Toivanen, Paula. ND. "Pasi Hellman and the Evolving Environment of Development Finance." Suomi/Africa. http://suomiafrica.org/pasi-hellman-on-development-finance.html.

Tok, Evren, Rachael Calleja, and Hanaa El-Ghaish. 2014. "Arab Development Aid and the New Dynamics of Multilateralism: Towards Better Governance?" *European Scientific Journal* Special Edition 1:591–604.

Troyjo, Marcos. 2017. "The Clash between Deglobalization and Reglobalization." *Huff Post*, 1 May. Accessed 3 August 2020. https://www.huffpost.com/entry/the-clash-between-deglobalization-reglobalization_b_586e8e2de4b0a5e600a78907.

Tudoroiu, Theodor. 2012. "Conceptualizing BRICS: OPEC as a Mirror." *Asian Journal of Political Science* 20 (1):23–45. doi: 10.1080/02185377.2012.673857.

Villanger, Espen. 2007. "Arab Foreign Aid: Disbursement Patterns, Aid Policies and Motives." *Forum for Development Studies* 34 (2):223–56. doi: 10.1080/08039410.2007.9666378.

Wang, Hongying. 2017. "New Multilateral Development Banks: Opportunities and Challenges for Global Governance." *Global Policy* 8 (1):113–18. doi: 10.1111/1758-5899.12396.

Wang, Hongying. 2019. "The New Development Bank and the Asian Infrastructure Investment Bank: China's Ambiguous Approach to Global Financial Governance." *Development and Change* 50 (1):221–44. doi: 10.1111/dech.12473.

Wihtol, Robert. 2013. "NDF and the Case for Niche Development Funds." Development Today. http://www.development-today.com/magazine/2013/dt_14-15/opinion/ndf_and_the_case_for_niche_development_funds.

Wihtol, Robert. 2014. Whither Multilateral Development Finance? In *AsDBI Working Paper Series*. Tokyo: Asian Development Bank Institute.

Wiklund, Claes, and Bengt Sundelius. 1979. "Nordic Cooperation in the Seventies: Trends and Patterns." *Scandinavian Political Studies* 2 (2):99–120. doi: 10.1111/j.1467-9477.1979.tb00209.x.

Williams, Maurice J. 1976. "The Aid Programs of the OPEC Countries." *Foreign Affairs* 54 (2):308–24. doi: 10.2307/20039574.

Wilson, Rodney. 1989. "The Islamic Development Bank's Role as an Aid Agency for Moslem Countries." *Journal of International Development* 1 (4):444–66. doi: 10.1002/jid.3380010403.

Woods, Ngaire. 2008. "Whose Aid? Whose Influence? China, Emerging Donors and the Silent Revolution in Development Assistance." *International Affairs* 84 (6):1205–21. doi: 10.1111/j.1468-2346.2008.00765.x.

Worrall, James. 2017. *International Institutions of the Middle East: The GCC, Arab League, and Arab Maghreb Union*. Abingdon, Oxon: Routledge.

Yousef, Tarik M. 2004. "Development, Growth and Policy Reform in the Middle East and North Africa since 1950." *Journal of Economic Perspectives* 18 (3):91–115. doi: 10.1257/0895330042162322.

Zamora, Stephen. 1980. "Voting in International Economic Organizations." *American Journal of International Law* 74 (3):566–608. doi: 10.2307/2201650.

Zavyalova, Natalya. 2016. "BRICS Money Talks: Comparative Socio-cultural Communicative Taxonomy of the New Development Bank." *Research in International Business and Finance* 39. doi: 10.1016/j.ribaf.2016.07.039.

Zimmermann, Felix, and Kimberly Smith. 2011. "More Actors, More Money, More Ideas for International Development Co-operation." *Journal of International Development* 23 (5):722–38. doi: 10.1002/jid.1796.

Zuvela, Maya. 2017. "Islamic Development Bank to Revamp, Decentralise Ops." *Reuters*, 23 May 2017. https://www.reuters.com/article/us-islamic-develop-strategy-interview/islamic-development-bank-to-revamp-decentralize-ops-idUSKBN18J1JY.

9 Infrastructure

Infrastructure is a broad sector. The World Bank (1994) says the sector incorporates power, telecommunications, water supply, sanitation and sewerage, solid waste, roads, railways, ports, airports, and major dams and canals. It is undoubtedly vital to development. Roads give people access not just to markets but to education and health care, water and sanitation are central to extending longevity, and energy and telecommunications are human rights. Infrastructure was the original focus of the multilateral development banks (MDBs) and retroliberalism has seen it return to the centre of the development agenda, aided by Chinese interests, international investors, and extravagant estimates of the value of infrastructure needs proposed by the MDBs. The Brookings Institute claimed that from 2016 to 2030 $90 trillion will be needed for infrastructure and the World Bank has adopted this estimate (Ahmad and Alawode 2017). In Asia, over the same period, the Asian Development Bank (AsDB) said that developing countries will need $26 trillion (Ahmad and Alawode 2017).

Infrastructure investment is written into the DNA of the MDBs. Only three of the 30 MDBs operating today do not make it a priority – the Council of Europe Development Bank (CEB), International Bank for Economic Cooperation (IBEC), and International Fund for Agricultural Development (IFAD). Infrastructure was a key focus during the 1950s and 1960s, although allocations declined in the crisis years of the 1970s as the focus on basic needs increased and declined further in the 1980s due to the hostility of the Washington Consensus to state investment. Attention returned from the late 1990s and today it is at the centre of development practice. Engen and Prizzon's (2018, 41) study of 22 MDBs found that for most of them 'infrastructure is the largest sector' and that 12 of them 'allocate more than 50% of their disbursements to infrastructure development,' with transportation and energy being the two largest sectors.

Neoliberalism's focus on limiting the size of governments has not disappeared and, as a consequence, the MDBs now define infrastructure as a problem arising from a lack of private finance (Ray 2015). Hence, the MDBs shifted from privatisation to public-private partnerships (PPPs) to de-risking infrastructure as an asset class, which is argued to multiply billions in investment into trillions (Gabor 2018). This has resulted in the MDBs doubling down in their efforts to develop innovative new financial instruments that expand private sector engagement in infrastructure to every corner of government operation. Still, private capital is hesitant to engage with the poorest states and in a range of sectors. Further, as infrastructure, it involves a high level of risk. There are environmental, social, political, and economic risks and a long history of poor planning and construction, particularly for large-scale, complex projects, which are back in fashion.

This chapter begins by explaining why infrastructure lending is a core business of the MDBs and equally why it is a risk-laden sector. The second section of the chapter outlines the history of MDB engagement with infrastructure and the third section explores the eruption of complex financial instruments in the context of rapidly expanding global debt. All in all, it is hard not to worry that the current boom in infrastructure investment may end with a bang.

9.1 Infrastructure: a core but high-risk business

Infrastructure lending was well suited to both the International Bank for Reconstruction and Development's (IBRD) structure and its early staffers concept of the Bank. The IBRD, like most MDBs, predominantly lends to nation states and its founding documents stipulated that loans must be mostly for specific projects and must have been evaluated and recommended by a 'competent committee.' Further, most MDBs have clauses in their founding agreements that they can only loan funds where they cannot be procured on market terms; in other words, they are meant to generate additionality for borrowers (Ryan-Collins and Spratt 2013). In addition, as Chapter 5 outlined, the MDBs are reliant on finance markets and credit rating agencies and so they need projects that bankers find acceptable. Infrastructure meets this brief perfectly; it involves specific projects that produce, on paper at least, the rates of return that finance markets want to see. Projects need to be substantial enough to warrant a good deal of technical expertise and study and still produce a scale of loan that is useful for a multilateral bank with a lending imperative; historically, the average World Bank loan size was around $100 million (Ranis 1997, 86). Moreover, the scale, risk, and timeframes of infrastructure investments mean that, all too often, private capital is not willing to lend, which is exactly why the MDBs were created. And, lastly, from the perspective of bankers, economists, and the IBRD's neoclassical growth model, infrastructure is the key driver of private sector growth.

Still, the scale of infrastructure projects means that they are often high-risk investments. As Flyvbjerg, Garbuio, and Lovallo (2009, 171–2) note,

> across the globe, large infrastructure projects almost invariably arrive late, over-budget and, and fail to perform up to expectations. Cost overruns and benefits shortfalls of 50 percent are common; cost overruns above 100 percent are not uncommon.

Given that the MDBs are not meant to fund commercially viable projects that can be financed by private capital, they are likely to be funding the riskiest infrastructure projects, though it is not always the case that they do. Delving deeper into the source of risk highlights that large infrastructure projects have long lead times, a high degree of complexity and sometimes a lack of clarity, technology is often uncertain, and geology, climate, and other issues create unforeseen and unbudgeted obstacles (Flyvbjerg 2009). In developing countries following the Second World War, there was an acute shortage of skilled personnel, especially engineers, and, as a consequence, complex infrastructure projects created an over-dependence on foreign skills and dependent development (Mold 2012, Sogge, Biekart, and Saxby 1996).

Infrastructure demand forecasts also tend to be dramatically wrong (Flyvbjerg 2009). Flyvbjerg, Garbuio, and Lovallo (2009, 172) argue that problematic forecasts do not just arise from delusions or genuine mistakes and bad luck but that 'deception' and the 'strategic manipulation of information' also play a role. This is because there are vested interests involved: politicians and policymakers who want to be seen leading projects of benefit to their communities, contractors and developers who stand to gain multimillion dollar contracts, not to mention the agendas of landowners, lawyers, financiers, and a host of others. For contractors, once they have won a contract, they can often renegotiate it to reflect 'unanticipated' costs and governments too often are left with all the risk and the private sector with the gains (Alston 2018).

All of this can influence the planning process and not everyone has the same level of information about the likely costs and benefits of proposals. In New Institutional Economics terms, there is asymmetric information. The long-term time horizon can serve to dampen risk concerns, such as for the politicians who leave office before a project is completed. The multiple parties involved mean it is often difficult to hold any one person or group to account for failures or cost overruns (Flyvbjerg, Garbuio, and Lovallo 2009). When investments are funded by MDBs, that adds yet another set of interests to be accounted for.

Projects in the Global South tend to have higher levels of corruption than those in the North. This meant that the infrastructure boom of the 1950s to 1970s produced many so-called 'white elephants' – status projects like highways to nowhere, dams that quickly silted up, poor quality roads that became impassable, and so on. The World Bank and other MDBs only finally admitted that corruption was an issue in the late 1990s but even then, they only focussed on corruption by government officials. They paid insufficient attention to reducing corruption in large-scale infrastructure projects and the (often Northern) 'corporations who supply the bribes' (Hostetler 2011, 235). The standard MDB refrain to such critiques is *that was in the past, things have changed now*, but recent examples are easy enough to find, for example, the International Finance Corporation (IFC) was implicated in a corruption scandal impacting a 2019 Colombian highway project (Goodman 2019).

MDB infrastructure projects have often negatively affected communities, including: 'loss of livelihoods; spread of communicable diseases; expansion of the production and trafficking of illicit goods; community conflicts; loss of life through dam collapses and construction accidents; and forced displacement and resettlement' (Sims 2020, 153). This happens despite the safeguard policies that most large MDBs have established because they are difficult to enforce. Further, gender policies tend not to be considered in the planning and implementation of World Bank infrastructure projects (Ferguson and Harman 2015). When infrastructure projects are privatised, the poor are unlikely to benefit because the private providers are interested in reducing costs and charging high user fees, which the poor can rarely afford, and thus they sometimes end up excluded from services (Alston 2018). In the case of the expensive and grossly under-funded area of sanitation, the World Bank – rather than help subsidise latrine construction costs – chose to use active shaming of the poor to trigger personal latrine construction. This approach is widely supported because its anti-subsidy model fits with neoliberalism's hostility to the state, but the programmes infringe human rights and mimic derogatory colonial programmes (Engel and Susilo 2014), while deliberate shaming harms the psychosocial well-being of the poor (Bateman and Engel 2018).

Large projects may offer sizeable economic benefits, but their environmental costs can be equally substantial. The Polonoroeste highway project outlined in Chapter 10 and the resultant mass deforestation of the Amazon is one of the better known examples (Rich 1994). Sims (2020, 153) offers this summary of the environmental impacts of recently funded MDB infrastructure investments: 'clearance of protected forest lands; increased pollutive outputs of expanding industries; species loss through habitat fragmentation, poaching, and vehicle-wildlife collisions; deterioration of riverine ecosystems including fisheries loss through hydropower development.' These concerns do not just relate to the World Bank but to the AsDB, Asian Infrastructure Investment Bank (AIIB), and other MDBs.

Maintenance of infrastructure has also been a huge challenge often exacerbated by infrastructure inappropriate for the economic or environmental conditions of a region (Mold 2012). The World Bank acknowledged the lack of attention to this challenge in documents published in the 1980s (Mold 2012). In the Pacific Islands, this situation is still so endemic that the Pacific Regional Infrastructure Facility (2013) contends that donors operate a build-neglect-rebuild paradigm, which is a reference to the PPP strategy of build-operate-transfer.

9.2 The evolution of MDB lending in infrastructure

Infrastructure did not just suit the structure of the MDBs, it was a core part of their initial Keynesian, welfare, modernisation model. Modernisation and Growth Theory both situated expanding capital formation as key to accelerating economic growth. Paul Rosenstein-Rodan's (1961) argument that capital produces increasing returns to scale thanks to the benefits of scale that accrue from development and that a 'big push' in infrastructure investment is needed to achieve this was particularly influential (Mold 2012). This was the World Bank's goal between the 1950s and 1970s. In the 1950s, infrastructure lending was 63% of total IBRD lending commitments and rose to a peak of 81% in the 1960s (World Bank 1994). The Bank at this time established the model that infrastructure and other projects must be tendered out to the market. Only on rare occasions does the Bank allow the use of a force account; that is, allowing governments to do the construction work themselves. This model was meant to ensure the most efficient use of Bank funds. Bank lending for infrastructure remained at a high 63% in the 1970s, even as it became interested in basic needs. Official flows were overrun by private finance in the 1970s, particularly re-invested petrodollars. These were the infrastructure boom decades, but they ended in a bust with project failures and poor maintenance on the one hand and general crisis in many developing countries on the other hand, caused by rising oil costs, decreasing prices for primary commodities, and general economic malaise.

Infrastructure investment declined rapidly with the rise of the Washington Consensus; structural adjustment lending came to total 43% of World Bank lending in the 1980s (World Bank 1994). This is not surprising, given that a key part of the neoliberal critique of statist development was that it focussed too much on the formation of physical capital, at the expense of 'human capital' (Toye 1993). Equally, neoliberalism in the 1980s was focussed on privatising state assets rather than constructing new ones, starting with those that operated in market sectors and then extending into natural monopolies or public utilities such as telecommunications, electricity, gas, water, and even sewerage, though this rarely proved profitable enough for privatisation.

By the late 1980s, some of the social and environmental costs of World Bank-funded infrastructure projects were becoming public, with civil society movements highlighting failures. This was another reason that infrastructure investments declined further in the early 1990s to just under 34% of lending commitments. The Bank responded with the development of a range of safeguard policies and – as outlined in Chapter 4 – other MDBs followed suit. Not all MDBs abandoned infrastructure, however. It remained a key focus for the Islamic Development Bank (IsDB); the Islamic MDB regards the sector as a key strength. IsDB Group (2016, 19) claims to prioritise more than 'most peer MDBs' and remarks that almost 80% of financial allocations 'are in infrastructure sectors – energy, water, transport, and telecommunication.' Infrastructure is a safe space for an MDB reliant on fossil fuel rents and working with conservative religious regimes (Engel and Bazbauers 2020). In Latin America, the Development Bank of Latin America (CAF) started to turn away from short-term credit for trade towards infrastructure from the early 1990s; from this time, it doubled its infrastructure commitments roughly every five years (CAF 2000, 2005). The CAF has consistently supported regional development with a focus on transport and energy projects.

The AsDB never abandoned infrastructure either. It is one of the most 'traditional' MDBs in that it lends as much as 80% of its funds for infrastructure (Park 2015, 456). Indeed, it has been known in the region as 'Asian Dams and Bridges.' It only created an accountability mechanism in 1995 largely thanks to US pressure and it managed to escape detailed scrutiny of the negative environmental and social impacts of most of its projects until 2000 when civil society groups made a major push for safeguard policies. In the late 1990s, the AsDB acted as a broker for regional initiatives in Southeast Asia with a strong focus on infrastructure, including the Greater Mekong Sub-Region (GMS) initiative. As Sims

(2020, 149) argues, this is one of the ways that the AsDB 'has sought to establish normative views on development' and it represents 'transnational (primarily infrastructure) connectivity as constitutive of development.' Still, these projects resulted in negative attention for the Asian MDB thanks to their environmental and livelihood costs (Sims 2015).

By the late 1980s and into the 1990s, the market was simply not supplying major infrastructure projects, as neoliberals had said it would. This is because, as Mold (2012, 246) comments at length, in

> many developing countries, the size of the market was too small to justify large-scale private participation in sectors such as the energy sector, and technological advances to provide a 'reasonable' minimum efficient scale of production were not forthcoming either. As a result, private investment in crucial sectors such as was rarely forthcoming on the anticipated scale.

With the 1980s debt crisis, infrastructure investment was often one of the first areas sacrificed by the state. Thus, investment fell below what was needed even to sustain existing infrastructure in some parts of the world, particularly in sub-Saharan Africa.

But, in the late 1990s, the tide started to turn for infrastructure. The AsDB's vocal support helped, though China's strong practical interest in and backing for the sector was even more important. In Latin America, neo-structuralism refocussed interest on infrastructure. There were quite a few regional infrastructure initiatives around the world and a number of these were centred on the MDBs, though some were initiatives of regional powers with leadership aspirations (Palestini 2016). Examples include the African Union's 2001 New Partnership for African Development and its associated Infrastructure Project Facility managed by the African Development Bank (AfDB) as well as the 2000 Initiative for the Integration of Regional Infrastructure of South America, proposed by Brazil but coordinated by the Inter-American Development Bank (IADB) and CAF with FONPLATA Development Bank and the Central American Bank for Economic Integration (CABEI) later involved (Palestini 2016). In addition, the AsDB and ASEAN established the ASEAN Infrastructure Fund (AIF) in 2012 to address infrastructure needs by mobilising regional savings and, of course, the AIIB was launched in 2015 to improve infrastructure connectivity in Asia.

Chinese development finance was a major driver of the infrastructure push in the 2000s. This was almost certainly a way of helping domestic Chinese firms deploy their surplus capacity. The largest Chinese public development banks are the China Development Bank and China Export-Import Bank (CHEXIM). By 2015, these two banks lent more in Latin America than the combined funds of the World Bank, IADB, and CAF (Palestini 2016) and they were major supporters of infrastructure in Africa too. The China Development Bank is the larger of the two and it mainly provides non-concessional loans for infrastructure and energy projects, while CHEXIM loans are concessional. CHEXIM and the IADB established a joint investment platform in 2012 focussing 'on infrastructure, mining, and energy projects' (Palestini 2016, 26). The Chinese interest in infrastructure also reflects their competitiveness in the sector, which has translated into winning contracts to implement MDB loans. In the early 1990s, firms from the US, Germany, Japan, France, and the UK won 50.5% of World Bank derivative procurement work and 96.8% of the AsDB and – with Italy – 96.5% of the IADB, although only 25% of AfDB Group contracts (Bracking 2009, 117). By 2002, however, China and India topped the list of suppliers for civil works contracts and China was also the number one supplier in goods contracts (Bracking 2009, 123).

In the 2000s, infrastructure became a cornerstone of the emerging retroliberal development agenda. The first step was viewing public investment in infrastructure as increasing the productivity of private investment, meaning the two were deemed complementary (Mold 2012). Next, plans for how infrastructure might be financialised by becoming an asset class made it a key part of the World Bank's Maximising Finance for Development (MFD) agenda. The rapid and multifaceted innovation in infrastructure contracting and financialisation is outlined in the next section of this chapter.

Interestingly, however, World Bank infrastructure lending commitments have not skyrocketed, though they have gone up. In the second half of the 2000s, infrastructure increased to 38% of lending commitments and in the second half of the 2010s they reached just over 40% (World Bank 2010, 2019). The CAF continued to expand its focus on infrastructure, with its cumulative loan portfolio as of March 2015 ranking transport in first place with 36% of approvals, followed by the energy sector in second place with 28% (CAF 2015). In the IsDB, the infrastructure sector accounted for 59% of OCR flows in 2018, a slight decline from 2010 to 2014 when it was 60.6% (Aid Flows 2019). Notably, the IsDB's 2018 Annual Report emphasised the importance of infrastructure contracts using neoliberal frameworks promoted by the World Bank like PPPs (IsDB 2018). Similarly, the Black Sea Trade and Development Bank (BSTDB), while largely focussing on private sector and trade lending, is shifting towards lending to governments for infrastructure as part of the 2019–22 Strategy (BSTDB 2019).

In Asia, the AsDB highlighted the region's infrastructure needs with its 2009 flagship report: Infrastructure for a Seamless Asia. The report estimates a large infrastructure gap and provides the standard case that closing this would improve efficiency and market access (O'Keeffe, Pryke, and Wurf 2017). It also notes that infrastructure financing 'is complicated because national governments are reluctant to finance infrastructure investment through foreign borrowing, while most of Asia's domestic savings are not at the disposal of national governments' (O'Keeffe, Pryke, and Wurf 2017, 36). Perhaps unwittingly, then, they provided part of the justification for China to create a new MDB focussed on infrastructure. Further, infrastructure is a priority of the AsDB's Strategy 2030 and it has taken a leaf out of the MFD playbook with a strong focus on leveraging bank resources to expand financing (AsDB 2018). On PPPs, the Asian MDB has even developed an operational framework to expand their use (Abon and Chiplunkar 2013). The AsDB has also devoted considerable amounts of technical assistance to infrastructure projects.

The AIIB, with its infrastructure-focussed mandate, has targeted a lending programme of $10–$15 billion annually, however it only reached $3.3 billion in loan commitments in 2018 and $4.5 billion in 2019. Most MDBs have taken some time to build their portfolio and, as outlined in Chapter 3, developing a project pipeline is difficult. Further, the AIIB focusses on the complex realm of infrastructure, making the situation more difficult. To achieve its current level of commitments, it has pursued a fair amount of co-financing and funding for financial intermediaries has increased significantly – more on this below.

Infrastructure is likely to remain a priority for the MDBs for the foreseeable future. It is a key focus of the MDBs and Chinese development finance, and the COVID-19 pandemic has led to the fast-tracking of infrastructure investments. There is legitimacy to the concern that the proliferation of bilateral and multilateral development finance programmes is causing inefficiencies and resource overlap. But the rapid build-up of infrastructure financing and the increasing financialisation of the sector are the reasons we ask, as Mold (2012) did, whether the infrastructure boom is again going to end in tears. To answer this question, a look at the contractual and financial innovations changing the sector is vital.

9.3 Financial innovation in infrastructure: the journey from competitive tendering to de-risking infrastructure as an asset class

The World Bank's Articles of Agreement have a range of clauses about the effective use of funds, but they did not originally specify international competitive bidding (ICB) for procurement. This was introduced in 1951 and, according to Mason and Asher (1973, 187), was 'one of the Bank's proudest moments.' ICB is not without its challenges, however. There are questions around the weighting for domestic procurement, the specifications for goods and services, the engagement of consultants in appraisal work that are also interested in providing inputs at the project stage, and more. In terms of consultants, today they frequently circumvent the Bank's prohibition by creating different consortiums for the appraisal and implementation stages of projects. Indeed, this is one reason why some of the supposed benefits of ICB have been overstated. Further, in major projects, there are generally only a handful of firms able to undertake the work, thus the bidding is often not as competitive as is made out. As noted above, this has resulted in a handful of Global North countries being the major beneficiaries of World Bank and other MDB work, with China and India now joining that group. In Africa, outside of the telecommunications sector, almost no African firms win major infrastructure projects (Mold 2012).

In the 1980s, the attention of the MDBs turned to corporatisation and privatisation of existing infrastructure projects. This often involved splitting firms or utilities into their component parts and privatising the most profitable parts, while corporatising the remainder with the view that one day it too would be privatised. In the case of electricity, for example, this means splitting services into three parts: generation, distribution, and supply. First, independent power providers are introduced into generation as a lead into privatising this component. Next, supply is privatised. Then, lastly, distribution is privatised as it is hard to make the poles and wires profitable on their own (Bayliss and Hall 2002, Yi-chong 2005). Still, it takes a lot of regulation and monitoring to create 'markets' in electricity as it is still largely a natural monopoly and the privatised sector has seen many scandals and market failures (Beder 2003). One illustration of the way that private capital is still being inserted into electricity markets is a 2018 project financed by the AIIB and IsDB supporting an independent gas power producer in Bhola, Bangladesh. The project was unsolicited and approved by the government without any open bidding, with the MDBs nevertheless providing finance; it demonstrates how the ideology of privatisation and neoliberalism take precedence over basic competitive practices. The project has also been subject to very critical reports by the NGO Forum on the AsDB for its impacts on the local environment and livelihoods.

The AIIB-IsDB project is what is called a build-own-operate model, but the growth of PPPs has led to the use of multiple modalities in MDB financing. As Abon and Chiplunkar (2013, 12) outline, the PPP modalities

> range from build-operate-transfer, build-own-operate-transfer, concession, private independent power producers, joint ventures, service contracts, build–own–operate, design–build–finance–operate, financing facility, and purely private sector investments such as direct loans to and equity investments in private organizations.

For infrastructure projects, it is common to see a special purpose vehicle (SPV) company created for the project that private investors and the government have equity shares in, with governments providing a capital subsidy through a range of possible mechanisms. Governments often guarantee tax breaks and revenues to the SPV, effectively de-risking it for private and institutional investors. Alston (2018) notes that this kind of privatisation of infrastructure has dramatically change the relationship between people and their governments and questions whether these arrangements can protect human rights in the face of the profit motive and corporate secrecy.

The World Bank's MFD agenda targets infrastructure and aims to turn it into an asset class. As Gabor (2018) argues, both the Bank and the G20 are focussed on de-risking projects, particularly infrastructure for private capital, and Gabor's parallel to David Harvey's accumulation by dispossession in the term accumulation by re-risking is apt. What we could add to Gabor's analysis, is that the traditional MDB approach of borrowing on bond markets to fund infrastructure that states would guarantee to repay, is also a way of de-risking private finance invested in MDBs. Still, extending de-risking to the asset and privatising its ownership extends the reach and power of private capital and interests over public ones in profound ways. The irony of the World Bank's approach to harnessing private finance in innovative ways is that the Bank was precisely meant to be an alternative to the dangers and violence of private capital. Instead, the Bank is expanding that influence.

States caught in the straitjacket of independent central banks and small government budgets are almost forced into privatisation and PPPs, assisted by the fact that accountancy rules mean PPPs can be excluded from public debt. Yet, PPPs are very often more expensive than traditional public investment though they are presented to citizens as more competitive (Alston 2018, Bayliss and Van Waeyenberge 2018) and their social outcomes are not satisfactory despite the multitude of safeguard policies that MDBs require (Alston 2018). The renewal of the austerity agenda following the 2008 Global Financial Crisis (GCF) saw a further growth in privatisation as a way of paying down state debt, which was created by bailing out private banks and businesses. PPPs are also being driven by the masses of surplus capital floating around the world looking for safe and profitable investments; investors are demanding states create these vehicles.

The AIIB's loans offer insights into the financialisation of infrastructure. Loans to financial intermediaries went from 15.4% of AIIB loan commitments in 2017 to 24.6% in 2018 and 28.8% in 2019. Of the 28 loan commitments in 2019, there were at least five PPPs and a further 15 loans to 'innovative' financial instruments including: financial intermediaries, private equity firms, climate bond portfolios, managed portfolios and the IFC's Emerging Asia Fund. One of the equity investments is in CITIC Capital's Pan Eurasian Fund. CITIC Capital calls itself an 'alternative investment management and advisory company' and its largest owner is CITIC Group, which is China's largest state-owned conglomerate and investment company. In other words, the AIIB is borrowing on bond markets to fund a Chinese state-backed private equity group, which will invest in projects and firms in Eurasia. This is a complex financial structure that requires profits to be paid to investors including the AIIB and salaries and bonuses to be paid to the fund managers as well as to the managers of the actual end projects. There will be very little transparency in the investments in Eurasian states.

AIIB loans to financial intermediaries include a subsidiary of the giant Indian conglomerate Tata – the Tata Cleantech Sustainable Infrastructure On-Lending Facility – and Turkiye Sinai Kalkinma Bankasi – Turkey's first privately owned development and investment bank, which is majority owned by Turkiye Is Bankasi Group, the country's largest private bank. In other words, these subsidiaries are both SPVs that reduce liability and accountability for their owners.

The $500 million AIIB investment to establish the Asia ESG (Environment, Social, and Governance) Enhanced Credit Managed Portfolio in 2019 looks like a way for the new MDB to rapidly increase its portfolio, though the Managed Portfolio will take some time to invest in projects. The ESG ratings are meant to signal to investors that the asset is not 'dirty' and hence this lowers its risk, though the contents of these ratings are deeply problematic. The administrative costs of establishing projects will be borne by the new entity and not the AIIB, making the AIIB look 'leaner' than it is. The fundamental issues with the intermediaries are their cost, lack of transparency around investments, and whether the projects eventually funded support basic human rights and poverty reduction.

A further irony here is that China itself used domestic and direct finance to support its rapid development in the 1980s and beyond with the state (through force account) or state-owned companies undertaking most infrastructure development. In its development finance, however, China is pushing other countries in the Global South to rely on international lending for finance and multinational corporations for construction. These examples show that China is pushing a retroliberal agenda that is 'kicking away the ladder for developing countries' (Yağcı 2016, 43).

9.4 Conclusion

Infrastructure is a core work area for the MDBs. It is also important for development and human well-being. There is, however, no simple relationship between the two. The type, quality, accessibility, and environmental impacts of infrastructure all need to be context-appropriate for large-scale, costly investments to be a net benefit. The MDBs discovered this with their early decades of investment producing poor outcomes and creating debt burdens in many countries. Notably, the MDBs now have access to better social cost benefit analysis tools than were available in the 1960s and 1970s (Mold 2012), so project selection should be better but these are not perfect and large infrastructure investments are still regularly subject to large cost overruns and overestimations of their benefits (Flyvbjerg 2009, Flyvbjerg, Garbuio, and Lovallo 2009). But infrastructure is back in fashion and it is a key part of the current retroliberal development agenda. The MDBs are being pressured to lend because of Chinese development finance and large quantities of surplus private capital seeking investments and they are increasingly using complex financial structures to do so.

This chapter has demonstrated how the MDBs have always promoted private sector participation in infrastructure regardless of its efficacy and they are now pushing complex financial mechanisms to increase sectoral investment. This is even though the MDBs were created to combat problematic private sector financial instruments and World Bank research demonstrating that every financial crisis of the post-Second World War period was preceded by 'innovative' financial tools (Kose et al. 2020). Further, this research shows that the current debt build-up is the fastest and most rapid in the post-war period. All of this suggests that the world is heading for another debt crisis and that many infrastructure investments from the MDBs will end up as debts, dragging down the prospects of states for decades.

Still, even with the World Bank and MDBs de-risking projects, there are limits to investments. The World Bank (2020) Private Participation in Infrastructure Dashboard tracks projects in 139 low- and middle-income countries and reveals that between 1990 and 2020 there have been close to 8,200 projects investing nearly $2 trillion. However, only 3.17% of this went to low-income countries. Indeed, five countries accounted for over 60% of investments – China, Brazil, India, Vietnam, and Russia – and China alone accounted for over 27% of investments in 2019. Electricity is the largest sector for investment, as it is one of the safest and most profitable sectors. Roads are a distant second, while sectors such as water, sanitation, and waste generate very little investment overall and even less in the poorest states. This suggests that direct MDB financing still has a role. The MDBs, however, are now more interested in promoting and working with financial sector actors than in the hard work of developing project pipelines in difficult though vital sectors like sanitation.

Bibliography

Abon, Aura, and Anand Chiplunkar. 2013. "ADB Assistance for Public-Private Partnership in Infrastructure Development (1998–2010): Charting a Way Forward." *GREAT Insights* 2 (4):11–12.

Ahmad, Aijaz, and Abayomi A. Alawode. 2017. *Mobilising Islamic Finance for Infrastructure Public-Private Partnerships*. Washington, DC: World Bank Group.

Aid Flows. 2019. World Bank. Accessed 17 September. http://www.aidflows.org/.

Alston, Philp. 2018. Report of the Special Rapporteur on Extreme Poverty and Human Rights. New York: UN General Assembly A/73/396.

AsDB. 2018. *Strategy 2030: Achieving a Prosperous, Inclusive, Resilient, and Sustainable Asia and the Pacific*. Manila: Asian Development Bank.

Bateman, Myles, and Susan Engel. 2018. "To Shame or Not to Shame – That Is the Sanitation Question." *Development Policy Review* 36 (2):155–73. doi: 10.1111/dpr.12317.

Bayliss, Kate, and David Hall. 2002. "Unsustainable Conditions — The World Bank, Privatisation, Water and Energy." Public Services International. Accessed April. http://www.psiru.org.

Bayliss, Kate, and Elisa Van Waeyenberge. 2018. "Unpacking the Public Private Partnership Revival." *The Journal of Development Studies* 54 (4):577–93. doi: 10.1080/00220388.2017.1303671.

Beder, Sharon. 2003. *Power Play: The Fight for Control of the World's Electricity*. Melbourne: Sage Publications.

Bracking, Sarah. 2009. *Money and Power: Great Predators in the Political Economy of Development*. London: Pluto Press.

BSTDB. 2019. Medium-Term Strategy and Busines Plan 2019–2022. Black Sea Trade and Development Bank.

CAF. 2000. *Annual Report 2000*. Caracas, Venezuela: Corporacion Andina de Fomento.

CAF. 2005. Annual Report 2005. Caracas, Venezuela: Corporacion Andina de Fomento.

CAF. 2015. Annual Report 2015. Caracas, Venezuela: Development Bank of Latin America.

Engel, Susan, and Adrian Robert Bazbauers. 2020. "Multilateral Development Banks: Washington Consensus, Beijing Consensus or Banking Consensus?" In *Rethinking Multilateralism in Foreign Aid: Beyond the Neoliberal Hegemony*, edited by Viktor Jakupc, Max Kelly and Jonathan Makuwira, 113–31. Abingdon, Oxon and New York: Routledge.

Engel, Susan, and Anggun Susilo. 2014. "Shaming and Sanitation in Indonesia: A Return to Colonial Public Health Practices?" *Development and Change* 45 (1):157–78.

Engen, Lars, and Annalisa Prizzon. 2018. A Guide to Multilateral Development Banks. London: ODI.

Ferguson, Lucy, and Sopie Harman. 2015. "Gender and Infrastructure in the World Bank." *Development Policy Review* 33 (5):653–71.

Flyvbjerg, Bent. 2009. "Survival of the Unfittest: Why the Worst Infrastructure Gets Built — And What We Can Do About It." *Oxford Review of Economic Policy* 25 (3):344–67.

Flyvbjerg, Bent, Massimo Garbuio, and Dan Lovallo. 2009. "Delusion and Deception in Large Infrastructure Projects: Tow Models for Explaining and Preventing Executive Disaster." *California Management Review* 51 (2):170–93.

Gabor, Daniela. 2018. Understanding the Financialisation of International Development through 11 FAQs. Washington, DC: Heinrich Böll Stiftung North America.

Goodman, Joshua. 2019. "World Bank Unit Implicated in Latin America Graft Scandal." AP, 2 July. Accessed 29 August. https://apnews.com/e2d43a7687724450a987d2649dc599bd?utm_source=emailmarketing&utm_medium=email&utm_campaign=news_lens_11_july_2019&utm_content=2019-07-12.

Hostetler, Courtney. 2011. "Going from Bad to Good: Combating Corporate Corruption on World Bank-Funded Infrastructure Projects." *Yale Human Rights and Development Law Journal* 14 (1):231–72.

IsDB. 2018. *Annual Report 2018*. Jeddah: Islamic Development Bank.

IsDB Group. 2016. *42 Years in the Service of Development*. Jeddah: Islamic Development Bank Group.

Kose, M. Ayhan, Peter Nagle, Franziska Ohnsorge, and Naotaka Sugawara. 2020. *Global Waves of Debt: Causes and Consequences*. Washington, DC: World Bank.

Mason, Edward S., and Robert E. Asher. 1973. *The World Bank Since Bretton Woods*. Washington, DC: The Brookings Institution.

Mold, Andrew. 2012. "Will It All End in Tears? Infrastructure Spending and African Development in Historical Perspective." *Journal of International Development* 24:237–54. doi: 10.1002/jid.2818.

O'Keeffe, Annmaree, Jonathan Pryke, and Hannah Wurf. 2017. Strengthening the Asian Development Bank in 21st century Asia. Sydney: Lowy Institute for International Policy.

Pacific Regional Infrastructure Facility. 2013. *Infrastructure Maintenance in the Pacific: Challenging the Build-Neglect-Rebuild Paradigm*. Sydney: Pacific Infrastructure Advisory Centre.

Palestini, Stefano. 2016. Development Banks and Regional Powers: An Analytical Framework. Berlin: KFG, Freie Universität Berlin.

Park, Susan. 2015. "Assessing Accountability in Practice: The Asian Development Bank's Accountability Mechanism." *Global Policy* 6 (4):455–65.

Ranis, Gustav. 1997. "The World Bank Near the Turn of the Century." In *Global Development Fifty Years After Bretton Woods: Essays in Honour of Gerald K. Helleiner*, edited by Roy Culpeper, Albert Berry and Frances Stewart, 72–89. London: North South Institute / Macmillan Press.

Ray, Shubhomoy. 2015. Infrastructure Financial and Financial Sector Development. Tokyo: Asian Development Bank Institute.

Rich, Bruce. 1994. *Mortgaging the Earth: The World Bank, Environmental Impoverishment, and the Crisis of Development*. Boston, MA: Beacon Press.

Rosenstein-Rodan, Paul N. 1961. "Notes on the Theory of the Big Push." In *Economic Development for Latin America, Proceedings of a Conference Held by the International Economic Association*, edited by Howard S. Ellis, 57–81. New York: St Martin's Press.

Ryan-Collins, Lily, and Stephen Spratt. 2013. "CAF Development Bank of Latin America's Approach for Infrastructure Financing." *GREAT Insights* 2 (4):4–5.

Sims, Kearrin. 2015. "The Asian Development Bank and the Production of Poverty: Neoliberalism, Technocratic Modernization and Land Dispossession in the Greater Mekong Subregion." *Singapore Journal of Tropical Geography* 36 (1):112–26. doi: 10.1111/sjtg.12093.

Sims, Kearrin. 2020. “The ADB and AIIB: Cooperation, Competition, and Contestation.” In *Rethinking Multilateralism in Foreign Aid: Beyond the Neoliberal Hegemony*, edited by Viktor Jakupec, Max Kelly and Jonathan Makuwira, 145–159. London: Routledge.

Sogge, David, Kees Biekart, and John Saxby, eds. 1996. *Compassion and Calculation: The Business of Private Foreign Aid*. London: Pluto Press with Transnational Institute.

Toye, John. 1993. *Dilemmas of Development*, 2nd ed. Oxford: Blackwell Publishers.

World Bank. 1994. *World Development Report 1994: Infrastructure for Development*. Oxford: Oxford University Press.

World Bank. 2010. *Annual Report 2010: Year in Review*. Washington, DC: World Bank.

World Bank. 2019. *Annual Report 2019: Ending Poverty. Investing in Opportunity*. Washington, DC: World Bank.

World Bank. 2020. “Private Participation in Infrastructure Dashboard.” Accessed 1 September. https://ppi.worldbank.org/en/visualization#sector=&status=&ppi=&investment=&region=&ida=&income=&ppp=&mdb=&year=&excel=false&map=&header=true.

Yağcı, Mustafa. 2016. “A Beijing Consensus in the Making: The Rise of Chinese Initiatives in the International Political Economy and Implications for Developing Countries.” *Perceptions* XXI (2):29–56.

Yi-chong, Xu. 2005. “Models, Templates and Currents: The World Bank and Electricity Reform.” *Review of International Political Economy* 12 (4):647–73.

10 Climate finance

Climate finance 'refers to local, national, or transnational financing – drawn from public, private, and alternative sources of financing – that seeks to support mitigation and adaptation actions that will address climate change' (UNFCCC 2020). Through their climate investments and advisory services, the multilateral development banks (MDBs) work as climate intermediaries. Exercising material, technical, and normative influence, they draw attention to climate issues and connect different actors in their efforts to adapt, mitigate, and build resilience to climate change. The MDBs frame climate action in terms of interventions made possible by financial investment, contributing to a narrative that exists largely within the bounds of a market-based, economistic, and quantifiable methodology.

The MDBs originally had fairly poor environmental records but have been reforming and have become influential actors in the global economic governance of sustainable development and climate change (Florini and Sovacool 2009, Käkönen and Kaisti 2012). They are only one part of complex environmental governance networks but are notable for their leadership in mainstreaming initiatives like the 2015 Paris Agreement and the Sustainable Development Goals (SDGs). They have introduced green and blue bonds to catalyse private investment. Indeed, 'multilateral lending is a defining feature of international finance and the environment' (Clapp and Dauvergne 2005, 196).

MDB climate actions are diverse. They range from project financing and resource mobilisation, including co-financing and on-lending to the public and private sectors, to building knowledge networks and communities of practice, to research and training. These actions make the MDBs climate intermediaries that draw together different actors and send signals to private capital about the feasibility of and potential rates of return on climate investments. The focus on private investment cannot be understated; the MDBs all acknowledge that public multilateral development finance (MDF) is required in the short-term but argue that successful climate interventions in the mid- to long-term need private capital. This somewhat naïve neoliberal climate mantra holds that with enough finance invested it is possible to manage climate change while promoting continuous economic growth.

The MDBs pursue climate actions to different degrees. Over the past few decades, international focus and institutional isomorphism has led almost all to adopt, at the least, corporate climate action plans to align their lending operations with sustainable best practice and participate in global climate forums. There are, however, differences due to capital availability, shareholder influence, and regional circumstance. Capital and mandate restrictions limit some MDBs from financing climate projects, but the larger MDBs are climate leaders, as are some of the smaller ones.

Shareholder influence and geography play key roles too. The Latin American MDBs are exemplars of proactive climate action as the region has been hit hard by climate-related disasters and progressive leaders have supported interventions, though regional politics has become more conservative in the last few years. Still, as an example, the Caribbean Community's 'early political championing of the climate change threat' shaped the Caribbean Development Bank's (CDB) robust environmental agenda (CDB 2012). In contrast, the Russian-led Eurasian Development Bank (EDB) and Black Sea Trade and Development Bank (BSTDB) are laggards and continue to heavily invest in petroleum, coal, and oil but the European Union (EU) has ensured that the European Investment Bank (EIB) has a strategic focus on climate change.

This chapter outlines the evolving role of the MDBs as climate intermediaries. The first section builds a history of the international climate regime, identifying key turning points in MDB climate action. Next, this chapter analyses initiatives by the MDBs to mainstream environmental and climate change objectives in their organisational activities. The third section evaluates MDB climate finance approvals, detailing both investment volumes and sectoral focuses. The final section examines climate bonds and climate finance facilities established, administered, or supported by the MDBs.

10.1 Climate history

The Intergovernmental Panel on Climate Change (IPCC), the leading United Nations (UN) body debating and coordinating global climate action, proclaimed in the early 2000s that 'there is now little doubt that human-induced climate change is happening' (cited in Adger et al. 2003, 180). The MDBs have largely taken this warning seriously, albeit with inter-organisational differences in practical action and some gaps and questions. Multilateral climate finance has evolved with the international climate regime – defined here as the global governance framework coordinating state and non-state climate action – over the past several decades. There have been four phases in the international climate regime: (i) 1970–87: Limits to Growth and Sustainable Development; (ii) 1987–2000: Formalising the International Climate Regime; (iii) 2000–10: From Sustainability to Climate Change; and, (iv) 2010–20: Adaptation, Mitigation, and Resilience. These phases, explored briefly below, align with key turning points in global climate action, which, in turn, saw organisational, operational, and policy shifts in the MDBs.

10.1.1 *Phase I: 1970–87: limits to growth and sustainable development*

Connections between development and the environment were first made by the MDBs in the 1970s. In 1971, the World Bank prepared the first MDB handbook linking environmental costs to long-term economic growth as an acceptable trade-off (Gutner 2002, 51, Lee 1985, x); they pioneered analysis of environmental factors in lending operations and conceptualised 'ways to stabilise the environment so that it could be commercialised and used to promote poverty alleviation' (Yudelman 1976). In other words, the environment was an input to economic growth, it was only a matter of finding the right level of exploitation. In 1972, the Club of Rome published the influential *Limits to Growth*, which modelled the consequences of exponential economic and population growth on finite natural resources (Meadows et al. 1972). *Limits to Growth* sparked debate about whether economic growth and sustainability are compatible as well as a reformist discussion on how best to manage natural resources while improving economic growth. This was a factor in the Inter-American Development Bank (IADB) becoming the first MDB to adopt an environmental policy in 1979.

Global concern over environmental sustainability grew throughout the 1970s and 1980s, spurred by heavily publicised human-made disasters including the 1978 Amoco Cadiz oil spill, 1984 Bhopal gas tragedy, and 1986 Chernobyl nuclear accident (Elliott 2004, 13). Further, the dire environmental consequences of numerous MDB, particularly World Bank, projects started to emerge. One of the most infamous was the World Bank Polonoroeste project paving 1,500 km of highway through the Brazil's Amazon, which resulted in mass deforestation and immiseration of the local Amerindian tribes (Rich 1994). Thus, environmental factors began to be incorporated into development assistance, though not very well.

Sustainable development emerged as a concept first in the 1980 UN-led *The World Conservation Strategy* before entering the official communiques of several MDBs, but it was not formalised in lending operations or project evaluations (Lee 1985, ix). The 1987 *Our Common Future*, the report drafted by the Brundtland Commission, articulated sustainable development as 'development that meets the needs of the present without compromising the ability of future generations to meet their own needs' (Brundtland 1987, 43). The Brundtland Report embedded the sustainable development concept in both policy and public discourse, an important step in mainstreaming environmental action (Redclift 2005). It was a key driver for MDBs revising their approach to environmental action throughout the 1990s.

10.1.2 *Phase II: 1987–2000: formalising the international climate regime*

The decade following the 1987 Brundtland Report saw the steady formalisation of the international climate regime, with the establishment of several environmental agencies. Among the first agencies was the IPCC set up in 1988 to assess existing scientific knowledge of human-caused climate change. The international community established the Global Environment Facility (GEF) in 1992, initially as a pilot programme with the World Bank. The 1992 UN Conference on Environment and Development – called the Rio Earth Summit – led to *Agenda 21* outlining a non-binding sustainable development agenda. With the adoption of the UN Framework Convention on Climate Change (UNFCCC) at the Rio Earth Summit, the GEF became the financing mechanism of both *Agenda 21* and the UNFCCC (Clapp and Dauvergne 2005, 208). The Kyoto Protocol of 1997, which entered into force in 2005, enacted greenhouse gas (GHG) emissions reduction targets. This was followed by the 2002 World Summit on Sustainable Development and the 2012 Rio +20 Summit.

The 1990s saw the steady formalisation of the environmental governance architecture, with the MDBs gradually aligning their operations to key international statements and agendas. Early on, the MDBs acted because of poor press and NGO pressure due to the significant environmental damage many of their projects were causing. The MDBs thus began to establish organisational departments to address sustainable development, as well as draft operational policy and guidelines. While relatively narrow in focus, the steady formalisation of the international climate regime led many MDBs to begin substantively engaging with environmental issues, framed in the 1990s in terms of sustainable development.

10.1.3 *Phase III: 2000–10: from sustainability to climate change*

The 2000s began with a highpoint of international collaboration – the launch of the Millennium Development Goals (MDGs) – but ended in a breakdown of inter-state cooperation with the failure of the 2009 COP-15 Copenhagen Summit to set emissions reduction targets. Two significant changes for the MDBs occurred. First, as outlined in Chapter 4, the MDGs became a unifying framework for the MDBs and Goal 8 was 'to ensure environmental sustainability,' which institutionalised it in the development banks (Alston 2005). In 2000, to better accommodate sustainable development and the MDGs, the GEF adopted a new policy giving the regional development banks (RDBs) access to GEF funding. This later expanded to include some sub-regional and specialised development banks, so there are now eight MDBs among the GEF's implementing agencies. The World Bank's Country Assistance Strategies – country-level diagnostics proposing loan schedules – began to ask sustainability questions from 2001 (Shyamsundar et al. 2001, 3).

The second significant development, identifiable from the late 2000s, saw the MDBs become key players in addressing climate change. With the collapse of COP-15 from stalled inter-state cooperation compounded by the spike in protectionist policies following the 2008 Global Financial Crisis (GFC), climate action lost priority for many countries, but this created more space for non-state actors in climate leadership. 2009 was a turning point for the MDBs; they demonstrated a concerted acceleration of interest in climate change adaptation, mitigation, and resilience, taking on the idea of climate-smart development and not just sustainable development (Lipper and Zilberman 2018).

10.1.4 Phase IV: 2010–20: adaptation, mitigation, and resilience

The 2010s saw accelerated concern for climate adaptation (purposive changes to better cope with climate change), mitigation (stabilisation or reduction of GHG emissions), and resilience (building infrastructure and services to better withstand climate shocks) (Ayers et al. 2014, Henstra 2012, Janetos et al. 2012). The rhetoric turned from *environmental factors are relevant to development* to *climate change shapes development*. During the 1990s, multilateral and bilateral climate finance had tended to be short-term funding for ad hoc projects. By the 2010s, it involved longer-term and more substantial investments (Peake and Ekins 2017, 833–4). The World Bank nearly doubled annual allocations between 2012 and 2018 and other MDBs increased from the mid-decade too.

The 2015 Paris Agreement and SDGs are the lodestars of current MDB climate finance, broadly aligning their lending, policy, and normative actions. A joint Climate Change Finance Statement released by several large MDBs in September 2019 showed their common approach: commitment to increase climate finance allocation over time; catalysing private finance; supporting the Paris Agreement; strengthening climate finance transparency reporting; and, transitioning operations away from fossil fuel projects (AfDB, AsDB, AIIB, et al. 2019). The priorities are clearly for more finance and more private sector finance.

The Paris Agreement entered into force in November 2016. Its centrepiece is the Nationally Determined Contributions (NDCs), the emissions reduction and adaptation commitments of countries. The Agreement outlined the need to build cooperative networks through the MDBs and climate financing mechanisms to achieve the NDCs (Peake and Ekins 2017, Sharma 2017). Many MDBs joined the NDC Partnership Agreement and built their own NDC advisory platforms: IADB launched NDC Invest in 2016, the African Development Bank (AfDB) unveiled the African HDC Hub in 2017, and the Asian Development Bank (AsDB) established NDC Advance in 2018 as a technical assistance platform. Other MDBs, such as EIB and CDB, have not developed their own platforms but incorporate measures to ensure lending operations align with recipient NDC strategies (Wright et al. 2018). Many MDBs also work with the Green Climate Fund (GCF), proposed in 2009 and established in 2011. It is the world's largest climate fund and was mandated to limit or reduce GHG emissions in developing countries and adapt vulnerable societies to climate change. It works through national and multinational implementing bodies including 11 MDBs.

The SDGs complement the Paris Agreement and the discursive shift from sustainability to climate action. The link between them is that global temperature increases above 1.5°C would make impossible the achievement of many of the SDGs and lead to worsening inequalities and a greater likelihood of conflict and humanitarian issues (IPCC 2018). The SDGs are much more comprehensive than the MDGs in their climate awareness and even imply that '[e]conomic growth can no longer be attained at the cost of the environment' (AsDB 2019, viii), but they do not go as far as suggesting that there is a trade-off between the two and they put a great deal of faith in technological fixes. While global agreements now indicate that ignoring anthropogenic climate change is no longer an option, the selfish retroliberal agenda has seen more and more states walk away from international agreements.

10.2 Climate mainstreaming

Every MDB has mainstreamed environmental actions, defined as 'the integration of environmental and climate change objectives into non-environmental sectors and the "greening" of public policies' (Benson et al. 2014, 606). While some have done far more and others far less, they have all acted, with the 2010s seeing a growth in mainstreaming. Only the Central American Bank for Economic Integration (CABEI), Development Bank of Latin America (CAF), European Bank for Reconstruction and Development (EBRD), and New Development Bank (NDB) explicitly refer to environmental factors in their establishing agreements; EBRD was 'the first MDB to be born with an environmental mandate' (Gutner 2002, 62), it being founded in the post-Brundtland milieu amidst the formalisation of the climate regime. The significance of so few MDBs formally mandated to support climate action shows that the growth of climate finance has been the result of efforts by management, member countries, and social movements to foster organisational change (Goldman 2001).

The World Bank was an early adopter of mainstreaming, albeit in somewhat limited forms. In 1987, it established an Environmental Department to set policy, planning, and research work but this was largely in response to public pressure related to environmental disasters and the Brundtland Report (Goldman 2001, Gutner 2002, Rich 1994). However, the Bank maintained a very narrow and neoliberal understanding that environmental degradation limited economic growth (Castro 2004). Mainstreaming saw the Bank become the largest environmental donor of the 1990s, providing a third of all multilateral environmental assistance, though this illustrates the lack of other resources as much as the Bank's engagement. Further, there were pertinent criticisms of the Bank's definition of environmental projects as it included large-scale dam projects that displaced large numbers of people including tribal communities (Zawahri and Weinthal 2014). Under pressure, the Bank established inspection panels and requirements that all projects must submit environmental impact assessments (O'Neill 2012, 155); the number of environmental staffers increased from five in 1987 to 200 by 1994. The 'significant shift in World Bank policies… in a relatively short period' (Clapp and Dauvergne 2005, 201) framed how other MDBs should restructure their own policies and lending operations, particularly the RDBs.

The RDBs began mainstreaming following the Brundtland Report. Prior to it, they were not aligned; earlier environmental policies were largely ad hoc, voluntary guidelines (Gutner 2002, 70). From 2000 onwards, isomorphic pressure framed by the Kyoto Protocol, MDGs, and growing public concern led the RDBs to deepen their mainstreaming activities. AsDB approved a new Environmental Policy in 2002, as did AfDB in 2004; these policies updated environmental assessment guidelines, revised country environmental analyses, and laid the groundwork to expand environmental and energy investments (Delina 2011, Posas 2011). Accelerated by the 2015 Paris Agreement and SDGs, the RDBs developed climate change action plans to increase their climate investments, establish policy platforms, and catalyse private climate finance. EBRD unveiled its Green Economy Transition (GET) framework in 2015, proposed to achieve a target of increasing climate finance to 40% of annual investments by 2020, and it became its main mechanisms to support borrower NDCs and the SDGs (EBRD 2018). Further, EIB sent strong signals to other MDBs and private capital with its announcement in July 2019 it would cease financing fossil fuel projects by the end of 2021 (Ambrose 2019).

Compared to the World Bank and RDBs, the other MDBs demonstrate greater variability in their climate actions. Various factors shape these differences, including limited capital availability constraining annual approvals and shareholder activism either promoting or demoting climate action as a strategic priority. The small scale of many of the sub-regional and specialised banks is also a factor. Climate-friendly changes include organisational pledges to carbon neutrality, such as the Council of Europe Development Bank (CEB) purchasing hybrid vehicles and CABEI maintaining a carbon neutral headquarters, and utilising renewable energy market mechanisms, with the East African Development Bank (EADB) purchasing UN-certified carbon emissions reduction credits from member countries.

Latin American and Caribbean MDBs have a strong history of climate mainstreaming. CAF, CDB, and CABEI have all developed robust policies, demonstrating what large and small MDBs are capable of with enough shareholder support. CAF started its Sustainable Development Coordination Office in 1994, which evolved to become the new Vice Presidency of Social and Environmental Development in 2004. Recently, it built a climate network with regional organisations to assemble alliances for climate finance action (CAF 2017), a move indicative of norm leadership. CDB and CABEI have similarly built strong climate frameworks, with CDB guided by its Climate Resilience Strategy 2019–24 drafted to develop its reputation and capabilities as a regional climate leader (CDB 2018a) and CABEI by its 2015–19 Institutional Strategy that recognises Central America as a disaster-prone region and therefore requires climate investments (CABEI 2015). Further, CABEI has developed strategic networks to support its climate actions – just like CAF – but has done so with non-regional actors, including the Climate Change Adaptation Fund and GCF. For smaller MDBs, accreditation with development funds and networks enables very small annual climate commitments to expand considerably.

Other MDBs have engaged less with climate mainstreaming, notably the Russian- and Arab-led MDBs. They do pursue some climate actions, but their approach is narrower and more conservative than other MDBs. To illustrate, the International Investment Bank (IIB) has an Environment and Social Policy

Framework, but its conceptualisation of climate action is narrowly limited to sustainable energy and infrastructure, while making considerable allowances for fossil fuel investments. This reflects the importance of carbon-based energy to its leading shareholders and their geopolitical pursuit of resource security. Further, while the Arab Bank for Economic Development in Africa (BADEA) became more rhetorically active in the 2010s, action lagged. BADEA's Seventh Five-Year Plan does not mention climate change, though it does discuss the importance of carbon-based and renewable energy sources (BADEA 2015), a position common across the Arab-led MDBs. The Islamic Development Bank (IsDB) has become somewhat more of a climate leader recently, publishing its 2019 Climate Change Policy that recognises its members are facing significant obstacles due to climate change (IsDB 2019). The Policy is aligned with a 10 Year Strategy that supports the achievement of the SDGs by 2030 (Sadik 2018) and has four policy pillars: mainstreaming climate action in lending operations; promoting climate change resilience; green growth and the transition to a green economy; and, leveraging resources for climate action (IsDB 2019). Yet, IsDB still allows projects to include fossil fuel elements, a reflection of the strategic importance of non-renewables to its main shareholders.

Despite achievements, troubling issues remain. Regarding environmental safeguards applied to projects, Humphrey (2016, 4–5) outlines that they are imposed over national laws and thus lead to sovereignty questions, are often one-size-fits-all, legalistic, and inflexible, and are expensive and time-consuming with costs paid by the borrower. Further, mainstreaming has revealed not a break from traditional MDB operations but attempts to integrate climate actions into the neoliberal model – emphasising market-based solutions and private sector finance to adapt, mitigate, and build resilience to climate change. As an illustration, most MDBS have climate risk management tools, including project exclusion lists prohibiting investments in non-renewables and screening tools to evaluate the climate impacts of projects. While such tools are important to minimise the negative effects of MDB operations, these tools do not fundamentally transform how development is understood or challenge the naïve faith that continuous economic growth is possible.

10.3 Climate finance

Annual sustainable development lending and climate finance by the MDBs has increased in volume and scope since the 1980s, paralleling climate mainstreaming. In absolute terms, the UN estimates global climate finance – public and private – to have been between $340 and $650 billion in 2014. However, global infrastructural, industrial, and energy investments – including carbon-based sectors – in the same year were estimated to be in the trillions (CEB 2016, Peake and Ekins 2017). This disparity is unsurprising, given the orientation of global investment patterns towards 'traditional' and 'bankable' sectors. But, despite risk aversion, over the 2010s there was increased support for climate action from both public and private capital, especially energy transition investments. Bell (2020, 59–64) identifies two phases in the gradual expansion of climate finance markets. First, state intervention prompted by popular pressure or political policy agendas encouraged a growth in renewables. Second, the expansion of state intervention signalled increasing market returns on investments, leading to greater engagement by private capital with new financial innovations emerging. This occurs even though 'the sunk costs and older path dependencies in the fossil fuel sector remain deeply entrenched in energy systems worldwide' (Bell 2020, 62). This analysis both provides a strong logic for MDBs to further engage in climate finance and frames the changes in MDBs. They have played an important role as 'market makers' for climate markets, catalysing private investment in environmental projects and setting common operational standards in project delivery and climate finance tracking (CEB 2016).

A 2019 AsDB Institute report, co-authored by Jeffrey Sachs, argues that the MDBs 'should help finance [environmental] programs in Asia and other regions by raising vastly more long-term debt from the capital markets at the prevailing low interest rates and then lending the money to governments and public-private investment entities' (Sachs et al. 2019, 3). The report reveals two important trends: first, the focus on public funding in the short-term to catalyse long-term private investment and, second, the increasing financialisation of climate action and use of debt. The need for public financial action is further articulated by Sachs et al. (2019, 5) because private banks 'consider most [renewable energy] projects to be risky' and their 'resources come from deposits, and deposits are usually short to medium term, whereas green infrastructure projects require long-term finance, resulting in a maturity mismatch for banks.'

AfDB, AsDB, EBRD, EIB, IADB, and the World Bank began publishing joint annual climate finance reports in 2011, following joint press releases starting with COP-15 in 2009. Since 2015, the reports have outlined projected climate finance allocations, with 2020 targets being to double or triple climate finance approvals. They are also a means to improve transparency, improve cooperation, and catalyse private finance. The 2018 Joint Report demonstrates a staggered increase in climate finance approvals after the 2015 Paris Agreement (AfDB, AsDB, EBRD, et al. 2019).

Several MDBs and the International Development Finance Club (IDFC) jointly agreed to the Common Principles for Climate Adaptation Finance Tracking in March 2015. The Principles were designed to align what previously had been ad hoc environmental investments and develop more systematic methodologies to track the movement of climate finance. Between 2015 and 2017, the Principles were applied to more than 1,000 projects with adaptation finance exceeding $18.6 billion. The IsDB applied the Principles to its climate actions beginning in 2018, demonstrating a rollout of the Principles as an institutional norm. Other MDBs have built their own methodologies for mapping climate finance. In addition to reporting, the Principles have been useful in drawing attention to MDB climate action and, as an attempt to 'crowd in' private capital, they have led the MDBs to build their capacity to assess climate finance vulnerabilities (Climate Finance Tracking Working Group 2018).

The World Bank, RDBs, and CAF and NIB are the largest MDB climate financiers. It is difficult to isolate the climate commitments of many MDBs; some do not list it as a discrete sector, for the NIB (2018) it is a cross-cutting theme. Others, like the World Bank, do, but such allocations reflect normative choices, for example, in determining what percentage of a sanitation project might count as climate finance. The World Bank's Environment and Natural Resources investment stream delivered 14% of all approvals between 2011 and 2015; the stream is one of eleven operational priorities. Between 2011 and 2016, the Bank Group committed $52 billion to over 900 climate projects, an annual average of $10.3 billion. In 2017, following a post-Paris Agreement spike, the percentage of climate finance increased to 31% (World Bank 2017). In 2018, the World Bank was the largest MDB climate financier, collectively approving close to 50% of all climate finance when ranked against the RDBs, followed by EIB and EBRD.

Like the World Bank, the RDBs have increased their climate finance commitments since the Paris Agreement. In 2017, AfDB had 28% of approvals as climate finance, up from 9% in 2016, AsDB listed 22% of approvals as climate interventions, and EBRD allocated 43% of OCR to its GET, up from 33% in 2016. Yet, the RDBs pursue different climate objectives. AfDB focusses on a 'New Deal on Energy' and policy environments attractive to private investment, AsDB on building climate-resilient infrastructure and low-carbon development, and EIB on targeting renewable energy projects and waste and wastewater reclamation. RDB climate finance focusses more on mitigation (70% in 2018) than adaptation (30% in 2018), with mitigation loans tending to be short-term responses compared to longer-term adaptation projects. In 2018, 71% of World Bank and RDB climate finance was delivered as investment projects and only 8% as policy loans, meaning that MDB climate finance is project-based. Lastly, sub-Saharan Africa (21%) and Latin America and the Caribbean (20%) are the two largest regional recipients of climate action from the World Bank and RDBs (AfDB, AsDB, EBRD, et al. 2019).

A 2018 report by E3G, an independent climate change thinktank, analysed the progress of the RDBs relative to the Paris Agreement (Wright et al. 2018). It found that while they all had aligned their practices with the Paris Agreement, the IADB and AfDB excelled as climate leaders in transitioning to low-carbon and resilient lending with their respective ratio of renewable climate finance to non-renewable finance as 13.9:1 and 5.3:1. The other RDBs performed less well: EBRD 1.2:1, EIB 1:1, and AsDB 0.9:1. These ratios are worrying. While the RDBs are committed to increasing their climate commitments and to divesting non-renewable energy investments, their critics rightly point out that they are not doing this fast enough given both the scale of the climate crisis and the role of the MDBs as market leaders.

The smaller MDBs demonstrate considerable variability in their climate commitments, reflecting their differences in climate mainstreaming as well as capital availability and shareholder influence. The Latin American and Caribbean MDBs are climate leaders, with 37% of CABEI approvals between 2015 and 2018 for climate interventions. CABEI also maintained a portfolio of $1 billion of GCF projects. Similarly, CEB allocated 30% of its annual approvals to environmental projects in 2015 and CDB committed 44% to environmental sustainability and disaster risk reduction in 2017. Other MDBs invest far less. BADEA did not approve any climate change projects in 2017, although 56% of its portfolio financed water, sanitation, and power projects, and the Eastern and Southern African Trade and Development Bank (TDB), despite policies mainstreaming sustainability, assigned 45% of its trade finance to petrochemical transactions in 2016 (BADEA 2017, TDB 2016). The BSTDB demonstrates the tension between renewable and non-renewable energy projects for smaller MDBs. In 2019, it approved several renewable energy projects, including the Syvash Wind Farm Project in Ukraine and a $65 million loan to the $970 million greenfield EFELER Geothermal Power Plant in Turkey. Yet, it also financed offshore oil and gas projects in Azerbaijan and Greece, a coal terminal in Russia, and a greenfield waste incineration plant in Turkey.

The AIIB and NDB claim to prioritise sustainable infrastructure investments. For AIIB, its sustainable energy infrastructure projects favour solar and hydro power (AIIB 2018), despite many climate experts not including hydropower as a sustainable source given its impacts on river flows and resettlement. But its lead shareholder China has made major investments in this area. NDB has a clear operational focus: sustainable infrastructure development, which is forecast to take two-thirds of total project commitments (NDB 2017). Of approved projects between 2016 and 2018, renewable energy and transportation projects were most common for NDB, typically involving highway upgrades and wind, hydro, and solar construction and storage projects. With a focus on project investment for climate action, the lending patterns of the new MDBs closely resemble those of the larger and more established MDBs, notably the presumption that infrastructural and technological reforms will solve climate challenges.

10.4 Climate bonds and facilities

MDF organisations have led the establishment and management of climate bonds and various funds and facilities to catalyse public and – especially – private investment for climate action. The rise of these funding mechanisms demonstrates the increasing financialisation of climate policy and the overreliance on global and regional financial markets (Layfield 2013). Environmental action has been a key part of the financialisation agenda of the MDBs and, as Layfield (2013, 901–2) remarks, a

> financialised policy goes further than simply relying on market-based instruments to achieve reductions in carbon emissions. In this context financialisation refers to the way in which governments identified a potentially global problem in the form of anthropogenic climate change, and then permitted a new global financial market to emerge as an important means to address this problem.

Still, there are large climate financing gaps and uncertainty whether private capital will

> meet the adaptation needs of the poorest and most marginalised people… The world's least developed countries received only 1.9 per cent of global foreign direct investment flows in 2012 and little of this money is focused in areas which are adaptation priorities.
>
> (Oxfam 2013)

Yet, the MDBs hold fast to the Maximising Finance for Development (MFD) view that 'capital markets can provide new solutions to age-old development challenges' (Gabor 2018, 16), be those challenges related to infrastructure, climate change, or human development.

Green bonds are the main financial instrument issued by the MDBs to mobilise private finance for climate change solutions. They were pioneered by the EIB in 2007, and their importance has increased since the 2015 Paris Agreement to catalyse green private investment (AsDB 2017). The green bond market grew considerably during the 2010s, increasing from $11 billion in 2013 to $42 billion in 2015 to $250 billion in 2018 (Chang 2019). Between 2007 and 2012, the green bond market was largely comprised of MDBs, notably the EIB, World Bank, and International Finance Corporation (IFC), with a few government funding agencies and national development banks also involved. The Paris Agreement and entrance of Chinese issuers gave the market a large boost (AsDB 2017, OECD 2017). Green bonds are structured like conventional bonds, because having the same or similar risk/return profiles and yield maturities encourages private investment (Banga 2019). The main point of difference is that proceeds must finance green projects. Blue bonds are a more recent innovation, designed to support the stable conservation and sustainable exploitation of the blue economy – sustainable economic activities directly related to oceans and seas (CDB 2018b), though it is worth pausing to ask if this is possible. Seychelles launched the world's first sovereign blue bond in 2018 to leverage finance for the blue economy, which led the CDB to express interest in issuing them.

The green bond market is governed by the voluntary Green Bond Principles. Established in 2014 by a consortium of investment banks including Deutsche Bank, JP Morgan, and HSBC, the Principles form an important structuring regime adopted by many MDBs, demonstrating their links to banking institutions. Updated in 2018, the Principles have four core components: the use of proceeds for actions with clear environmental benefits; processes of project evaluation and selection aligned to sustainability objectives and eligibility; management of proceeds allowing tracking of investment operations; and, up-to-date reporting on proceeds use (ICMA 2018). AfDB, AsDB, CEB, EBRD, EIB, NIB, and the World Bank are all member issuers of the Green Bond Principles, and the West African Development Bank (BOAD) is an observer. Despite the structuring regime of the Principles, criticisms have been raised that the green bond market is far too broad to meaningfully identify clear environmental benefits, leading to the potential 'greenwashing' of non-renewable sectors (Doran and Tanner 2019). Further, while the green bond market has been effective in financialising 'concerns' about climate change, questions remain whether it has led to quantifiable environmental improvements (Tripathy 2017).

The EIB issued the first green bond in 2007, labelled a Climate Awareness Bond. Between 2007 and 2018, it raised €23.5 billion across 11 currencies, making it the world's largest green bond issuer (Wright et al. 2018). In April 2018, EIB introduced Sustainability Awareness Bonds, with an initial €500 million offering. The World Bank issued its own green bonds in 2008, responding to a request from Scandinavian pension funds seeking to support climate projects. It achieved issuances of over $10 billion by 2017. EBRD commenced bond issuances in 2010 and NIB in 2011. AfDB began in 2013, raising $15 billion between 2013 and 2018, which is significant given that the African green bond market only reached $3 billion in 2017. AsDB was comparatively slow to enter the market given that the Asia-Pacific region already had a green bond market and was the second largest region for climate-aligned bonds in 2017. In regions where bond markets are underdeveloped, the MDBs have taken a leading role in cultivating green and blue bond transactions and in assisting governments to issue their own green bonds (Wright et al. 2018).

Smaller MDBs have also engaged with climate bonds, though in more marginal ways compared to the RDBs. CABEI is relatively active and in November 2019 it issued a $375 million floating-rate five-year Green Bond, listed on the Luxembourg and Taipei Stock Exchanges, demonstrating the complexity of global finances; the issuance led to an aggregate demand of $974 million, driven by Asian (75%) and European (25%) investors. The ECOWAS Bank for Investment and Development (EBID) has expressed interest in green bond issuances, but it is currently limited to policy discussions. In 2017, ECOWAS announced the intention to establish a platform for climate finance at COP-23 in Bonn. The statement was preceded by the Declaration of Abidjan in June 2017 at the ECOWAS Green Investment Catalyst Roundtable, which discussed the potential for green investment in West Africa and constraints posed by a lack of adequate financing and stable legal frameworks. The smaller MDBs recognise the utility of climate bond issuances as bolstering their limited capital to finance climate interventions. In November 2019, IsDB issued a Green Sukuk, which is a Shari'ah compliant green bond. The Islamic MDB has issued sukuks, or Islamic bonds, since 2003 and total international sukuk issuances reached $95 billion in 2017 (Sadik 2018, 72–4). Under the Sustainable Finance Framework, IsDB is authorised to issue Green Sukuk and Sustainability Sukuk, the main difference between them being that Sustainability Sukuk proceeds can be allocated to both environmental and social projects. The AIIB and NDB have also issued green bonds, following trends set by the more established MDBs. Indeed, they began issuing them almost immediately after their establishment.

There is a chaotic network of actors, funds, and financing mechanisms supporting the international climate regime; 'the current world of climate change finance…, with its multiplicity of funds, funding sources, and new financial mechanisms for climate change, makes organising climate change finance in an orderly way a daunting task' (Gomez-Echeverri 2013, 644), leading to coordination difficulties and donor overlap. Administered by or in collaboration with the MDBs, climate funds and facilities range from the GEF and GCF to smaller multi-donor trusts such as AsDB's Climate Change Fund established in May 2008 and AfDB's Africa Climate Change Fund founded in April 2014. Despite governance complexity, the growth of these funds and facilities has increased access to climate finance and made possible more robust pre-investment and technical assistance project support. A range of examples follow.

Financial mechanisms such as the GEF and GCF are beneficial for the smaller MDBs in accessing climate finance. As an example, BOAD is limited in its annual approvals and only recently engaged substantively with climate action. After receiving accreditation with GEF in 2015 and GCF in 2016, BOAD developed a pipeline of projects for WAEMU member countries, receiving over $23 million from GEF and $255 million from GCF. Bowman and Minas (2019, 351) regard GCF favourably, arguing that it 'could be a key interlocutor between law- and policy-makers and private sector financiers,' thereby connecting finance with action. In contrast, Kumar (2015) identifies criticisms of GCF, including concerns that it does not adequately consult indigenous communities, its processes lack transparency, and it funnels money via large MDBs and private banks instead of directly to local institutions in the countries where projects take place.

The MDBs have developed and engaged with numerous other small-scale climate funds and facilities. AsDB manages its Climate Change Fund and the Clean Energy Financing Partnerships Facility launched in 2007, NIB runs Climate Change, Energy Efficiency, and Renewable Energy lending facility founded in 2008 endowed with €1 billion, and EIB operates three facilities established in 2004. The creation of these funds and facilities illustrates not only the growing demand for climate investments but also the limitations of traditional OCR and concessional lending for climate interventions.

To demonstrate the multitude of climate funds and facilities interacting with one MDB, consider the AfDB. The African RDB works with the Climate Investment Funds (CIFs), is accredited with GEF, GCF, and the Climate Change Adaptation Fund, and established several regional bodies including the Africa Climate Change Fund, ClimDev-Africa Special Fund, Congo Basin Forest Fund, Sustainable Energy Fund for Africa, and African Water Facility. The CIFs, announced in February 2008 by Japan, the UK, and the US, provide grants, concessional loans, risk mitigation instruments, and equity to over 70 developing countries. A third of CIF funding goes to sub-Saharan Africa and well over half of that goes to the AfDB (AfDB 2017). The complex arrangement of funds and facilities engaged by even one MDB demonstrates the problems in donor coordination, at the same time the system enables MDBs to access different climate finance sources.

Climate bonds and funds and facilities are important instruments to catalyse investment in a sector that suffers considerable public and private financing gaps.

The growth of green and blue bonds and alternate financing mechanisms has not been without risks, however. While making capital available that previously was not, the risks include the duplication of scarce resources and expertise resulting in high transaction costs, weak visibility and high complexity for recipients, resource competition at the expense of demand-driven projects, and poor strategic coordination (Brouder and Garreta 2009).

10.5 Conclusion

Since the 1987 Brundtland Report, there have been concerted efforts to financialise climate action and catalyse private investment as argued necessary for long-term climate adaptation, mitigation, and resilience. Writing on the World Bank's environmental lending, Nielson and Tierney (2003, FN120) contended that critics

> are wrong when they conclude that the Bank is conducting business as usual when it comes to the environment. Environmental lending has increased significantly since 1987, the Bank has institutionalized checks on the dysfunctional behavior of its staff, the Bank has dramatically decreased lending for traditional 'dirty' loans, and member governments have significantly increased their ability to monitor and sanction behavior that is not consistent with official Bank lending practices.

Though this comment was written almost two decades ago, the fact remains that the MDBs have changed significantly since the 1980s and in fact the 2010s saw further improvements.

While environmentally questionable lending practices remain, the evidence reveals that through climate mainstreaming, increased climate finance levels, and the emergence of green and blue bonds and new financing windows, the MDF architecture has institutionalised sustainable development and climate actions as legitimate and expected organisational behaviours, with the MDBs exercising influence as climate intermediaries. The business-as-usual of the MDBs in 2020 is that climate change is an existential threat to 21st-century development. Still, the major limitation that must be laid bare is that the MDBs plan to address environmental challenges through a market-based capitalist system that still regards growth and sustainability as compatible. The MDBs also remain strongly influenced by their shareholders and the retroliberal era has seen many countries back or even walk away from meaningful climate action; the Spring 2020 Meetings of the World Bank and IMF did not discuss the role of climate action in the COVID-19 recovery. Further, the mechanisms the MDBs favour to address climate change – green bonds and related financialisation – may not be suited to achieve a just and equitable transition to a sustainable future. Still, the fondness of the MDBs and private capital for new bonds may be a sustaining force for the multilateral promotion of climate action.

Bibliography

Adger, W. Neil, Saleemul Huq, Katrina Brown, Declan Conway, and Mike Hulme. 2003. "Adaptation to Climate Change in the Developing World." *Progress in Development Studies* 3 (3):179–95. doi: 10.1191/1464993403ps060oa.

AfDB. 2017. Growing Green: The AfDB and CIF for a Climate-Smart Afric. Tunis: African Development Bank.

AfDB, AsDB, AIIB, EBRD, EIB, IADB, IsDB, NDB, and World Bank Group. 2019. High Level MDB Statement: Climate Change Finance.

AfDB, AsDB, EBRD, EIB, IADB, IsDB, and World Bank Group. 2019. 2018 Joint Report on Multilateral Development Banks' Climate Finance. London: European Bank for Reconstruction and Development.

AIIB. 2018. Financing Asia's Future. Beijing: Asian Infrastructure Investment Bank.

Alston, Philip. 2005. "Ships Passing in the Night: The Current State of the Human Rights and Development Debate Seen through the Lens of the Millennium Development Goals." *Human Rights Quarterly* 27 (3):755–829. doi: 10.1353/hrq.2005.0030.

Ambrose, Jillian. 2019. "EIB Plans to Cut All Funding for Fossil Fuel Projects by 2020." *The Guardian*, 27 July 2019. https://www.theguardian.com/environment/2019/jul/26/eib-plans-to-cut-all-funding-for-fossil-fuel-projects-by-2020.

AsDB. 2017. Catalysing Green Finance: A Concept for Leveraging Blended Finance for Green Development. Manila: Asian Development Bank.

AsDB. 2019. Strengthening the Environmental Dimensions of the Sustainable Development Goals in Asia and the Pacific: Stocktake of National Responses to Sustainable Development Goals 12, 14, and 15. Manila: Asian Development Bank.

Ayers, Jessica, Saleemul Huq, Helena Wright, Arif M. Faisal, and Syed Tanveer Hussain. 2014. "Mainstreaming Climate Change Adaptation into Development in Bangladesh." *Climate and Development* 6 (4):293–305. doi: 10.1080/17565529.2014.977761.

BADEA. 2015. Seventh Five-Year Plan 2015–2019. Khartoum: Arab Bank for Economic Development in Africa.

BADEA. 2017. Annual Report 2017. Khartoum: Arab Bank for Economic Development in Africa.

Banga, Josué. 2019. "The Green Bond Market: A Potential Source of Climate Finance for Developing Countries." *Journal of Sustainable Finance & Investment* 9 (1):17–32. doi: 10.1080/20430795.2018.1498617.

Bell, Stephen. 2020. "The Renewable Energy Transition Energy Path Divergence, Increasing Returns and Mutually Reinforcing Leads in the State-Market Symbiosis." *New Political Economy* 25 (1):57–71. doi: 10.1080/13563467.2018.1562430.

Benson, Emily, Alex Forbes, Mika Korkeakoski, Razi Latif, and Dechen Lham. 2014. "Environment and Climate Mainstreaming: Challenges and Successes." *Development in Practice* 24 (4):605–14. doi: 10.1080/09614524.2014.911819.

Bowman, Megan, and Stephen Minas. 2019. "Resilience through Interlinkage: The Green Climate Fund and Climate Finance Governance." *Climate Policy* 19 (3):342–53. doi: 10.1080/14693062.2018.1513358.

Brouder, Alan, and Catherine Garreta. 2009. "Global Environment Facility." In *Handbook of Transnational Economic Governance Regimes*, edited by Christian Tietje and Alan Brouder, 899–914. Leiden: Koninklijke Brill NV.

Brundtland, Gro Harlem. 1987. *Our Common Future*. Oxford: Oxford University Press for the World Commission on Environment and Development.

CABEI. 2015. 2015–2019 Institutional Strategy: Integrating Sustainable Development and Competitiveness. Tegucigalpa: Central American Bank for Regional Integration.
CAF. 2017. Sustainability Report CAF 2015–2016. Caracas: Development Bank of Latin America.
Castro, Carlos J. 2004. "Sustainable Development: Mainstream and Critical Perspectives." *Organization & Environment* 17 (2):195–225. doi: 10.1177/1086026604264910.
CDB. 2012. Action on Climate Change: Climate Resilience Strategy 2012–2017. St. Michael: Caribbean Development Bank.
CDB. 2018a. "CDB Adopts Updated Climate Resilience Strategy." Caribbean Development Bank, Last Modified 14 December 2018. https://www.caribank.org/newsroom/news-and-events/cdb-adopts-updated-climate-resilience-strategy.
CDB. 2018b. Financing the Blue Economy: A Caribbean Development Opportunity. St. Michael: Caribbean Development Bank.
CEB. 2016. Supporting the Transition to a Low-Carbon and Climate-Resilient Economy: The Role of Climate Finance. Paris: Council of Europe Development Bank.
Chang, Youngho. 2019. Green Finance in Singapore: Barriers and Solutions. In *ADBI Working Paper Series*. Manila: Asian Development Bank Institute.
Clapp, Jennifer, and Peter Dauvergne. 2005. *Paths to a Green World: The Political Economy of the Global Environment*. Cambridge, MA: The MIT Press.
Climate Finance Tracking Working Group. 2018. Lessons Learned from Three Years of Implementing the MDB-IDFC Common Principles for Climate Change Adaptation Finance Tracking. Climate Finance Tracking Working Group.
Delina, Laurence L. 2011. "Asian Development Bank's Support for Clean Energy." *Climate Policy* 11 (6):1350–66. doi: 10.1080/14693062.2011.579288.
EBRD. 2018. Implementing the EBRD Green Economy Transition: Technical Guide for Consultants: Reporting on Projects Performance Against the Green Economy Transition Approach. London: European Bank for Reconstruction and Development.
Elliott, Lorraine. 2004. *The Global Politics of the Environment*, 2nd ed. Hampshire: Palgrave Macmillan.
Florini, Ann, and Benjamin K. Sovacool. 2009. "Who Governs Energy? The Challenges Facing Global Energy Governance." *Energy Policy* 37 (12):5239–48. doi: https://doi.org/10.1016/j.enpol.2009.07.039.
Gabor, Daniela. 2018. Understanding the Financialisation of International Development through 11 FAQs. Washington, DC: Heinrich Böll Stiftung North America.
Goldman, Michael. 2001. "The Birth of a Discipline: Producing Authoritative Green Knowledge, World Bank-Style." *Ethnography* 2 (2):191–217. doi: 10.1177/14661380122230894.
Gomez-Echeverri, Luis. 2013. "The Changing Geopolitics of Climate Change Finance." *Climate Policy* 13 (5):632–48. doi: 10.1080/14693062.2013.822690.
Gutner, Tamar L. 2002. *Banking on the Environment: Multilateral Development Banks and Their Environmental Performance in Central and Eastern Europe*. Cambridge, MA: The MIT Press.
Henstra, Daniel. 2012. "Toward the Climate-Resilient City: Extreme Weather and Urban Climate Adaptation Policies in Two Canadian Provinces." *Journal of Comparative Policy Analysis: Research and Practice* 14 (2):175–94. doi: 10.1080/13876988.2012.665215.
Humphrey, Chris. 2016. Time for a New Approach to Environmental and Social Protection at Multilateral Development Banks. In *Briefing Paper*. London: Overseas Development Institute.
ICMA. 2018. Green Bond Principles: Voluntary Process Guidelines for Issuing Green Bonds. International Capital Markets Association.

Doran, Michael and James Tanner. 2019. "Critical Challenges Facing the Green Bond Market." International Financial Law Review. Accessed 23 September 2019. https://www.iflr.com/article/b1lmxbv3f6b5td/critical-challenges-facing-the-green-bond-market

IPCC. 2018. "Global Warming of 1.5°C." https://www.ipcc.ch/sr15/.

IsDB. 2019. Climate Change Policy. Jeddah: Islamic Development Bank.

Janetos, Anthony C., Elizabeth Malone, Erin Mastrangelo, Karen Hardee, and Ariane de Bremond. 2012. "Linking Climate Change and Development Goals: Framing, Integrating, and Measuring." *Climate and Development* 4 (2):141–56. doi: 10.1080/17565529.2012.726195.

Käkönen, Mira, and Hanna Kaisti. 2012. "The World Bank, Laos and Renewable Energy Revolution in the Making: Challenges in Alleviating Poverty and Mitigating Climate Change." *Forum for Development Studies* 39 (2):159–84. doi: 10.1080/08039410.2012.657668.

Kumar, Sanjay. 2015. "Green Climate Fund Faces Slew of Criticism." *Nature* 527 (7579):419. doi: 10.1038/nature.2015.18815.

Layfield, David. 2013. "Turning Carbon into Gold: The Financialisation of International Climate Policy." *Environmental Politics* 22 (6):901–17. doi: 10.1080/09644016.2012.737252.

Lee, James A. 1985. The Environment, Public Health, and Human Ecology. Washington, DC: World Bank.

Lipper, Leslie, and David Zilberman. 2018. "A Short History of the Evolution of the Climate Smart Agriculture Approach and Its Links to Climate Change and Sustainable Agriculture Debates." In *Climate Smart Agriculture: Building Resilience to Climate Change*, edited by Leslie Lipper, Nancy McCarthy, David Zilberman, Solomon Asfaw and Giacomo Branca, 13–30. Cham: Springer.

Meadows, Donella H., Dennis L. Meadows, Jorgen Randers, and William W. Behrens III. 1972. *The Limits to Growth: A Report for the Club of Rome's Project on the Predicament of Mankind*. New York: Universe Books.

NDB. 2017. General Strategy 2017–2021. Shanghai: New Development Bank.

NIB. 2018. Sustainable Financing. Helsinki: Nordic Investment Bank.

Nielson, Daniel L., and Michael J. Tierney. 2003. "Delegation to International Organizations: Agency Theory and World Bank Environmental Reform." *International Organization* 57 (2):241–76.

O'Neill, Kate. 2012. *The Environment and International Relations*. New York: Cambridge University Press.

OECD. 2017. Mobilising Bond Markets for a Low-Carbon Transition. In *Green Finance and Investment*. Paris: OECD Publishing.

Oxfam. 2013. "Adaptation and the $100 Billion Commitment." https://www.oxfam.org/en/research/adaptation-and-100-billion-commitment.

Peake, Stephen, and Paul Ekins. 2017. "Exploring the Financial and Investment Implications of the Paris Agreement." *Climate Policy* 17 (7):832–52. doi: 10.1080/14693062.2016.1258633.

Posas, Paula. 2011. "Climate Change in Development Bank Country Environmental Analyses." *Journal of Environmental Assessment Policy and Management (JEAPM)* 13:459–81. doi: 10.1142/S1464333211003961.

Redclift, Michael. 2005. "Sustainable Development (1987–2005): An Oxymoron Comes of Age." *Sustainable Development* 13 (4):212–27. doi: 10.1002/sd.281.

Rich, Bruce. 1994. *Mortgaging the Earth: The World Bank, Environmental Impoverishment, and the Crisis of Development*. Boston, MA: Beacon Press.

Sachs, Jeffrey D., Wing Thye Woo, Naoyuki Yoshino, and Farhad Taghizadeh-Hesary. 2019. Why is Green Finance Important? In *AsDBI Working Paper Series*. Manila: Asian Development Bank Institute.

Sadik, Abdul-Karim. 2018. "The Role of Arab Development Institutions in Financing Sustainable Development." In *Financing Sustainable Development in Arab Countries*, edited by Najib Saab and Abdul-Karim Sadik, 63–84. Beirut: Arab Forum for Environment and Development.

Sharma, Anju. 2017. "Precaution and Post-caution in the Paris Agreement: Adaptation, Loss and Damage and Finance." *Climate Policy* 17 (1):33–47. doi: 10.1080/14693062.2016.1213697.

Shyamsundar, Priya, Kirk Hamilton, Lisa Segnestam, Maria Sarraf, and S. Frankhauser. 2001. Country Assistance Strategies and the Environment. Washington, DC: World Bank.

TDB. 2016. Annual Report 2016. Bujumbura: Eastern and Southern African Trade and Development Bank.

Tripathy, Aneil. 2017. "Translating to Risk: The Legibility of Climate Change and Nature in the Green Bond Market." *Economic Anthropology* 4 (2):239–50. doi: 10.1002/sea2.12091.

UNFCCC. 2020. "Introduction to Climate Finance." United Nations Framework Convention on Climate Change. https://unfccc.int/topics/climate-finance/the-big-picture/introduction-to-climate-finance.

World Bank. 2017. World Bank Annual Report 2017. Washington, DC: World Bank.

Wright, Helena, James Hawkins, Dileimy Orozco, and Nick Mabey. 2018. Banking on Reform: Aligning Development Banks with the Paris Climate Agreement. E3G.

Yudelman, Montague. 1976. "The Role of Agriculture in Integrated Rural Development Projects: The Experience of the World Bank." *Sociologia Ruralis* 16 (4):308–25.

Zawahri, Neda, and Erika Weinthal. 2014. "The World Bank and Negotiating the Red Sea and Dead Sea Water Conveyance Project." *Global Environmental Politics* 14 (4):55–74.

11 Human development

The multilateral development banks (MDBs) have long used the rhetoric of human development and social progress to shape their operational strategies. For some, such as the World Bank, ending extreme poverty and promoting shared prosperity guide their current missions, while for others like the African Development Bank (AfDB) their revised establishing agreements explicitly include social progress as an organisational purpose. This chapter analyses MDB financing for human development, defined here broadly as investing in people to improve quality and duration of life (Lind 2019, 422), with a focus on education, health, and gender.

This chapter arrives at two significant conclusions. First, although finance for education and health can be dated to the 1960s, the MDBs only began investing in people in earnest in the late 1980s and some only since the early 2000s. With operational histories prioritising infrastructural investment and private sector growth, human development is often a secondary consideration, if considered substantively at all. This takeaway is important, given that so many MDBs use the rhetoric of human development and social progress to defend their investment priorities. Second, human development financing has generally favoured investing in people to improve economic growth rather than improve quality of life. Given that the MDBs first articulated their education, health, and gender policies in the Washington Consensus era, revising those policies time and again during the post-Washington Consensus and retroliberal eras, the resultant legacy has been to classify people as economic units; human development has come to mean human capital development, which focusses on the utility of people as per their productive capacity. This is problematic, as a neoliberal 'common sense' understanding of human capital necessarily constricts the breadth of options available that the MDBs can pursue in promoting human development.

There is, nevertheless, considerable variation between the MDBs in their human development financing. Some have engaged substantively. For example, 'social services' was the fourth largest investment sector of the Caribbean Development Bank (CDB) between 1970 and 2000. Similarly, 'social development' was one of three strategic axes of the Central American Bank for Economic Integration (CABEI) in 2015, accounting for 38.7% of annual approvals. In contrast, other MDBs, including the International Investment Bank (IIB) and ECO Trade and Development Bank (ETDB), barely reference the concept outside public statements affirming the importance of investing in people for economic growth. Further, a handful of MDBs such as the Development Bank of Central Africa States (BDEAC) and West African Development Bank (BOAD) do not disclose sufficient public information to identify lending patterns, although the limited data suggests very low engagement. A few reasons explain the poor commitment of select MDBs to human development, low engagement of select MDBs with human development, including limits on annual lending capacity, difficulties in assuring loan repayments for social sector investments compared to infrastructural investments, and a lack of borrower interest. Instead of focussing on why certain MDBs do not invest substantively in education, health, and gender, this chapter analyses those that do, evaluating how they have done so and the policies that have guided their actions. The remainder of this chapter is divided into four sections. After first reviewing the literature and MDB financing for human development, the chapter turns to education, health, and then gender.

11.1 Human development

Human development entered the lexicon of development in the early 1990s. While initiatives to invest in people first emerged in the 1970s in discussions about poverty and basic needs (Javed Burki and Ul Haq 1981, Streeten 1979), targeted interest in human development was a late Cold War construct (Cammack 2017). Human development posits that people are the ends as well as the means of development, challenging the conventional view of development understood as per capita economic growth (Ponzio and Ghosh 2016). It combines a multidimensional conceptualisation of human well-being and poverty through a focus on the social, cultural, political, and economic institutions which enhance or curtail human capabilities. The works of Streeten (1981), Ul Haq (1995), Sen (1990) were foundational to building the concept. The UNDP's *Human Development Reports*, published annually since 1990, were effective in mobilising support from governments, MDBs, and civil society organisations, though they did maintain an understanding of people as units in economic growth (Cammack 2017).

The World Bank played a leading role in shaping human development in multilateral development finance (MDF), comparable to its role in other debates about development. During the Bank's early decades, it minimised social sector financing, prioritising a growth-only agenda via macroeconomic reforms and capital inputs to achieve economic growth (Ponzio and Ghosh 2016). Between the 1950s and 1960s, the Bank and others argued that investment in social development, including education and healthcare, was counterproductive and 'would only squander limited national resources' (Kapur, Webb, and Lewis 1997, 115). Robert Cavanaugh, the Bank's liaison between the MDB and Wall Street during the 1950s and 1960s, said,

> If we got into the social field… then the bond market would definitely feel that we were not acting prudently from a financial standpoint… If you

> start financing schools and hospitals and water works, and so forth, these things don't normally and directly increase the ability of a country to repay a borrowing.
>
> (cited in Kapur, Webb, and Lewis 1997, 119–20)

It was not until 1968 and the appointment of President Robert McNamara that the Bank shifted from a financial institution to a 'development agency' (Bazbauers 2018). McNamara, supported by the Bank's first Chief Economist, Keynesian development economist Hollis Chenery, argued that in the absence of redistribution of growth, socioeconomic development would be stymied by inequality (Ponzio and Ghosh 2016). From McNamara onwards, three broad anti-poverty initiatives emerged from the Bank: anti-poverty as welfare, as protection, and as social development.

Anti-poverty as welfare came in the form of investments in education, health, population planning, and nutrition, and they occupied a third of the World Bank's loan portfolio between 1968 and 1981. The rationale behind these investments was that enhancing human capital – or the ability of people to perform labour – would increase economic growth, a basic needs tenet (Hall 2007, Hunter and Brown 2000). With the arrival of President Tom Clausen in 1981, the Bank altered its a poverty strategy by aligning it with the nascent Washington Consensus. As a result, it became a model to limit welfare budgets and encourage private sector participation in and delivery of welfare services. There was thus a shift to short-term welfare projects with a productivity objective, rationalised by the human capital principle that investments in education and health would enhance productivity and lead to higher economic growth (Hall 2007).

Yet, the severe social consequences of neoliberal structural adjustment exposed problems in the neoliberal poverty strategy and, buttressed by UNICEF's 1987 call for 'adjustment with a human face' (Jolly 1991), the Bank under President Barber Conable introduced moderate pro-welfare, anti-poverty measures and built minimalist safety nets using social emergency programmes and social action funds (Hall 2007). The Bank's *World Development Report 1990: Poverty* and *World Development Report 2000: Attacking Poverty* highlight the operational shift, with the former focussed on poverty reduction through enhanced productivity and economic growth and the latter on empowerment via pro-poor institutions and the introduction of insurance mechanisms such as cash transfers to protect against risks and shocks (World Bank 2000), which informed the Bank's anti-poverty as protection initiative.

Anti-poverty as protection was a response to criticisms posed of neoliberal adjustment. In many developing countries, welfare provision services bore the brunt of public spending cutbacks, exacerbating poverty and vulnerability (Thomson, Kentikelenis, and Stubbs 2017). In belated response, the World Bank drafted programmes to support safety net mechanisms, coming in the forms of conditional income transfers, food programmes, price subsidies, microcredits, and fee waivers for health services. These fell under the responsibility of the Social Protection Unit launched in the Bank's Human Development Network in 2001. Conditional cash transfer (CCT) programmes, as a social protection measure, started in Latin America in the late 1990s and became popular with the MDBs only in the late 2000s once their poverty reduction impacts could not be ignored. They preferred minimalist programmes that still posited development as an individual responsibility before that, in particular the very problematic intervention of microfinance (Bateman 2010, Engel and Pedersen 2019, Mader 2015). The main objectives of CCTs are short-term poverty alleviation via cash transfers and long-term alleviation through human capital development (Barham, Maluccio, and Stampini 2018). The core difference between anti-poverty as welfare and as protection is in the more targeted approach of the latter (Fiszbein 2009). Nonetheless, both approaches align on the premise that enhanced human capital will lead to increased economic growth.

Anti-poverty as social development dates to social components integrated in World Bank projects approved in the 1970s but became increasingly institutionalised from the late 1990s following the advent of the post-Washington Consensus. In 1996, Bank President James Wolfensohn established a Social Development Task Force to measure the social impact of the Bank's lending operations. This was a reply to the 'Fifty Years is Enough' campaign as well as Wolfensohn's personal commitment to enhancing participatory development (Hall 2007). It provided an important context for the adoption of Poverty Reduction Strategy Papers as a Bank tool as well as new conditional lending modalities, such as development policy loans replacing structural adjustment loans in 2004. Whereas anti-poverty as welfare and protection were temporary solutions pursued through emergency financing, anti-poverty as social development focussed on social analysis inputs to support such initiatives as community-driven development, participation and civic engagement, culture, indigenous peoples, conflict prevention, youth, and social accountability during the post-Washington Consensus era. This was a more holistic approach than pure neoliberalism, though still a largely instrumentalist and constrained approach to human welfare (Cammack 2012, Carroll 2010). Whereas Bank social development lending accounted for 5.1% of annual lending in 1980, human development lending totalled 14% in 2015. While still a rather modest commitment, the elevated importance of human development is visible.

The current MDB discourse on human development prioritises human capital development. Entering the mainstream of development assistance in the 1990s (Gundlach 1996), the concept of human capital rose to prominence in the 2000s and 2010s as part of a reconfiguration of welfare, poverty, employment, and market competition. The Asian Development Bank (AsDB), Council of Europe Development Bank (CEB), European Investment Bank (EIB), Inter-American Development Bank (IADB), Nordic Investment Bank (NIB), and World Bank all promote human capital growth as human development. EIB regards education and health investments as necessary to building a competitive and diversified workforce, CEB in 2005 allocated 13.4% of sectoral approvals to human capital development, and IADB identifies labour market insertion – or measures to improve employability and reduce barriers to labour market entry – as a human development sub-sector. For NIB, 'human capital and equal economic opportunities' are one of four institutional drivers, arguing that the 'quality of labour inputs and accumulation of knowledge stock in an economy boost productivity in a similar manner as accumulation and improved quality of physical capital' (Normann 2019). For AsDB, human capital investments have 'intrinsic value,' being 'regarded at the macro level as a key factor of production in the economywide production function' (Son 2010, 2). Lastly, the World Bank established the Human Capital Project in 2017 as a research and policy toolkit and the *World Development Report 2019: The Changing Nature of Work* argues that enhanced human capital is a prerequisite for sustained, inclusive economic growth (World Bank 2019). Thus, a persistent focus on human development remains, but it is pursued as investments in human capital; a means to invest in people to ensure long-term economic growth (Rossi 2018).

11.2 Education

The right to education was accepted as a fundamental human right under the Universal Declaration of Human Rights in 1948. Yet, in international development assistance, education as a sectoral investment stream has a rocky history, with the definition of education fluidly evolving over time and annual financial commitments fluctuating greatly. During the 1950s and 1960s, education investments prioritised technical and vocational education – skills-based approaches then deemed necessary to supplement rapid infrastructural growth (Kenneth 2015). Education policy, development, and funding in low-income countries were aligned under the modernisation paradigm (Cox 1968). The newly formed discipline of the economics of education emerged and ushered in a wave of optimism about the role of education in facilitating economic growth. The optimism for skills training and development was short-lived, however, when target-driven plans for education in Africa did not generate expected economic outcomes (Kenneth 2015). By the 1980s, education priorities shifted for many MDBs following the neoliberal turn, as deregulation and privatisation eroded public education programmes. It was not until the 1990 World Conference on Education for All that the rationale for education development reverted to its human rights origins, reinforced by the 2000 launch of the Millennium Development Goals (MDGs) and the 2015 Sustainable Development Goals (SDGs). A key part of this change was the turn away from user fees for primary education. However, even after the MDGs, MDB education investments remained small. Further, sectoral investments have largely aligned with human capital understandings, with education positioned as a contributing factor to improving workforces, employability, and competitive economic growth as opposed to improving quality of life.

The World Bank's education programme began in 1962, with a project approved to Tunisia to finance middle and secondary school building construction. Over the next two decades, education lending comprised a very small percentage of annual approvals – in 1970, of $2.2 billion approved, the Bank allocated $79.9 million to education projects, prioritising construction and equipment financing for secondary and vocational schools as well as curriculum studies. Education was viewed instrumentally, in terms of relevance to economic growth: 'further education and training beyond the basic level should be provided selectively to improve the knowledge and skills needed to carry out economic, social, and other developmental roles' (World Bank 1975, 18).

From the Washington Consensus era onwards, World Bank education lending increased but remained a small portion of annual approvals, 6.3% in 1985 and 7.25% in 1990. By 1995, the Bank's education portfolio grew to include initiatives to promote equitable access to education for girls and indigenous children, while maintaining a strong focus on vocational skills training. The post-Washington Consensus and retroliberal eras under the MDGs and SDGs saw little change though emphasised the public savings generated by contracting out textbook and supply services to private providers in another example of the marketisation agenda. Throughout the 2000s and 2010s, annual education approvals averaged 8% of total annual approvals and committed to 'interventions to help ensure that education builds relevant skills to meet labour market demands' (World Bank 2010, 16); a human capital agenda.

The regional development banks (RDBs) largely followed the World Bank's lead, although the two European RDBs – the EIB and European Bank for Reconstruction and Development (EBRD) – have been far less active. This reflects the fact that in most European countries the state plays an active role in education and provides the bulk of primary and secondary education – the MDBs do not need to encourage investment. The EIB, after decades of little engagement with the sector, approved projects in the 2000s and 2010s for primary, secondary, tertiary, and vocational education, but at a small percentage of annual approvals; 1.3% in 2000 and 5.5% in 2015. Despite comprising only 5.5% of 2015 approvals, that figure was €4.3 billion, larger as a net amount compared to the other RDBs. Building on the European Union's 2020 Strategy, EIB's current education portfolio prioritises those areas that promote market competitiveness and economic sustainability.

IADB and AsDB have financed education projects far longer than their European counterparts. Between 1960 and 1995, IADB approved 153 education loans totalling $2.8 billion, just 3.6% of the $78 billion allocated across 2,248 loans. This was maintained in 2005 but increased to 7.2% in 2010; it has since maintained an average comparable to the World Bank. Its approach to education sees a balance between human development and human capital development, with projects over the 2010s supporting equitable education access and adequate school supplies as well as building labour market skills. For AsDB, vocational and higher education loans totalled just over 1% of annual approvals between 1966 and 1975, delivered mostly as small loan components rather than stand-alone projects. By 1990, however, AsDB (1990, 33–4) shifted its approach 'from a rather narrow human capital rationale, typified by an almost exclusive emphasis on technical and vocational education, to an approach that embraces the entire sector, including primary, non-formal and environmental education.' During the 2000s, its approach to education drew heavily on new communication technologies and private service delivery. By 2010, education investments amounted to 10% of annual approvals, with AsDB arguing that projects should be oriented to skills training and employability, a return to its human capital approach of the 1970s.

Of the sub-regional development bank (SRDBs), only three devote significant resources to education: CABEI, CDB, and the Development Bank of Latin America (CAF). FONPLATA also finances education projects, but publicly available information is limited and, in 2019, health and education projects collectively totalled 4% of new commitments, compared to 63% for logistics and transportation. Thus, the SRDBs most active in education financing all operate in Latin America. Yet, the sector still comprises a small percentage of annual and cumulative approvals. CABEI approved $24.8 million in education investments in 2018 of $2.44 billion in new approvals and, between 1970 and 2018, CDB allocated $707.7 million to the sector of a total of $5.2 billion, around 13.6%. CDB's education portfolio covers a broad agenda, ranging from human development projects that improve access to quality early childhood development and teacher effectiveness to human capital projects that ensure training is relevant to increased workforce participation and promote gender-equitable access to non-traditional occupational areas. CAF, while also a relatively small education lender, launched a $140 million education bond in July 2019, reflecting the financialisation agenda. It is guided by its 2018–22 Educational Agenda that details three strategic guidelines: increased access to education, improved education quality, and strengthened education relevance, drawing connections between education providers, skills development, and employability (CAF 2018); again demonstrating an instrumental focus around human capital development.

Education investments by the specialised development banks also exist on a spectrum: (i) not financing education projects, as is the case with the newly formed New Development Bank (NDB) and Asian Infrastructure Investment Bank (AIIB) – the closest connection made by the NDB has been in noting that transportation projects enable greater access to health, education, and social services; (ii) financing small-scale education projects, such as NIB supporting the construction of a multipurpose education facility in Rovaniemi, northern Finland, in 2015; and, (iii) relatively active lenders, such as the CEB and Arab-led MDBs. To illustrate, 8.77% of CEB's approvals between 1989 and 1997 were for education sector projects, a considerable portion given that its two largest sectors were social housing (15.9%) and rural modernisation (14.4%). In 2015, however, the sector comprised only 1.5% of new approvals. With the refugee crisis taking off in that year, it appears other investments were prioritised. Overall, CEB mirrors other MDBs in that agreed projects are informed by the human capital tenet that an educated and skilled workforce improves a country's market competitiveness.

The four Arab-led MDBs have all financed education projects, though there are differences between them. Between 1974 and 2018, the Arab Fund for Economic and Social Development (AFESD) and Arab Bank for Economic Development in Africa (BADEA) allocated 7% and 10.4% of the cumulative approvals to the social sector, which is a broad field including the health, education, housing, and microfinance sub-sectors. To illustrate priorities, BADEA in 2018 approved a school construction education project, indicative of its infrastructure-focussed portfolio. For the OPEC Fund for International Development (OFID), new education sector approvals amounted to 2% of annual approvals in 2010 and 2.9% in 2018, with projects financing school facility upgrades, again suggesting an infrastructure-based approach, like AFESD and BADEA. The approach of the Islamic Development Bank (IsDB) has been more comprehensive. While only 3.2% of its total approvals between 1975 and 2019 were for education, its core education priorities in the 2010s were universal basic education, science and mathematics education for technological advancement, vocational training to enhance youth employability, and non-formal education through vocational literacy programmes for employability (IsDB Group 2016); a combination of human development and human capital investments.

In summary, statistical studies of the MDBs reveal them to be bit players in the education field (Morozkina and Sabelnikova 2017), prioritising human capital development by financing infrastructural upgrades and mechanisms to improve employability. While sectoral investments have expanded in recent decades, causes for concern remain, particularly since the MDBs tend to finance ad hoc projects that do not adequately address systemic issues related to educational inequalities and ineffective service provision.

11.3 Health

Health was an early arena of international cooperation, predating MDF. International Sanitary Conferences started in 1851 and the League of Nations had a Health Organisation. Since 1948, the World Health Organization (WHO) has been the main international health body promoting and protecting health globally (McInnes 2015). During the Keynesian, welfare, modernisation era, there was intense advocacy for strong government intervention to overcome systemic health impediments, including poverty, unequal access to health services, and assuring high quality care (Zwi and Mills 1995). However, once health became a sectoral focus for the MDBs, its conceptualisation – as with education – fluctuated between a rights-based focus on improving quality of life for the poor and a human capital-focus on ensuring a healthy, working population to bolster economic growth (Sastry and Dutta 2013). In evaluating World Bank health projects, Noy (2018, 17) identified that project rationales vary greatly, from prioritising market efficiencies to equity and social development, and that they are shaped in part by the strategies and goals of borrowers.

Like education, the health sector has remained at the periphery of MDB action, particularly when compared to infrastructure investments. The World Bank did not adopt a formal health policy until 1974. Prior to that, the Bank's focus was limited to financing health components in projects addressing other sectors and the odd project on population or family planning. By the end of the Keynesian era, the Bank's (1980) engagement in the sector was limited to addressing life expectancy, mortality rates, and temporary illnesses that impacted worker output; its understanding of health was technical and instrumental, a factor potentially impeding economic growth.

With the neoliberal turn, the World Bank maintained its instrumental outlook but added in the privatisation and decentralisation of healthcare. A Bank (1987) policy paper argued that the main problems facing the health sector in developing countries were poor resource allocation, wasteful(!) public health programmes, and inequitable service distribution. Solutions included introducing user fees and private insurance as well as privatising public health facilities. The Bank did envisage a residual public system for the poor, though circumscribed by a very limited definition of public health goods: basic preventative healthcare, infectious and easily transmittable diseases, and basic maternal and child health services; essential, low-cost, high-return interventions. The focus on efficiency and limiting state expenditures had little consideration of the catastrophic effect of degrading healthcare, which was to be greatly exacerbated by the emerging HIV/AIDS crisis in the 1980s (Birn 2009, Thomson, Kentikelenis, and Stubbs 2017). Other MDBs such as the AfDB and AsDB followed the Bank's lead, adopting similar health policy prescriptions (Coburn, Restivo, and Shandra 2015, Larmour 2002). By 1990, Bank health sector financing equalled just 4.5% of annual approvals, with sector priorities being healthcare modernisation, immunisation programmes, and construction, equipment, and training.

The graphic consequences of a lack of healthcare support in developing countries was part of what drove the shift to the post-Washington Consensus, which promised a slightly friendlier approach to public health but delivered little. Even the MDGs did not stop the push for the further privatisation of health services. The MDGs listed three health-related goals: reduce child mortality, improve maternal health, and combat HIV/AIDS, malaria, and other diseases (Komatsu, Low-Beer, and Schwartländer 2007). Influential in setting MDF targets, the World Bank and other MDBs aligned their health sector investments behind the MDGs (Roth et al. 2018). Alongside the MDGs, the 2002 establishment of the Global Fund to Fight AIDS, Tuberculosis, and Malaria helped centre HIV/AIDS as *the* priority of global health investments during the 2000s (Lisk 2009). Funding commitments for HIV/AIDS increased from $300 million in 1996 to $8.8 billion in 2011. The focus on HIV/AIDS transformed the narrative from health-to-development to AIDS-to-development, leading to a seismic shift in investment priorities away from broader health issues to narrower, target-led goals (Dennis and Zuckerman 2008, Woodling, Williams, and Rushton 2012). Further, the HIV/AIDS epidemic was narrowly framed as a loss of labour potential, fitting neoliberal the 'common sense' of viewing health as a factor in economic productivity, and 'limiting the range of articulations and actions in response to HIV/AIDS' (Sastry and Dutta 2013, 36). Particularly relevant is that HIV/AIDS programmes have been criticised as inadequately addressing gender dynamics, with 'fundamentally patriarchal' programmes placing 'women in the global South at increased risk of HIV/AIDS' (Sastry and Dutta 2013, 36) and often focussing on maternal health issues above 'reproductive and sexual health rights more broadly' (Dennis and Zuckerman 2008, 298).

The RDBs all finance health projects, except for the EBRD, which does not have a health sector investment stream but rather references 'public health benefits' as components of loan appraisals. Annual RDB health sector approvals are low, however. In 2019, the World Bank allocated 7.6% of annual approvals ($3.41 billion) to health sector projects, EIB allocated 2.3%, AfDB 2.4%, and IADB and AsDB 3%. These percentages fluctuate, with IADB health sector approvals at 8% in 2015 and 0.2% in 2000. Cumulative EIB health sector investments were €30 billion over its several-decade history, a relatively small amount considering that it approved €69 billion across all sectors in 2018. Thus, although a sector promoted by the World Bank and RDBs as vital to human development, financing levels are low. The AfDB, AsDB, and IADB prioritise investments for communicable diseases, rural and urban health, hospital management, and public-private healthcare delivery. Following a pattern, EIB 'has implicitly taken the view that health is mostly equivalent to healthcare. Indeed, it has concentrated its financing mainly on the creation or improvement of hospital infrastructure' (Schmidt, Moreno, and Goodwin 2007, ii); an infrastructure-based human development approach.

In the sub-regional and specialised development banks, project data and annual approvals reveal the health sector to be a low priority, with many not investing at all. There are, however, exceptions, notably IsDB and CEB. IsDB invested 2.9% of its cumulative lending portfolio in the health sector between 1975 and 2019, with health projects approved during the 2010s prioritising two areas: prevention and control of communicable and non-communicable diseases and health system strengthening to improve healthcare quality and access (IsDB Group 2016). These areas reflect the post-Washington consensus agenda, with the specific diseases used to limit expenditures and the governance focus to ensure technocratic efficiencies. CEB allocated 12.1% of its 2015 approvals to the health sector, predominantly co-financing projects for modernising and increasing accessibility to medical infrastructure. Other MDBs that invest only marginally in the sector include BADEA, which approved only one health project in 2018 – financing the construction of buildings at a hospital site in Mauritius. In 2018, OFID invested 5% of new approvals in the health sector ($140.5 million), focussing on high-burden diseases (HIV/AIDS) and non-communicable diseases (cancer and diabetes), again demonstrating a disease-specific focus rather than a comprehensive approach to public services.

The initial response of the MDBs to COVID-19 between March and May 2020 was quick and large. Most MDBs devised COVID-19 response plans, ranging from short-term financing during the initial outbreak to long-term programmes. The World Bank Group allocated $160 billion to address health, economic, and social shocks experienced over 2020 and 2021 and the RDBs provided a further $80 billion. Priorities were medical supplies, transmission surveillance, and clinical care facilities, as well as direct cash transfers to the poor and vulnerable. A few also utilised previously established pandemic financing mechanisms, such as the World Bank's Pandemic Emergency Financing Facility founded in July 2017 to address to the 2014–15 West Africa Ebola outbreak and EIB's Infectious Disease Financing Facility that held a €5 billion project pipeline in mid-2020. Emerging financing arrangements were also approved by many sub-regional and specialised

MDBs, including CABEI, CAF, CDB, IsDB, NIB, and the Black Sea Trade and Development Bank (BSTDB). Though smaller in size than the World Bank and RDBs, they demonstrated the capacity of MDBs to quickly allocate emergency finance. Even MDBs that would not normally finance the health sector, like AIIB, drafted pandemic response plans.

COVID-19 revealed the dominance of the retroliberal development agenda. Even with a global pandemic and many countries facing unmanageable levels of debt, there was no expansion of grant resources for the Global South. Indeed, the US cut funding to WHO. The MDBs, development finance institutions (DFIs), and some Chinese funds were the main financing mechanisms available to many countries. Indeed, there was a very large outflow of private capital from the Global South. Further, MDB finance was used to plug holes in health systems that had been eroded over decades. Public systems are underfunded, have not focussed sufficiently on pandemic preparedness, and have no spare capacity thanks to the relentless neoliberal focus on efficiency. We expect to see MDB funds propping up private health providers in developing countries as they are facing financial stress and crisis (Williams 2020). This is because many of their most profitable procedures are either being delayed by patients or governments or because insurance schemes are struggling due to the level of claims and the associated economic disruptions meaning many people cannot pay their insurance premiums.

11.4 Gender

The nexus between women, gender, and development has long been a point of contest. Until very recently, the MDBs have largely sidestepped substantive recognition of the significance of women to and gendered inequalities in development. This is not to suggest that they have not engaged with gender, but rather that such issues have been treated as incidental. There are serious questions about whether MDB gender actions genuinely address inequalities or whether they are more rhetorical responses to expectations that they should be part of an international organisation's operations (Aasen 2009).

Many MDBs over the 2010s published reports discussing gender dynamics in their organisations, including attempts to better manage corporate diversity. The AfDB released an internal gender equality strategy in 2014 that detailed male to female employment ratios and promotion opportunities as well as guidelines for an inclusive workplace. In 2018, CEB enacted a gender equality strategy for organisational reform. Such reforms are important, for they expose and attempt to redress gendered biases. To illustrate, EIB has a severe gender imbalance for internal promotions, with 'numerous complaints by female employees in recent years about the lack of gender diversity and career advancement for women and a generally misogynistic culture at the bank' (De La Baume 2017). The EIB's lack of gender diversity is not unique, with most MDBs disproportionately staffed by men, particularly in management positions, from presidents to senior leadership to members of boards of governors and executive directors. This topic is important and would benefit from detailed future research, but our focus in this chapter is on MDB lending operations.

Since the 1970s, three primary perspectives on women, gender, and development have evolved: women in development (WID), women and development (WAD), and gender and development (GAD). Each of the gender-based paradigms occupies a different space in development discourse, offering alternate accounts of the impacts of and solutions to reduce inequalities for women (and men), while being unified in encouraging greater participation and empowerment of women, and stressing the harm of gender exclusion to progressive societal change (Momsen 2004). For the MDBs, actions to address gendered inequalities began with the adoption of WID policies in the 1980s but more recently shifted towards a neoliberal variant of GAD; WAD has not entered the policy documents or lending operations of the MDBs.

WID was the first academic paradigm drawing women into development discourse, led by Ester Boerup's (1970) *Women's Role in Economic Development*. Adopting a liberal feminist lens, WID challenged modernisation theory's exclusion of women from development. The paradigm was criticised, however, for its oversimplification of women's work and role in society and its argument that legal and administrative reforms were sufficient to address systemic gendered inequalities (Pearson and Jackson 1998, Rathgeber 1990, see Benería and Sen 1981, Tinker 1990). Next, WAD came from neo-Marxist feminist analyses in the mid-1970s to address WID's limitations. It asserts that women have always been important economic actors and their work inside and outside the household has been critical to the maintenance of (capitalist) society (Pala 1977). WAD regards the perpetuation of dependency and global inequalities as the key determinant facing developing countries and women in those societies (Rathgeber 1990), and attention thus focusses on the unequal gendered impact of modernisation (Griffin 2009). It has been criticised for inadequate attention to social and patriarchal divisions between men and women and for discounting the intersectionality of other identities which perpetuate inequalities between women themselves (Parpart 1993). Lastly, GAD emerged in the 1980s as a response to silences in WID and WAD. It represents a more holistic approach and 'is not concerned with women per se but with the social construction of gender and the assignment of specific roles, responsibilities, and expectations to women and to men' (Rathgeber 1990, 494); the focus turns to the relationships between women and men and the impact different gendered roles have on development. For GAD, development is multidimensional and is not merely the process of integrating women into productive labour but to ensuring women and men benefit from development.

Beginning in the 1980s, the MDBs slowly began to incorporate 'gender' into their operations. Unlike education and health, 'women' and 'gender' for the MDBs are not investment sectors but rather issues that are taken into consideration when drafting loan agreements. While gender mainstreaming has made progress over the past few decades, it remains a less than important issue for most MDBs; common statements appear as 'it is our aim to embed gender issues in all that we do' as opposed to committing substantive resources to addressing gendered inequalities. Since the 1980s, three phases demarcate MDB gender strategies: mid-1980s to mid-1990s and WID, mid-1990s to mid-2000s and GAD, and 2010s (OVE 2018). The 2010s are particularly significant not only because they have seen an integration of WID and GAD approaches but also because this was when many of the smaller MDBs began engaging with gender issues.

Between 1984 and 1990, the World Bank, IADB, AfDB, and AsDB introduced their initial WID policies, prioritising actions that increased women's access to employment, markets, education, and material resources (OVE 2018). These policies predated initiatives by other MDBs by at least a decade. Still, projects were often small. For example, under its 1984 WID Gender Directive, the World Bank approved a $7.5 million project to the Gambia to improve women's economic productivity and income earning potential. IADB pursued a WID agenda in projects as early as 1978, but it published its first WID policy in 1987 that focussed on economic growth and poverty alleviation for women through increased access to credit, microenterprise loans, and institutional support for women entrepreneurs. Microfinance, as noted earlier, is very problematic as a poverty reduction programme and its construction of gender relations and women's empowerment has been the subject of powerful critiques (Karim 2011, Yeboah et al. 2015). Still, it remains a preferred policy for many MDBs. Turning to AfDB, in 1987 it established a WID Unit designed to evaluate WID components in the project cycle. AsDB's approach mirrored the World Bank and other RDBs, with an economistic and growth-oriented WID model. Reflecting Japanese government hostility to gender equality action, between 1992 and 1995 the Asian RDB only approved two WID projects – it had a policy but little substantive action.

By the mid-1990s, the WID policies of the larger MDBs were replaced by new strategies aligned more with a neoliberal GAD paradigm; it was more holistic in addressing social, political, and economic structures but favoured market-centric responses. The World Bank (2000) outlined a revised Gender Sector Strategy with measures addressing barriers to women and men gaining equal access to credit, education, and healthcare. For IADB, in 1995 then Executive Vice President Nancy Birdsall outlined an initiative to ensure that half of projects had gender components by 2000, which was followed in 2003 by a Gender Mainstreaming Action Plan to increase the volume of loans, country strategies, and advisory services targeting gender issues. AfDB turned towards GAD in its 2001 Gender Policy that sought to embed gender as a crosscutting issue alongside the environment, civil society participation, and institutional development and AsDB's 1998 Policy on Gender and Development proposed a GAD-oriented roadmap, broadly focussing on mainstreaming gender in lending operations as well as setting the foundations for a multi-donor Gender and Development Cooperation Fund launched in 2003.

The World Bank, IADB, AfDB, and AsDB again drafted new gender policy documents in the 2010s, merging WID and GAD into 'twin-track strategies' (OVE 2018, 8). The World Bank Group's (2015) current 2016–23 Gender Equality Strategy prioritises closing education and health inequalities, removing employment and land ownership obstacles for women, and enhancing women's voice and agency. IADB's (2019) 2019–21 Diversity Action Plan for Operations lists five action lines: agenda setting and policy development, operational mainstreaming, direct investment, knowledge and dissemination, and technological innovation.

In 2010, AfDB unveiled a Gender and Social Development Monitoring Division, followed by a new Gender Strategy in 2014 and a Gender Marker System in 2018 to track gender mainstreaming in its operations. Prügl (2017, 47) describes such initiatives as

> the reconstruction of neoliberalism so that it dons a feminist face. This reconstruction preserves the privileges of private enterprise, individual responsibility, and the wisdom of the market while recognising the inequality-producing force of institutional biases, informal, norms, unequal endowments, and power relations in the household and society.

In 2010, EBRD implemented the first phase of its Gender Action Plan, which was approved in May 2009, drafted to support equal opportunity and to promote women entrepreneurship. The Gender Action Plan was replaced in 2015 by the Strategy for the Promotion of Gender Equality 2016–20, which Shields and Wallin (2015) and Shields (2020) regard as proposing a neoliberal 'business case' for gender mainstreaming, framing women as individualistic workers operating in a market economy; a clear articulation of human capital development as opposed to human development.

For the SRDBs and specialised development banks, available data reveals considerably less substantive gender interventions than the World Bank and RDBs. There are, without question, a few MDBs with robust diversity policies that have been translated into action, including CDB and IFAD, while others have not developed clear gender policies, such as the Russian- and Arab-led MDBs, with the notable exception of IsDB. The NDB and AIIB to date have not financed gender projects, although they have disseminated boilerplate press releases stating the importance of women to development. Other MDBs have only very recently engaged with gender and therefore details remain scant, such as IsDB and its Women's Empowerment Policy published in February 2019, which is designed to mainstream gender in its lending, analytical work, and organisational practices. Similarly, CAF created a Gender Equity and Inclusion Unit in 2015 to provide gender oversight in projects, but only began applying gender safeguards to its entire loan portfolio in 2019.

As a gender leader, CDB introduced gender mainstreaming in 2005, with initiatives to incorporate gender analyses into lending operations, develop gender analytical frameworks and indicators as part of country surveys, and improve gender equality awareness. In December 2008, it approved a Gender Equality Policy, followed by its 2015 Gender Equality Policy and Operational Strategy. In 2015, 57% of its projects included gender components and between 2012 and 2015 it conducted ten Country Gender Assessments of member countries. CDB thus appears to be one of the most progressive MDBs, prioritising economic empowerment for women. Similarly, IFAD has a long gender history, almost rivalling the World Bank and RDBs. This history dates to 1992 when it led the Summit on the Economic Advancement of Rural Women that argued WID approaches to be ineffectual in addressing systemic issues leading to gendered inequalities in development (IFAD 2018). In 1998, IFAD published its *Lending Policies and Criteria* that directed operational resources to poor rural women and in 2012 it approved the Gender Equality and Women's Empowerment Policy. This policy focussed on economic empowerment for rural women, equal voice for women and men in rural organisations, and more equitable workloads between women and men, pursued through country programmes and projects, advocacy initiatives, and public and private sector capacity building. In 2016, IFAD's Strategic Framework 2016–25 identified gender equality as one of five guiding principles, shaping not only lending operations but also internal organisational practices. Like CDB, IFAD is a very progressive MDB.

The approach taken by the MDBs to women and gender in development is largely one that regards gendered inequalities as objects that can be 'fixed' through the application of the right resources. While attempts to mainstream gender actions and support women's empowerment and inclusion are essential pursuits by the MDBs, the broad approach taken is one that focusses on economic opportunities through resource investment, without significantly addressing entrenched cultural values and norms that maintain structural gender imbalances;

> failure to acknowledge the role of neoliberal economics – privatization and deregulation – and depoliticization in consolidating social inequalities leads to the World Bank advocating a developmental paradigm that will perpetuate poverty and thus gender inequality.
>
> (Power 2020, 29)

11.5 Conclusion

There has been a lot written about the World Bank's role in human development interventions, and a little about some of the other MDBs. We cannot do justice to the literature in this chapter. There are many important qualitative analyses of MDB-funded development interventions that shed light on the nature of human development, capabilities, and participation. There is important work on the rights of indigenous people, minority groups, the disabled, and more that we do not have the space to engage with here. Our focus was to provide an overview of the ideas and policies that shaped MDB actions in a few key areas. We demonstrated that human development is a difficult space for the MDBs, as they were conceived to fund profitable projects with clear quantitative returns on investment. As they shifted from their banking focus towards development, they could not ignore the field and did not want to as it gave them a whole new arena to finance. Still, their engagement with human development is restrained, despite influencing global discourse on education, health, and gender. Ultimately, their approach to human development is framed by neoliberalism. It is thus not surprising that, in education, the human capital approach of creating productive workers trumps cultivating educated citizens with rights. In health, the MDBs still extoll market forces despite decades of failures and inefficiencies associated with private healthcare provision. And, in gender, we see the agenda of 'fixing women' to ensure that they are more efficient economic units. Still, the chapter highlighted some differences between the MDBs, and such subtleties matter, particularly when considering whether to invest in people to improve their productive capacity or to improve quality of life.

Bibliography

Aasen, Berit. 2009. Gender Equality and the Multilateral Development Banks (MDBs): How the World Bank, the African Development Bank, the Asian Development Bank and the Inter-American Bank Work on Women Empowerment and Gender Equality. In *NIBR Working Paper*: Norwegian Institute for Urban and Regional Research.

AsDB. 1990. Annual Report 1990. Manila: Asian Development Bank.

Barham, Tania, John Maluccio, and Marco Stampini. 2018. "Long-Term Impacts of Conditional Cash Transfers: Review of the Evidence." *IDEAS Working Paper Series from RePEc*.

Bateman, Milford. 2010. *Why Doesn't Microfinance Work?: The Destructive Rise of Local Neoliberalism*. New York: Zed Books.

Bazbauers, Adrian Robert. 2018. *The World Bank and Transferring Development: Policy Movement through Technical Assistance*, International Political Economy Series. Cham: Palgrave Macmillan.

Benería, Lourdes, and Gita Sen. 1981. "Accumulation, Reproduction, and "Women's Role in Economic Development": Boserup Revisited." *Signs* 7 (2):279–98. doi: 10.1086/493882.

Birn, Anne-Emanuelle. 2009. "The Stages of International (Global) Health: Histories of Success or Successes of History?" *Global Public Health* 4 (1):50–68. doi: 10.1080/17441690802017797.

Boerup, Ester. 1970. *Woman's Role in Economic Development*. London: Allen & Unwin.

CAF. 2018. Educational Agenda 2018–2022. Caracas: CAF.

Cammack, Paul. 2012. "Risk, Social Protection and the World Market." *Journal of Contemporary Asia* 42 (3):359–77. doi: 10.1080/00472336.2012.687627.

Cammack, Paul. 2017. "The UNDP, the World Bank and Human Development through the World Market." *Development Policy Review* 35 (1):3–21. doi: 10.1111/dpr.12198.

Carroll, Toby. 2010. *Delusions of Development: The World Bank and the Post-Washington Consensus in Southeast Asia*. Houndmills, Basingstoke: Palgrave Macmillan.

Coburn, Carolyn, Michael Restivo, and John M. Shandra. 2015. "The African Development Bank and Infant Mortality: A Cross-national Analysis of Structural Adjustment and Investment Lending from 1990 to 2006." *International Journal of Comparative Sociology* 56 (3–4):275–96. doi: 10.1177/0020715215610799.

Cox, Robert W. 1968. "Education for Development." *International Organization* 22 (1):-310–31. doi: 10.1017/S0020818300013588.

De La Baume, Maïa. 2017. "Macho Time Warp at the European Investment Bank." *Politico*. https://www.politico.eu/article/european-investment-bank-a-mens-club-at-the-top/.

Dennis, Suzanna, and Elaine Zuckerman. 2008. "Mapping Multilateral Development Banks' Spending on Reproductive Health and HIV and AIDS." *Gender and Development* 16 (2):287–300.

Engel, Susan, and David Pedersen. 2019. "Microfinance as Poverty-Shame Debt." *Emotions and Society* fast tracked:1–16. doi: 10.1332/263168919X15653391247919.

Fiszbein, Ariel. 2009. *Conditional Cash Transfers Reducing Present and Future Poverty*, edited by Norbert Rüdiger Schady and Francisco H. G. Ferreira, *A World Bank policy research report*. Washington, DC: World Bank.

Griffin, Penny. 2009. *Gendering the World Bank: Neoliberalism and the Gendered Foundations of Global Governance*. Hampshire: Palgrave Macmillan.
Gundlach, Erich. 1996. Human Capital and Economic Development: A Macroeconomic Assessment. Kiel: Kiel Institute for the World Economy (IfW).
Hall, Anthony. 2007. "Social Policies in the World Bank: Paradigms and Challenges." *Global Social Policy* 7 (2):151–75. doi: 10.1177/1468018107078160.
Hunter, Wendy, and David Brown. 2000. "World Bank Directives, Domestic Interests, and the Politics of Human Capital Investment in Latin America." *Comparative Political Studies* 33 (1):113–43. doi: 10.1177/0010414000033001005.
IADB. 2019. Diversity Action Plan for Operations: 2019–2021. In *Social Sector*, edited by Gender and Diversity Division: Inter-American Development Bank.
IFAD. 2018. Agents of Rural Change: The IFAD Story. Rome: International Fund for Agricultural Development.
IsDB Group. 2016. *42 Years in the Service of Developmennt*. Jeddah: Islamic Development Bank Group.
Javed Burki, Shahid, and Mahbub Ul Haq. 1981. "Meeting Basic Needs: An Overview." *World Development* 9 (2):167–82. doi: 10.1016/0305-750X(81)90011-5.
Jolly, Richard. 1991. "Adjustment with a Human Face: A UNICEF Record and Perspective on the 1980s." *World Development* 19 (12):1807–21. doi: 10.1016/0305-750X(91)90026-E.
Kapur, Devesh, Richard Charles Webb, and John P. Lewis. 1997. *The World Bank: Its First Half Century*, edited by Richard Charles Webb and John P. Lewis. Washington, DC: Brookings Institution.
Karim, Lamia. 2011. *Microfinance and Its Discontents: Women in Debt in Bangladesh*. Minneapolis: University of Minnesota Press.
Kenneth, King. 2015. "The History and Future of International Cooperation in Education." In *Routledge Handbook of International Education and Development*, edited by Simon McGrath and Qing Gu, Chapter 27, 375–389. Abingdon: Routledge.
Komatsu, Ryuichi, Daniel Low-Beer, and Bernhard Schwartländer. 2007. "Global Fund-supported Programmes Contribution to International Targets and the Millennium Development Goals: An Initial Analysis." *Bulletin of the World Health Organization* 85 (10):805–11. doi: 10.2471/blt.06.038315.
Larmour, P. 2002. "Conditionality, Coercion and Other Forms of 'Power': International Financial Institutions in the Pacific." *Public Administration and Development* 22 (3):-249–60. doi: 10.1002/pad.228.
Lind, Niels. 2019. "A Development of the Human Development Index." *Social Indicators Research* 146 (3):409–23. doi: 10.1007/s11205-019-02133-9.
Lisk, F. 2009. *Global Institutions and the HIV/AIDS Epidemic: Responding to an International Crisis*. Abingdon: Routledge Taylor & Francis Group.
Mader, Philip. 2015. *The Political Economy of Microfinance*. New York: Palgrave Macmillan.
McInnes, Colin. 2015. "WHO's Next? Changing Authority in Global Health Governance after Ebola." *International Affairs* 91 (6):1299–316. doi: 10.1111/1468-2346.12454.
Momsen, Jane Henshall. 2004. *Gender and Development*. London: Routledge.
Morozkina, Alexandra, and Ekaterina Sabelnikova. 2017. "Education Systems and Multilateral Development Banks: International Practices and Perspectives." *International Organisations Research Journal* 12 (1):24–42. doi: 10.17323/1996-7845-2017-01-24.
Normann, Henrik. 2019. Nordic Investment Bank – Henrik Normann – Answers to UNSW Survey 15.5.2019, interviewed by Adrian Robert Bazbauers: UNSW Canberra.
Noy, Shiri. 2018. "Healthy Targets? World Bank Projects and Targeted Health Programmes and Policies in Costa Rica, Argentina, and Peru, 1980–2005." *Oxford Development Studies* 46 (2):164–83. doi: 10.1080/13600818.2017.1346068.

OVE. 2018. Evaluation of the Bank's Support for Gender and Diversity. Office of Evaluation and Oversight (Inter-American Development Bank).

Pala, Achola O. 1977. "Definitions of Women and Development: An African Perspective." *Signs: Journal of Women in Culture and Society* 3 (1):9–13. doi: 10.1086/493434.

Parpart, Jane L. 1993. "Who Is the 'Other'?: A Postmodern Feminist Critique of Women and Development Theory and Practice." *Development and Change* 24 (3):439–64. doi: 10.1111/j.1467-7660.1993.tb00492.x.

Pearson, Ruth, and Cecile Jackson. 1998. "Introduction: Interrogating Development: Feminism, Gender, and Policy." In *Feminist Visions of Development: Gender Analysis and Policy*, edited by Ruth Pearson and Cecile Jackson. 4–16. London: Routledge.

Ponzio, Richard, and Arunabha Ghosh. 2016. *Human Development and Global Institutions: Evolution, Impact, Reform*, edited by Arunabha Ghosh, *Global institutions series; 115*. Abingdon, Oxon: Routledge.

Power, Luke. 2020. "New Ways or Old Tricks? The World Bank's Gender Strategy and Its Implications for Health." *International Journal of Health Services* 50 (1):21–31. doi: 10.1177/0020731419885090.

Prügl, Elisabeth. 2017. "Neoliberalism with a Feminist Face: Crafting a New Hegemony at the World Bank." *Feminist Economics* 23 (1):30–53. doi: 10.1080/13545701.2016.1198043.

Rathgeber, Eva M. 1990. "WID, WAD, GAD: Trends in Research and Practice." *The Journal of Developing Areas* 24 (4):489–502.

Rossi, Federico. 2018. Human Capital and Macro-Economic Developemnt: A Review of the Evidence. In *Policy Research Working Paper*: World Bank Group.

Roth, Gregory A., Degu Abate, Kalkidan Hassen Abate, Solomon M. Abay, Cristiana Abbafati, Nooshin Abbasi, Hedayat Abbastabar, Foad Abd-Allah, Jemal Abdela, Ahmed Abdelalim, Ibrahim Abdollahpour, Rizwan Suliankatchi Abdulkader, Haftom Temesgen Abebe, Molla Abebe, Zegeye Abebe, Ayenew Negesse Abejie, Semaw F. Abera, Olifan Zewdie Abil, Haftom Niguse Abraha, and Aklilu Roba Abrham. 2018. "Global, Regional, and National Age-sex-specific Mortality for 282 Causes of Death in 195 Countries and Territories, 1980–2017: A Systematic Analysis for the Global Burden of Disease Study 2017." *The Lancet* 392 (10159):1736–88. doi: 10.1016/S0140-6736(18)32203-7.

Sastry, Shaunak, and Mohan Jyoti Dutta. 2013. "Global Health Interventions and the "Common Sense" of Neoliberalism: A Dialectical Analysis of PEPFAR." *Journal of International and Intercultural Communication* 6 (1):21–39. doi: 10.1080/17513057.2012.740682.

Schmidt, Werner, Monica Lledó Moreno, and Judith Goodwin. 2007. Operations Evaluation: Evaluation of EIB Financing of Health Projects: Synthesis Report. EIB Operations Evaluation.

Sen, Amartya. 1990. "Development as Capability Expansion." In The Community Development Reader, edited by James DeFilippis and Susan Saegert: 41–58. Oxon: Routledge.

Shields, Stuart. 2020. "The EBRD, Fail Forward Neoliberalism and the Construction of the European Periphery." *The Economic and Labour Relations Review* 31 (2):230–48. doi: 10.1177/1035304620916652.

Shields, Stuart, and Sara Wallin. 2015. "The European Bank for Reconstruction and Development's Gender Action Plan and the Gendered Political Economy of Post-Communist Transition." *Globalizations* 12 (3):383–99. doi: 10.1080/14747731.2015.1016307.

Son, Hyun H. 2010. Human Capital Development. In *ADB Economics Working Paper Series*: Asian Development Bank.

Streeten, Paul. 1979. "Basics Needs: Premises and Promises." *Journal of Policy Modeling* 1 (1):136–46.

Streeten, Paul. 1981. *First Things First: Meeting Basic Human Needs in the Developing Countries*. New York: Published for the World Bank by Oxford University Press.

Thomson, Michael, Alexander Kentikelenis, and Thomas Stubbs. 2017. "Structural Adjustment Programmes Adversely Affect Vulnerable Populations: A Systematic-Narrative Review of Their Effect on Child and Maternal Health." *Public Health Reviews* 38 (1):13. doi: 10.1186/s40985-017-0059-2.

Tinker, Irene. 1990. *Persistent Inequalities: Women and World Development*. New York: Oxford University Press.

Ul Haq, Mahbub. 1995. *Reflections on Human Development: How the Focus of Development Economics Shifted from National Income Accounting to People-centred Policies, Told by One of the Chief Architects of the New Paradigm*. New York: Oxford University Press.

Williams, Owain D. 2020. "Market Failure, COVID and Private Healthcare." Accessed 17 August. https://covid19healthdiaries.com/diary?did=274.

Woodling, Marie, Owain D. Williams, and Simon Rushton. 2012. "New Life in Old Frames: HIV, Development and the 'AIDS Plus MDGs' Approach." *Global Public Health* 7 (sup2):S144–58. doi: 10.1080/17441692.2012.728238.

World Bank. 1975. Annual Report 1975. Washington, DC: World Bank.

World Bank. 1980. Annual Report 1980. Washington, DC: World Bank.

World Bank. 1987. Financing Health Services in Developing Countries: An Agenda for Reform. Washington, DC: World Bank.

World Bank. 2000. World Bank Report 2000/2001: Attacking Poverty. Washington, DC: World Bank.

World Bank. 2010. Annual Report 2010. Washington, DC: World Bank.

World Bank. 2019. World Development Report 2019: The Changing Nature of Work. Washington, DC: World Bank.

World Bank Group. 2015. World Bank Group Gender Strategy (FY16–23): Gender Equality, Poverty Reduction and Inclusive Growth. Washington, DC: World Bank.

Yeboah, Thomas, Albert Arhin, Emmanuel Kumi, and Luch Owusu. 2015. "Empowering and Shaping Gender Relations? Contesting the Microfinance–Gender Empowerment Discourse." *Development in Practice* 25 (6):895–908.

Zwi, Anthony B., and Anne Mills. 1995. "Health Policy in Less Developed Countries: Past Trends and Future Directions." *Journal of International Development* 7 (3):299–328. doi: 10.1002/jid.3380070302.

12 Conclusion

We set ourselves a difficult task in writing a single volume about 30 multilateral development banks (MDBs) operating in every corner of the globe over the past 80 years. Undoubtedly, in this breadth we have missed important details and writing a simple conclusion about the complex and interdependent architecture of MDF is daunting. And, yet, the breadth of the volume has, we think, been useful in unearthing many questions, particularly those highlighted by the title of the book. Are the MDBs a system? What is the relationship between the MDBs, financial markets, and debt? And what kind of vision of development do the MDBs promote? After we respond to these three questions, this concluding chapter briefly considers a future research agenda for the MDBs before turning to how COVID-19 is demonstrating the continued significance of the development banks and what we need to be reviewing about them in the context of a global pandemic.

12.1 The MDBs as a system

The book demonstrates that the 30 MDBs largely have the same lineage. They evolved from the post-Second World War Keynesian, modernisation, welfare project that sought to tame capitalism but relied on capitalist tools to do so, such as banks in the form of the MDBs. Mandate, structure, and governance similarities illustrated in Chapters 3–5 makes it evident that the MDBs can be regarded as a system. The establishment of the IDA in the World Bank and not in the UN was a key turning point in the history of development finance, promoting a banking model for the MDBs over a cooperative focus (Shaw 2005). Still, between 1946 and 1979, the MDBs followed the Keynesian formula of promoting balanced investment and economic development, with an expansion of that agenda to include social, regional, and sub-regional development. Even MDBs created in and by the Global South, which emerged from an anti-colonial and generally developmentalist agenda, largely followed the same model. With the rise of neoliberalism, there came the first neoliberal MDB, the EBRD, with its focus on creating market-oriented economies and multi-party democracies. Many other MDBs became partners in the neoliberal paradigm or had to admit new shareholders to accommodate the changing exigencies of the global financial system.

Chapter 5 demonstrated that all the MDBs basically follow the organisational blueprint laid down by the World Bank, with variations emerging due to differences in capital, shareholders, capabilities, and mandates. There is good evidence that the World Bank, RDBs, and a handful other MDBs have followed each other in establishing accountability mechanisms, safeguard policies, and anti-corruption mechanisms (Komori 2016, Park 2014, 2017). Several international development initiatives also align the MDBs, including the 2005 Multilateral Debt Relief Initiative and a few OECD Development Assistance Committee (DAC) proposals, for example, the Aid Effectiveness Agenda, which involved 13 of the then 28 MDBs. The MDBs are thus networked in a myriad of ways, though the larger MDBs are more networked than most of the smaller ones.

One main networking and cooperation forum for the MDBs is the Annual and Spring IMF and World Bank Group Meetings. There are also regular Heads of MDBs and IMF Meetings, which include the AfDB, AsDB, EBRD, EIB, IADB, IsDB, World Bank, and IMF. In 2016, the BRICS-led NDB and China-led AIIB joined these meetings. Further, the MDBs have issued joint statements on a range of issues over the past two decades, particularly on the Millennium and Sustainable Development Goals and the 2015 Paris Agreement. And there have been and are a range of formal and informal working groups on specific topics, for example:

- Heads of procurement from at least ten MDBs have been meeting since 2000 to enhance their work;
- The Evaluation Cooperation Group was established between the World Bank and AfDB, AsDB, EBRD, and IADB in 1996 and since then the evaluation groups of the BSTDB, EIB, IFAD, IMF, and IsDB have joined;
- Several MDBs and the International Development Finance Club (IDFC) jointly agreed to the Common Principles for Climate Adaptation Finance Tracking in March 2015; and,
- The Global Infrastructure Forum was launched in 2016, as was a platform to coordinate on economic migration and forced displacement which included seven MDBs.

The World Federation of Development Finance Institutions was established in 1979 to promote more efficient development banking, increase opportunities for development banks, and expand coordination. It is made up of four regional groupings, which all have RDBs and SRDBs as special members and other DFIs (including national development banks and export-import banks) as ordinary members. The African association includes the five functional African SRDBs as special members and the IBRD and IFC as honorary members. The Asia Pacific grouping's 117 members include AsDB, PIDB, the IsDB Group's Islamic Corporation for the Development of the Private Sector (ICD), and the IIB. The Latin American group's 80 members include IADB, CABEI, CAF, FONPLATA Development Bank, and EIB. There is also a special grouping for IsDB members.

The IDFC is another coordinating body for the MDBs. It was established in 2011 to help DFIs set agendas on development finance and share know-how. Today it has 26 members including six SRDBs – BOAD, BSTDB, CABEI, CAF, IIB, and TDB – and IsDB through the ICD, along with national development banks from both the Global North and South and one export-import bank; this demonstrates the connections between the MDBs and between the MDBs and other DFIs. It claims to have $4 trillion in combined assets and annual commitments over $850 billion. The IDFC and World Federation of Development Finance Institutions sponsored a joint summit in November 2020 called Finance in Common, which brought together 450 global development institutions.

The MDBs also co-finance each other's projects; EIB's first loan in 1958 was co-financed by the IBRD. They in addition coordinate their lending with each other in different ways, a major one being country-level donor coordination groups. Finally, there have been numerous reviews of the MDB system by US and international agencies indicating that the global community regards the MDBs as a networked system, though they do not always cover the full suite of MDBs.

12.2 The MDBs, financial markets, and debt

The first IFIs were created in the wake of a series of crises in the 19th and 20th centuries culminating in the 1929 Great Depression. They were the product of an increasingly globalised network of money and debt built up with the state system. International financial cooperation emerged slowly from the mid-19th century and Chapter 2 identified a range of precedents for MDBs, most specifically a Mexican proposal for a development finance element to be added to the inter-American bank idea, which was discussed on-and-off from the late 1800s. Still, formal IFIs only emerged at the end of the Second World War and they were designed to promote financial openness while controlling the problems that international finance markets had already brought.

The MDBs were designed to ensure that states received the investment flows they needed to promote development but, in setting up the IBRD as a 'bank,' Harry Dexter White and John Maynard Keynes inadvertently created an organisation that would not overcome 'the somewhat violent and not too enlightened motives of capital' (White cited in Oliver 1975, 97). Or, equally to the point, the MDBs could not overcome the violence of capital in the absence of an orderly system of default for nation-states. Indeed, the MDBs have and continue to provide loans directly – and facilitate private lending for – what the Committee for the Abolition of Illegitimate Debts calls illegitimate, odious, and unsustainable debts. That is to say, the MDBs lend to regimes simply because they control a territory; they loan regardless of a regime's legitimacy, respect for human rights, or whether the loan benefits the local population (Toussaint 2019). Safeguard policies have been established by the MDBs to limit the latter situation, but the literature is still littered with far too many examples of project-linked human rights failings, which is only likely to increase with the greater infrastructure focus discussed in Chapter 9.

The MDBs also helped financialisation in the 1970s thanks to their promotion of lending to the Global South and, once the 1982 Debt Crisis hit, the World Bank became a major debt-collector for the Global North. After the 1980s, most MDBs became proponents of a neoliberal approach to development, which led to a dramatic increase in financialisation. But this financialised capitalism has not proved to be as super-efficient as its proponents claimed. Rather, it has been prone to crisis, with major debt crises in 1997 and 2008. As outlined in Chapter 4, 2010–20 saw the 'largest, fastest and most broad-based increase' in EMDE debt of the past 50 years, even once the impacts of China's corporate debt bubble were excluded (Kose et al. 2020, 111). This has occurred along with low interest rates and the growth of new financial 'innovations,' which were present in the previous three debt crises (Kose et al. 2020). Earlier debt crises tended to be triggered by banking or financial crises. This time the trigger may be the current global pandemic.

Regardless, the book has demonstrated how the MDB system is entwined with debt networks from other DFIs and private finance and that the MDBs play a pivotal role in this system as direct lenders, signallers, facilitators, creators of 'common sense' policy frameworks, financial innovators, de-riskers, and more. With the shift to the retroliberal development paradigm, states have been encouraged to take on more and more debt for development, but the development model is a shadow of its former self, mostly just recycling old ideas in a way that sets them on a problematic detour when many should have gone straight to landfill.

12.3 The MDBs and framing development discourse

Most MDBs emerged and grew up with the Keynesian, modernisation, welfare model, but their banking DNA meant that they tended to focus on the modernisation element and, within that, on bankable projects that demonstrated returns to the market. This drive did not disappear even with greater lending for basic needs from the 1970s and certainly not with the emergence of the Washington Consensus in the 1980s. When the human cost became too high, the post-Washington Consensus arrived to renew the palatability of neoliberalism. What followed was a brief progressive interlude, with the Millennium and Sustainable Development Goals targeting poverty alleviation and human development. But the penny-pinching returned with the Beyond Aid initiative, and this fed into the rise of the current retroliberal development agenda. The influence of China can be seen in an old-school focus on infrastructure as facilitating economic growth and an increased emphasis on state sovereignty and concurrent dismantling of human rights-based approaches to development.

Chapters 9 through 11 explored three main areas of MDB operations: infrastructure, climate finance, and human development. Our choice in selecting these areas reflect the fact that Engen and Prizzon (2018) found that in 2015 infrastructure was the largest MDB sector in terms of disbursements, while the World Bank and CDB had the social sector as their largest area of support, with BADEA and IADB also being quite active. Importantly, as revealed by their human development actions and climate interventions, the MDBs tend to finance social and environmental programmes that promote increased productivity as opposed to 'solving' climate change or improving the lives of people. The three chapters demonstrated how most MDBs follow an instrumentalist approach in each of these areas, and that the larger MDBs play a key role in setting the normative agenda.

Lastly, the two new MDBs led by the BRICS and China not only replicated the MDB model, they opted for a donor-recipient blueprint, which is less development-friendly than the member-owned, financial cooperative agenda envisaged by some the founders of the IBRD. Still, member-led MDBs remain and there are examples of innovative, growing banks in the Global South, most notably CAF.

12.4 Some thoughts on a future research agenda

Turning very briefly to academic research on the MDBs, it is clear from the book that this is a huge field and there is much left unexplored. Historical research on almost all the MDBs, apart from the World Bank and a few RDBs, remains very limited. Archival access would be a fruitful avenue for expanding understandings of development priorities, challenges, and drivers. Equally, an historical analysis of the relationship between states and the MDBs both as recipients and donors would reveal much, especially since this has only been done for a handful of borrowing states and most research on donor countries focusses on the US. For recipient states, questions and topics could include why they have engaged with MDBs, differences in borrowing country portfolios, long-term studies of project outcomes, comparative studies of conditionalities and safeguards, the relationships between political and business interests in MDB lending (see Bond 2016, 2020), and the political economy and practices of MDB procurement (Bracking 2009, Williams-Elegbe 2017). There has also been limited research on the impact of the MDBs on labour markets (Murphy 2014) and, while there are many important project studies, we think there is space for additional comparative project analyses at the meso or macro level.

The complex relationships between the MDBs could use further investigation. This could focus on the World Bank and RDBs, or the RDBs and SRDBs in their regions. And the ideas and programmes of the RDBs and SRDBs could give historical and contemporary insights into the role of regionalism in development thinking and practice (Bruszt and Palestini 2016). Equally there is more scope for research on the RDBs and some of the sub-regional and specialised banks as intellectual actors, as Shields (2015) has done on the EBRD. Organisational research on MDB leadership would be interesting, from issues of poor gender representation in most MDBs to the professional and personal backgrounds linking MDB staff.

There is very little research on the SRDBs, which is peculiar given that they are fascinating and have diverse histories and outcomes. Humphrey (2019) has provided some excellent research with a focus on MDB banking imperatives but there are other avenues, for example: the pros and cons of the quirks of the SRDBs, such as having other DFIs and commercial banks as shareholders; the story of why and how non-regional members joined, like Belarus in the TDB or Barclays Bank and the Consortium of Yugoslav Institutions in the EADB; or, why the CDB provides a very high level of budgetary support lending. Research on the SRDBs could be useful for IR and IPE to better understand cooperative relations between smaller or less powerful nation-states. Similarly, the dominance of hegemons in the SRDBs would be quite illustrative; for example, Russia's role in the IBEC, IIB, and EDB could shed light on the financial dimension of Russia's relations with its neighbours and former Soviet states and the relative degrees of coercion and consent involved. Research on the extent to which the SRDBs follow mainstream development discourse is very scarce and would be illuminating in shedding light on policy diffusion from a constructivist perspective or on neoliberal hegemony from a Gramscian one. Finally, research on the SRDBs could be useful for developing a model about what kinds of innovations are possible for states genuinely wanting more progressive and equal relationships between members in an MDB.

12.5 COVID-19

Amid a global pandemic, it would be wrong not to close this book with a few thoughts on how the MDBs are responding to COVID-19. Indeed, it is vital as the MDBs will be one of the main sources of funding for the Global South, if not the main source, given that the Beyond Aid Agenda has seen decreases in grant financing and increases in loans. The World Bank has so far committed to providing $160 billion to help states address the crisis and a handful of others will provide a further $80 billion. The World Bank is also frontloading grants through its COVID-19 Fast Track Facility with more lending to follow. Some of the funding is of course supporting healthcare. Yet, as Chapter 11 briefly demonstrated, historical MDB financing to the health sector has been limited and what they have provided has tended to support the privatisation and deregulation of public health services. The resultant mixed public-private systems in developing countries are often poorly coordinated and do not have the capacity to respond to public health emergencies let along a pandemic. The private sector provides most of the hospital beds in many developing countries, but many private operators are unwilling to treat COVID-19 patients and others are using the crisis as an opportunity to price gouge and some from both these groups are struggling financially because of the pandemic's impacts. Yet, the MDB response to date appears to be a doubling-down on support for the private sector; public sector healthcare remains underfunded. This support is unlikely to assist the poorest, most vulnerable, and people in rural and remote areas. Indeed, much of it may just bail-out urban-based private medical centres. Hence, MDB health financing needs close monitoring and critical scrutiny.

The COVID-19 response of the MDBs is not limited to healthcare concerns. They have allocated significant financial allotments to budgetary support, emergency liquidity, and investment loans for economic recovery in infrastructure and other areas. Loans to financial intermediaries are proving popular for the World Bank, IFC, AIIB, CEB, and others, which is one of the least transparent forms of MDB lending. For example, the AIIB COVID-19 Crisis Recovery Facility is set to provide $10 billion to public and private organisations from April 2020 to October 2021, with considerable support directed to on-lending facilities and credit lines to financial institutions and immediate fiscal and budgetary support, including a $500 million credit line to Turkey to alleviate capital shortages. Just as in the healthcare sector, close monitoring of loans will be vital to ensure that their benefits are not mostly captured by elites, with the middle class and poor ultimately left to pay the bill. The likelihood of misappropriation and outright corruption is high across the globe, but higher in states in the Global South dominated by predatory domestic power configurations. When COVID-19 hit, rapidly increasing debt was already a concern. Thus, it may not be long before the MDBs switch from being vital sources of funds in a pandemic to debt-collectors and austerity promoters.

Bibliography

Bond, Patrick. 2016. "BRICS Banking and the Debate over Sub-imperialism." *Third World Quarterly* 37 (4):611–29.

Bond, Patrick. 2020. "BRICS Banking and the Demise of Alternatives to the IMF and World Bank." In *International Development Assistance and the BRICS*, edited by Jose A. Puppim de Oliveira and Yijia Jing, 189–218. London: Palgrave Macmillan.

Bracking, Sarah. 2009. *Money and Power: Great Predators in the Political Economy of Development*. London: Pluto Press.

Bruszt, Lazlo, and Stefano Palestini. 2016. "Regional Development Governance." In *The Oxford Handbook of Comparative Regionalism*, edited by Tanja A. Börzel and Thomas Risse, 374–404. Oxford: Oxford University Press.

Engen, Lars, and Annalisa Prizzon. 2018. *A Guide to Multilateral Development Banks*. London: ODI.

Humphrey, Chris. 2019. "'Minilateral' Development Banks: What the Rise of Africa's Trade and Development Bank Says about Multilateral Governance." *Development and Change* 50 (1):164–90. doi: 10.1111/dech.12467.

Komori, Yasumasa. 2016. "The Asian Development Bank: Joining the Fight against Corruption?" In *Global Economic Governance and the Practices of the Multilateral Development Banks*, edited by Susan Park and Jonathan R. Strand, 21–38. London: Routledge.

Kose, M. Ayhan, Peter Nagle, Franziska Ohnsorge, and Naotaka Sugawara. 2020. *Global Waves of Debt: Causes and Consequences*. Washington, DC: World Bank.

Murphy, Hannah. 2014. "The World Bank and Core Labour Standards: Between Flexibility and Regulation." *Review of International Political Economy* 21 (2):399–431. doi: 10.1080/09692290.2013.779591.

Oliver, Robert W. 1975. *International Economic Co-operation and the World Bank*. London and Basingstoke: Macmillan Press.

Park, Susan. 2014. "Institutional Isomorphism and the Asian Development Bank's Accountability Mechanism: Something Old, Something New, Something Borrowed, Something Blue?" *The Pacific Review* 27 (2):217–39.

Park, Susan. 2017. "Accountability as Justice for the Multilateral Development Banks? Borrower Opposition and Bank Avoidance to US Power and Influence." *Review of International Political Economy* 24 (5):776–801. doi: 10.1080/09692290.2017.1363798.

Shaw, D. John. 2005. "Turning Point in the Evolution of Soft Financing: The United Nations and the World Bank." *Canadian Journal of Development Studies* XXVI (1):43–61.

Shields, Stuart. 2015. "The European Bank for Reconstruction and Development as Organic Intellectual of Neoliberal Common Sense in Post-Communist Transition." In *Global Economic Governance and the Development Practices of the Multilateral Development Banks*, edited by Susan Park and Jonathan R. Strand, 167–86. Abingdon: Routledge.

Toussaint, Eric. 2019. *The Debt System: A History of Sovereign Debts and Their Repudiation*. Chicago, IL: Haymarket Books.

Williams-Elegbe, Sope. 2017. *Public Procurement and Multilateral Development Banks: Law, Practice and Problems*. Oxford: Hart.

Index

Note: Bold page numbers refer to tables.

FSC
www.fsc.org
MIX
Papier | Fördert
gute Waldnutzung
FSC® C083411

Kolibri 360 GmbH
Ferdinand-Jühlke-Straße 7
99095 Erfurt, Deutschland
produktsicherheit@kolibri360.de